World in Denial

Defiant Nature of Mankind
~ A Biblical Account ~

Prophetic Evidence for a Divine Creator

Roger G. Gallop, Ph.D.

Copyright © 2017 by Red Butte Press, Inc.

Revised (2019, 2021)

All rights reserved. No portion of this book may be reproduced in any form without written permission of the publisher, except in the case of brief quotations in articles and reviews.

Roger G. Gallop, Ph.D.
World In Denial - Defiant Nature of Mankind - A Biblical Account (Prophetic Evidence for a Divine Creator)

Library of Congress Control Number: 2016913954

ISBN-13:   978-0-9829975-0-5 (paperback)
ISBN-13:   978-0-9829975-1-2 (case laminate)
ISBN-13:   978-0-9829975-5-0 (eBook)

Red Butte Press, Inc.
P. O. Box 711
Ponte Vedra Beach, Florida 32004-0711

Scripture quotations marked NIV are taken from the *Holy Bible, New International Version®*, Copyright © 1973, 1978, 1984, 1985 by International Bible Society. Used by permission of Zondervan Publishing House. Also, some Scripture quotations are taken from Bible Gateway, www.biblegateway.com.

Scripture quotations marked NAS are taken from the *New American Standard Bible®*, Copyright © 1960, 1962, 1963, 1968, 1971, 1972, 1973, 1975, 1977, 1995 by The Lockman Foundation. Used by permission. (www.Lockman.org)

Scripture quotations marked KJV are taken from the King James Version. Scripture quotations marked ESV are taken from English Standard Version.

Photographs and illustrations are by Roger G. Gallop or by authors who have granted permission; other photographs and illustrations have been released into the public domain by their author or U.S. Government agency, or the copyright has expired.

Graphics: Roger G. Gallop, or as shown on drawing

Book Design/Layout: Roger G. Gallop

This book was written for educational and ministerial purposes.

Roger G. Gallop is also author of the books:
evolution - The Greatest Deception in Modern History (Scientific Evidence for Divine Creation)
Defeating Evil - God's Plan Before the Beginning of Time (Planet Earth - God's Testing Ground)

Visit www.CreationScienceToday.com

World In Denial

With the miraculous rebirth of the State of Israel on May 14, 1948, after 1,878 years of worldwide exile, and Israel's repossession of the ancient City of Jerusalem during the Six Day War on June 5-10, 1967, all in fulfillment of Old and New Testament prophecy; the ever-increasing economic debt of the U.S., the European Union, and the rest of the world; the nuclear and military alliance of Russia with Iran and Turkey, and Russia's preparatory military incursion into Syria (2015); the increase of immorality, violence, and lawlessness in the U.S. and worldwide; and the disappearance of honor, integrity, and the moral code in our society (including government and public schools) and throughout the world; and then after a 20-year military occupation, the utter incompetent U.S. withdrawal from Afghanistan on August 31, 2021, which, in turn, opened the door to China (see chapter 12, p. 196) in this region of the world—now you would think people would be just a little more than curious if such events relate somehow to end time Bible prophecy.

One would logically assume people would keep an open mind and consider the evidence. After all, according to the Bible, there's **more than a lot riding on a person's decision to accept or reject the gift of pardon** (see p. xvii). Yet unbelievably, a large segment of the world remains indifferent, uncaring, and unconcerned, and many are ferocious in their anti-Biblical and anti-Christian sentiment. Do you ever wonder why people have such an inclination? The fact is, there is an undeniable tendency by human beings throughout history to turn away from the truth **without reason**—hence, the book title, *World in Denial - Defiant Nature of Mankind (Prophetic Evidence for a Divine Creator)*—a tendency or drive that would lead most rational people to believe there is a force in the world in opposition to God of the Holy Bible. There are reasons for this indifference:

> Many people dismiss evidence for a Divine Creator because of an enormous predisposition against the supernatural.[1] If a person's mind is closed to Scripture, no amount of evidence (scientific and theological) will change his/her mind. This *"hardening of their hearts"* (Ephesians 4:18; Mark 8:17) is an unseen phenomenon we witness in the world today.

> The phenomena of evil (sin, iniquity, wickedness, immorality, depravity, violence, terrorism, corruption, and pride) prevalent throughout the world cause people to 'turn away'—to *"willfully forget"* without reason! (See 2 Peter 3:5-6.) In Luke 8:10-12, Jesus described such people as *"though seeing, they may not see; though hearing, they may not understand."* (See Matthew 13:14.)

> In addition, many people 'turn away' because the secular, atheistic world is telling them there is no hope—that death is the end. Yet, scientific evidence supporting Creation is overwhelming (see first book by R. Gallop), and prophetic evidence in the Bible is telling the world that God is real and totally Sovereign—and there is great hope of life after death through Jesus Christ.

Scientific evidence and **fulfilled Bible prophecies** (ancient world and most especially, what we can actually see in today's world) provide some of the strongest reasons to believe the Truth of the Holy Bible and accept Jesus Christ as Lord and Savior. People can look no farther than Biblical prophecy to see God interceding in the activities of nations and individuals alike—**yet most people are completely unaware of such prophetic events and the end times in which we are now living.**

Seek the Truth. Read this book and the book, *evolution - The Greatest Deception in Modern History (Scientific Evidence for Divine Creation),* and the Holy Bible, the book of revelation.

---

notes:
1. Burrows, M. (1956). *What Mean These Stones?* NY: Meridian Books, 291, 1; as cited in McDowell, J., (1972). *Evidence that Demands a Verdict.* San Bernardino, CA: Campus Crusade for Christ, 69.

contents

Preface ix
   Who is God? x
   The Seven Dispensations xii
      Antediluvian Period xii
      Immediate Postdiluvian Period xiii
   In Reading This Book xiii

Prologue xv
   Nature of Mankind xv
   Freedom of Choice xvii
   Pain and Suffering and its Origin xix
   Good and Evil xxi

Chapter 1: The Bible's Truth and Accuracy 1
   Scientific Evidence for Divine Creation 1
   The Bible's Unity 4
   The Bible's Historical Accuracy 5
   The Bible's Preservation 6
      The Old Testament 7
      The New Testament 10
      Attempts to Destroy the Bible 11
   The Bible's Uniqueness 12
   The Bible's Prophetic Accuracy 12

Chapter 2: Early Jewish History and Divine Covenants 17
   The Abrahamic Covenant 17
      Abraham and His Sons Isaac and Ishmael 19
      The Seed of Everlasting Hatred 19
      Isaac and His Twin Sons Esau and Jacob 20
   The Twelve Sons of Jacob 21
      Jacob and His Family Travel to Egypt 22
      The Twelve Tribes of Israel 22
   Moses and Aaron 23
      Liberation of the Jewish People 24
      Exodus of the Jewish People 24
   The Mosaic Covenant 26
      Beginnings of Disobedience 27
      Continual Grumbling and Disobedience 28
      Renewal of the Mosaic Covenant 30
   The Ethical Question of War 31

Chapter 3: Warnings, Blessings, and Punishment for Disobedience 35

    Decrees and Warnings 36

    Blessings for Obedience and Punishment for Disobedience:
        Warnings to the Jewish People and All of Humanity 37

        Blessings for Obedience 37

        Punishment for Disobedience 38

    Moses Predicts the Future 41

    The Lord Reaffirms Israel's Future Rebellion 43

    Israel's Triumph in the Land of Canaan 44

    Promises Fulfilled Despite Continued Disobedience 45

        Period of Judges (c. 1400 BC to 1050 BC) 46

        United Kingdom (c. 1050 BC to 930 BC) 47

Chapter 4: Jewish History and Consequences for Disobedience 51

    Divided Kingdom (c. 930 BC – 586 BC) 51

    Assyrian Empire Conquers the Northern Kingdom (Israel) (c. 721 BC) 52

    Babylonians Conquer the Assyrian Empire and
        the Southern Kingdom (Judah) (c. 612 BC) 52

        Destruction of Solomon's Temple and Jerusalem (c. 586 BC) 53

        Prophets Who Foresaw These Events 54

    Medo-Persians (Iran) Conquer the Babylonians (c. 538 BC) 55

        Rebuilding the Temple and the Walls of Jerusalem (c. 516 BC) 55

        Disappearance of the Prophets (c. 430 BC) 57

    Grecian Empire Conquers the Medes and Persians (c. 331 BC) 58

    Roman Republic Conquers the Grecian Empire (c. 146 BC):
        Emergence of the Roman Empire (c. 27 BC) 59

    The Life and Ministry of Jesus Christ (c. 1 BC – AD 32) 60

        61 Prophecies Fulfilled Pertaining to Jesus Christ (c. 1 BC – AD 32) 64

        Jesus Christ Teaches About Sin and Repentance 66

        Rejection of Jesus Christ by the Jewish People (c. AD 30 – AD 70) 68

Chapter 5: Worldwide Dispersion of the Jewish People 71

    Why This Fierce Punishment for Disobedience? 72

        Persecution is Not from God 74

        Scripture about Persecution 76

    What Became of the Land of Palestine? (AD 70 – 1948) 77

        Roman Occupation and Parthians in the East (27 BC – AD 500) 77

        Arab Occupation (AD 500 – AD 979) 78

        Turko-Persian Empire (aka Seljuk Empire) (AD 979 – AD 1215) 78

Mongol Empire of Asia (AD 1215 – AD 1453) ... 79
Ottoman Empire (AD 1453 – AD 1917) ... 79
British and French Control (1917 – 1948) ... 80
Nazi Germany and the Holocaust (1933 – 1945) ... 81

Chapter 6: Miraculous Rebirth of the State of Israel (May 14, 1948) ... 83
Old Testament Scripture Pertaining to the Rebirth of Israel ... 84
New Testament Scripture Pertaining to the Rebirth of Israel ... 87
Prophecies Fulfilled on May 14, 1948 ... 89
God's Chosen People and Prophecy Fulfilled ... 90
Fallacy of Replacement Theology ... 91
Anti-Semitism and Wholesale Attempts to Eradicate the Jewish People ... 93

Chapter 7: Renewal of the Ancient Conflict Between Isaac and Ishmael ... 97
War of Independence (1948 and 1949) ... 97
1956 Sinai and Suez Crisis ... 98
The Six Day War (June 5 – 10, 1967) ... 99
Fulfillment of Bible Prophecy ... 101
Israelis Are Aware of Bible Prophecy ... 102
The City of Jerusalem: The Temple Mount and the Western Wall ... 103
1973 Yom Kippur War (October 6 – 25, 1973) ... 107
Camp David Accords and Return of the Sinai to Egypt (1978 and 1982) ... 108
1982 Lebanon Crisis (1982 – 2000) ... 108
The Oslo Accords (1993 – 1995) ... 110
Israel Disengages from Gaza and Parts of the West Bank (2005) ... 111
The Gaza Strip ... 111
The West Bank and Golan Heights ... 111
Surrendering Land for Peace (1982 and 2005) ... 112
2006 Lebanon War (July 12 – August 14, 2006) ... 112
The Gaza Wars ... 113
First Gaza Conflict (2008 – 2009) ... 114
Second Gaza Conflict (2012) ... 114
Third Gaza Conflict (2014) ... 114
Conclusion ... 115

Chapter 8: Prophetic Super Signs Before the Seven Year Tribulation ... 117
Rebirth of the State of Israel (May 14, 1948) ... 118
Repossession of Jerusalem by the State of Israel (June 5 – 10, 1967) ... 119
Israel Surrounded by Hostile Arab Nations ... 120

    Fallacy of an Arab Palestinian State ... 121
    Discarded Solution to the Palestinian Dilemma ... 123
    Stated Goals of Arab Nations ... 124
    God Blesses Israel with a Warning to Other Nations ... 125
    Psalm 83 ... 126
Increase in Arrogance, Immorality, and Lawlessness - Worldwide ... 127
Rise of Russia and Its Alliance with Muslim States ... 131
Modern Transportation and Increase in Knowledge ... 133

Chapter 9: Decline of the United States: Part 1 ... 135
Arrogance, Immorality, Violence, and Lawlessness ... 136
Economic Decline ... 141
A Deep Knowing Something is Wrong ... 146

Chapter 10: Decline of the United States: Part 2 ... 151
Political Correctness ... 152
    Appeasement of Evil Political Ideologies ... 153
    Appeasement of All Religions (except Christianity and Judaism) ... 155
Moral Decline of Public Schools and Universities ... 159
    Public Middle Schools and High Schools ... 159
    Public Colleges and Universities ... 163
Compromised Teaching of the Bible ... 164

Chapter 11: What Can We Expect in the Near Future? ... 167
Pre-Tribulation Prophetic Signs ... 168
Rapture of the Church ... 171
Rise of the Antichrist ... 175
The Coming Seven Year Tribulation ... 176
    Daniel's 70th Week ... 177
    Increase in the Severity of Signs ... 178

Chapter 12: The Seven Year Tribulation Period ... 185
Seals, Trumpets, and Bowls ... 186
First 3 ½ Years of the Tribulation Period ... 187
    Invasion by Russia and Its Allies ... 188
    Rebuilding the Third Temple ... 191
Second 3 ½ Years of the Tribulation Period ... 194
    Persecution and Desolation ... 194
    Armageddon: The Great Tribulation ... 196
    The Second Coming of Jesus Christ and the Millennial Period ... 199

Epilogue 202
   Questions and Answers 202
   The Bible Warns: There is Only One Way to Heaven 224
   Final Message 226

Appendix A – Glossary 229
Appendix B – Establishment of a New Covenant 245
Appendix C – Satan's Attempts to Seize Total Control 248
Appendix D – The Rapture and the Second Coming 251

Index 254

preface

> ### *Do Not Turn Your Back — Do Not Walk Away*
> *"In the time of my favor I heard you, and in the day of salvation I helped you. I tell you, now is the time of God's favor, now is the day of salvation."* —2 Corinthians 6:2, NIV

This book describes the nature of mankind, both Jew and Gentile, from the beginning of history and prophetic evidence for Divine Creation. We begin with a discussion of man's natural tendency to sin, ensuing pain and suffering, good and evil, overwhelming scientific evidence for Creation, a young earth and Noah's Flood, and the integrity of the Bible. But the primary focus of the book is on a defiant, morally corrupt, arrogant humanity and indisputable prophetic evidence for Divine intercession into man's activities and God's plan for the redemption of mankind.

The theme centers on God's irrevocable and everlasting covenant with the Jewish people, God's *"chosen... people"* and *"treasured possession"* (Genesis 13:14-15; Deuteronomy 7:6-9, 28:46, 29:24-29; Psalm 105:8-10; Jeremiah 31:35-37); the continual disobedience of the Jewish people (as a whole); and the depraved, paganistic culture of surrounding Gentile nations and their influence on the State of Israel during its early history.

Other central topics include Divine punishment of both Jews and Gentiles for their continued idolatry and defiance of God's laws and decrees; Old Testament prophecies leading to the First Coming of Jesus Christ, the Son of God (1 BC - AD 32); exile of the Jewish people worldwide (beginning AD 70) for their disobedience and ultimately, for their rejection of the Messiah, Jesus Christ (Luke 19:44); the miraculous prophetic rebirth of the State of Israel on May 14, 1948 (Deuteronomy 30:1-5; Isaiah 43:5-7, 66:7-8; Ezekiel 34:13, 36:22-24, 37:1-6, 11-14, 21-23, 39:27-29; Hosea 3:4-5; Jeremiah 31:10, 31:35-36; and Amos 9:14-15) as God honors His covenant with Israel; the miraculous repossession of the City of Jerusalem on June 5-10, 1967; and other indisputable prophetic signs.

This book also reviews the decline of the U.S.; rise of Russia, Iran, and China; the removal of the church; the seven year tribulation; and the abomination of desolation, Armageddon, and the Second Coming. It is not the intent of this book to provide a detailed analysis of these subjects, but rather provide a reasonable, intellectual basis for faith in a Divine Creator—that God is real and Sovereign, and He continually intercedes into the activities of nations and individuals alike.

God is the Author of Life and Creator of all that exists (John 1:1-3; Colossians 1:16; Hebrews 1:2; Jeremiah 10:12-16, 51:15-19); omnipotent, omnipresent, and omniscient (Romans 8:29; Ephesians 1:4-5; 1 Corinthians 2:7; Jeremiah 23:24, 32:27); and beyond our understanding.

who is God?

The proper name for God is Yahweh, or "the Lord", *"...the name of the Lord, the Eternal God"* (Genesis 21:33, NIV); *"His ways are eternal"* (Habakkuk 1:12, 3:6, NIV); *"...everlasting to everlasting"* (1 Chronicles 16:36, 29:10; Nehemiah 9:5; Psalm 103:17, 106:48, NIV); *"Your throne, O God, will last for ever and ever"* (Hebrews 1:8, NIV); *"I am the Alpha and the Omega, the First and the Last, the Beginning and the End"* (Revelation 1:8, 21:6, 22:13, NIV); "*And they will reign for ever and ever"* (Revelation 22:13, NIV); and *"As God told Moses, 'I AM WHO I AM'"* (Exodus 3:14, NIV).

The Lord is omnipresent, omnipotent, and omniscient (Romans 8:29; Ephesians 1:4-5; 1 Corinthians 2:7); and He is the Creator of the heavens and the earth and all that exists (Genesis 1-2; Jeremiah 10:12-16, 51:15-19; Isaiah 40:28, 42:5; Zechariah 12:1-3). The Bible teaches that God is without sin (1 Peter 2:22; 1 John 3:5; Habakkuk 1:13), and He is completely just and holy (Isaiah 6:1-3, 57:15; Psalm 99:5).

Most importantly, *"God is love"* (1 John 4:8, 4:16, NIV). The word "love" in this verse is translated 'agape love' found only in humans and God (Romans 5:8)—an unconditional, self-sacrificing love. (See Prologue, Good and Evil.) He created us to have fellowship with Him, and He sacrificed His Son to restore that fellowship, *"For God so loved the world that he gave his one and only Son, that whoever believes in him shall not perish but have eternal life"* (John 3:16, NIV).

> "In many Scripture passages, God calls upon us to fear Him. But once our sins are confessed, He tells us in Romans 8:15 that we can come to Him saying, "Abba! Father!" (meaning "Papa" or "Daddy"). We are welcome to go boldly before His throne with the access permitted only to the King's children. We still fear Him but in a way that does not diminish our love for Him or His for us."[2]

And finally, we lest not forget *"the Lord is a warrior"* (Exodus 15:3, NIV)—*"He does whatever pleases Him"* (Psalms 115:3, 135:6; Job 23:13; Daniel 4:35, NIV), and *"He is to be feared"* (1 Chronicles 16:25; Psalm 96:4; Isaiah 8:13; Job 25:15-16; Matthew 10:28, NIV). Fearing God helps us overcome our own sinful nature. If a man is known to be God-fearing, we know that he will keep his word and we can trust that person.[1] Our primary sin throughout history is that *"there is no fear of God before their [our] eyes"* (Romans 3:18, NIV).

The following passage was taken from the book by Roger Gallop, *evolution - The Greatest Deception in Modern History*, chapter 3, Human Nature and the Moral Law.

Moral Law was examined by C. S. Lewis in his book, *Mere Christianity*—a universal law of decent behavior or morality—a law of "right and wrong" behavior.[3] Unlike other natural laws, the Moral Law is a law that human beings are free to disobey.

Since the rebellion by Adam, humanity has had an inherited or inborn tendency to sin and rebel—to oppose the Creator's sovereignty over their lives. In the days of Noah (c. 4004 BC – 2385 BC), mankind was rebellious and exceedingly wicked—and with this came eventual consequences—the Flood that destroyed all of humanity. Rebellion and wickedness have been continually present throughout the history of mankind.

In opposition to this tendency, the Moral Law motivates humans to make personal sacrifices that may lead to suffering, injury, and even death without the possibility of personal benefit. Such behavior is in direct conflict with nonhuman primates and other animals. According to Lewis, man has two impulses: the first is to provide help and the second is to avoid danger, but the overriding drive is to help—not to run away. (See Lewis, p. 9-10.) Although we are free to disobey (free will) this inner voice of conscience, the motivation to do the right thing is real. The Moral Law will ask me to save a drowning man with personal sacrifice, even if he is an enemy or stranger. (See Lewis p. 10.)

The reality is, not one person keeps the Moral Law all the time and many of us never keep the law at all—and in the act of not keeping the law, most humans try to shift the blame or alleviate their wrong behavior with all types of excuses. Quarrelling between two individuals, for example, is "appealing to some kind of standard of behavior which he expects the other man to know about." (See Lewis, p. 3.) Lewis sums it up: "human beings, all over the world, have this curious idea that they ought to behave in a certain way...[but] they do not in fact behave in that way." (See Lewis, p. 8.) The question is, what lies behind this law? (See Lewis, p. 13.)

As Lewis explains, "If there was a controlling power *outside the universe*, it could not show itself to us as one of the facts inside the universe—no more than the architect of a house could actually be a wall or staircase or fireplace in that house. The only way in which we could expect it to show itself would be inside ourselves as an influence or a command trying to get us to behave in a certain way. And that is just what we do find inside ourselves. Surely this ought to arouse our suspicions?" (See Lewis, p. 24.) [Italics added]

God wants man to behave in a certain way, urging man to do what is right and just, and if he does not, he is made to feel uncomfortable. (See Lewis, p. 23.) One must conclude that this must be a holy and righteous God who despises evil. This is certainly proclaimed throughout the Bible. **If God is outside the universe—outside the natural world—the tools of science cannot find God**. Ultimately, the decision to acknowledge and accept God is based on personal choice and faith (Matthew 17:20; Romans 1:17, 3:22, 3:28); and *"We live by faith, not by sight"* (2 Corinthians 5:7, NIV).

The following was taken from the book by Roger Gallop, *evolution - The Greatest Deception in Modern History*, chapter 9, The Big Bang and Its Problems.

How did the universe progress from nothing without a causal agent (that is, Divine Creator), thus denying the First and Second Laws of Thermodynamics, and the Law of Causality (cause and effect; every effect has a cause), and how did life and human consciousness come into existence? Regarding the Law of Causality, "the following reasoning stands up to scrutiny:

- Everything which has a beginning has a cause
- The universe has a beginning
- Therefore the universe has a cause."[4]

> God is *outside and inside the universe*, and *He created matter and energy*; *time is linked to matter and energy*; so therefore *He is not limited by time.*

As authors explain in *The Creation Answers Book*, "It is important to stress the words 'which has a beginning.' The universe requires a cause because it had a beginning... God, unlike the universe, had no beginning, so does not need a cause. In addition, Einstein's general relativity [theory], which has much experimental support, shows that time is linked to matter and space. So, time itself would have begun along with matter and space at the beginning of the universe. Since God, by definition, is the creator of the whole universe, He is the creator of time. Therefore, He is not limited by the time dimension He created, so He has no beginning in time. Therefore, He does not have, or need to have, a cause."[5]

World in Denial - Defiant Nature of Mankind

the seven dispensations

In reading this book, please keep in mind the **seven dispensations of time** (periods or ages) in which God dealt with mankind. Scripture divides time (from the creation of Adam in Genesis to the *"new heaven and a new earth"* of Revelation 21:1) into seven unequal periods, or dispensations (Ephesians 2:7, 3:2); each period continues into each of the succeeding periods.

These periods are 1) **Innocence** which extends from the creation of Adam in Genesis 2:7 to the expulsion of Adam and Eve from Eden (Genesis 3:23-24), 2) **Conscience** which extends from expulsion from Eden to the Flood (c. 2385 BC), 3) **Government** which extends from post-Flood to Abram (c. 2166 BC - 1991 BC), 4) **Promise** which extends from Abraham to Moses (c. 1526 BC - 1406 BC), 5) **Law** which extends from Moses and the Ten Commandments to the time of our Lord Jesus Christ (c. 1 BC - AD 32), 6) **Grace** which extends from the crucifixion of Christ (AD 32) to the Second Coming (near future), and 7) **Millennium** which extends from the Second Coming for another 1,000 years. (See chapter 12, The Second Coming of Jesus Christ and the Millennial Period.)

Each period marks a change in God's method of dealing with mankind with respect to sin and man's responsibility. Each of the dispensations may be regarded as a new test, and **each ends in judgment, marking mankind's complete failure in every dispensation.** At this current time in history, five of these dispensations, or periods of time, have been fulfilled—and we are living at the close of the sixth and facing the seventh and last dispensation, the millennium.

antediluvian period

The first two ages, Innocence and Conscience, are antediluvian or pre-Flood. During this 1,619 year period (c. 4004 BC - 2385 BC), people had no institution of civil government and law, and they could only distinguish between good and evil by their own conscience and personal Divine revelations. During the Age of Conscience, mankind was given the individual and moral responsibility to pursue goodness and virtue and turn away from evil. But humanity abandoned its relationship with God—and ultimately, mankind was consumed with wickedness and violence continually. *"Now the earth was corrupt in the sight of God, and the earth was filled with violence"* (Genesis 6:11, NAS). The human race became morally depraved, which is thoroughly described in Genesis 6.

> *"Then the Lord saw that the wickedness of man was great on the earth, and that every intent of the thoughts of his heart was only evil continually. And the Lord was sorry that He had made man on the earth, and He was grieved in His heart. And the Lord said, 'I will blot out man whom I have created from the face of the land, from man to animals to creeping things and to birds of the sky; for I am sorry that I have made them'"* (Genesis 6:5-7, NAS).

> *"Now the earth was corrupt in the sight of God, and the earth was filled with violence. And God looked on the earth, and behold, it was corrupt; for all flesh had corrupted their way upon the earth"* (Genesis 6:11-12, NAS).

W. Graham Scroggie has graphically depicted the biblical picture of antediluvian humanity.[6]

"The appalling condition of things is summed up in a few terrible words, words which bellow and burn: wickedness, evil imagination, corruption, and violence; and these sins were great, widespread, 'in the earth,' continuous, 'only evil continually,' open and daring, 'before God,' replete, 'filled,' and universal, 'all flesh.'... This is an astounding event! After over 1,600 years of human history the race was so utterly corrupt morally that it was not fit to live; and of all mankind only four men and four women were spared, because they did not go with the great sin drift."

> More information about the antediluvian and post-flood periods can be found in the book, *evolution - The Greatest Deception in Modern History*, chapter 10.

This period reached a point of continuous utter depravity. The degradation and wickedness of the antediluvians have been affirmed by an astonishing collection of Scriptural testimony. (See Genesis 6:1-6, 11-13; Luke 17:26-27; 1 Peter 3:20; 2 Peter 2:5; & Jude 14-15.)

immediate postdiluvian period

Immediately following the Flood, God commanded the descendants of Noah to *"increase in number and fill the earth"* (Genesis 9:1, NIV), but within just a few hundred years people chose to locate in the area of Mesopotamia in direct disobedience to God. Mesopotamia (Greek meaning "between two rivers") is an area located between the Tigris and Euphrates rivers, corresponding to modern-day Iraq and the western part of Iran (south of Mt. Ararat)—an area commonly known as the "cradle of civilization." During the third dispensation, a human organization known as civil government was divinely established to control the wickedness of men.

in reading this book

This book begins with the Age of Promise—the time of Abraham, Isaac, Jacob, and Moses; and ends with the sixth dispensation. Through all these dispensations or ages, mankind (as a whole) remains disobedient, idolatrous, arrogant, immoral, and corrupt.

Chapter 1 is devoted to the truth and accuracy of the Bible. Chapters 2 through 5 are devoted to Jewish history, Divine Covenants, disobedience of Jews and Gentiles, and reasons for worldwide dispersion of the Jewish people in AD 70. **These chapters will help the reader understand the defiant nature of mankind throughout history, including modern times, and how Old Testament prophecies relate to end time events in today's world.**

Chapters 6 through 12 describe the fulfillment of end time prophecy including the miraculous rebirth of the State of Israel on May 14, 1948 (in just one day), and repossession of the ancient City of Jerusalem on June 5-10, 1967, which are "fundamental to end time Bible prophecy." Other prophetic signs include renewal of ancient conflicts between Israel and their Arab neighbors; decline of the United States; rise of Russia, Iran, and China; and what we can expect in the near future!

> Technical terms are defined in Appendix A (Glossary), and some terms or explanations are found in "text boxes." Appendices (B through D) provide a slightly more in-depth review of various topics. All Scripture is italicized. Some words are also italicized or bold for emphasis. Circa, cir., or c. placed before dates of antiquity (e.g., c. 1526 BC - 1406 BC) mean 'about' or 'approximately.' Also, 'United Kingdom' refers to the United Kingdom of Israel (c. 1400 BC to 1050 BC).

notes: preface

1. Reardon, J. (2013). What does it mean to fear God? Christianity Today International; Retrieved July 2016, from http://www.christianitytoday.com/biblestudies/bible-answers/spirituallife/what-does-it-mean-to-fear-god.html.

2. Alcorn, R. (2017). *Seeing the Unseen*. Colorado Springs, CO: Multnomah Books, 11.

3. Lewis, C.S. (1952). *Mere Christianity*. New York: Harper Collins Publishers, chapters 1-4. Also see Collins, Francis S. (2006). *The Languages of God*. New York: Free Press, chapter 1. See the book by Roger Gallop, *evolution - The Greatest Deception in Modern History*, chapter 3, Human Nature and the Moral Law.

4. Catchpoole, D., Sarfati, J., and Wieland, C. (2008). *The Creation Answers Book*. (D. Batten, Ed.). Atlanta, GA: Creation Book Publishers, 18.

5. Ibid.

6. Scroggie, W. Graham (1953). *The Unfolding Drama of Redemption*. London: Pickering & Inglis Ltd., I: 74, 77. Also cited in Whitcomb, J.C., and Morris, H.M. (1961). *The Genesis Flood*. Phillipsburg, NJ: The Presbyterian and Reformed Publishing Company, 18.

prologue

> "For God so loved the world that he gave his one and only Son, that whoever believes in him shall not perish but have eternal life." — John 3:16, NIV "The reason the Son of God appeared was to destroy the devil's work." — 1 John 3:8, NIV

nature of mankind

Many have asked the question, "Is there an intellectual basis for faith in Jesus Christ as the Son of God?"[1] This question was asked by Josh McDowell in his book, *Evidence That Demands a Verdict*. Theological scholars, students, and adults over the span of history, and esteemed scientists in the fields of geology, biology, genetics, physics, astronomy, and medicine, answer this question with a resounding, Yes!

My personal basis for faith in God of the Holy Bible is based on a number of reasons: 1) scientific evidence for Divine creation presented in the book, *evolution – The Greatest Deception in Modern History*, 2) unity, historical accuracy, preservation, and uniqueness of the Bible, 3) fulfillment of testimony (forecasts) by Old Testament prophets (including historical events in Old and New Testament times), and 4) physical signs existing in today's world that directly pertain to fulfillment of end time Bible prophecy. Also, the undeniable corruption and moral depravity of mankind, as described in the Bible, the presence of good and evil (love and hatred), and pain and suffering, all support the truth and message of the Bible and the fundamental need for redemption by a holy and righteous God.

"Human beings can absorb many pressures in life, but a lack of hope is not one of them. The world in which we live has no hope. Looking back, we see an unending history of war, hatred, and cruelty, all of which reveals the inhumanness of mankind. The very study of history is a study of war and man's inhumanity to his fellow man. The whole world yearns for peace, but knows no peace. Mankind's problems continually worsen, leaving people without hope."[2] Not only does the Bible provide that hope, but it tells us about the end times (last days) in which we now live through Bible prophecy and what we must do to be saved—which gives us hope and confidence in the future.

One would logically assume that maintaining an open mind and seeking the truth about the Divinity of our Lord Jesus Christ and creation as described in the Book of Genesis would be of utmost importance to every person living today. After all, in the scheme of things, life here on earth is a very short time (a vapor in the wind) when compared to eternity, *"...a mist that appears for a little while and then vanishes"* (James 4:14, NIV). Seeking answers to relevant questions (i.e., theological and scientific) about origin and purpose should be at the top of our list of priorities—but sadly, it is not. Most people want to avoid the subject because the secular, atheistic world is telling them there is no hope—that death is the end.

Contrary to such secular doctrine, the evidence supporting Divine creation and the deity of Jesus Christ is overwhelming. If someone just takes the time, McDowell says that he has "never heard a single individual—who honestly considered the evidence—deny that Jesus Christ is the Son of God and the Savior of men."[3] While a large segment of the world remains indifferent, many others are ferocious in their anti-Biblical and anti-Christian sentiment. Do you ever wonder what motivates people to have such an inclination? The fact is there is an undeniable tendency by all human beings to sin (committing acts of evil to varying degrees)—a tendency or drive that would lead most rational people to believe there is an evil (supernatural) force in the world—the exact opposite of holy, righteous, and merciful.

Rebellious and idolatrous history of humanity and the natural tendency for moral decay are graphically portrayed throughout the Bible (Old and New Testaments). Examples include paganistic cultures of the antediluvian period (c. 4004 BC to 2385 BC); in the time of Mesopotamia (c. 2200 BC); in ancient Egypt and Assyria (c. 2000 BC); Canaanite people of the Middle East (c. 1600 BC to 1400 BC); and the empires of Babylonia (c. 612 BC to 539 BC), Medo-Persia (c. 538 BC to 334 BC), Greece (c. 334 BC to 146 BC), and Rome (c. 146 BC to AD 476); and in historical accounts of the Dark Ages (c. 6th to 14th century), World War I and World War II, and by today's continual worldwide ethnic conflicts.

> **Sin** is breaking the moral law (see chapter 3, Human Nature and the Moral Law in the book, *evolution – The Greatest Deception in Modern History*), or any one of the Ten Commandments, or a departure from goodness. **Evil** is sin, iniquity, wickedness, immorality, or corruption. "Evil, in its essence, refuses to accept God as God and puts someone or something else [idolatry] in His place... For this reason, the Bible treats idolatry as the ultimate sin, since it worships as God what is not God."[4]

> **Terrorism** is the face of evil today—the horrific beheadings, crucifixion, torture, and persecution of Christians (including women, children, and their families) by Islamic extremists in the Middle East and worldwide.
>
> **Immorality** and deviant behavior are being tolerated and accepted as the 'new normal' by much of our youth in America and throughout the world.

Consider the world today, with its political corruption, lying, slander, public displays of moral depravity, bizarre behavior, violent crimes against humanity, abortion, theft, adultery, drug-taking, drunkenness, gambling, greed of all kinds, prostitution, sexual perversions, trafficking of children and teenagers for sex, wars and rumors of wars, and terrorism.

The nature of mankind throughout history is to 'harden their hearts.' (See Mark 8:17-18; Ephesians 4:18.) This hardening of the heart is a supernatural phenomenon, an unseen battle between good and evil we witness in the news and in our everyday lives. The evil nature of mankind is also portrayed by the exceedingly repugnant behavior of some clergymen over the ages—physical cruelty, collusion with political dictators, and abhorrent sexual abuses—detestable behavior that has alienated many from the Christian faith.

Immorality is tolerated and accepted as the norm by our youth. The problem has never been with the God of the Holy Bible but with the corruption and moral depravity of humankind. Take a moment to read Romans 1, verses 18–32—it reads like a commentary of today's world.

freedom of choice

In the beginning God created man (male and female) in His image and gave man dominion over the entire world (Genesis 1:26-28, 5:1-2). God created a perfect world (Genesis 1:31)—no death, struggle, violence, cruelty, or bloodshed—and everything was "upheld" by God (Colossians 1:17 and Hebrews 1:3). God also allowed man to be a free moral being—that is, He gave man the ability "to choose what is true, what is right, what is good."[5] (The question of divine election or predestination is reviewed in end note 6.)

There are multitudes of verses in the Bible supporting 'free will'—among them, Genesis 2:16-17, 3:5; Joshua 24:15; Psalm 119:30; Isaiah 7:15, 66:3; Ezekiel 33:11; Matthew 16:24; Romans 10:13; 1 Corinthians 7:37; 2 Peter 3:9; and Revelation 22:17. For example, Joshua 24:15 (NIV) proves that man is a free moral agent: *"...choose for yourselves this day whom you will serve."* 'Free will' simply means "the ability of an individual to make his or her personal choice for or against God, and it is an indisputable fact of Scripture."[6]

Why did God give humanity the choice between good and evil as described in Joshua 24:15? The answer can be simply stated: without 'free will' there is no love or fellowship between humans and their Creator but 'free will' also makes evil possible.

With 'free will' could evil have been avoided? Unfortunately, the answer is No. There are always people who will 'harden their hearts' and choose evil (sin). The only way God could destroy evil is to destroy 'free will' and the consequences of destroying 'free will' would be to destroy the possibility to love— "there is no love without freedom." Without free will, God would simply be creating robots.

God chose the best world possible—a world of 'free will' where love is preserved and sin is tried (even with ensuing pain, suffering, decay, disease, and death) and defeated rather than a world where there is no 'free will,' no love, and no sin. Man's purpose is to be part of the Kingdom and family of God, but we can only reach this destiny through a process of trials (ordeals) of this world and perseverance—a testing ground to either accept or reject the free gift of pardon through Jesus Christ.

For more information about 'free will,' sin, God's testing ground, the purpose of mankind, and making the right choice, see the book by Roger Gallop, *Defeating Evil — God's Plan Before the Beginning of Time*, specifically chapters 7 and 8, and epilogue.

Humans chose to walk out of God's will with its ensuing pain and suffering. Because of sin (rebellion) by the first man, Adam, against his Creator (Genesis 3:6; Romans 5:12), creation was cursed by God (Genesis 3:14–19)—in effect leading to a contaminated and corrupt world. Creatures under man's rule, though morally innocent, shared in God's judgment—death and deterioration. While this may seem implausible to many, in fact, creation, rebellion, and the curse are in perfect alignment with scientific laws and the moral nature of man.

Since the beginning of human history, humans have always had an inherited or inborn tendency to sin and rebel—that is, oppose the Creator's sovereignty over their lives. We see this every day in our own individual lives. In the days of Noah (c. 4004 BC–2385 BC), mankind was rebellious and exceedingly wicked—they abandoned God and, ultimately, they were consumed with wickedness and violence continually. In the eyes of God, their "measure of sin was now full" (see Genesis 15:16), and with this rebellion and wickedness came eventual consequences—the Flood that destroyed humanity. (Read the book by Roger Gallop, *evolution - The Greatest Deception in Modern History (Scientific Evidence for Divine Creation).*

In Genesis 6:5 (NIV), *"The Lord saw how great man's wickedness on the earth had become, and that every inclination of the thoughts of his heart was only evil all the time. The Lord was grieved that He had made man on the earth, and His heart was filled with pain. So the Lord said, 'I will wipe mankind, whom I have created, from the face of the earth—men and animals, and creatures that move along the ground, and birds of the air—for I am grieved that I have made them.'"*

In Matthew 24:37-39 (NIV), Jesus Christ says, *"As it was in the days of Noah, so it will be at the coming of the Son of Man. For in the days before the Flood, people were eating and drinking, marrying, and giving in marriage, up to the day that Noah entered the ark, and they knew nothing about what would happen until the Flood came and took them all away. That is how it will be at the coming of the Son of Man."* (See chapter 11, Rapture of the Church.)

The purpose for this prophetic warning (as described in Matthew 24) is to help people discern the times in which we are now living and understand how to prepare for what is coming.

During the Jewish exodus from Egypt (c. 1446 BC - 1406 BC), the 12 tribes of Israel and Judah ignored the law of Moses (the Ten Commandments as described in Exodus 20:1-17), and during the times of Judges (c. 1400 BC - 1050 BC), they forgot their Creator when no one was leading them in obedience and faithfulness to God, *"...everyone did what was right in his own eyes"* (Judges 21:25, NAS), and chaos reigned.

> What are idols and false gods? Idolatry is the inclination of man to worship idols in place of God. Idols can take the form of statues; moon and stars; material possessions; music, movie, and sports celebrities; kings and queens; and even dictators. All of this is a form of idolatry. This is described in more detail in section, Good and Evil.

As described in the Old and New Testaments, people turned their backs on God (*turned away without reason*) and worshipped idols and false gods. Eventually they faced harsh punishment with the fall of the Northern Kingdom (Israel and Samaria) to the Assyrians c. 721 BC; the fall of the Southern Kingdom to the Babylonians (Judah c. 621 BC, the City of Jerusalem and the Temple c. 586 BC); and then the fall of Judah to the Romans and worldwide exile of the Jewish people in AD 70. **People in today's world and throughout history are no different from people in the days of the Old and New Testaments.**

Countries such as Great Britain and the United States, where people once honored God, experienced unprecedented security and prosperity for their faithfulness. But these same countries today are morally bankrupt and collapsing economically as people *turn away* from God. *"Righteousness exalts a nation, but sin is a disgrace to any people"* (Proverbs 14:34, NIV). **When nations turn their backs on God and live as if He does not exist, corruption and wickedness flourish.** Economic woes follow as taxes increase and governments print more and more money to pay for the myriad of social maladies (e.g. drug addiction). Does this sound familiar?

The increase in arrogance, immorality, violence, and lawlessness in society including our high schools and universities is described in chapters 9 and 10.

pain and suffering and its origin

The first man, Adam, decided to walk out of God's will (Genesis 3)—a moral decision that brought death and corruption to a perfect creation (Genesis 3:14-19; Romans 5:12, 6:23) and to all mankind. If Adam and Eve had remained loyal to their Creator and chosen what was good and right at that moment in time, **evil would have been defeated** (as it was eventually defeated at the Cross of Calvary). Wickedness and depravity with its ensuing pain and suffering are "man's fault, not God's." People ask why would a loving God create a world full of pain and suffering—but the real question is, "why would a loving God come into the world He created to suffer and die to pay for my sin?"[7]

The Bible tells us about the entry of evil into the universe—how Lucifer and 1/3 of the angels chose to rebel against God the Creator by attempting to usurp God's power or authority (Ezekiel 28:1, 14–15; Revelation 12:3-9, 9:1; and Luke 8:30).[8] Rebellion by these angelic beings (now demonic beings) led ultimately to the temptation and fall of mankind. Allowing evil, hence pain and suffering, "was a necessary price to achieve a far greater eternal result."[9]

As the apostle Paul explains, *"...our present sufferings are not worth comparing with the glory that will be revealed in us"* (Romans 8:18, NIV), and *"For our light and momentary troubles are achieving for us an eternal glory that far outweighs them all"* (2 Corinthians 4:17, NIV).

"From the beginning, God planned that his Son [Jesus Christ] should deal the death blow to Satan, evil, and suffering, to reverse the Curse, redeem a fallen humanity, and repair a broken world."[10] The apostle John explains, *"The reason the Son of God appeared was to destroy the devil's work"* (1 John 3:8, NIV).

The Holy Bible, open to Psalm 118

See the book by Roger Gallop, *Defeating Evil - God's Plan Before the Beginning of Time*, specifically chapter 8 and epilogue.

The problem of evil and suffering has been addressed by theologians and authors throughout the centuries; more prominently by C. S. Lewis in *The Problem of Pain* (1940, restored 1996); by Randy Alcorn in his book, *If God Is Good – Faith in the Midst of Suffering and Evil* (2009); by Dr. N. L. Geisler in his book, *If God, Why Evil?* (2011); *and* by Dr. Carl Wieland in his book, *Beyond the Shadows - Making Sense of Personal Tragedy* (2011).

Also see articles by Dr. T. Mitchell (December 2011). Death and Steve Jobs. *Answers Update*, 18 (12), Hebron, KY: Answers in Genesis, 1-2 (answersingenesis.org), and Dr. J. Johnson (November 2011). Human suffering: Why this isn't the "best of all possible worlds." *Acts & Facts*, 40 (11), Dallas, TX: Institute for Creation Research, 8-10. (ICR.org)

"God does not allow us to suffer for no reason, and even though the reason may be hidden in the mystery of his divine purpose (see Isaiah 55:8-9)—never for us to know in this life—we must trust in him as the God who does only what is right."[11]

> **The two distinct natures of our Lord Jesus Christ are united as one person**—total deity and total human. The Lord Jesus is equal to God the Father and God the Holy Spirit, yet different in that He is also a true man, yet sinless.
>
> **Why did Jesus have to be the sacrificial Lamb of God?** Because of sin (rebellion) by the first man, Adam, against his Creator (Genesis 3:6; Romans 5:12), creation was cursed by God (Genesis 3:14-19)—in effect leading to a contaminated and corrupt world. Only Jesus, the Son of God, could be the Mediator between God the Father and desperately sinful mankind, and without Jesus, there would be no reconciliation and no redemption (salvation; restoration) for humanity. The complexity of the concept of the God-Man in Jesus Christ is especially difficult to comprehend, but **it was necessary to redeem creation lost to sin**. God loved us so much that He provided a "second Adam" in His Son Jesus to take our place and become our "redeemer."[12]

God's redemptive plan was first announced (prophesied) in Genesis 3:15 (NIV) and is carried throughout the Bible. In this verse (v. 15), the Lord says *"**And I will put enmity between you and the woman, and between your seed and her Seed; he will crush your head, and you will strike** [bruise] **his heel.**"* [Bold added] The offspring of the woman (offspring being Jesus Christ) will eventually crush the serpent's head, a promise fulfilled in Christ's victory over Satan—a victory in which all believers will share.

> ### Meaning of Genesis 3:15[13]
>
> *"And I will put enmity"*—This verse concerns the fall of Adam and Eve. God is speaking to the serpent who is an embodiment of Satan. God desires no alliance with Satan and the two are mutually exclusive.
>
> *"**between you and the woman** [Eve]**, and between your seed** [Satan's seed] **and her Seed** [Jesus]"*—God makes a distinction between "your seed" (Satan's seed; spiritual descendants such as demons or fallen angels) and "her Seed" (Jesus). "Her Seed" refers to the humanity or the incarnation of Christ in human form through the virgin birth. The New Testament refers to Jesus as the "Seed" (Galatians 3:16). (The expression "the woman" is mentioned eight times in Genesis 3; each time refers to Eve.)
>
> *"...he will crush your head, and you will strike his heel."*—God forecasts the defeat of Satan by the incarnation (God in human form) of Christ, the Messiah. The battle lines were drawn between God and Satan. *"He will crush your head"* is a mortal wound as the power of Satan is crushed by Christ who bears the weight of humanity's sin. *"And you will strike* [bruise] *his heel"* refers to the immeasurable sacrifice and death of Christ on the cross (Isaiah 53:10).
>
> At the fall of man (when man turned away from God in the Garden of Eden), God promised a solution to their sin (Genesis 3:15). Sin was the cause of Christ suffering and dying on the cross and this sacrifice crushed Satan's head. **Christ not only fully paid for the sins of the world on the cross but he defeated Satan as well** (Colossians 2:14-15).

good and evil

The presence of good and evil (love and hatred) in the world is a testament to the spiritual battle being waged today. Good and evil are polar opposites, and they have no quantifiable mass or energy—it is a supernatural phenomenon no matter how you might try to define it. If one believes in such concepts (and one would have to be blind, deaf, and dumb not to believe that good and evil exist), **then one is compelled to believe in the supernatural.** Let's look at these terms briefly.

What is good? Goodness, morality, and virtue refer to qualities of character or conduct usually based on a code of conduct (see section, Human Nature and the Moral Code, in the book, *evolution – The Greatest Deception in Modern History*). Throughout history, that code of conduct has been based on the Ten Commandments as described in Exodus 30 and Deuteronomy 5 (which, by the way, public school systems throughout America have systematically removed from the classroom). Morality indicates conformity to a recognized standard of right or good behavior, and virtue suggests high moral standards—standards that are maintained in spite of temptations or evil influences.

Are you personally fighting or enduring within yourself a spiritual war? If so, this is a very good indication that your heart (your soul and spirit) is pursuing goodness, which causes your sinful nature (that natural inclination from the time of Adam and Eve) to fight back.[14] According to the Bible, sin comes naturally: Psalm 51:5; Romans 7:6, 18, 8:4, 8-9, 13; Galatians 5:13, 16, 19, 24. As the apostle John explained, "*Anyone who does what is good* [as a way of life] *is from God. Anyone who does what is evil* [as a way of life] *has not seen God* [has not come to really know Him]" (3 John 11, NIV).

What is Love? Love is an intense feeling of affection. There are four forms of love: friendship (platonic), romantic, natural affection (familial), and agape. The first three can be understood in terms of shared mutual benefit that is found in all animals.

Agape is a self-sacrificing love found only in humans and God. It is described in John 3:16 (NIV), *"For God so loved the world that he gave his one and only Son, that whoever believes in him shall not perish but have eternal life."* The word "love" in this verse is translated 'agape.' When 1 John 4:8 says "*God is love,*" the Greek New Testament uses the word agape to describe God's love. (See section, Forms of Life and Love, in the book, *evolution – The Greatest Deception in Modern History.*)

What is Evil? Evil is sin, iniquity, wickedness, immorality, or corruption.[15] Sin is breaking the moral law, or any one of the Ten Commandments, or a departure from goodness. We associate evil with tyrants and dictators, terrorists and mass murderers, and people twisted into psychotic monsters of crime against the innocent. Evil is "a fundamental and troubling departure from goodness." And as mentioned in the section, Freedom of Choice, "Evil, in its essence, refuses to accept God as God and puts someone or something else [idolatry] in His place... [it is] the refusal to accept the true God as God...For this reason, the Bible treats idolatry as the **ultimate sin**, since it worships as God what is not God."[16] [Bold added]

Idolatry is the inclination of man to worship idols in place of God. Idols can take the form of statues such as golden calf idols, African idols, Hindu idols, Buddha idols,

Krishna idols, just to name a few. It can also mean worshiping the sun, moon, and stars; and material possessions such as money, automobiles, and boats (the standard for success today is material wealth and social status); sports, movie and music celebrities; political figures; kings and queens; and even dictators. Some argue that even big businesses have turned their back on God and worship at the altar of the dollar. All of this is a form of idolatry.[17]

How can mankind ignore the reality of evil—a supernatural phenomenon we see all around us in every country, state, city, and neighborhood in the form of corruption, violence, theft, adultery, drug addiction, abortion, gambling and greed of all kinds, not to mention ethnic wars, rumors of wars, and terrorism? Most notably, how can mankind ignore the indiscriminate shootings in every American city and the savagery (torture and barbaric killings of families—men, women, and children) by Islamic extremists in the Middle East and in other regions of the world?

This is just a trace sampling of what is happening in our midst. Paul wrote to Timothy that "*There will be **terrible times** in the last days.*" [Bold added] And then just a few verses later he warned, "*...evil men and impostors will go from bad to worse, deceiving and being deceived*" (2 Timothy 3:1, 13, NIV). **Those days are here, and it will only grow worse. Wake up America!!**

"*For our struggle is not against flesh and blood, but against the rulers, against the authorities, against the powers of this dark world and against the **spiritual forces of evil** in the heavenly realms*" (Ephesians 6:12, NIV). [Bold added] "*The one who does what is sinful is of the devil, because the devil has been sinning from the beginning. The reason the Son of God appeared was to destroy the devil's work*" (1 John 3:8, NIV).

The spiritual forces of evil cause people to *turn away without reason*—to willfully forget! (See 2 Peter 3:5-6.) In Luke 8:10-12 (NIV), Jesus described such people as "***though seeing, they may not see; though hearing, they may not understand.***" [Bold added] (Also see Matthew 13:14.) For whatever reason, if a person's mind is closed to Scripture, no amount of evidence will change him. This "hardening of the heart" (see Ephesians 4:18) against God is a supernatural phenomenon, an unseen battle between good and evil we witness in the news and in our everyday lives. Many people dismiss such claims because they have "**an enormous predisposition against the supernatural.**"[18]

We live in a troubled world (to put it mildly) and many bad things happen—often at the hands of corrupt people. It is clear that evil exists. What is surprising is that the Bible teaches that **evil is close to each one of us**.

What is Hatred? Hatred is an intense animosity or hostility that can be directed against individuals, groups of people, or beliefs or ideas. Love and hate are polar opposites, and they have no quantifiable mass or energy. Hatred is often associated with feelings of anger and hostility. Hatred can also manifest itself with the persecution of Christians, Jews, and the State of Israel. This type of hatred is described throughout this book. "*He did evil because he had not set his heart on seeking the Lord*" (2 Chronicles 12:14, NIV).

Christians and Jews are under attack throughout the world today, and it will continue to get worse. Although Christians in the United States still enjoy freedom to worship God without bias and prejudice, such freedom is rapidly being eroded. In many other countries such as China, Sudan, Africa, Saudi Arabia, North Korea, Russia, and most Muslim nations (e.g., Afghanistan) throughout the Middle East, Christians and Jews suffer great persecution and often times suffer terrible death for their faith. During the tribulation such suffering will be worldwide.

notes: prologue

1. McDowell, J. (1972). *Evidence that Demands a Verdict.* San Bernardino, CA: Campus Crusade for Christ, i. Also, see Craig, W.L. (2008). *Reasonable Faith.* Crossway Books. Wheaton, IL. (Josh McDowell is a Christian apologist, evangelist, and writer. He is associated with the Evangelical tradition of Protestant Christianity. His best-known book is *Evidence That Demands a Verdict*, which was ranked 13th in Christianity Today as one of the most influential evangelical books.) These books are highly recommended.

2. LaHaye, T. and Ice, T. (2001). *Charting the End Times.* Eugene, OR: Harvest House Publishers, 14.

3. McDowell, J., op. cit., i.

4. Alcorn, R. (2009). *If God Is Good – Faith in the Midst of Suffering and Evil.* Colorado Springs, CO: Multnomah Books, 24-25.

5. Johnson, J. (November 2011). Human suffering: Why this isn't the "best of all possible worlds." *Acts & Facts*, 40 (11), Dallas, TX: Institute for Creation Research, 10. (ICR.org)

6. Hagee, J. (2006). *Jerusalem Countdown: A Warning to the World.* Lake Mary, FL: FrontLine, 145-146. Also see Gallop, R. (2014, 2nd ed., revised 2016, 2018). *evolution – The Greatest Deception in Modern History,* xvi. Order on www.CreationScienceToday.com, www.Creation.com, www.Amazon.com/books, and www.Christianbook.com (Christian Book Distributors).

John 6:44 (NIV) states, *"No one can come to me unless the Father who sent me draws him, and I will raise him up at the last day."* Although this Scripture implies election or predestination, an individual must first make a personal choice, either to accept or deny the Creator.

God gives every human being the freedom to believe or not believe that Jesus Christ is the Son of God and to choose good or evil (that is, either choosing to live a righteous life or sinful life). In Matthew 4:19 (NAS), Jesus said to his disciples, *"Follow Me, and I will make you fishers of men"* and in 2 Peter 3:9 (NAS), *"The Lord is not slow about His promise...not wishing for any to perish but for all to come to repentance"*—implying that all men have freedom of choice.

Once a person *"calls on the name of the Lord"* (Romans 10:13, NIV), the Holy Spirit *"draws him..."* (John 6:44, NIV) into a spiritual union that cannot be broken or removed (John 10:27-28). Believing or calling on the name of the Lord is a continual and sincere desire of the heart, and people do not come to Christ strictly on their own initiative, but the Father draws them. God is omnipotent, omnipresent, and omniscient—He knew you in ancient times (Romans 8:29; Ephesians 1:4-5; 1 Corinthians 2:7) and foreknew the choice you will make (thus, there is the component of predestination), although you still have freedom of choice today.

In Revelation 1:7-8, John describes God the Father as *"who is and who was and who is to come."* There is no better way to describe the continuous existence of being. The best definition of a life source that philosophy can give us is "an unmoved mover." John's God goes way back before that! **He continuously existed before the beginning of all things** (John 1:1).

Regarding election or predestination, many were divinely selected in advance (for example, Abraham, Isaac, Jacob, Moses, Joshua, David, the disciples, John the Baptist, Paul, Timothy, and all the Old Testament Prophets to just name a few) for specific divine purposes—God knew them in advance and knew they would believe and dedicate their lives to God of the Holy Bible.

7. Mitchell, T. (December 2011). Death and Steve Jobs. *Answers Update*, 18 (12), Hebron, KY: Answers in Genesis, 1-2. (answersingenesis.org)

8. Alcorn, op. cit., 48-49.

9. Ibid., 41-42.

10. Alcorn, op. cit., 51.

11. NIV Bible end notes, Job 42:12-16.

12. Hal Lindsey (March 20, 2015; March 27, 2015; September 4, 2015). The Hal Lindsey Report, News from Hal Lindsey Media Ministries. (www.hallindsey.org)

13. Richison, G.C. (December 23, 2001). Genesis 3:15; as cited in http://versebyversecommentary.com/christmas/genesis-315/.

14. Hooser, D. (2014). The Fruit of the Spirit - Goodness: God's Character and Man's Potential. United Church of God, An International Association; as cited in http://www.ucg.org/christian-living/fruit-spirit-goodness-gods-character-and-mans-potential/.

15. What is Evil According to the Bible; as cited in http://godlovesyou-adron.blogspot.com/2011/03/what-is-evil-according-to-bible.html. Also see Alcorn, op. cit., 24-25.

16. Alcorn, R., op. cit., 25.

17. Hal Lindsey (March 4, 2014), op. cit.

18. Burrows, M. (1956). *What Mean These Stones?* New York: Meridian Books; as cited in McDowell, J., 69.

Chapter 1

The Bible's Truth and Accuracy

> *"In the beginning was the Word, and the Word was with God, and the Word was God. He was in the beginning with God. All things came into being through Him; and apart from Him nothing came into being..."* —John 1:1–3, NAS

Scientific Evidence for Divine Creation

Because science is incapable of penetrating the supernatural (the spiritual and the many theoretical dimensions in an infinite universe), it certainly does not mean a supernatural infinite God does not exist. One would logically theorize that in an infinite universe, with no valid (verifiable) explanation as to the cause, a supernatural cause would be a real or certain possibility—the only logical possibility. Nevertheless, secular scientists today are totally dedicated to a naturalistic explanation of origin although they have to "explain how nothing became everything" and thereby "invoke their own supernatural 'first act'."[1] For whatever reason, if a person's mind is closed to Scripture, no amount of evidence (scientific and theological) will change his or her mind.

Josh McDowell states, "Over and over again, like a broken record, I hear the phrase, 'Oh, you don't read the Bible do you?' or sometimes it is phrased, "...the Bible is just another book..."

Then there is the professor or teacher who ridicules the Bible to his students and snickers at the thought of anyone reading it.[2] And when asked why he/she (the teacher or student) doesn't believe in God and Creation (as opposed to atheism and evolution), typically the response would be, "There is overwhelming evidence for evolution, so why bother." Is that really true? The answer is a **most resounding No!!** Just take the time to read the book *evolution – The Greatest Deception in Modern History*.[3]

> Evolution is a belief system that many, if not most, scientists assume as fact and routinely use to interpret their observations. Instead of gathering scientific data, testing, and forming a conclusion (i.e., using the scientific method - see glossary), evolutionists first form their conclusion, and then search for evidence to support it.

When evolutionists are presented with an array of scientific laws and evidence supporting Creation and the statistical odds against

---

> The supernatural is that which is not subject to the laws of physics or that which is said to exist apart from nature as we know it.
>
> The spiritual forces of evil cause people to turn away—to willfully forget without reason! (See 2 Peter 3:5-6.) In Luke 8:10-12 (NIV), Jesus described such people as *"though seeing, they may not see; though hearing, they may not understand."* [Bold added] (Also see Matthew 13:14.) For whatever reason, if a person's mind is closed to Scripture, no amount of evidence will change his/her mind.
>
> This "hardening of the heart" against God (Ephesians 4:18) is a supernatural phenomenon—an unseen battle between good and evil not only found in the Bible and throughout history, but also most poignantly found in today's news and in our everyday lives. Many people dismiss such phenomena "not from a careful evaluation of the available data, but from an **enormous predisposition against the supernatural**."[5]

evolution, they seem unconcerned about these laws, evidence, or the statistical odds (see chapter 3, Evolution - A Statistical Impossibility in the above cited book)—they merely (glibly) state that "since life has naturally appeared, we merely beat the odds."[4]

When an evolutionary biology professor was presented the same evidence, the professor proposed "an infinite number of parallel universes, with ours happening to be the one in which the odds were beaten." Where's the scientific evidence in that response? "No amount of evidence can 'prove' God to people with this kind of [atheistic] mindset."[6]

Dr. Henry M. Morris, Ph.D., once stated, "The fact is that **evolutionists believe in evolution because they want to**. It is their desire at all costs to explain the origin of everything without a Creator. Evolutionism is thus intrinsically an atheistic religion....Whether atheism or humanism (or even pantheism), the purpose is to eliminate a personal God from any active role in the origin of the universe and all its components, including man."[7] [Bold added]

What many people today never hear and realize is the fact that scientific creation is based on scientific evidence—and such evidence is *overwhelming*. So why do secular scientists continue to adhere to a false evolutionary doctrine? The book, *evolution – The Greatest Deception in Modern History (Scientific Evidence for Divine Creation)*, provides the reasons and summarizes much of the evidence for scientific creation, including research by esteemed scientists in almost all fields of science.[8] See list of some of the evidence from the above cited book.

- Evolution is contrary to the First and Second Laws of Thermodynamics (see chapt. 2), the Law of Biogenesis (see chapt. 3), and the Law of Causality (see glossary) whereas creation is consistent with such laws.[3] These laws have always proved valid whenever tested. Many scientists believe the 2nd Law is enough to disprove evolutionary theory and is one of the important reasons why many esteemed scientists have abandoned evolutionary doctrine in favor of creationism.

- Students in public schools (middle schools, high schools, colleges, and universities) are taught as scientific fact that "survival of the fittest" caused evolution of life on Earth—but this is a complete falsehood. Natural selection (or survival of the fittest, adaptation, or speciation) is, in fact, a '**thinning out process**' that leads to loss of genetic information. So called "adaptive evolution" selects gene traits from an already existing gene pool best suited for a specific environment. No one has ever observed uphill drift or the addition of genetic information to the gene pool.

- Evolution has no known biological processes or mechanisms to form higher levels of organization and complexity—gene mutations are overwhelmingly degenerative and none are "uphill" (i.e., unequivocally beneficial) in the sense of adding new genetic information to the gene pool.

- The probability of getting an average-size protein of left-handed amino acids (found only in living cells) by random, natural processes is zero. And the probability of getting a living cell, synonymous to the most sophisticated supercomputer yet microscopic in size, is likewise zero, and consciousness (awareness, perception) would only be expected from a Divine creator.

- Geologic landforms and sedimentary features throughout the world are completely consistent with a worldwide flood as described in the Book of Genesis. For many esteemed geologists who have researched geologic landforms and catastrophic processes, evidence of a global flood is indisputable.

- A worldwide flood as described in Genesis 6–8 is within the boundaries of known geophysics—see phase diagram in chapter 4 of the book, *evolution – The Greatest Deception in Modern History* and **Pangaea Flood Video** at www.CreationScienceToday.com.

- Enormous limestone formations, huge coal and oil formations, and immense underground salt layers are indicative of a worldwide flood—not slow and gradual processes over billions of years. Such features are satisfactorily explained by a global flood and known geophysical and geochemical processes.

- There is no credible technique for establishing the age of sedimentary rock—fossil dating used to establish the age of sedimentary rock suffers from circular reasoning and guesswork, all based on the assumption of evolution.

- The standard geologic and fossil column, as depicted in most science textbooks with transitional creatures evolving toward more complex forms, is utterly fictitious and misleading and does not represent the real world. In reality, it perfectly represents the aftermath of a worldwide flood.

- There are no transitional fossils or living forms—there is not one single example of evolution! Evolutionists look for "the" missing link—ironically, they are in desperate search for just one! But there should be billions of examples of transitional forms with transitional structures if evolution were true, but there are none. This one fact alone should convince most rational people that evolution is a false doctrine—a great deception.

- Irreducible complexity (IC) is another reason why evolution is impossible. A practical household analogy is the common mousetrap—its individual parts have no transitional value or function yet the trap could not function if any of the parts were missing. A biological example is the human eye comprising the iris, pupil, cornea, sclera, lens, macula, retina, optic disk, and optic nerve. The individual parts have no transitional value yet the eye could not function if any of the parts were missing. Amniotic eggs and the flagellum of bacteria are other examples of IC. These and other biologic systems of the body could not have evolved piece by piece (according to Darwinian gradualism) because the entire system must be present at the start for the system to work. See Appendix B.

- Contrary to popular belief, evidence indicates that early man was intelligent and highly skilled with an advanced social structure. There is also evidence suggesting their belief in the existence of an afterlife.

- Soft tissue with traces of red blood cells has been found in dinosaur fossils supposedly 70 to 250 million years old but soft tissues and red blood cells have relatively short life spans.

- Carbon-14 has been found in coal and diamonds and in deep geological strata, all supposedly hundreds of millions of years old. Researchers have been unable to find carbon (stable forms: carbon-12 and -13) without carbon-14 (unstable form). (C-14 has a relatively short life span.)

- Radioisotope dating suffers from broken, unprovable assumptions. The technique is "fatally flawed"—yet scientists contend as fact what they cannot prove primarily because of their desire to explain the origin of the universe without a Creator.

- Abundant daughter isotopes are indicative of accelerated nuclear decay associated with creation (expansion, stretching out, or acceleration of the universe from an extremely hot, dense phase when matter and energy were concentrated) and a worldwide flood with massive restructuring of the earth's lithosphere—not slow and gradual processes over billions of years.

- Powerful evidences of accelerated nuclear decay in igneous rocks found worldwide are helium in zircon crystals, radiohalos and fission tracks, and rapid magnetic field reversals and decay.

- Gravitational time dilation offers a credible explanation for a young earth—that is, it explains how light from the extremities of the universe has the potential of reaching the earth in a relatively short period of time (from earth's perspective).

- Over a hundred geochronometers (techniques to date the earth and universe) indicate a young earth and universe (e.g., carbon-14 found in coal and diamonds, and lack of continental erosion, lack of ocean sediments, and lack of salt in the sea.

Each one of these evidences is enough to convince most rational people that evolution is a false doctrine and the earth is, in fact, young!

The Bible's Unity

The Bible comprises 39 Old Testament Books and 27 New Testament Books and was written over a span of nearly 1600 years by more than 40 authors from various occupations and social classes including kings, peasants, philosophers, fishermen, herdsmen, physicians, businessmen, poets, statesmen, scholars, military generals, etc. (beginning with Genesis and the Torah written by Moses about 1450 BC and ending with Revelation written by the apostle John about AD 95).

Furthermore, the Bible was written in different places (Moses in the wilderness; Jeremiah in a dungeon; Daniel in a palace [ruins have been discovered; see chapter 3, United Kingdom]; Paul inside a Roman prison; Luke while traveling; John on the Isle of Patmos, a small Greek island in the Aegean Sea; and others during military crusades); in different times (David in times of war and Solomon in times of peace); different moods (times of joy and during times of great sorrow and despair); on different continents (Asia, Africa, and Europe); and in three languages (Hebrew-Old Testament, Aramaic-language of Christ, and Greek-New Testament).

The Bible is consistent in its message and form (composition, symmetry, style, and agreement) from beginning to end: creation and fall of mankind (Genesis), disobedience and moral depravity of mankind (throughout the Old and New Testaments), and God reaching out to mankind offering redemption or a bridge to salvation (New Testament). The theme throughout the Bible is 'God's plan of redemption' for sinful and immoral humanity. (See book by Roger Gallop, *Defeating Evil - God's Plan Before the Beginning of Time*.)

The first and last Books of the Bible—Genesis and Revelation, written by Moses and John, respectively—fit together perfectly in describing "paradise lost" and "paradise regained"—in Genesis 1-3 and Revelation 21-22. From the first book of Genesis to the last book of Revelation, the Bible is perfectly unified, impeccably written, and the most widely distributed book of all time. Mere human genius could never have accomplished such an extraordinary feat.[9] Such unity is **humanly impossible—man with his immoral nature, arrogance, and self-absorption could not have written this book.**

As Kyle Butt states in Apologetics Press, "To say that the writers of the Bible were diverse would be an understatement. Yet, though their educational and cultural backgrounds varied extensively, and though many of them were separated by several centuries, the 66 books that compose the Bible fit together perfectly. **To achieve such a feat by employing mere human ingenuity and wisdom would be impossible.** In fact, it would be impossible from a human standpoint to gather the writings of 40 men from the same culture, with the same educational background, during the same time period, and get anything close to the unity that is evident in the Bible. The Bible's unity is a piece of remarkable evidence that proves its divine origin."[10] [Bold added]

The Bible was written from God's perspective, not from a human perspective. The history of man throughout the Bible is depicted with all his failures, sinfulness (arrogance, self-absorption, bias, sexual immorality and

---

The Bible's major categories and books: Creation (Genesis); Law (Exodus through Deuteronomy); History (Joshua through Esther); Poetry (Job through Song of Solomon); Major Prophets (Moses, Isaiah, Jeremiah, Ezekiel, and Daniel); Minor Prophets (Hosea, Joel, Amos, Asaph, Obadiah, Jonah, Micah, Nahum, Habakkuk, Zephaniah, Haggai, Zechariah, and Malachi); Life of Christ (Matthew, Mark, Luke, and John); History of the church (Acts); Epistles and Letters (Romans through Jude); and Prophecy (Revelation).

perversions, cruelty, corruption, theft, adultery, greed, and the list goes on), and unfaithfulness to God (idolatry)—laid "open and bare" for all to see. **Self-centered, arrogant, and egotistical man could never have written such a book.** Even the heroes of the Bible have their moral failures recorded for all to read, including Noah (Genesis 9:20-24), Moses (Numbers 20:7-12), David (2 Samuel 11), Solomon (1 Kings 11:1-13), Elijah (1 Kings 19), Peter (Matthew 26:74), and Paul (Acts 7:58, 8:2-3, 9:1). *"For all have sinned and come short of the glory of God"* (Romans 3:23, NIV).

According to Scripture, the Bible is God-breathed (2 Timothy 3:16; 2 Peter 1:21; Genesis 2:7; Exodus 24:3, 4, 7; Jeremiah 36:1-4; 1 Corinthians 14:37; Revelation 1:1, 2, 10, 11, 19; and Ephesians 3:3-5). Although 2 Timothy 3:16 is the only place in the Bible where the phrase *"God-breathed"* is used, Scripture is filled with similar meanings. All Scripture is inspired

> **Disciple** (in Greek) means student or follower while **apostle** (in Greek) means a messenger or sent one. Disciples were followers or students of Christ. Jesus chose twelve to travel and learn from him; eventually, eleven plus one added later (Matthias in Acts 1:26) were sent to foreign lands to act as messengers of the good news (the gospel). Not all of the disciples were apostles though all apostles were disciples.

by God and was given through Old Testament prophets and New Testament apostles to instruct men how to live righteously before God.

The late Dr. David L. Cooper, one of the most esteemed Bible scholars in the world, said of the Bible, "Abundant and overwhelming is the proof that the Scriptures are God-breathed. No open-minded truthseeker can weigh the evidence for the divine origin of the Scriptures and can arrive at the conclusion that the books of the Bible were written by uninspired men."[11]

The Bible's Historical Accuracy

If the Bible is divinely inspired, it must be historically accurate—and if the Bible is accurate, then this is strong evidence that the authors were divinely inspired. Over the last several hundred years enemies of Christianity have attacked the Bible's historical accuracy but, in every case, the Bible has been proved correct through archaeological excavations: stone ruins, relics, monuments, tombs, and artifacts of ancient civilizations. Peoples and events, known only previously in Scripture, have been verified through such excavations and, in every instance, the Bible has always been proven right.[12]

The Old and New Testaments make abundant references to nations, kings, battles, cities, rivers and mountains, buildings, customs, politics, dates, etc. Because historical accounts described in the Bible are so specific, many details are subject to archaeological examination and verification. Critics in the 19th century made many accusations in an attempt to disprove the reliability of the Bible but the astonishing increase of archaeological facts in the 20th century has overturned all these skeptical claims. For example, at one time the Bible was ridiculed for mentioning previously unknown names such as Assyria,

> **Archaeology** is the study of human activity in the past, primarily through the recovery and analysis of material culture such as relics, monuments, inscriptions, tombs, and artifacts of ancient civilizations.

Nineveh, and kings not mentioned in other historical documents but this and much more has been confirmed through archaeological excavations.[13]

Archaeological discoveries this past century have confirmed many hundreds of biblical statements. Dr. Henry M. Morris concluded his study of archeological evidence of the Bible by stating, "It must be extremely significant that, in view of the great mass of corroborative evidence regarding the Biblical history of these periods, there exists today not one unquestionable find of archaeology that proves the Bible to be in error at any point."[14]

Nelson Glueck, renowned Jewish archaeologist, wrote that "It may be stated categorically that no archaeological discovery has ever controverted a biblical reference." He continued by stating "...the almost incredibly accurate historical memory of the Bible, and particularly so when it is fortified by archaeological fact."[15] Josh McDowell, in his book, *Evidence that Demands a Verdict*, cites example after example of esteemed archaeologists and historians who attest to the accuracy of the Bible.

William F. Albright, one of our great archaeologists, states that "There can be no doubt that archaeology has confirmed the substantial historicity of Old Testament tradition." Albright adds, "The excessive skepticism shown toward the Bible by important historical schools of the eighteenth and nineteenth centuries, certain [skeptical] phrases which still appear periodically, have been progressively discredited. Discovery after discovery has established the accuracy of innumerable details, and has brought increased recognition to the value of the Bible as a source of history."[16]

The late Millar Burrows, an American biblical scholar, a leading authority on the Dead Sea scrolls, and professor emeritus at the Yale Divinity School, exposed the **cause of excessive unbelief**. Burrows stated that "Archaeology has in many cases refuted the views of modern critics. It has been shown in a number of instances that **these views rest on false assumptions and unreal, artificial schemes** of historical development." He explained the cause of unbelief by stating, "The excessive skepticism of many liberal theologians stems not from a careful evaluation of the available data, but from an ***enormous predisposition against the supernatural.***"[17] [Bold and italics added]

The Bible's Preservation

The Bible was preserved through a process called canonization. Our English word canonization comes from the Greek word kanon, which means 'a straight edge or ruler.' In other words it is a rigorous review process using precise rules and standards. See text box.

The books of the Bible have been canonized and have been determined to be Holy Scripture, or the divinely inspired Word of God. Canonization could not have been done without using such standards. "Determining the standards was a process conducted first by Jewish rabbis and scholars and then later by early Christians. Ultimately, it was God who decided which books belonged in the biblical canon."[18]

One might logically assume that because the Bible has been copied and translated many hundreds or even thousands of times, there might be a greater likelihood of numerous errors and changes. So let's examine why the Bible (Old and New Testaments) remains accurate when compared with the original manuscript.[19]

> The word canon means 'standard' which denotes rules to measure and evaluate.[20] Five guiding principles include: 1) Is it authoritative? Does the book come from "the hand of God?" 2) Is it prophetic? Do prophecies come from prophets of the Old or New Testament? 3) Is it authentic? Does the book come from Divine inspiration? 4) Is it dynamic? Did it come from "the life transforming power of God?" and 5) Was it received, read, and used by the people of God?
>
> The process of "collection and recognition" was conducted first by Jewish rabbis and scholars. "Compared to the New Testament, there was much less controversy over the canon of the Old Testament. Hebrew believers recognized God's messengers [apostles] as prophets and accepted their writings as inspired of God." For the New Testament, the process of "collection and recognition" began by early Christians and later by Christian scholars and theologians. Ultimately, God in His sovereignty decided what books belonged in the biblical canon.[21]

The Old Testament

The quantity of Old Testament Hebrew manuscripts is small (as compared with the New Testament) because imperfect, worn, or damaged manuscripts were "formally buried" by Jewish scribes. The sole mission of Aaronic priests and scribes was the safeguarding and preservation of OT Scriptures. *"Unto them were committed the oracles of God"* (Romans 3:2, KJV). Old Testament manuscripts were standardized (canonized) by Masoretic Jews by 6th century AD. (See canonization in Glossary – Appendix A.)

Because of this extreme care, the quality of Hebrew manuscripts exceeds all other ancient documents. The 1947 discovery of the Dead Sea Scrolls provided a significant check or verification of the accuracy because these ancient scrolls predate (exist before) the earliest Masoretic Old Testament manuscripts by about 1,000 years. Regardless of this time span, the number of alternative interpretations between the Dead Sea Scrolls and the Masoretic Text is very small, and most are slight changes in spelling and style. As Sir Frederic Kenyon said, "the Christian can take the whole Bible in his hand and say without fear or hesitation that he holds in it the true Word of God, handed down without essential loss from generation to generation throughout the centuries."[22]

As explained by Dr. Kenneth Boa, "Because of the great reverence the Jewish scribes held toward the Scriptures, they exercised extreme care in making new copies of the Hebrew Bible. The entire scribal process was specified in meticulous detail to minimize the possibility of even the slightest error. The number of letters, words, and lines were counted, and the middle letters of the Pentateuch and the Old Testament were determined. If a single mistake was discovered, the entire manuscript would be destroyed."[23]

The late Robert D. Wilson, an American linguist and Presbyterian scholar who devoted his life to studying and proving the reliability of the Hebrew Bible (Old Testament), states: "In 144 cases of transliteration from Egyptian, Assyrian, Babylonian, and Moabite into Hebrew and in 40 cases of the opposite, or 184 cases in all, the evidence shows that for 2,300 to 3,900 years the text of the proper names in the Hebrew Bible has been transmitted with the most minute accuracy. That the original scribes should have written them with such close conformity to correct philological [lingual, dialectal] principles is a wonderful proof of their thorough care and scholarship; further that the Hebrew text should have been transmitted by copyists through so many centuries is a phenomenon unequalled in the history of literature."[24]

> The **Masoretic Text** is the authoritative Hebrew and Aramaic text of Rabbinic Judaism (mainstream form of Judaism since 6th century AD). Jewish and Christian scholars have used a wide range of sources to augment the Hebrew text including the Septuagint, Samaritan Pentateuch, and the Dead Sea Scrolls.[25]
>
> **Septuagint** is the primary third century BC Greek translation of the Old Testament. It is the oldest Greek version of the Old Testament, translated by Jewish scholars during the reign of Ptolemy II Philadelphus, king of Ptolemaic Egypt (c. 285 to 246 BC).
>
> **Samaritan Pentateuch** is the first five books of the Bible authored by Moses (the Pentateuch) written in the Samaritan alphabet. Most likely the Torah was available in northern Israel when the Assyrians led the Northern Kingdom (Israel) into exile in 721 BC. See chapter 4, Assyrian Empire Conquers the Northern Kingdom.
>
> **Dead Sea Scrolls** were discovered during the years 1947 and 1956 in 11 caves along the northwest shore (about 1.2 km inland) of the Dead Sea in the Qumran Mountains of Israel. The scrolls were written by the Essenes, Jewish community of faith, between 200 BC and AD 68. Thirty-eight of the thirty-nine Old Testament books were included in these texts. The discovery confirms that we have the same Old Testament Scripture that existed in the day of Jesus. One of the remarkable finds is a 24 foot-long scroll of Isaiah. (See photo below.)
>
> These sources reveal an amazing consistency with the Masoretic Text which gives us assurance that God divinely and sovereignly protected His Word through thousands of years of meticulous copying and translating.
>
> The survival of thousands of New Testament manuscripts confirms New Testament writings were also carefully preserved. While copies of major portions of the New Testament survive from documents dated around AD 300, most other classic books survive no older than around AD 900.

Dead Sea Scroll, Book of Isaiah, Ancient Caves at Qumran near the Dead Sea, Israel. *Photo by Roger Gallop, March 11, 2016*

The Palms scroll. *Public Domain, Wikipedia.*

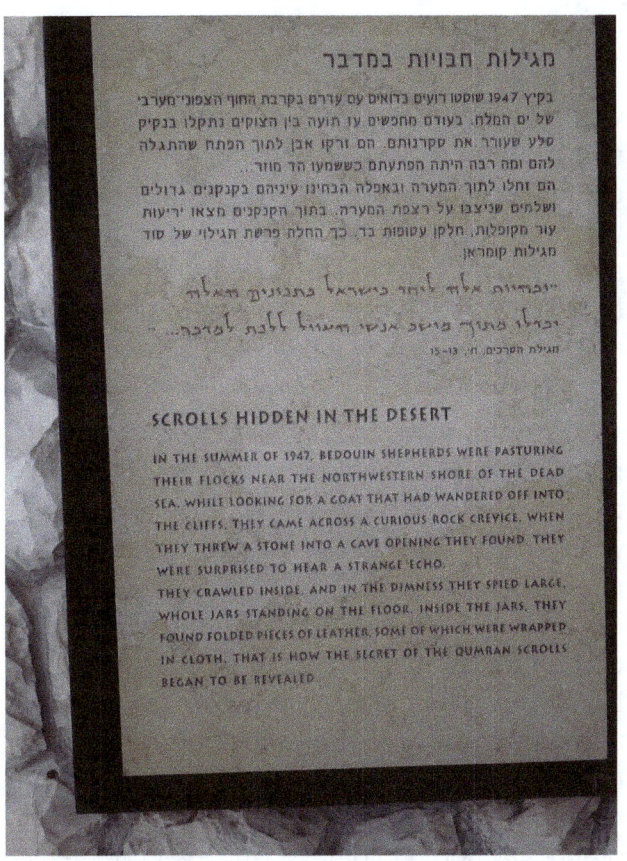

Scrolls hidden in ancient caves at Qumran near the Dead Sea, Israel. *Photos by Roger Gallop, March 11, 2016*

Qumran Cave, *Public Domain, Wikipedia*

The Communal House, Qumran Mountains, Israel
Photo by Roger Gallop, March 11, 2016

The New Testament

The quantity of New Testament manuscripts is unsurpassed in ancient literature. There are about 8,000 Latin manuscripts, over 5,000 Greek manuscripts, and at least 1,000 in other languages. "In regard to the New Testament there are about thirteen thousand manuscripts, complete and incomplete, in Greek and other languages that have survived from antiquity. No other works from classical antiquity has such attestation."[26] In comparison, the usual number of existing manuscripts for works of Greek and Latin authors, such as Plato, Aristotle or Caesar, ranges from 1 to 20.

Scripture has been translated into hundreds of languages (both ancient and modern)—and comparisons can be made to determine the possibility of errors or changes. Such extensive comparisons of these ancient manuscripts have found very little variance. Of this little variance, "only a small number of these differences affect the sense of the passages, and only a fraction of these have any real consequences."[27] Many of the earliest surviving manuscripts (such as Syriac and Coptic versions) show that God's Word has been precisely preserved in many languages.

New Testament preservation of Scriptures occurred through the priesthood of believers. After the crucifixion of Christ, every believer was a priest under Christ. Scripture was safeguarded by faithful Christians in every walk of life through guidance of the Holy Spirit. *"But when he, the Spirit of truth, comes, he will guide you into all the truth. He will not speak on his own; he will speak only what he hears, and he will tell you what is yet to come"* (John 16:13, NIV).

Scripture "written on material [papyrus, parchment, or vellum] that perishes, having to be copied and recopied for hundreds of years before the invention of the printing press, did not diminish its style, correctness nor existence."[28] The "Jews preserved it as no other manuscript has ever been preserved... they kept tabs on every letter, syllable, word and paragraph. They had special classes of men within their culture whose sole duty was to preserve and transmit these documents with practically perfect fidelity...Who ever counted the letters and syllables and words of Plato or Aristotle?"[29]

According to Josh McDowell, "After trying to shatter the historicity and validity of the Scripture, I came to the conclusion that they [ancient manuscripts] are historically trustworthy. If one disregards the Bible as being unreliable, then he must disregard almost all literature of antiquity."[30]

Attempts to Destroy the Bible

Over the many centuries the Bible has withstood fierce attacks like no other book in history. Many have tried to burn it or ban it, and "outlaw it from the days of Roman emperors to present-day Communist dominated countries."[31] Despite vicious attacks and efforts to destroy the Bible, it remains the greatest book throughout all time.

Greek ruler Antiochus Epiphanes, who ruled the Seleucid Empire (Syrian region of Judah; see glossary and chapter 4, Grecian Empire Conquers...) from c. 175 BC to 164 BC, tried to eradicate Judaism (the religion, culture, and way of life of the Jewish people) by destroying all copies of the Torah, the first five books of the Bible. He also defiled the Temple in Jerusalem; he ordered the killing of tens of thousands of Jewish men, women, and children; and he ordered the Jews to destroy their Hebrew Scripture and worship Zeus as their supreme god. But Judas Maccabeus saved the Hebrew books and led a revolt that won independence for the Jewish people (chapter 4, Grecian Empire Conquers...). The Jewish holiday, Hanukkah, commemorates the rededication of the Holy Temple following the Maccabaen revolt.

Another example is the Roman emperor Diocletian who issued an edict in AD 303 to kill all Christians and destroy their Bibles: "...an imperial letter was everywhere promulgated, ordering the razing of the churches to the ground and the destruction by fire of the Scriptures, proclaiming that those who held high positions would lose all civil rights, while those in households, if they persisted in their profession of Christianity, would be deprived of their liberty."[32] The next emperor, Constantine, legalized Christianity and paid for the production of fifty new hand-written copies of the Bible just 25 years later.

In his book, *All About the Bible*, author Sidney Collett, says "Voltaire, the noted French infidel who died in 1778, said that in one hundred years from his time Christianity would be swept from existence and passed into history. But what has happened? Voltaire has passed into history; while the circulation of the Bible continues to increase in almost all parts of the world, carrying blessing wherever it goes."[33]

Jesus Christ made a remarkable prophesy about the preservation of His Word: *"Heaven and earth will pass away, but My words will never pass away"* (Mark 13:31, NIV; also Matthew 24:35). God's Word is indestructible: *"It is easier for heaven and earth to disappear than for the least stroke of a pen to drop out of the Law"* (Luke 16:17, NIV). In addition, Jesus stated that His words would spread around the world: *"And this gospel of the kingdom will be preached in the whole world as a testimony to all nations, and then the end will come"* (Matthew 24:14, NIV). *"And the gospel must first be preached to all nations"* (Mark 13:10, NIV). What we find today is that God's Word has been preserved and has been preached throughout the world.

The Bible is the most read and studied of all historical books and remains available in many languages, more than any other book. Yet *people today resist reading and studying the Bible* for reasons given in the Prologue, Nature of Mankind.

The Bible teaches that God is all-powerful and can do anything He chooses (Jeremiah 32:17, 27; Matthew 19:26; Mark 14:36; Job 42:2). If He therefore chooses to preserve the Scriptures so that man cannot destroy it, or if He chooses to whisper in someone's ear to change the course of history or to bless just a single individual (a child, a mother, a father, a family), He is certainly able to do so. See http://av1611.com/kjbp/articles/moorman-preservation.html, The King James Bible Page by Jack Moorman (2014).

The Bible's Uniqueness

And then finally, the Bible's uniqueness cannot be ignored. Why has the Bible become the most widely distributed and most influential book of all time? And what are the chances that such a small nation of people (Israel) would write a book that would have the greatest influence worldwide? Certainly, the odds for such a book would favor a more ancient society such as Egypt, Mesopotamia (cradle of civilization), or any one of the other great empires.[34]

But instead, the world's most prominent and influential book comes from the Jewish people of tiny Israel—who from the time of Moses and all the major and minor prophets until the time of Jesus and His apostles (a span of more than 1,600 years) was inspired by God (God-breathed; 2 Timothy 3:16; 2 Peter 1:21; Genesis 2:7; Exodus 24:3,4,7; Jeremiah 36:1-4; 1 Corinthians 14:37; Revelation 1:1, 2, 10, 11, 19; and Ephesians 3:3-5) to record the words of the Bible through the prophets, disciples, and apostles. And these words included assurances and prophecies that information about God would reach the ends of the earth.[35]

In addition, Jesus stated in Matthew 24:14 and Mark 13:10 that His words would spread around the world. And in Psalm 48:10 and Psalm 22:27 are references to God being known and praised throughout the world and in Isaiah 45:22 is the offer of salvation to all people. The Bible became the first religious book to be distributed worldwide and is the predominant religious book in Europe, and North and South America; also, it has an influential presence throughout Africa, Asia including Hong Kong, the Philippines, Russia, and South Korea.[36]

The Bible's Prophetic Accuracy

Prophecy is "history written in advance"—and could only be given by the omnipresent, omnipotent, and omniscient God of the Holy Bible. The apostle Peter states in 2 Peter 1:21 (NIV), *"For prophecy never had its origin in the human will, but prophets, though human, spoke from God as they were carried along by the Holy Spirit."*

People can look no farther than Biblical prophecy to see God working in our world today—**yet most people are completely unaware of such miraculous events** (as described in chapters 4 - 12). Jesus described this inability to understand as ***"though seeing, they may not see; though hearing, they may not understand"*** (Luke 8:10-12, NIV; Matthew 13:14). [Bold added] **Fulfilled prophecies that**

Biblical prophecy plays two roles. It foretells future events, and it explains positive or negative results. Prophecy announces events that bring joy and pleasure or fear and foreboding. When prophecy is ignored, it is usually **because people don't like what they hear**. Biblical prophecy is **always accurate and precise**.

In Matthew 24, Jesus spoke of wars, famines, earthquakes, persecutions, apostasy, and betrayals in the last days, and finally of His own return, but *most incredibly* even in light of current worldwide events including the rebirth of the State of Israel and its possession of the City of Jerusalem (see chapters 6 - 8), **such prophecy is widely rejected today**. This and other end time prophecies are as dependable as Noah's warning of the Flood. Consider 2 Peter 3:3-7: **a modern day warning!**

we can actually see today provide some of the strongest reasons to believe the Truth of the Holy Bible and are evidence proving the Bible's credibility as a product of supernatural Divine Creation.

Prophecy illustrates the power of God through the fulfillment of impossible predictions—specific human events predicted thousands of years in advance—**events that we can see and understand today.** Wilbur Smith, worldwide bestselling author, concludes that:[37]

> "...whatever one may think of the authority of and the message presented in the book we call the Bible, there is worldwide agreement that in more ways than one it is the most remarkable volume [book] that has ever been produced in these some five thousand years of writing on the part of the human race."

> "It is the only volume ever produced by man, or a group of men in which is to be found a large body of prophecies relating to individual nations, to Israel, to all the peoples of the earth, to certain cities, and to the coming One who was to be the Messiah. The ancient world had many different devices for determining the future, known as divination, but not in the entire gamut of Greek and Latin literature, even though they use the words prophet and prophecy, can we find any real specific prophecy of a great historic event to come in the distant future, nor any prophecy of a Savior to arise in the human race..."

> "Mohammedanism **cannot** point to any prophecies of the coming of Mohammed uttered hundreds of years before his birth. Neither can the founders of any cult in this country rightly identify any ancient text specifically foretelling their appearance."

Prophet of the Old Testament is an individual who actually spoke with God and received Divine knowledge, and in turn served as an intermediary with humanity, delivering knowledge from the Lord God. The message that the prophet conveys is called **prophecy**.

As stated previously, the Bible is God-breathed (2 Timothy 3:16; 2 Peter 1:21; Genesis 2:7; Exodus 24:3, 4, 7; Jeremiah 36:1-4; 1 Corinthians 14:37; Revelation 1:1, 2, 10, 11, 19; and Ephesians 3:3-5). All Scripture is inspired by God and was given through Old Testament prophets and New Testament apostles to instruct men how to live righteously before God.

About **33 percent** of the Bible focuses on prophecy and the majority of these prophecies focuses on the amazing end time prophecies happening in today's world: the rebirth of the State of Israel, the nations of the world, signs of the end times, the rapture of the church, the seven year tribulation period, and the Second Coming of our Lord Jesus Christ.

Prophecy concerning the history of Israel and current end time events is found in the Major Prophets (Isaiah, Jeremiah, Ezekiel, and Daniel) and Minor Prophets (Hosea, Joel, Amos, Asaph, Obadiah, Jonah, Micah, Nahum, Habakkuk, Zephaniah, Haggai, Zechariah, and Malachi) of the Old Testament. End time prophecy in the New Testament is found in Matthew, Mark, Luke, John, First and Second Thessalonians, First and Second Timothy, First and Second Peter, and Revelation.

Many people "attack predictive prophecy **from the viewpoint of post-dating,"** that is, writing the prophecy after the event rather than before. McDowell shows how these prophecies are **NOT** "post-dictions" (that is, written after the event).[38] Ancient hand-written scrolls were copied and recopied and then distributed and redistributed throughout the known world of that time. It is logical to understand that no one could possibly have collected all the copies, from Egypt to Babylon to Greece, to make modifications after the event. And enough copies have been found among ancient artifacts during archaeological excavations to confirm they were written long before the events were accurately prophesied.

In Isaiah 41:23 (NIV), the prophet emphatically made a challenge to heathen gods: *"tell us what the future holds, so we may know that you are gods."* The true God accepted this challenge. "He predicted multitudes of events to happen in the future. They have come true exactly as predicted, even though in some cases thousands of years have elapsed before their fulfillment. God has proven that He is our supernatural God with all wisdom. We have no alternative but to believe."[39]

This book is about prophetic evidence for Divine creation. To understand Bible prophecy one must first have a good, basic understanding of Old and New Testament (Jewish) history. The next four chapters (chapters 2 - 5) focus on the fulfillment of God's covenant to Abraham, Isaac, and Jacob; disobedience of the Jewish people; God's enduring patience waiting for His chosen people to return to the Lord; continued disobedience of the Jewish people; and the scattering of the Jewish people throughout the world (Diaspora) in AD 70.

And then against all odds and in fulfillment of Old and New Testament prophecy, the Jewish people returned and reestablished the State of Israel on May 14, 1948, after 1,878 years of worldwide exile. The rebirth of Israel and repossession of the ancient City of Jerusalem following the Six Day War on June 5–10, 1967 (prerequisites to rebuilding the Temple and the Second Coming) are pre-tribulation super signs.

Many other end time prophetic events pertaining to Israel and surrounding countries (European Union, Russia, Iran, Arab countries and China) are currently being fulfilled in today's world, but most people seem oblivious to end time Bible prophecy.

A professor once remarked to McDowell, **"If you are an intelligent man, you will read the one book that has drawn more attention than any other, if you are searching for the truth."**[40] [Bold added] If you are seeking the truth about what is going on in the world today, then read the Bible—devote 15 to 20 minutes each night starting with the New Testament. Purchase an NIV Study Bible with explanation notes at the bottom of each page. Also read McDowell, J. (1972). *Evidence that Demands a Verdict.* San Bernardino, CA: Campus Crusade for Christ, and end times books by Hal Lindsey, Jack Van Impe, Tim LaHaye-Thomas Ice, John Hagee, David Jeremiah, Chuck Missler, Mark Hitchcock, and many others.

notes: Chapter 1

1. Bates, G. Who made God? Can there be an uncreated creator? CD Produced by Creation Ministries International, www.Creation.com.

2. McDowell, J. (1972). *Evidence that Demands a Verdict.* San Bernardino, CA: Campus Crusade for Christ, 17.

3. Gallop, R.G. (2014, Second Ed., revised 2016, 2018). *evolution – The Greatest Deception in Modern History.* Red Butte Press, Inc. Order on www.Amazon.com/books, www.Christianbook.com (Christian Book Distributors).

4. Stout, T.R. (2013). Can true science prove God? *Creation Matters.* Creation Research Society, 18(4), 7.

5. Burrows, M. (1956). *What Mean These Stones?* New York: Meridian Books, 1; as cited in McDowell, J. (1972), op. cit., 69.

6. Stout, T. R. (2013), op. cit.

7. Morris, H.M. The scientific case against evolution. Institute for Creation Research. Retrieved October 2014, from http://www.icr.org/home/resources/resources_tracts_scientificcaseagainstevolution/.
(Dr. Henry M. Morris (1918-2006) was Founder of the Institute for Creation Research.)

8. Gallop, R.G. (2014, revised 2016), op. cit.

9. Ham, K., Sarfati, J., and Wieland, C. (1990). *The Revised & Expanded Answers Book.* Green Forest, AR: Master Books, 17. Also see Butt, Kyle (2007). The Unity of the Bible. Montgomery, AL: Apologetics Press. Retrieved 2014, from http://www.apologeticspress.org/APContent.aspx?category=13&article=2151.

10. Butt, K. (2007), op. cit.

11. Cooper, David L. (1942). *The World's Greatest Library Graphically Illustrated.* Los Angeles, CA: *Biblical Research Society*, 7; as cited in LaHaye, T. and Ice, T. (2001). *Charting the End Times.* Eugene, OR: Harvest House Publishers, 15-16.

12. Sasser, J. (2003). The Historical Accuracy of the Bible. La Vista Church of Christ. Retrieved 2014, from http://www.lavistachurchofchrist.org/LVarticles/HistoricalAccuracyOfTheBible.htm.

13. LaHaye, T. and Ice, T. (2001), op. cit., 14.

14. Morris, H.M. (1956). *The Bible and Modern Science.* Chicago: Moody Press; as cited in http://www.seeking4truth.com/historical_accuracy_of_the_bible.htm.

15. Glueck, N. (1969). *Rivers in the Desert; History of Neteg.* Philadelphia: Jewish Publications Society of America; as cited in McDowell, J. (1972), op. cit., 68 (69-76).

16. Albright, W.F. (1956). *Archaeology and the Religions of Israel.* Baltimore: Johns Hopkins University Press; as cited in McDowell, J. (1972), 68; and Albright, W.F. (1960). *The Archaeology of Palestine.* Rev. ed. Harmondsworth, Middlesex: Pelican Books; as cited in McDowell, J., op. cit., 68.

17. Burrows, M. (1956), op. cit., 291, 1; as cited in McDowell, J., op. cit., 69.

18. Got Questions.org; Retrieved http://www.gotquestions.org/canon-Bible.html; and All About Truth. Retrieved 2014, from http://www.allabouttruth.org/bible-manuscripts-faq.htm.

19. Boa, Kenneth (2006). How Accurate is the Bible? Retrieved 2014, from https://bible.org/article/how-accurate-bible. (Dr. Kenneth Boa is an evangelical author, speaker, and the president of Reflections Ministries. He teaches a weekly Bible and Faith study at Peachtree Presbyterian Church in Atlanta and offers these talks and other resources free online at KenBoa.org. His talks on biblical doctrines, apologetics, and even modern literature captivate and encourage and are valuable for people involved in ministry.)

20. McDowell, J., op. cit., 33-34.

21. Got Questions.org. Retrieved http://www.gotquestions.org/canon-Bible.html.

22. Kenyon, F.G. (1941). *Our Bible and the Ancient Manuscripts*. New York: Harper and Brothers, 25; as cited in McDowell, J., op. cit., 56.

23. Boa, K. (2006). op. cit.

24. Wilson, R.D. (1959). *A Scientific Investigation of the Old Testament*. Chicago: Moody Press; as cited in McDowell, J., op. cit., 58.

25. McDowell, J., op. cit., 59-62.

26. Ramm, B. (1957). *Protestant Christian Evidences*. Chicago: Moody Press, 230; as cited in McDowell, J., op. cit., 22; and Boa, K. (2006), op. cit.

27. Boa, K. (2006), op. cit.; and McDowell, J., op. cit., 43-76 (chapter 4).

28. McDowell, J., op. cit., 21.

29. Ramm, B. (1957), op. cit., 230; as cited in McDowell, J., op. cit., 22.

30. McDowell, J., op, cit., 76.

31. Ramm, B. (1957), op. cit., 232; as cited in McDowell, 22; and Matthews, M. (May 25, 2014). The Preservation of the Bible. *Answers in Genesis*; retrieved from https://answersingenesis.org/the-word-of-god/the-preservation-of-the-bible/.

32. McDowell, J., op. cit., 23.

33. Collett, S., *All About the Bible*. Old Tappan: Revell, n.d., 63; as cited in McDowell, J., op. cit., 22.

34. Konig, G. and Konig, R. (1984; 3rd Edition revised). *100 prophecies*. George Konig and Ray Konig, 1-3. See www.100prophecies.org and McDowell, J., op. cit., 17-28.

35. Ibid.

36. Id.

37. Smith, W. (1961). *The Incomparable Book*. Beacon Publications, 9-10; as cited in McDowell, J., 24.

38. McDowell, J., op. cit., 280.

39. Ibid., 332.

40. Ibid., 26.

Chapter 2

Early Jewish History and Divine Covenants

> **Note to reader:** Chapter 2 reviews the early history of the Jewish people, Divine Covenants, and Scripture that is fundamental to Bible prophecy. **This information will help the reader understand end time prophetic events, especially those occurring in today's world.**

> *"The LORD had said to Abram, 'Go from your country, your people and your father's household to the land I will show you. I will make you into a great nation, and I will bless you; I will make your name great, and you will be a blessing. I will bless those who bless you, and whoever curses you I will curse; and all peoples on earth will be blessed through you.'* —Genesis 12:1-3, NIV

The Abrahamic Covenant

Abram was born in Ur of the Chaldeans in 2166 BC (today, Ur is located on the Euphrates River in southern Iraq). As a young man, he and his wife Sarai, and his father Terah, moved to Haran (see map next page). Abram was faithful and believed in the one true God. After his father died (Abram was about 73 years old), the Lord came to Abram with the **first covenant** (Genesis 12:1-5, 7; 13:14-15, NIV)—an **unconditional covenant,** commonly known as the **Abrahamic Covenant.**

"The LORD had said to Abram, 'Go from your country, your people and your father's household to the land I will show you. **I will make you into a great nation, and I will bless you; I will make your name great, and you will be a blessing. I will bless those who bless you, and whoever curses you I will curse; and all peoples on earth will be blessed through you.'** *So Abram went, as the LORD had told him; and Lot went with him. Abram was seventy-five years old when he set out from Haran. He took his wife Sarai, his nephew Lot, all the possessions they had accumulated and the people they had acquired in Haran, and they set out for the* **land of Canaan,** *and they arrived there"* (Genesis 12:1-5, NIV). [Bold added]

"The LORD appeared to Abram and said, **'To your offspring I will give this land.'** *So Abram built an altar there to the LORD, who appeared to him"* (Genesis 12:7, NIV). [Bold added]

"The LORD said to Abram after Lot had parted from him, 'Look around from where you are, to the north and south, to the east and west. All the land that you see I will give to you and your offspring **forever'"** (Genesis 13:14-15, NIV). [Bold added]

> The approximate period in which Abraham lived was c. 2166 BC to 1991 BC. The book of Genesis explains that Abraham was faithful and that he believed in the one true God. God tested Abraham by asking him to leave his country and go to a land that God would show him (the land of Canaan, which later became Israel). Details about Abraham's life are provided in Genesis, chapters 11 through 25.

Abrahamic Covenant: God promised Abram, *"To your offspring [descendants] I will give this land"* (Genesis 12:7, NIV). God told Abram to move to the *"land I will show you"* (Genesis 12:1, NIV)—the land of Canaan. In an unconditional covenant, no conditions must be met by human beings. The covenant cannot end; it remains in effect **forever** (Genesis 13:15), and that makes it essential to Bible prophecy.[1] An 'everlasting covenant' is described in chapter 6, section The Fallacy of Replacement Theology.

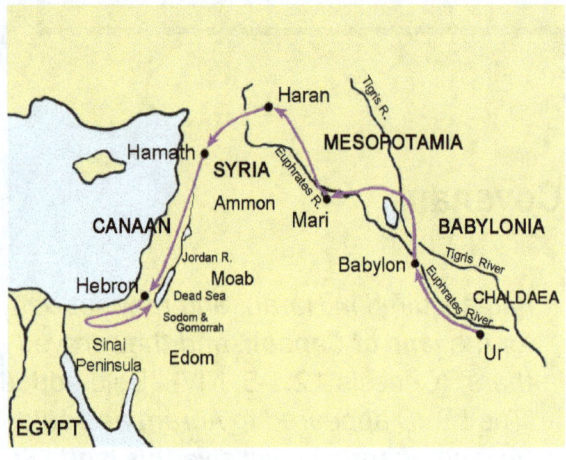

Abraham's Journeys

About 2091 BC when Abram was 75 years old, he departed Haran (Harran) and headed south-southwest to the land of Canaan with his wife Sari and nephew Lot. Upon arriving in Hebron, Lot and Abram parted ways: Abram settled in the area of Hebron west of the Dead Sea and Lot settled east of the Dead Sea near Sodom and Gomorrah (becoming father of the Moabites and Ammonites).

When in Hebron, God **reaffirmed the covenant** with Abram with boundaries of the promised *"land of Canaan"* (Genesis 15:16, 18-21, NIV). This Promised Land (Holy Land or Land of Israel) stretched from the Sinai Desert northeast to the Euphrates River which would include present-day Israel, Lebanon, and Jordan plus substantial portions of Syria, Iraq, and Saudi Arabia.

*"In the fourth generation your descendants will come back here, for the **sin of the Amorites has not yet reached its full measure.**"* (Genesis 15:16, NIV) [Bold added] *"...On that day the LORD made a covenant with Abram and said, 'To your descendants I give this land, from the Wadi of Egypt to the great river, the Euphrates—the land of the Kenites, Kenizzites, Kadmonites, Hittites, Perizzites, Rephaites, Amorites, Canaanites, Girgashites and Jebusites'"* (Genesis 15:18-21, NIV).

The descendants of **Canaan** are listed in Genesis 10:15-19. It was Canaan, the son of Ham and grandson of Noah, who Noah cursed in Genesis 9:25. The **Canaanites** are a tribe that lived west of the Dead Sea and who conquered areas east of the Jordan River. This term describes "all the inhabitants" of the land of 'ancient Israel.'

The three sons of Noah are **Ham** whose descendants populated the ancient land of Canaan, and adjoining parts of Africa and Asia; **Japheth** whose descendants populated Europe, Russia, Turkey, Iran, and some parts of northern Asia; and **Shem** whose descendants were the Jews and the Arabs.

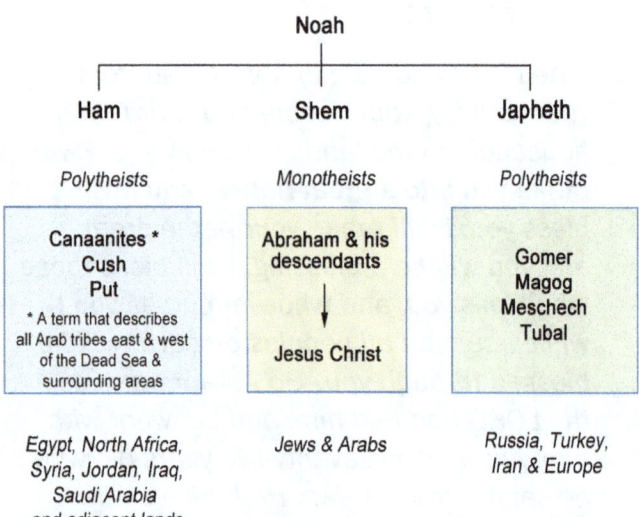

Noah's Sons and Descendants

Abraham and His Sons Isaac and Ishmael

Twelve years had now gone by since the initial promise by God (first covenant). Sarai was now 76 years old and barren, and Abram was 85. Sarai was doubtful about ever being able to conceive and so she decided to help carry out the promise of the Lord by giving Abram her Egyptian handmaiden, Hagar, as a concubine (Genesis 16:1-4). From that union came **Ishmael** and after he reached the age of about 12-13 years, he was certainly told of the promises of God. (Sarai was 77 and Abram was 86 when Ishmael was born.)

As Abram reached his 99th year (Genesis 1:1) and Sarai her 90th year (Genesis 1:17), **the Lord reaffirmed the original covenant** with Abram by stating *"I will confirm my covenant between me and you and will greatly increase your numbers"* (Genesis 17:2, NIV). Also, God **changed Abram's name to Abraham** and reaffirmed he will be *"a father of many nations"* (Genesis 17:1-8) and **changed Sarai's name to Sarah** (Genesis 17:15) and reaffirmed that Sarah *"will be the mother of nations; kings of peoples will come from her"* (Genesis 17:16, NIV).

> Abraham (according to a footnote in the NIV English translation of the Bible) means "Father of many nations". Abram is defined as "exalted father" and he lived 175 years (2166 BC to 1991 BC).

> In Genesis 16:12 (NIV), an angel of the Lord described Ishmael to Hagar: *"He will be a wild donkey of a man; his hand will be against everyone and everyone's hand against him, and he will live in hostility toward all his brothers."* [Bold added]
> This is exactly what we see today—ethnic fighting and conflicts and an inability of the descendants of Ishmael (Arabs) to get along with each other and their neighbors.

Abraham reminded God (as if God needed reminding) that he already had a son, Ishmael, but God **reaffirmed the original covenant** by stating, *"Then God said, 'Yes, but your wife Sarah will bear you a son, and you will call him Isaac. I will establish my covenant with him as an everlasting covenant for his descendants after him. And as for Ishmael, I have heard you: I will surely bless him; I will make him fruitful and will greatly increase his numbers. He will be the father of twelve rulers, and I will make him into a great nation'"* (Genesis 17: 9-20, NIV).

The Seed of Everlasting Hatred

Abraham's first born son with his wife, Sarah, was named **Isaac** (Genesis 17:19). With the birth of Isaac, Ishmael, the son of a concubine, lost his rights of inheritance including the land promised to Abraham by God. At a birthday celebration for Isaac, Sarah, the mother of Isaac, saw Ishmael mocking Isaac (Genesis 21:8-10, 26:2-4.) The mocking resulted in the expulsion of Ishmael and his mother, Hagar, from Abraham's household (verse 10) and in verses 12-13, this banishment was upheld by God.

This expulsion eventually led **Ishmael to become the patriarch of the Arab nations** through his 12 sons (Genesis 25:12-16, 17:20). (See graphic in section, The Twelve Sons of Jacob.) Although this happened about 4,000 years ago, the feud between the families (descendants) of Isaac and Ishmael initiated the "seed of everlasting hatred" of the Arabs toward the Jews and a continual effort by the Arabs to seize or occupy the land of Israel by force. In today's world and throughout history, the Islamic faith is the catalyst in keeping the Arabs' ancient hatred of the Jews in a highly frenzied state.

Isaac and His Twin Sons Esau and Jacob

Abraham begot Isaac who begot twin boys, Esau and Jacob, by his wife Rebekah. The babies jostled (an expression of aggression or hostility) in her womb, and she asked the Lord "*why is this happening to me?'... The Lord said to her, "Two nations are in your womb, and two peoples from within you will be separated; one people will be stronger than the other, and the older will serve the younger*" (Genesis 25:23, NIV). When the boys were older, Esau (the older of the twins) sold his birthright to his brother Jacob for a bowl of red stew as described in Genesis 25:31-33.

God **reaffirmed the covenant** to Abraham's son, Isaac, in Genesis 26:2-4, and then to Isaac's son, Jacob, **it was reaffirmed** in Genesis 28:4, 13. According to Isaiah 14:1, Ezekiel 36:22, 24, and Amos 9:14-15, the land was to be occupied by the Jewish people. Esau took his wives from the women of Canaan and moved to an area south-southeast of the Dead Sea, and there **Esau became the father of the Edomites** (Genesis 36: 1-43).

> Jacob, the son of Isaac who is the son of Abraham, was born in Canaan, the land which later became Israel. Jacob's name was changed to Israel (Genesis 35:10), and he had 12 sons for whom the 12 tribes of Israel were named.

"'I have loved you,' says the LORD. But you ask, 'How have you loved us? Was not Esau Jacob's brother?' declares the LORD. 'Yet I have loved Jacob, but Esau I have hated, and I have turned his hill country into a wasteland and left his inheritance to the desert jackals'" (Malachi 1:2-3, NIV).

Malachi 1:3 is quoted in Romans 9:10-13, *"Not only that, but Rebekah's children had one and the same father, our father Isaac. Yet, before the twins were born or had done anything good or bad—in order that God's purpose **in election might stand: not by works but by him who calls**—she was told, 'The older will serve the younger.' Just as it is written: 'Jacob I loved, but Esau I hated'"* (Romans 9:10-13, NIV).

Why did God love Jacob and hate Esau?[2] If God is love (1 John 4:8), how could He hate anyone? This was **not a matter of human emotions of 'love' and 'hate'** but rather **a matter of divine election by a Sovereign God**—God chose Jacob over Esau. Of the two twin sons, God chose Jacob (whom He later renamed "Israel") to be the father of His chosen people, the Israelites.

So, the choice had **nothing to do with any human emotions of love and hate**. It was simply a matter of God choosing one man and his descendants and rejecting another man and thereby also rejecting his descendants. Romans chapter 9 makes it abundantly clear that **loving Jacob and hating Esau was entirely related to which of them God chose**—God is Sovereign, omnipotent, omnipresent, and omniscient (Romans 8:29; Ephesians 1:4-5; 1 Corinthians 2:7), and He does what pleases Him (Job 23:13; Psalms 115, 135; Daniel 4:35). Despite the divine election of Jacob, the descendants of Esau, the Edomites, were blessed by God (Genesis 33:9; Genesis 36).

Hundreds of years after Jacob and Esau had died, the Israelites and Edomites became bitter enemies as the Edomites often aided Israel's enemies in attacks on Israel. **By siding with Israel's enemies, Esau's descendants brought the curse of God on themselves.** Genesis 27:29 tells Israel, *"May nations serve you and peoples bow down to you. Be lord over your brothers, and may the sons of your mother bow down to you. May those who curse you be cursed and those who bless you be blessed."* [Bold added]

Likewise, God chose Abraham from all the men in the world at that time. The Bible could have said, "Abraham I loved, and every other man I hated." God chose Abraham's son Isaac instead of Abraham's son Ishmael. The **choice had nothing to do with human emotions**—it was **simply a matter of God choosing one man and his descendants and rejecting another man and his descendants**.

The Twelve Sons of Jacob

Jacob's name was symbolically changed to Israel (Genesis 35:10) and he had 12 sons: 1) Reuben, 2) Simeon, 3) Levi (Levi was not included among the 12 tribes but was set apart as belonging to the Lord), 4) Judah, 5) Issachar, and 6) Zebulon, all 6 sons from wife Leah; and 7) Gad and 8) Asher from wife Zilpah (Leah's maidservant); and 9) Dan and 10) Naphtali from Bilhah (Rachel's maidservant); and 11) Benjamin and 12) Joseph, from wife, Rachel.

The Twelve Sons of Israel

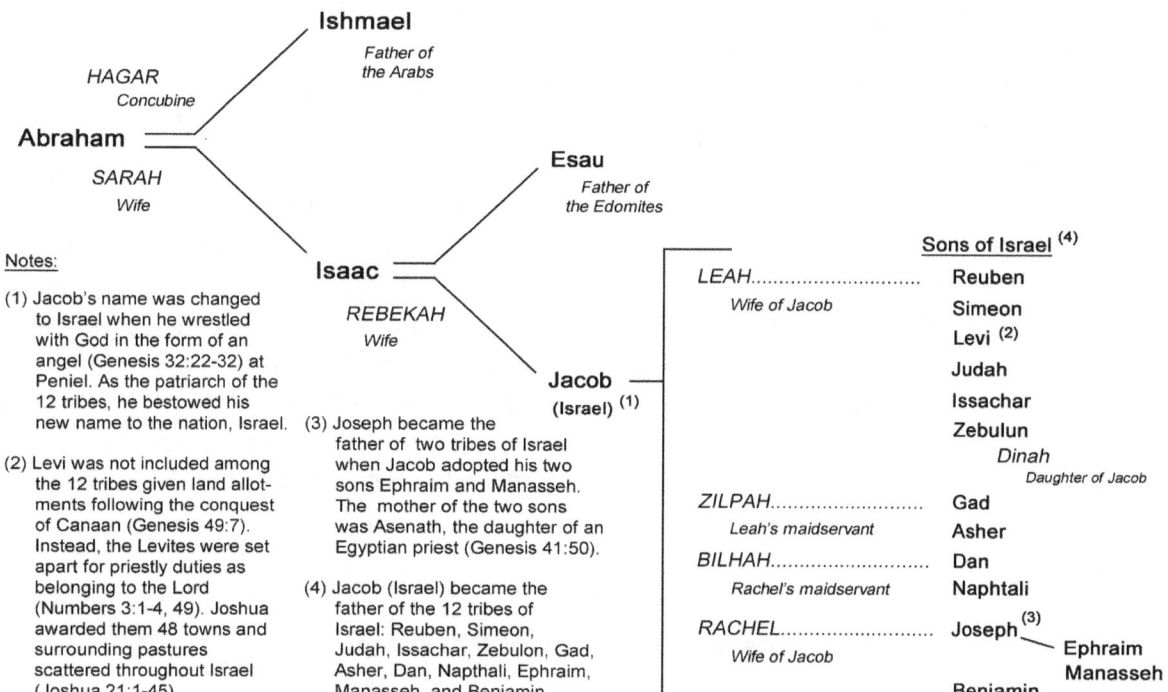

Notes:

(1) Jacob's name was changed to Israel when he wrestled with God in the form of an angel (Genesis 32:22-32) at Peniel. As the patriarch of the 12 tribes, he bestowed his new name to the nation, Israel.

(2) Levi was not included among the 12 tribes given land allotments following the conquest of Canaan (Genesis 49:7). Instead, the Levites were set apart for priestly duties as belonging to the Lord (Numbers 3:1-4, 49). Joshua awarded them 48 towns and surrounding pastures scattered throughout Israel (Joshua 21:1-45).

(3) Joseph became the father of two tribes of Israel when Jacob adopted his two sons Ephraim and Manasseh. The mother of the two sons was Asenath, the daughter of an Egyptian priest (Genesis 41:50).

(4) Jacob (Israel) became the father of the 12 tribes of Israel: Reuben, Simeon, Judah, Issachar, Zebulon, Gad, Asher, Dan, Napthali, Ephraim, Manasseh, and Benjamin.

Jacob (Israel) loved his son Joseph (familial love) more than his other sons and gave Joseph a beautiful coat (Genesis 37:3). Because Joseph unwisely told his brothers about a dream that they would serve and bow down to him, his brothers hated him (intense hostility) and plotted to kill him. They took his coat and threw him into an empty well, and then sold him as a slave to Midianite (Ishmaelite) merchants travelling to Egypt (c. 1896 BC). The brothers spattered the coat with goat's blood and then returned home to their father Jacob who concluded that his son Joseph was killed by wild animals. Jacob mourned for his son (Genesis 37:31-35).

Meanwhile, Joseph was sold to one of Pharaoh's officials, the captain of the guard. Because the Lord had blessed Joseph in all that he did, Joseph was placed in charge of his master's household, but Joseph was falsely accused of making unwanted advances toward his master's unscrupulous wife. (Genesis 39) Joseph was thrown in prison (verse 20), but while confined, he successfully interpreted dreams of the chief cupbearer and baker. When Pharaoh heard this, he sent for Joseph and told Joseph about his dreams. Joseph successfully interpreted Pharaoh's dreams (Genesis 41:26-32)—that Egypt and the surrounding region would have seven years of great abundance followed by seven years of severe famine. Pharaoh then placed Joseph in charge of the palace and all the people were to submit to his orders (verse 40). He had sons, **Ephraim and Manasseh**, by Asenath, the daughter of an Egyptian priest (Genesis 41:50).

Jacob and His Family Travel to Egypt

During the seven year period of abundance, Joseph ordered the storage of vast quantities of grain in each city of Egypt in preparation for the coming seven years of famine. When the period of famine began, there was enough food for all of Egypt, but there was also famine throughout the general region including the land of Canaan (Genesis 41). As a result of this famine, the ten brothers of Joseph (Jacob's sons) travelled to Egypt to find food (Benjamin, the youngest, did not go). (See Genesis 42:4.)

Upon their arrival in Egypt, Joseph immediately recognized his brothers but his brothers were unable to recognize their brother Joseph (likely due to the fine clothing, grooming, and his high position in the Egyptian inner circle). Without divulging who he was, Joseph told the ten brothers to leave Simeon, return to Canaan (carrying grain for their household), and bring back the youngest brother, Benjamin, as a requirement for the family to continue trading in Egypt.

Joseph's bothers returned to Canaan and explained everything to their father, Jacob. Because of the severe famine, Jacob and his sons, including the youngest son Benjamin, and their families travelled to Egypt, and they were ultimately reunited with Joseph who forgave his brothers for their treachery.

The Twelve Tribes of Israel

According to Exodus 12:40-41, the Jewish people remained in Egypt for more than 430 years (1876 BC – 1446 BC), likely reaching a population of 2 to 3 million—but during this period the Jewish people were enslaved and oppressed by the Egyptians. And during this time Jacob (Israel) become the father of the **12 tribes of Israel: 1) Reuben, 2) Simeon, 3) Judah, 4) Issachar, 5) Zebulon, 6) Gad, 7) Asher; 8) Dan, 9) Naphtali, 10) Ephraim, 11) Manasseh, and 12) Benjamin.**

The two grandsons of Jacob, Ephraim and Manasseh (the sons of Joseph from wife Asenath; see previous section), were adopted by Jacob. Levi was not included among the 12 tribes—the Levites were set apart and devoted to the Lord as priests.

> Refer to the Lord's promise to Abraham in Genesis 15:16 (NIV), *"In the fourth generation your descendants will come back here, for the sin of the Amorites has **not yet reached its full measure.**"* [Bold added] Abraham's descendants would return to the land of Canaan in four generations, or the age of a man when his first son was born, or 100 years in the case of Abraham. (Generation is the age of a man when his first son is born according to Genesis 15:16, or one cycle in the succession of parents and children; today's generation is about 30 to 40 years.)

Moses and Aaron

While the Jewish people were in Egypt (1876 BC – 1446 BC), a Levi man (Amram) married a Levi woman (Joshebed) and they had a daughter, Miriam, and a son, **Aaron** (born c. 1529 BC). When they had their second son, **Moses** (born c. 1526 BC), their daughter Miriam was 7 years old and the other son, Aaron, was 3 years old.

> The Egyptians enslaved and oppressed the Jewish people *"and worked them ruthlessly."* (Exodus 1: 1) Over time the Egyptians began to fear the Jews because they had multiplied greatly—so in order to decrease their number, Pharaoh (probably Ahmose of the 18th dynasty) ordered the killing of every Hebrew newborn boy but the girls were to be spared (Exodus 1:16, 22).

Because Pharaoh ordered the killing of every newborn Jewish male, the mother, Joshebed, hid her son for three months. But when she could no longer hide him, she placed the baby in a papyrus basket coated with tar and placed the basket amongst the reeds of the Nile, an area of shoreline frequented by Pharaoh's daughter. When she saw the basket, she sent her maidservant to retrieve it. Miriam, the sister of the baby boy, waited and noticed that Pharaoh's daughter felt great sympathy and concern for the Hebrew child.

Miriam approached and asked Pharaoh's daughter if she could find a Hebrew woman to nurse the baby for her (Pharaoh's daughter)—and she said yes and even offered to pay the surrogate mother. Miriam got her mother, Joshebed, to nurse the baby, and when the Hebrew baby grew a little older, Miriam took the baby to Pharaoh's daughter and he became her son. She named him Moses, which means, *"I drew him out of the water"* (Exodus 2:10, NIV).

Moses grew up as the grandson of Pharaoh and was educated in the palaces of Egypt. Joshebed, the mother of Moses, continued to act as the nanny or caregiver. Consequently, Moses never lost his Jewish heritage and connection to his people, especially the Levites. Later on as a young man, Moses saw an Egyptian taskmaster beating a Jew. Moses intervened and killed the taskmaster (c. 1500 BC) but incredibly, some Jews informed on Moses to the Egyptian authorities and Moses was forced to flee.

During this time, Moses lived in the land of Midian which is across the Sinai Peninsula and Gulf of Aqaba (see map in section, Exodus of the Jewish People). Moses married Zipporah, the daughter of an excommunicated priest, and had a son, Gershon. Moses became a shepherd, following the traditions of other great leaders of the Jewish people: Abraham, Isaac, Jacob, and Jacob's twelve sons who were all shepherds.

> A **shepherd** is symbolic of Jesus and all the patriarchs. The vocation provides good preparation for dealing with the many difficulties and challenges of unifying and leading a very large group of people.

Liberation of the Jewish People

After more than 400 years of enslavement and oppression (Exodus 1:11-14), the Lord saw the people's distress and sent Moses to Pharaoh with a message: *"How long will you refuse to humble yourself before me? Let my people go, so that they may worship me"* (Exodus 10:3, NIV). But despite numerous warnings from the Lord, Pharaoh refused to follow the Lord's command. The Lord then sent ten devastating plagues upon Egypt: blood, frogs, gnats, flies, plague on the livestock, boils, hail, locusts, darkness, and death of the firstborn son in Egypt. See Exodus 7-12.

The last of the plagues was by far the worst—the death of all firstborn of Egypt. The Lord spared the children of Israel during this last great plague by "passing over" their homes—hence the name of the holiday, **Passover**. (See glossary for more information about Passover or Pesach, an important Jewish celebration.) Pharaoh's resistance to the Lord's commands was finally broken (Exodus 12:31-32), and he allowed the Jewish people to leave Egypt. Approximately 3 million men, women, and children left Egypt that day and began the journey to Mount Sinai. **This event (c. 1446 BC) marked the birth of Israel as God's chosen people.**[3]

God's purpose for Israel:[4] 1) receive and record God's revelation to man, 2) protect and preserve the accuracy of the Scriptures, 3) serve as the human family for the Messiah, Jesus Christ, 4) witness to the world there is only one true God, the God of the Holy Bible, and 5) to spread the gospel of Jesus Christ, the Messiah, throughout the pagan world (with 144,000 Jewish evangelists; see Appendix B).

Exodus of the Jewish People

When Moses and Aaron brought the Jewish people out of Egypt, there were as many as 2.5 to 3 million men, women, and children comprising the 12 tribes of Israel and the Levites. But soon after releasing the Jewish people, Pharaoh changed his mind and pursued this great exodus (Exodus 14:5). By Divine intervention the Lord parted the Red Sea, and the Jewish people were able to cross safely (Exodus 14:21-22) at Pi-hahiroth while the sea flowed back over the pursuing Egyptian army, swallowing their chariots and horsemen (Exodus 14:26-28).

The exodus comprised the 12 tribes of Israel c. 1446 BC. The tribe of Levi was set apart from the 12 tribes as belonging to the Lord. Joseph became the father of two tribes when Jacob adopted his two sons, Ephraim and Manasseh. The other 10 tribes are Reuben, Simeon, Judah, Issachar, Zebulon, Gad, Asher, Dan, Naphtali, and Benjamin.

Exodus 12:37 indicates 600,000 walking men plus wives and children. In the census taken about a year after the Exodus, recorded in Numbers 1:2, 3, 45, 46, there were 603,550 males (20 years old and older) plus 22,000 male Levites over one month old (Numbers 2:32, 33; 3:39). If all the men had one wife, that would make 1,200,000 adults. If each of the 600,000 families had three children with them, that would be 1,800,000 children (although many Jewish families would have had more than three children). Total number of Jews: approximately 3 million.

> It is baffling when people state that it is impossible for the Red Sea to part, or the earth to flood, or the world to be created in six literal solar days. People are unable to concede that their minds are finite, and their attitudes are arrogant and corrupt, and never give a thought to the possibility and reality of an infinite God who created the heavens and earth and all that exists (Jeremiah 10:12-16, 51:15-19, and Isaiah 40:28, NIV)—omnipotent, omnipresent, and omniscient (Romans 8:29; Ephesians 1:4-5; 1 Corinthians 2:7; Jeremiah 23:24, 32:27)—and certainly beyond our understanding.

Exodus of the Jewish People

Israel liberated from Egypt (Exodus 12; Numbers 33:5).

Succoth – The Lord led Israel in a cloud by day and in a pillar of fire by night (Exodus 13:20-22).

Pi-hahiroth – Israel passed through the Red Sea (Exodus 14; Numbers 33:8).

Marah – The Lord healed the waters of Marah (Exodus 15:23-26).

Elim – Israel camped by 12 springs (Exodus 15:27).

Wilderness of Sin – The Lord sent manna and quail to feed Israel (Exodus 16).

Rephidim — Israel fought the Amaleks (Exodus 17:8-16).

Mount Sinai – The Lord revealed the Ten Commandments (Exodus 19-20).

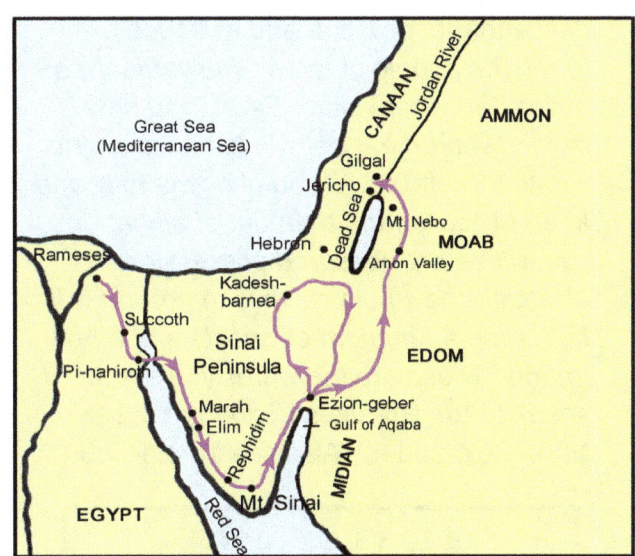

Exodus of the Jewish People

Sinai Wilderness – Israel constructed the tabernacle (Exodus 25-30).

Wilderness Camps – Seventy elders were called to help Moses govern the people (Numbers 11:16-17).

Ezion-geber – Israel peacefully passed through the lands of the Edomites, Moabites, and Ammonites (Deuteronomy 2).

Kadesh-barnea – Moses sent 12 men (one from each tribe) into the promised land; although they confirmed that the land 'flowed with milk and honey', only Caleb amd Joshua believed the Lord would help them conquer the Canaanites and take possession of the land. Kadesh served as the main camp of Israel for many years (Numbers 13:1-3, 17-33, 14, 32:8; Deuteronomy 2:14).

Eastern Wilderness – Israel avoided conflict with Edom and Moab (Numbers 20:14-21; 22-24).

Arnon Valley – Israel fought and destroyed the Amorites (Deuteronomy 2:24-37).

Mount Nebo – Moses saw the promised land (Deuteronomy 34:1-4); delivered his last three sermons (Deuteronomy. 1-32).

Plains of Moab – The Lord told Israel to divide the land and dispossess the inhabitants (Numbers 33:50-56).

Jordan River – Israel crossed the Jordan River (on dry ground) near Gilgal; stones from the bottom of the Jordan River were placed as a monument (Joshua 3:1-5:1).

Jericho – Israel captured and destroyed the city (Joshua 6).

Reference: Bible Maps, Israel's Exodus from Egypt and Entry into Canaan, the 17 locations cited above retrieved from http://classic.scriptures.lds.org/en/biblemaps/2?sr=1, and NIV Study Bible, New International Version, Map 3: Exodus and Conquest of Canaan. Grand Rapids, MI: Zondervan Publishing House.

The Mosaic Covenant

On the third month after fleeing Egypt, the Jewish people eventually encamped at Mount Sinai.

"Then Moses went up to God, and the LORD called to him from the mountain and said, 'This is what you are to say to the descendants of Jacob and what you are to tell the people of Israel: You yourselves have seen what I did to Egypt, and how I carried you on eagles' wings and brought you to myself. Now if you obey me fully and **keep my covenant,** *then out of all nations you will be my* **treasured possession.** *Although the whole earth is mine, you will be for me* **a kingdom of priests and a holy nation.***' These are the words you are to speak to the Israelites"* (Exodus 19:3-6, NIV). [Bold added] (Also see 1 Peter 2:9.)

> In Exodus 19:3-6, God describes the Jewish people as *"a kingdom of priests and a holy nation"* **with the responsibility of bringing the word of God to the entire world.** These people (Jews) are a separate and distinct people apart from the world (the rest of the world being Gentiles, or non-Jews).

"So Moses went back and summoned the elders of the people and set before them all the words the LORD had commanded him to speak. **The people all responded together, 'We will do everything the LORD has said.' So Moses brought their answer back to the LORD.** *The LORD said to Moses, 'I am going to come to you in a dense cloud, so that the* **people will hear me speaking with you and will always put their trust in you.'** *Then Moses told the LORD what the people had said"* (Exodus 19:7-9, NIV). [Bold added]

Moses went up to Mount Sinai (accompanied by Joshua, who would later lead the Israelites into the land of Canaan) and God spoke the words of the Ten Commandments. Then Moses went down to the people and told them what God had said. (Exodus 20; Deuteronomy 5) **God warned the people through Moses not to make or worship any idols—gods of silver and gold** (Exodus 20:22-23). Moses summoned all Israel, and said to them,

> *"Hear, O Israel, the statutes and the ordinances which I speak in your hearing this day, and you shall learn them and be careful to do them. The LORD our God made* **a covenant [Mosaic Covenant]** *with us in Horeb. It was not with our fathers that the LORD made this covenant, but with us, with all of us who are alive here today. The LORD spoke with you face to face at the mountain, out of the midst of the fire, while I stood between the LORD and you at that time, to declare to you the word of the LORD"* (Deuteronomy 5:1-5, NIV). [Bold added]

Mosaic Covenant is conditional between the Jewish people and God: *"Now if you obey me fully and* **keep my covenant,** *then out of all nations you will be my* **treasured possession.** *Although the whole earth is mine, you will be for me* **a kingdom of priests and a holy nation.** *These are the words you are to speak to the Israelites"* (Exodus 19:5-6, NIV). [Bold added]

Under the **Mosaic Covenant,** the **responsibility of the Israelites** is to obey all of the statutes, ordinances and decrees established by God—obedience added to faith. The **responsibility of God** is to bless Israel when they obey those laws and commandments, and to curse Israel when they do not.

"Then God said to Moses, 'Come up to me on the mountain and stay here, and I will give you the tablets of stone, with the law and commands I have written for their instruction'" (Exodus 24:12, NIV). *"Then Moses entered the cloud as he went on up the mountain. And **he stayed on the mountain forty days and forty nights**"* (Exodus 24:18). [Bold added] *"When the Lord finished speaking with Moses on Mount Sinai, he gave him two tablets of the Testimony, the tablets of stone inscribed by the finger of God"* (Exodus 31:18, NIV).

> Unlike the Abrahamic Covenant, **the Mosaic Covenant is temporary** because man is incapable of keeping the law. In Jeremiah 31:31, *"Behold, the days are coming, declares the Lord, when I will make a **new covenant** with the house of Israel and the house of Judah"* (Jeremiah 31:31, NIV). [Bold added] See Appendix B, Establishment of a New Covenant.

Beginnings of Disobedience

Despite the people actually witnessing (first-hand) the miracles of God—miracles that included their release from Egyptian enslavement and oppression; the crossing of the Red Sea; being told that they (the Jewish people) will be '*a kingdom of priests and a holy nation*'; God leading them in a cloud by day and fire by night; and then being allowed to see God in a dense cloud and to actually hear God speaking with Moses—but instead of showing excitement and great anticipation of God's promises, the Jewish people exhibited little faith and understanding (like many people in today's world), and began to grumble and protest (Exodus 15:24).

"When the people saw that Moses was so long in coming down from the mountain, they gathered around Aaron and said, 'Come, make us gods who will go before us. As for this fellow Moses who brought us up out of Egypt, we don't know what has happened to him'" (Exodus 32:1, NIV).

Despite warnings by God not to worship idols of other gods (Exodus 20:22-23), the Jewish people, and incredibly even with the tacit approval of Aaron, began making an idol: a golden calf (Exodus 32). While on the mountain,

*"Then the LORD said to Moses, 'Go down, because your people, whom you brought up out of Egypt, have become corrupt. They have been **quick to turn away** from what I commanded them and have made themselves an idol cast in the shape of a calf. They have bowed down to it and sacrificed to it and have said, These are your gods, Israel, who brought you up out of Egypt. I have seen these people,'* the LORD said to Moses, *'and they are **a stiff-necked people**. Now leave me alone so that my anger may burn against them and that I may destroy them. Then I will make you into a great nation'"* (Exodus 32:7-10, NIV). [Bold added]

Upon the pleadings of Moses, *"The Lord relented and did not bring on his people the disaster he [the Lord] had threatened"* (Exodus 32:14, NIV).

Upon seeing the golden calf and the people dancing and celebrating, the anger of Moses burned against the people. Moses broke the tablets, burned the calf in the fire, and then ground the calf into powder and made the people drink it (Exodus 32:19-20).

Aaron said to Moses, *"Do not be angry, my lord...You know how prone these people are to evil."* (Of course, Aaron was speaking about himself as well.) This was a great sin the people committed against God and there were consequences for their evil behavior. Due to God's mercy (grace) and compassion, new stone tablets were made by Moses (Exodus 34) and the words of the covenant, the Ten Commandments, were again written on the tablets by God at the top of Mount Sinai.

Continual Grumbling and Disobedience

The Lord had Moses send 12 men (one from each tribe) to explore the land of Canaan. Upon their return after 40 days they confirmed that the land *"does flow with milk and honey! Here is its fruit. But the people who live there are powerful, and the cities are fortified and very large"* (Numbers 13:27, NIV). But only Caleb and Joshua (2 of the 12 explorers) believed the Lord would help the Israelites conquer the Canaanites and take possession of the land.

Despite the Lord's assurance of victory for the Jewish people, *"...which I am going to give to the sons of Israel...."* (Numbers 13:1, NAS), they feared their wives and children would be taken as plunder and they rebelled against the Lord.

"All the Israelites grumbled against Moses and Aaron, and the whole assembly said to them, "If only we had died in Egypt! Or the desert!" (See Numbers 14:2, NIV.)

These same people who had been redeemed from slavery and witnessed first-hand (with their own eyes) the miracles of God, and with whom God made a **covenant** at Mount Sinai, responded not with faith, gratitude, determination, and obedience but with **continual disobedience, unbelief, and grumbling**, which resulted in their refusal to commence the conquest of Canaan. (See Numbers, chapter 14.)

The Book of Numbers describes the journey from Mount Sinai to the plains of Moab east of the Jordan River along the eastern border of Canaan. **The book also describes the disobedience of God's people including their continual idol worship and subsequent judgment.**

> *"The Lord said to Moses, 'How long will these people treat me with contempt? How long will they refuse to believe in me, in spite of all the miraculous signs I have performed among them?'"* (Numbers 14:11, NIV) Moses again pleaded with the Lord and *"The Lord replied [to Moses], I have forgiven them, as you asked. Nevertheless...as surely as the glory of the Lord fills the whole earth, not one of the men who saw my glory and the miraculous signs I performed in Egypt and in the desert but who disobeyed me and tested me... —not one of them will ever see the land I promised on oath to their forefathers"* (Numbers 14:20-23, NIV).

This first generation of Jewish people forfeited their inheritance of the Promised Land and would live the remainder of their

---

After being enslaved for 430 years, Moses and the Jewish people left Egypt and headed toward Mount Sinai and eventually to the land of Canaan. **Because of disobedience and continual idol worship**, Moses and the Israelites wandered the desert for 40 years before reaching the border of Canaan.

lives in the desert—only their children would see and enjoy God's promise. The Israelites spent an extended 40 years wandering in the Sinai desert (Numbers 14:34, 32:13; Deuteronomy 29:5; Acts 7:30-50) because of their **continual grumbling, disobedience, and idol worship** (Numbers 14; Deuteronomy 32:16).

> *"For forty years—one year for each of the forty days you explored the land—you will suffer for your sins and know what it is like to have me against you"* (Numbers 14:34, NIV). As for the children that the Israelites feared would be taken as plunder by the Canaanites, the Lord said, *"...I will bring them in to enjoy the land you have rejected"* (Numbers 14:31, NIV).

"During the forty years that I led you through the desert, **your clothes did not wear out, nor did the sandals on your feet...I did this so that you might know that I am the Lord your God"** (Deuteronomy 29:5, NIV). [Bold added]

What did the Lord do exactly?

He suspended the 1st and 2nd Laws of Thermodynamics (laws of physics); that everything in our world is decaying or running down. While the Jewish people were in the desert, the Lord demonstrated **He has complete control (omnipotent) over all that exists.**

When Adam and Eve sinned, not only was harmony between God and man destroyed, but also the 1st and 2nd Laws came into existence (Romans 8:19-22). When Christ died on the Cross, He made peace possible between God and man, and He restored in principle the harmony in the physical world, although the full realization of this harmony (removal of the 1st and 2nd Laws) will come only when Christ returns.

See glossary in this book and chapter 2 and glossary of the book by Roger Gallop, *evolution - The Greatest Deception in Modern History,* for information about laws of science.

After wandering the desert for 40 years, the next generation—children who were now 20 to 60 years of age—was about to begin their conquest of the land of Canaan. The Lord told Moses to bypass the land of the Edomites (descendants of Esau) and the land of the Moabites and Ammonites (descendants of Lot) because of their blood relationship with the Israelites (Deuteronomy 2:5).

Even Moses, the great prophet and servant of the Lord, was not allowed to enter the Promised Land *"because you did not trust in me [the Lord] to honor me as holy in the sight of the Israelites"* (Numbers 20:12, NIV). (The specific reason is described in verses 6-12. Also see Deuteronomy 1:37, 3:23-29; 31:1-3.) Subsequently, **Moses was told to commission Joshua** to lead the Israelites across the Jordan River (Deuteronomy 1:37-38, 31:7-8). Despite the judgment on his rebellious people, God was **steadfast in upholding the covenant** and bringing the Israelites into the land of Canaan—the Land of Promise.

The Lord again defined the boundaries of the land and how the land would be divided among the 12 tribes (Numbers 34; Deuteronomy 3:12-20). Moses reminded the people that by obeying the Lord and keeping his commands and decrees, the Jewish people would enjoy a long prosperous life and a long national existence (Deuteronomy 6:1-3, NIV).

> *"These are the commands, decrees and laws the LORD your God directed me to teach you to observe in the land that you are crossing the Jordan to possess, so that you, your children and their children after them may fear the LORD your God as long as you live* **by keeping all his decrees and commands that I give you,** *and so that you may enjoy long life. Hear, Israel, and* **be careful to obey so that it may go well with you** *and that you may increase greatly in* **a land flowing with milk and honey,** *just as the LORD, the God of your ancestors, promised you"* (Deuteronomy 6:1-3, NIV). [Bold added]

Renewal of the Mosaic Covenant

On the plains of Moab by the Jordan River, the Lord set forth conditions for the Jewish people before they set out for the land of Canaan. Moses delivered his farewell address—a covenant renewal—to prepare the people just before they crossed the Jordan River into Canaan.

*"When the LORD your God brings you into the land you are entering to possess and drive out before you many nations—the Hittites, Girgashites, Amorites, Canaanites, Perizzites, Hivites and Jebusites, seven nations larger and stronger than you— and when the LORD your God has delivered them over to you and you have defeated them, **then you must destroy them totally**. [See next section, The Ethical Question of War.] **Make no treaty with them, and show them no mercy. Do not intermarry with them.** Do not give your daughters to their sons or take their daughters for your sons, for they will turn your children away from following me to serve other gods, and the LORD's anger will burn against you and will quickly destroy you. This is what you are to do to them: Break down their altars, smash their sacred stones, cut down their Asherah poles and burn their idols in the fire"* (Deuteronomy 7:1-5, NIV). [Bold added]

In Deuteronomy 7:6-9 (NIV), God again explains why He chose the Jewish people:

*"For you are **a people holy to the LORD your God**. The LORD your God has **chosen you** out of all the peoples on the face of the earth to be his people, his **treasured possession**. The LORD did not set his affection on you and choose you because you were more numerous than other peoples, for you were the fewest of all peoples. **But it was because the LORD loved you and kept the oath he swore to your ancestors** that he brought you out with a mighty hand and redeemed you from the land of slavery, from the power of Pharaoh king of Egypt. Know therefore that the LORD your God is God; he is the faithful God, keeping his covenant of love to a thousand generations of those who love him and keep his commandments"* (Deuteronomy 7:6-9, NIV). [Bold added]

About 1406 BC Moses died and Joshua led the Israelites into Canaan and began the conquest of the Promised Land, and established the State of Israel for the first time in history.

Don't make the terrible mistake by turning away from God. God is holy, righteous, and merciful, and through our Lord Jesus Christ offers the gift of eternal salvation (John 3:16, 5:24, 14:6; Romans 10:9, 13; and Ephesians 2:8-9) to those who do not turn away and are willing to repent of their sins and accept through faith the free gift of pardon—so by grace [mercy] you are saved through faith (Ephesians 2:8-9).

People should not forget that the Lord is **omnipresent, omnipotent, and omniscient** (Romans 8:29; Ephesians 1:4-5; 1 Corinthians 2:7) and *"the Lord is a warrior"* (Exodus 15:3)—*"He does whatever pleases Him"* (Psalms 115:3, 135:6; Job 23:13; Daniel 4:35, NIV), and *"He is to be feared"* (1 Chronicles 16:25; Psalm 96:4; Isaiah 8:13, NIV). [Bold added] See Prelude, Who is God?

The Ethical Question of War[5]

The conquest of Canaan was not for political reasons, but rather it was about how God, to whom the entire world belongs, reclaimed a small portion of the earth from **exceedingly wicked, paganistic powers whose measure of sin was now full.** (See Genesis 15:16, NIV.)

The conquest was God's holy war, an endeavor to claim lands given to the Jewish people through an **unconditional covenant** with patriarchs Abraham, Isaac, and Jacob (the **Abrahamic covenant**) and then a **conditional covenant** through Moses (the **Mosaic covenant**). The land was the Lord's, and it had to be cleansed of a **depraved paganistic culture and idol worship.** God gave the Israelites conditional occupancy of the land as fulfillment of the covenant.

> The conquest can only be understood in the framework of Divine judgment and an overall plan of redemption of all mankind. God gave the Israelites a "limited undertaking" **to cleanse the land of all traces of paganism**—but it was made clear that these paganistic people (the 'Canaanites') and **their wealth would not be seized as plunder** (Joshua 6:17).

The religious practices of these paganistic people (that is, the Hittites, Girgashites, Amorites, Canaanites, Perizzites, Hivites, and Jebusites) included **idol worship, child sacrifice in fire as food to the idols (an unspeakable horror), religious prostitution, orgies, and divination embedded in the worship of demonic gods (demons).** God was long-suffering and tolerant in his judgment, even with the **exceedingly wicked 'Canaanites'** (a term used to describe all the paganistic people of that region). They worshipped Baal and his wife Ashtoreth, fertility deities. Archaeology has revealed the immoral behavior and terrible cruelty of these people.

> Just how wicked these religious practices were is now known from archaeological artifacts and from their own classic literature, discovered at Ras Shamra on the north Syrian coast beginning in 1929. In addition, pagan temples, altars, tombs, and ritual vessels have been uncovered, exposing more of their culture and customs. **Just like in the days of Noah, these people were evil all the time.**

Detestable practices of the Canaanites are described in Deuteronomy 18:9-13, NIV. It states,

> *"When you enter the land the Lord your God is giving you, **do not learn to imitate the detestable ways of the nations there.** Let no one be found among you who sacrifices his son or daughter in the fire, who practices divination or sorcery, interprets omens, engages in witchcraft, or cast spells, or who is a medium or spiritist or who consults the dead. Anyone who does these things is detestable to the Lord, and because of these detestable practices the Lord your God will drive out those nations before you. You must be blameless before the Lord your God"* (Deuteronomy 18:9-13, NIV).

> *"However, in the cities of the nations the LORD your God is giving you as an inheritance, do not leave alive anything that breathes. **Completely destroy them**—the Hittites, Amorites, Canaanites, Perizzites, Hivites and Jebusites—as the LORD your God has commanded you. **Otherwise, they will teach you to follow all the detestable things they do in worshiping their gods,** and you will sin against the LORD your God"* (Deuteronomy 20:16-18, NIV). [Bold added]

> *"After the LORD your God has driven them out before you, do not say to yourself, 'The LORD has brought me here to take possession of this land because of my righteousness.' No, it is on account of the wickedness of these nations that the LORD is going to drive them out before you.* **It is not because of your righteousness or your integrity that you are going in to take possession of their land; but on account of the wickedness of these nations, the LORD your God will drive them out before you,** *to accomplish what he swore to your fathers, to Abraham, Isaac and Jacob"* (Deuteronomy 9:4-5, NIV). [Bold added]

Triumph over the Canaanites was a witness to the world that the God of Israel is the true living God—the God of the Holy Bible. The conquest and occupation of the land of Canaan **served as a warning to the world**—a warning that the God of Israel would ultimately destroy all pagan cultures and idolatry and would ultimately support only those (individuals and nations) who acknowledge and serve Him. And this also gives witness to all nations today of the final outcome of humanity—that humanity has a natural tendency to degenerate, and its ultimate destiny is like in the days of Noah.

Although God of the Holy Bible is holy, righteous, merciful, compassionate, patient, and offers eternal salvation (John 3:16, 5:24, 14:6; Romans 10:9, 13; and Ephesians 2:8-9), don't make the terrible mistake of turning away and not realizing **"The Lord is a warrior"** (Exodus 15:3, NIV) [Bold added] who will ultimately **disinherit** all those who reject His offer of salvation. The seven year tribulation (**unbeknownst or unperceived by most people of the world today**) is soon coming, and the second Joshua will wield the sword of judgment (Revelation 19:11-16).

> War is a terrible curse that humans bring upon themselves when they oppose God's rule and do not observe God's warnings and, ultimately, reject his offer of salvation. Now for a time, in the Age of Grace, He reaches out to the entire world with the gospel of salvation through our Lord Jesus Christ, and **terrible judgment waits in the wings** (Revelation 19:11-16, 20:11-15).
>
> **Revelation 20:11-15 should give people great pause (serious reflection) about their eternal destiny—do not turn your back on the Lord but accept the free gift of salvation while you can.**

> The Bible Warns: There is Only One Way to Heaven (see epilogue). The Lord Jesus Christ offers the gift of eternal salvation (John 3:16, 5:24, 14:6; and Romans 10:9, 13) to those who do not 'turn away' and are willing to accept—so by grace [mercy] you are saved through faith (Ephesians 2:8-9).
>
> **Don't make the terrible mistake by turning away from God. God is holy, righteous, and merciful, and through our Lord Jesus Christ offers the gift of eternal salvation** (John 3:16, 5:24, 14:6; Romans 10:9, 13; and Ephesians 2:8-9) to those who do not turn away and are willing to repent of their sins and accept through faith the free gift of pardon—so by grace [mercy] you are saved through faith (Ephesians 2:8-9).

Historical marker at the entry of ruins of City of Megiddo. *Photos by Roger Gallop*

"The city of Megiddo played a prominent role in the history of the ancient Near East. Strategically located…Megiddo controlled access to the road that linked Egypt with Mesopotamia and Anatolia – the most important trade and military route of that time. Megiddo is the only site in the Land of Israel mentioned in the records of all Near Eastern ancient powers and was one of the most fought-over cities in the region. The first fully-recorded battle in history, in which Pharaoh Thutmose III's army faced a coalition of Canaanite kings, took place here in 1479 BC.

Megiddo is mentioned in many biblical narratives. Its king was one of the Canaanite rulers defeated by Joshua…it was the site where two Judahite kings–Ahaziah and Josiah–met their deaths. For millions of Christians, Megiddo (the Valley of Jezreel or Yizreel) is the Armageddon site of St. John's Revelation where the forces of Good will defeat the forces of Evil in the Final Battle at the End of Days." (Ref. from marker)

"The Late Bronze period (1550-1150 BC) is marked by Egyptian rule of Canaan. At that time, Megiddo was one of the country's major city-states and its king a loyal vassal of the Egyptian pharaoh. The city-gate and the elaborate palace located just inside the gate are the best known remains of this period…" (Ref. from marker)

Historcal marker at the entry of ruins of City Gate.
Photos by Roger Gallop

Megiddo ruins — Pagan culture which included child sacrifice, idol worship, religious prostitution, orgies, and divination embedded in the worship of demonic gods.

Photos by Roger Gallop

Ruins of Megiddo overlooking the Valley of Yizreel — the site of the future Armageddon (the great tribulation) as described in the Book of Revelation. See chapter 12 for more information.

notes: **Chapter 2**

1. Lindsey, H. (February 13, 2015). Hal Lindsey Report. Hal Lindsey Media Ministries. (www.hallindsey.org)

2. Got Questions Ministry, GotQuestions.org, "Why did God love Jacob and hate Esau (Malachi 1:3; Romans 9:13)?" Retrieved 2015, from http://www.gotquestions.org/Jacob-Esau-love-hate.html.

3. What is Passover? Chabad.org. Retrieved 2015, from http://www.chabad.org/holidays/passover/pesach_cdo/aid/871715/jewish/What-Is-Passover.htm.

4. Lindsey, H. (1973, 1984). *There's A New World Coming.* Eugene, OR: Harvest House Publishers, 101-103.

5. NIV Study Bible, New International Version, Introduction to the Book of Joshua, The Conquest and the Ethical Question of War. Grand Rapids, MI: Zondervan Publishing House.

Chapter 3

Warnings, Blessings, and Punishment for Disobedience

> **Note to reader:** Chapter 3 reviews Scripture that pertains to warnings, blessings, and punishment for disobedience of the Jewish people—Scripture that is fundamental to Bible prophecy. **This information will help the reader to fully understand end time prophetic events, especially those occurring in today's world.**

> *"...'Now if you obey me fully and keep my covenant, then out of all nations you will be my treasured possession. Although the whole earth is mine, you will be for me a kingdom of priests and a holy nation.'"* —Exodus 19:5-6, NAS

This chapter begins with a review of the two covenants—Abrahamic and Mosaic—because **these covenants are "fundamental to Bible propehcy."**[1]

The **Abrahamic Covenant**, the original covenant with Abram, Isaac, and Jacob, and their descendants, is an unconditional covenant found in Genesis 12:1-3, 13:14-15.

The **Mosaic Covenant** is a conditional covenant found in Exodus 19 – 24. This covenant is an expansion of the original covenant with The Ten Commandments as specified in Exodus 20 and in Deuteronomy 5, and in other decrees and warnings. In the Mosaic Covenant, God promises to make Israel His *"treasured possession"* among the people of the land and to make Israel *"a kingdom of priests and a holy nation"* (Exodus 19:5-6, NIV). God then enacted laws and decrees.

The Ten Commandments were part of God's covenant with Israel. *"Then the Lord said to Moses, 'Write down these words, for in accordance with these words I have made a covenant with you and with Israel.' Moses was there with the Lord forty days and forty nights without eating bread or drinking water. **And he [the Lord] wrote on the tablets the words of the covenant—The Ten Commandments"*** (Exodus 34:27-28, NIV). [Bold added]

> In the Bible, God makes two kinds of covenants with human beings—conditional and unconditional (as described in chapter 2; also see glossary). A **covenant** is a binding agreement between two or more parties; in legal terms, it is a formal sealed agreement or contract.
>
> An **unconditional covenant** is predicated on God saying to man, 'I will do this. Period.' The Lord came to Abram with the first covenant (Genesis 12:1-3, 13:14-15)—known as the **Abrahamic Covenant**. God promised him *"To your offspring [descendants] I will give this land"* (Genesis 12:7, NIV). There are no conditions that have to be fulfilled by human beings. An 'everlasting covenant' is described in chapter 6, section The Fallacy of Replacement Theology. **The covenant cannot end; it remains in effect today and forever and that makes it fundamental to Bible prophecy.**[2]
>
> A **conditional covenant** is predicated on God saying to man, *'If you will do this, I will do that'*— known as the **Mosaic Covenant**. God promises *"'Now if you obey me fully and keep my covenant, then out of all nations you will be my **treasured possession. Although the whole earth is mine, you will be for me a kingdom of priests and a holy nation.'** These are the words you are to speak to the Israelites"* (Exodus 19:5-6, NIV). [Bold added]

Decrees and Warnings

On the plains of Moab by the Jordan River (c. 1406 BC), before the Israelites crossed into the land of Canaan, Moses warns the Israelites to be faithful and follow the commands and decrees of the Lord your God. *"Moses summoned all Israel and said: Hear, O Israel, the decrees and laws I declare in your hearing today. Learn them and be sure to follow them"* (Deuteronomy 5:1, NIV; The Ten Commandments).

And Moses asks the Israelites, what is the greatest commandment? *"Love the LORD your God with all your heart and with all your soul and with all your strength. These commandments that I give you today are to be on your hearts. Impress them on your children. Talk about them when you sit at home and when you walk along the road, when you lie down and when you get up. Tie them as symbols on your hands and bind them on your foreheads. Write them on the doorframes of your houses and on your gates"* (Deuteronomy 6:5-9, NIV).

Moses warns the Israelites, *"So be careful to do what the LORD your God has commanded you;* **do not turn aside to the right or to the left. Walk in obedience to all that the LORD your God has commanded you,** *so that you may live and prosper and prolong your days in the land that you will possess"* (Deuteronomy 5:32-33, NIV). Additional decrees are set forth in chapters 6 through 26, but **most important, 1) love the Lord your God, 2) do not forget the Lord, 3) fear and obey the Lord, and lastly, 4) do not worship other gods.**

"Be careful, or you will be enticed to turn away and worship other gods and bow down to them. Then the LORD's anger will burn against you...." (Deuteronomy 11:16-17, NIV) *"...when you have driven them out and settled in their land, and after they have been destroyed before you,* **be careful not to be ensnared by inquiring about their gods, saying, 'How do these nations serve their gods? We will do the same.' You must not worship the LORD your God in their way, because in worshiping their gods, they do all kinds of detestable things the LORD hates. They even burn their sons and daughters in the fire as sacrifices to their gods"** (Deuteronomy 12:29-31, NIV). [Bold added]

Follow the Lord's commands: *"The LORD your God commands you this day to follow these decrees and laws; carefully observe them with all your heart and with all your soul. You have declared this day that the LORD is your God and that you will walk in obedience to him, that you will keep his decrees, commands and laws—that you will listen to him. And the LORD has declared this day that you are his people, his* **treasured possession** *as he promised, and that you are to keep all his commands. He has declared that he will set you in praise, fame and honor high above all the nations he has made and that you will be a* **people holy to the LORD your God,** *as he promised"* (Deuteronomy 26:16-19, NIV). [Bold added]

When the Israelites assembled before Moses in the plains of Moab before setting out for the Promised Land (the land of Canaan), Moses spoke of 'blessings for obedience' and 'curses for continued disobedience.' **The blessings for obedience and curses for disobedience under the Mosaic Covenant are laid out in just one chapter: Deuteronomy 28.** The **"blessings"** are found in verses 1-14 and the **"curses"** are found in verses 15-68.

The Law of Moses is also called the Book of the Covenant, Book of the Law, Mosaic Law, or the Ordinances and Ceremonial Law. The Ten Commandments are called the Moral Law, a reflection of God's character.

Blessings for Obedience and Punishment for Disobedience
Warnings to the Jewish People and All of Humanity

Blessings for Obedience

The blessings for obedience are found in Deuteronomy 28:1-14, NIV:

"If you fully obey the LORD your God and carefully follow all his commands I give you today, the LORD your God will set you high above all the nations on earth. All these blessings will come on you and accompany you if you obey the LORD your God:

You will be blessed in the city and blessed in the country.

The fruit of your womb will be blessed, and the crops of your land and the young of your livestock—the calves of your herds and the lambs of your flocks.

Your basket and your kneading trough will be blessed.

You will be blessed when you come in and blessed when you go out.

The LORD will grant that the enemies who rise up against you will be defeated before you. They will come at you from one direction but flee from you in seven.

The LORD will send a blessing on your barns and on everything you put your hand to. The LORD your God will bless you in the land he is giving you.

The LORD will establish you as his holy people, as he promised you on oath, if you keep the commands of the LORD your God and walk in obedience to him. Then all the peoples on earth will see that you are called by the name of the LORD, and they will fear you. The LORD will grant you abundant prosperity—in the fruit of your womb, the young of your livestock and the crops of your ground—in the land he swore to your ancestors to give you.

The LORD will open the heavens, the storehouse of his bounty, to send rain on your land in season and to bless all the work of your hands. You will lend to many nations but will borrow from none. The LORD will make you the head, not the tail. If you pay attention to the commands of the LORD your God that I give you this day and carefully follow them, you will always be at the top, never at the bottom. Do not turn aside from any of the commands I give you today, to the right or to the left, following other gods and serving them."

Blessings for obedience given to the people by Moses are also listed in Leviticus 26:1-13. The contents of Leviticus were given to Moses by God at Mount Sinai.

Punishment for Disobedience

The curses for disobedience are found in Deuteronomy 28:15-63, NIV. [Bold added]

"However, if you do not obey the LORD your God and do not carefully follow all his commands and decrees I am giving you today, all these curses will come on you and overtake you:

[16]You will be cursed in the city and cursed in the country. [17]Your basket and your kneading trough will be cursed. [18]The fruit of your womb will be cursed, and the crops of your land, and the calves of your herds and the lambs of your flocks. [19]You will be cursed when you come in and cursed when you go out.

[20]The LORD will send on you curses, confusion and rebuke in everything you put your hand to, until you are destroyed and come to sudden ruin because of the evil you have done in forsaking him. [21]The LORD will plague you with diseases until he has destroyed you from the land you are entering to possess. [22]The LORD will strike you with wasting disease, with fever and inflammation, with scorching heat and drought, with blight and mildew, which will plague you until you perish. [23]The sky over your head will be bronze, the ground beneath you iron. [24]The LORD will turn the rain of your country into dust and powder; it will come down from the skies until you are destroyed.

[25]The LORD will cause you to be defeated before your enemies. You will come at them from one direction but flee from them in seven, and you will become a thing of horror to all the kingdoms on earth. [26]Your carcasses will be food for all the birds and the wild animals, and there will be no one to frighten them away. [27]The LORD will afflict you with the boils of Egypt and with tumors, festering sores and the itch, from which you cannot be cured. [28]The LORD will afflict you with madness, blindness and confusion of mind. [29]At midday you will grope about like a blind person in the dark. You will be unsuccessful in everything you do; day after day you will be oppressed and robbed, with no one to rescue you.

[30]You will be pledged to be married to a woman, but another will take her and ravish her. You will build a house, but you will not live in it. You will plant a vineyard, but you will not even begin to enjoy its fruit. [31]Your ox will be slaughtered before your eyes, but you will eat none of it. Your donkey will be forcibly taken from you and will not be returned. Your sheep will be given to your enemies, and no one will rescue them. [32]Your sons and daughters will be given to another nation, and you will wear out your eyes watching for them day after day, powerless to lift a hand. [33]A people that you do not know will eat what your land and labor produce, and you will have nothing but cruel oppression all your days [oppressed and crushed continually]. [34]The sights you see will drive you mad. [35]The LORD will afflict your knees and legs with painful boils that cannot be cured, spreading from the soles of your feet to the top of your head.

[36]The LORD will drive you and the king you set over you to a nation unknown to you or your ancestors. There you will worship other gods, gods of wood and stone. [37]You will become a thing of horror, a byword and an object of ridicule among all the peoples where the LORD will drive you.

³⁸You will sow much seed in the field but you will harvest little, because locusts will devour it. ³⁹You will plant vineyards and cultivate them but you will not drink the wine or gather the grapes, because worms will eat them. ⁴⁰You will have olive trees throughout your country but you will not use the oil, because the olives will drop off. ⁴¹You will have sons and daughters but you will not keep them, because they will go into captivity. ⁴²Swarms of locusts will take over all your trees and the crops of your land.

⁴³The foreigners who reside among you will rise above you higher and higher, but you will sink lower and lower. ⁴⁴They will lend to you, but you will not lend to them. They will be the head, but you will be the tail.

⁴⁵All these curses will come on you. They will pursue you and overtake you until you are destroyed, because you did not obey the LORD your God and observe the commands and decrees he gave you. ⁴⁶They will be a sign and a wonder to you and your descendants forever. ⁴⁷Because you did not serve the LORD your God joyfully and gladly in the time of prosperity, ⁴⁸therefore in hunger and thirst, in nakedness and dire poverty, **you will serve the enemies the LORD sends against you. He will put an iron yoke on your neck until he has destroyed you.**

⁴⁹The LORD will **bring a nation against you** from far away, from the ends of the earth, like an eagle swooping down, a nation whose language you will not understand, ⁵⁰a fierce-looking nation without respect for the old or pity for the young. ⁵¹They will devour the young of your livestock and the crops of your land until you are destroyed. They will leave you no grain, new wine or olive oil, nor any calves of your herds or lambs of your flocks until you are ruined. ⁵²They will lay siege to all the cities throughout your land until the high fortified walls in which you trust fall down. They will besiege all the cities throughout the land the LORD your God is giving you.

⁵³Because of the suffering your enemy will inflict on you during the siege, you will eat the fruit of the womb, the flesh of the sons and daughters the LORD your God has given you. ⁵⁴Even the most gentle and sensitive man among you will have no compassion on his own brother or the wife he loves or his surviving children, ⁵⁵and he will not give to one of them any of the flesh of his children that he is eating. It will be all he has left because of the suffering your enemy will inflict on you during the siege of all your cities. ⁵⁶The most gentle and sensitive woman among you—so sensitive and gentle that she would not venture to touch the ground with the sole of her foot—will begrudge the husband she loves and her own son or daughter ⁵⁷the afterbirth from her womb and the children she bears. For in her dire need she intends to eat them secretly because of the suffering your enemy will inflict on you during the siege of your cities.

⁵⁸If you do not carefully follow all the words of this law, which are written in this book, and do not revere this glorious and awesome name—the LORD your God— ⁵⁹the LORD will send fearful plagues on you and your descendants, harsh and prolonged disasters, and severe and lingering illnesses. ⁶⁰He will bring on you all the diseases of Egypt that you dreaded, and they will cling to you. ⁶¹The LORD will also bring on you every kind of sickness and disaster not recorded in this Book of the Law, until you are destroyed. ⁶²**You who were as numerous as the stars in the sky**

will be left but few in number, because you did not obey the LORD your God. ⁶³*Just as it pleased the LORD to make you prosper and increase in number, so it will please him to ruin and destroy you.* **You will be uprooted from the land you are entering to possess**" (Deuteronomy 28:15-63, NIV). [Bold added]

Punishment for disobedience given to the people by Moses is listed in Leviticus 26:14-39. **Moses warned the Jewish people that if they continue their sin against their covenant with God, a horrible fate would fall upon them as listed in Leviticus 26:31-33.** The contents of Leviticus were given to Moses by God at Mount Sinai.

> *"I will turn your cities into ruins and lay waste your sanctuaries, and I will take no delight in the pleasing aroma of your offerings. I myself will lay waste the land, so that your enemies who live there will be appalled. I will scatter you among the nations and will draw out my sword and pursue you. Your land will be laid waste, and your cities will lie in ruins"* (Leviticus 26:31-33, NIV).

Note that there are **many more verses related to curses than blessings. God wanted to get the attention of the Israelites. Outlining the curses in greater detail was meant as a 'driving motivation' to the Jewish people to follow the decrees and commands of the Lord.** It also serves to show us that **war, occupation, and Diaspora** (worldwide exile) were among the curses.

Diaspora refers to the Jews who were exiled from the land of promise (Promised Land, Holy Land or Land of Israel) during the Babylonian occupation (597 BC and 586 BC) and the Roman occupation (AD 70). Throughout much of Jewish history, most Jews have lived in Diaspora. Today, the world's Jewish population is primarily concentrated in two countries, the United States and Israel. About half of the Jewish people live in Israel while most of the rest reside in the U.S.

These **curses were a prophecy of events that later transpired** (721 BC, 586 BC, and AD 70; see chapter 4). And yet, the fact that these curses have befallen Israel **does not imply that God has forsaken the Jews** as some today might suggest. If the people do not obey these commands and decrees, they will suffer plagues, harsh and prolonged disasters, and banishment from one end of the earth to the other (Deuteronomy 28: 58-68)—but **if the people should return to the Lord, even if they have been scattered to the ends of the earth, the Lord will gather them up and return them back to land that belonged to their fathers, and they would be blessed** (Deuteronomy 30:1-10).

Moses Predicts the Future

And then Moses predicts the dispersion of the Jewish people in the latter years due to their disobedience and idol worship. (Deuteronomy 28:64-68, NIV, a continuation of blessings and punishment in Deuteronomy 28:1-63; see previous section.)

> *⁶⁴**Then the LORD will scatter you among all nations, from one end of the earth to the other.** There you will worship other gods—gods of wood and stone, which neither you nor your ancestors have known. ⁶⁵Among those nations you will find no repose, no resting place for the sole of your foot. There the LORD will give you an **anxious mind, eyes weary with longing, and a despairing heart.** ⁶⁶You will live in constant suspense, filled with dread both night and day, never sure of your life. ⁶⁷In the morning you will say, "If only it were evening!" and in the evening, "If only it were morning!"—because of the terror that will fill your hearts and the sights that your eyes will see. ⁶⁸The LORD will send you back in ships to Egypt on a journey I said you should never make again. There you will offer yourselves for sale to your enemies as male and female slaves, but no one will buy you"* (Deuteronomy 28:64-68, NIV). [Bold added]

Renewal of the unconditional covenant of Abraham, Isaac, and Jacob with the Israelites before the conquest of the Promised Land is found in Deuteronomy 29:12-15, NIV.

> *"You are standing here in order to enter into a covenant with the LORD your God, a covenant the LORD is making with you this day and sealing with an oath, **to confirm you this day as his people, that he may be your God as he promised you and as he swore to your fathers, Abraham, Isaac and Jacob.** I am making this covenant, with its oath, not only with you who are standing here with us today in the presence of the LORD our God but also with those who are not here today"* (Deuteronomy 29:12-15, NIV). [Bold added]

Why This Fierce Punishment for Disobedience? (See Deuteronomy 29:24-29, NIV, and chaper 5, Why This Fierce Punishment for Disobedience?)

> *"All the nations will ask: 'Why has the LORD done this to this land? Why this fierce, burning anger?'*
>
> *And the answer will be: 'It is because this people abandoned the covenant of the LORD, the God of their ancestors, the covenant he made with them when he brought them out of Egypt. They went off and worshiped other gods and bowed down to them, gods they did not know, gods he had not given them. Therefore the LORD's anger burned against this land, so that he brought on it all the curses written in this book. In furious anger and in great wrath the LORD uprooted them from their land and thrust them into another land, as it is now.'*

On the plains of Moab by the Jordan River (c. 1406 BC), before the Israelites crossed into the land of Canaan, Moses viewed the promised land (Deuteronomy 34:14) and delivered his last three sermons (Deuteronomy 1-32) with decrees and warnings of exile for **disobedience and idol worship**. About 800 years later the first **Diaspora** began in the year 597 BC when a portion of the population of Judea was deported to Babylonia by the Babylonians, under the reign of King Nebuchadnezzar, and then a second significant deportation to Babylonia occurred in 586 BC when the First Jewish Temple (Solomon's Temple) was destroyed. The Jewish exile worldwide occurred in AD 70 when the Second Jewish Temple was destroyed by the Roman Empire. Some time later the Romans crushed a Jewish rebellion for independence in a three-year war ending in AD 135.

> *The secret things belong to the LORD our God, but the things revealed belong to us and to our children forever, that we may follow all the words of this law"* (Deuteronomy 29:24-29, NIV).

Moses predicts the restoration of the Jewish people and renewal of the Mosaic covenant in Deuteronomy 30:1-5, NIV. (Restoration of the State of Israel occurred May 14, 1948; see chapter 6.)

> *"When all these blessings and curses I have set before you come on you and you take them to heart wherever the LORD your God disperses you among the nations, and when you and your children return to the LORD your God and obey him with all your heart and with all your soul according to everything I command you today, then the LORD your God will restore your fortunes and have compassion on you and* **gather you again from all the nations where he scattered you. Even if you have been banished to the most distant land under the heavens, from there the LORD your God will gather you and bring you back. He will bring you to the land that belonged to your ancestors, and you will take possession of it.** *He will make you more prosperous and numerous than your ancestors"* (Deuteronomy 30:1-5, NIV). [Bold added]

Moses forewarns the Israelites before setting out for the land of Canaan, *"This day I call heaven and earth witnesses against you that* **I have set before you life and death, blessings and curses. Now choose life,** *so that you and your children may live and that you may love the Lord your God, listen to his voice, and hold fast to him. For the Lord is your life, and he will give you many years in the land he swore to give to your fathers, Abraham, Isaac and Jacob"* (Deuteronomy 30:19-20, NIV). [Bold added]

Moses was told to commission Joshua to lead the Israelites across the Jordan River and into the land of Canaan (Deuteronomy 1:37-38, 31:23, 34:9; Numbers 27:12-23).

> *"Then Moses summoned Joshua and said to him in the presence of all Israel, 'Be strong and courageous, for you must go with this people into the land that the LORD swore to their forefathers to give them, and you must divide it among them as their inheritance.* **The LORD himself goes before you and will be with you; he will never leave you nor forsake you.** *Do not be afraid; do not be discouraged'"* (Deuteronomy 31:7-8, NIV). [Bold added]

The Lord Reaffirms Israel's Future Rebellion

The Lord reaffirms Israel's future rebellion and the coming disasters that will befall Israel (Deuteronomy 31:14-29, NIV). [Bold added]

"The LORD said to Moses, 'Now the day of your death is near. Call Joshua and present yourselves at the tent of meeting, where I will commission him.' So Moses and Joshua came and presented themselves at the tent of meeting.

Then the LORD appeared at the tent in a pillar of cloud, and the cloud stood over the entrance to the tent. And the LORD said to Moses: 'You are going to rest with your ancestors, and these people will soon prostitute themselves to the foreign gods of the land they are entering. They will forsake me and break the covenant I made with them. And in that day I will become angry with them and forsake them; I will hide my face from them, and they will be destroyed. Many disasters and calamities will come on them, and in that day they will ask, 'Have not these disasters come on us because our God is not with us?' And I will certainly hide my face in that day because of all their wickedness in turning to other gods.

Now write down this song [see The Song of Moses in Deuteronomy 32:1-43] and teach it to the Israelites and have them sing it, so that it may be a witness for me against them. When I have brought them into the land flowing with milk and honey, the land I promised on oath to their ancestors, and when they eat their fill and thrive, they will turn to other gods and worship them, rejecting me and breaking my covenant. And when many disasters and calamities come on them, this song will testify against them, because it will not be forgotten by their descendants. ***I know what they are disposed to do, even before I bring them into the land I promised them on oath.'*** *So Moses wrote down this song that day and taught it to the Israelites.*

(The song is found in Deuteronomy 32.)

The LORD gave this command to Joshua son of Nun: 'Be strong and courageous, for you will bring the Israelites into the land I promised them on oath, and I myself will be with you.'

After Moses finished writing in a book the words of this law from beginning to end, he gave this command to the Levites who carried the ark of the covenant of the LORD: [Moses speaking] *'Take this Book of the Law and place it beside the ark of the covenant of the LORD your God. There it will remain as a witness against you.* ***For I know how rebellious and stiff-necked you are. If you have been rebellious against the LORD while I am still alive and with you, how much more will you rebel after I die!*** *Assemble before me all the elders of your tribes and all your officials, so that I can speak these words in their hearing and call the heavens and the earth to testify against them.* ***For I know that after my death you are sure to become utterly corrupt and to turn from the way I have commanded you.*** *In days to come, disaster will fall on you because you will do evil in the sight of the LORD and arouse his anger by what your hands have made'"* (Deuteronomy 31:14-29, NIV). [Bold added]

Israel's Triumph in the Land of Canaan

Joshua leads the Israelites across the **Jordan River and into the land of Canaan** (c. 1406 BC) (Joshua 3-4)—see map in chapter 2, Exodus of the Jewish People.

"The Lord your God himself will cross over ahead of you [and] He will destroy these nations [Canaanites] before you, and you will take possession of their land" (Deuteronomy 31:3, NIV).

"I will send My terror ahead of you, and throw into confusion every nation you encounter. I will make all your enemies turn their backs and run. I will send **hornets** *ahead of you so that they will drive out the Hivites, the Canaanites, and the Hittites before you. I will not drive them out before you in a single year, that the land may not become desolate and the beasts of the field become too numerous for you"* (Exodus 23:27-29, NIV). [Bold added]

"Moreover, the Lord your God will send **the hornet** *among them until even the survivors who hide from you have perished. Do not be terrified by them, for the Lord your God, who is among you, is a great and awesome God"* (Deuteronomy 7:20-21, NIV). [Bold added]

The word 'hornet' used in these passages describes some agent that caused great panic amongst the Canaanites in front of the advancing Israelites. Some believe that the word hornet was used metaphorically as a feeling of 'sheer panic'—a *"terror of God"* (Genesis 35:5). The Septuagint (Greek translation of the OT) interpretation of "hornet" is the word 'wasp'—but whatever it was, it caused panic and confusion amongst the peoples of Canaan.

The conquest of the Promised Land took about 6 years. Following the conquest, the land was divided amongst the 12 tribes (Joshua 13-21), and the Levites were assigned 48 cities and surrounding pasturelands (Joshua 20-21). Victory over the Canaanites validated to surrounding peoples and the world that **the God of Israel is the only true and living God whose claim on the world is supreme (sovereign or absolute).** This was also a warning that the God of Israel would ultimately destroy all pagan cultures and would support only those who acknowledge and serve Him. (This applies to all peoples and nations today.)

> In the Land of Israel there are four species of hornets which are larger in size than those found in America. They "attack human beings in a very furious manner. The furious attack of a swarm of hornets drives cattle and horses to madness, and has even caused the death of the animals."³

Tribes of Israel

Promises Fulfilled
Despite Continued Disobedience

After the conquest and the taking of the land of Canaan (the Promised Land), the people were inclined to disregard the commandments, decrees, and laws stated in the Book of Deuteronomy. Before his death Joshua warned the people of the consequences for disobedience and idolatry and reaffirmed the Mosaic covenant (Joshua 24:19-28, NIV).

> *"Joshua said to the people, 'You are not able to serve the LORD. He is a holy God; he is a jealous God. He will not forgive your rebellion and your sins. ^{20}If you forsake the LORD and serve foreign gods, he will turn and bring disaster on you and make an end of you, after he has been good to you.'*
>
> *^{21}But the people said to Joshua, 'No! We will serve the LORD.'*
>
> *^{22}Then Joshua said, 'You are witnesses against yourselves that you have chosen to serve the LORD.' 'Yes, we are witnesses,' they replied.*
>
> *^{23}'Now then,' said Joshua, 'throw away the foreign gods that are among you and yield your hearts to the LORD, the God of Israel.'*
>
> *^{24}And the people said to Joshua, 'We will serve the LORD our God and obey him.'*
>
> *^{25}On that day Joshua made a covenant for the people, and there at Shechem he reaffirmed for them decrees and laws. ^{26}And Joshua recorded these things in the Book of the Law of God. Then he took a large stone and set it up there under the oak near the holy place of the LORD.*
>
> *^{27}'See!' he said to all the people. 'This stone will be a witness against us. It has heard all the words the LORD has said to us. It will be a witness against you if you are untrue to your God.' ^{28}Then Joshua dismissed the people, each to their own inheritance"* (Joshua 24:19-28, NIV).

The Jewish people were **warned continually** (Exodus 20:23, 32:7-10; Joshua 24:15, 19-20; Judges 2:6-23; Samuel 8:6-20, 12:25; 2 Kings 17:7-23; Isaiah 65:1-7; Amos 9:1-10), but they would not listen. Over the course of the next 800 years (c. 1375 BC – 586 BC), the Jewish people were inclined to turn their back on God and worship idols (the ultimate sin) and intermarry with people from paganistic cultures.

> The **Mosaic covenant** called for the Jewish people to drive out the Canaanites and to cleanse the region of paganism, and to obey the Lord's commands and decrees—then *"he will set you high above all nations that he has made, in praise and in fame and in honor, and that you shall be a **people holy to the LORD your God**, as he has spoken"* Deuteronomy 26:16-19. [Bold added]

The Lord said to Moses on Mount Sinai, this is what you are to tell the people of Israel,

> *"...'Now if you obey me fully and keep my covenant, then out of all nations you will be my treasured possession. Although the whole earth is mine, you will be for me a kingdom of priests and a holy nation.' These are the words you are to speak to the Israelites"* (Exodus 19:5-6, NIV). [Bold added] See chapter 2, The Mosaic Covenant.

The Jewish people forgot all the many acts of God that established Israel in the Promised Land—miracles witnessed firsthand (with their own eyes) during the exodus from Egypt—and additionally, **they forgot their unique identity as God's chosen people and the blessings and the curses and punishment for disobedience.**

World in Denial - Defiant Nature of Mankind

Period of Judges
Judges 1:1 - 1 Samuel 9
c. 1400 BC to 1050 BC

Many of the 'covenant promises' God had given to the patriarchs (Abraham, Isaac, and Jacob) and to the Jewish people in the desert had been fulfilled. The Jewish people occupied the promised land—it was now time to completely cleanse the land of its paganistic culture and for the Jewish people to form a self-governing nation-state (homeland).

But in the land of Canaan **Israel soon forgot the many acts of God** that established the Jewish people in the land. They failed to remember their unique identity as God's people—people chosen to be *"a kingdom of priests and a holy nation."* Rather, the **Jewish people immersed themselves in the Canaanite culture and became devoted to false gods (idols) and pagan beliefs and practices.**[4]

"In those days Israel had no king; everyone did as he saw fit." (Judges 17:6, NIV). Israel had essentially departed from the covenant standards found in the law and did not truly acknowledge or obey the Lord, their heavenly King.[5] To settle disputes, the land of Israel was ruled by a succession of judges, some of them receiving only a brief mention in the Book of Judges.

Samuel was the last of the Hebrew Judges and **the first of the major prophets** who began to prophesy inside the land of Israel. He lived during the time between two eras: Judges and Kings.

> List of Judges from the Book of Judges: Shamgar 3:31; Tola 10:1-2; Jair 10:3-5; Ibzan 12:8-10; Elon 12:11-12; Abdon 12:13-15; Othniel 3:7-11; Ehud 3:12-30; Jephthah 11:1 – 12:7; Gideon 6:11 – 8:35 (led 300 Israelites to defeat the entire army of the Midianites); Samson 13:1 – 16:31 (known for his great strength; delivered Israel from the Philistines); Deborah 4:1 — 5:31; and Samuel (1 Samuel and 2 Samuel).

When Samuel was about 65 years of age, all the elders of Israel gathered together at Ramah and said to Samuel, *"Give us a king to lead us"* (1 Samuel 8:5-9, NIV).

> *"They said to him, 'You are old, and your sons do not follow your ways; now appoint a king to lead us, such as all the other nations have.' But when they said, 'Give us a king to lead us,' this displeased Samuel; so he prayed to the LORD. And the LORD told him: 'Listen to all that the people are saying to you;* **it is not you they have rejected, but they have rejected me [the Lord] as their king.** *As they have done from the day I brought them up out of Egypt until this day, forsaking me and serving other gods, so they are doing to you. Now listen to them; but warn them solemnly and let them know what the king who will reign over them will claim as his rights'"* (1 Samuel 8:5-9, NIV). [Bold added]

Samuel explained to the people what the kings will do (1 Samuel 8:10-17)—the king will take your sons to build chariots and weapons of war, and to plow his land and gather his harvest; and he will take your daughters to work in the kitchens as cooks and bakers, and as personal attendants; he will take your pasturelands, vineyards, and olive groves; and he will take a portion of your produce (grain, grapes, and olives); and he will take your cattle, donkeys, and flocks; and you will become his slaves.

Samuel warned the people in 1 Samuel 8:18-22, NIV:

> *"When that day comes, you will cry out for relief from the king you have chosen, but the LORD will not answer you in that day. But the people refused to listen to Samuel. 'No!' they said. 'We want a king over us.* **Then we will be like all the other nations,**

with a king to lead us and to go out before us and fight our battles.' [This was a defiant act of forgetting their unique identity and the true God of Israel.]

When Samuel heard all that the people said, he repeated it before the LORD. The LORD answered, 'Listen to them and give them a king.' Then Samuel said to the Israelites, *'Everyone go back to your own town'"* (1 Samuel 8:18-22, NIV). [Bold added]

Despite the warnings from Samuel, the people wanted a human king to lead them. God used Samuel to establish a kingship in Israel by anointing the first two kings: Saul and David. Samuel also provided 'covenant continuity' during the transition from judges to kings (monarchy).

United Kingdom
Kings Saul, David, and Solomon
1 Samuel 10 - 1 Kings 11
c. 1050 BC to 930 BC

After about 350 years of being governed by judges, the 12 tribes of Israel demanded **a human king**—a king like the surrounding pagan nations—and by demanding a human king, the people continued to **turn away from their "faith and obedience" to the one true God.** Saul became the first king of Israel and reigned about 40 years (c. 1050 – 1010 BC); then David (c. 1010 – 970 BC), and Solomon (c. 970 - 930 BC), the son of David. How remarkable it is, even today, that people still demand their kings or queens; for example, United Kingdom of Great Britain and Northern Ireland (although actual power is vested in the legislative and/or executive cabinet).

Saul (c. 1082 BC – 1010 BC) was the first king of a United Kingdom of Israel and Judah. He was anointed by the prophet Samuel and reigned from the town of Gibeah located just north of Jerusalem. He fell on his sword to avoid capture in the battle against the Philistines at Mount Gilboa, during which three of his sons were also killed.

David (c. 1010 BC – 970 BC) was born in Bethlehem and became the second king of Israel. King David, unlike Saul, followed the commands of God and although he committed

> Today, other countries that still have royalty include, but not limited to, Belgium, Cambodia, Canada, Denmark, Jamaica, Japan, Jordan, Kuwait, Lesotho (in southern Africa), Luxembourg, Malaysia, Monaco, Morocco, Netherlands, New Guinea, New Zealand, Norway, Oman, Qatar, Saudi Arabia, Spain, Swaziland (in southern Africa), Sweden, Thailand, United Arab Emirates, and the Vatican City State. Most government types are constitutional; others are absolute such as Oman, Qatar, Saudi Arabia, Swaziland, and the Vatican. https://en.wikipedia.org/wiki/List_of_current_sovereign_monarchs.

> There was a difference between a king and a judge. A **judge** was a leader elevated by God to meet a specific need usually during times of crisis. When the crisis was over the judge would return to his normal occupation. **Kings** established a political government (monarch) with a bureaucracy. A king held his title of king as long as he lived and upon his death, the title was usually passed to his firstborn son.

sins, he repented and sought to please God. David reigned for 7 years in Hebron (and had 6 sons with 6 different wives, Ahinoam, Abigail, Maacah, Haggith, Abital, and Eglah) and then 33 years in Jerusalem (and had 4 sons with Bathsheba, none with Michal, and 9 sons with concubines). See 1 Chronicles 3:1-9. During his reign, he expanded the overall territory of Israel. See 2 Samuel 3.

Solomon (c. 970 – 930 BC), the fourth son of David by his wife, Bathsheba, became the third king of Israel. Like David, he also reigned for 40 years. King Solomon built the First Temple (c. 957 BC) in Jerusalem to honor God, but eventually Solomon turned away from God and married women from surrounding pagan cultures. As a result of Solomon's unfaithfulness, the popularity of pagan religions and moral degeneration increased amongst the Jewish people.

> The **First Temple** was built under King Solomon, the son of King David, c. 957 BC. The kingdom of Israel under Solomon controlled most of the land God had promised Abraham, stretching from the Nile in Egypt to the river Euphrates in Persia. Because of **continued disobedience during the time of Judges and under the kingship of Saul, David, and Solomon**, the land was never fully occupied by the Jewish people. Clearly, this was not the time the land was to be claimed as an "everlasting covenant."

Looking west from the Mount of Olives across the Eastern and Southern Walls, Dome of the Rock, al-Asqa mosque, Kidron Valley at bottom, and ruins of King David's palace. *Photo by Roger Gallop, March 14, 2016*

Looking South to the Kidron Valley and south along the Eastern Hill at a point about 500 feet south of the Southern Steps of Temple Mount. The area of archaeological excavation of David's palace is right-center. *Photo by Roger Gallop, March 13, 2016*

Historical Marker indicating site that may be the remains of King David's Palace. *Photos by Roger Gallop, March 13, 2016*

Excavated remains of what may be King David's Palace. *Photos by Roger Gallop, March 13, 2016*

> The name Mount Zion has referred successively to three locations: 1) Lower Eastern Hill was the name of the "Jebusite fortress" that was conquered by King David c. 1003 BC, then renamed the "City of David" where he built his palace, 2) later expanded northward to the top of the Eastern Hill where King Solomon built the first temple c. 957 BC, The Temple Mount, and 3) then later, it expanded to the Western Hill separated from the lower Eastern Hill by the Tyropoeon Valley. The Western Hill became more populated by the first century because of the (by-then) lost palace of King David. The Western Hill is what today is called Mount Zion.

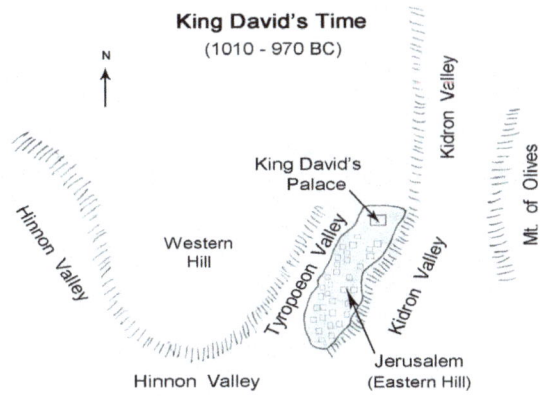

King David's Jerusalem. Note location of David's Palace. See chapter 7, The City of Jerusalem for additional sketches.
Sketch by Roger Gallop

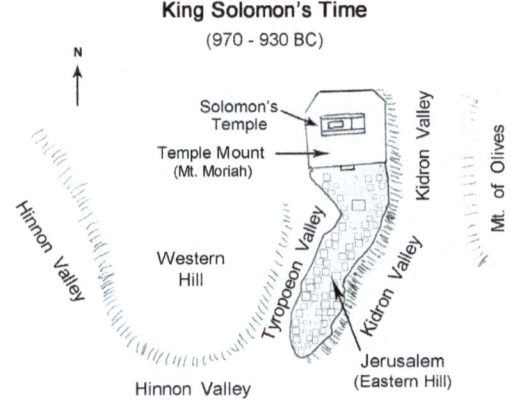

King Solomon's Jerusalem. See chapter 7, The City of Jerusalem for additional sketches.
Sketch by Roger Gallop

notes: Chapter 3

1. Hal Lindsey (February 13, 2015). Hal Lindsey Report, Hal Lindsey Media Ministries. (www.hallindsey.org)

2. Ibid.

3. M.G. Easton, M.A., D.D. (1897). *Illustrated Bible Dictionary*. Third Edition, published by Thomas Nelson. Public Domain, copy freely.

4. NIV Study Bible, New International Version, Introduction to the Book of Judges. Grand Rapids, MI: Zondervan Publishing House.

5. Ibid. and Judges 17:6.

Chapter 4

Jewish History and Consequences for Disobedience

> *"The LORD, the God of their ancestors, sent word to them through his messengers again and again, because he had pity on his people and on his dwelling place. But they mocked God's messengers, despised his words and scoffed at his prophets until the wrath of the LORD was aroused against his people and there was no remedy. He brought up against them the king of the Babylonians..."* —2 Chronicles 36:15-17, NIV

Divided Kingdom
1 Kings 12 - 2 Kings 17
c. 930 BC - 586 BC

Shortly after the reign of King Solomon, Israel became a divided kingdom. This was the result of the Jewish people continually **"turning away" from the Lord and worshiping pagan gods.** The Southern Kingdom, Judah, included the city of Jerusalem and the Temple and was composed of the two tribes, Judah and Benjamin. The northern kingdom retained the name of Israel with its capital Samaria and was composed of the other ten tribes.

During this period (following the reign of Saul, David, and Solomon), the Southern Kingdom (Judah; Judea; capital Jerusalem) had 5 good kings (Asa, Jehoshaphat, Jotham, Hezekiah, and Josiah) and 15 kings who did 'evil in the eyes of the Lord.' The Northern Kingdom (Israel; capital Samaria) had 20 kings, all who 'did evil in the eyes of the Lord.' The northern and southern kingdoms had on-going disputes and battles with each other and with surrounding nations, and they continued to turn their backs on the Lord and worshipped pagan gods and followed the immoral practices of their neighbors. Such failings led to many of the "curses" that the Jews experienced over the years.

Kingdoms of Israel and Judah

The ten tribes of the northern kingdom of Israel were Asher, Dan, Gad, Issachar, Joseph (2 tribes: sons Ephraim and Manasseh), Naphtali, Reuben, Simeon, Zebulun. The two tribes of the southern kingdom of Judah were Judah and Benjamin.

Judea corresponds to part of the ancient **Kingdom of Judah**, also known as the Southern Kingdom. **Samaria** corresponds to the capital of the ancient Kingdom of Israel, also known as the Northern Kingdom.

Assyrian Empire Conquers the Northern Kingdom (Israel)
c. 721 BC

The Assyrian Empire (c. 900 – 607 BC), under the rule of Shalmaneser (c. 726 - 721 BC), conquered the Northern Kingdom of Israel c. 721 BC. This was the result of the Northern Kingdom continually turning away from the Lord and worshiping pagan gods. It was a time of idolatry, child sacrifice, decadence, indulgent living, materialism, sexual immorality, oppression of the poor, and rampant corruption.

The Assyrian invaders tortured and mutilated many of the Israelites before they were executed—and ultimately, the 10 tribes of Israel were replaced with foreigners (Isaiah 7:7-9; 2 Kings 17:24). The people of Israel were "shattered [crushed] as a people, losing their identity as distinct tribes of Israel."[1]

The Assyrians turned their attention to the Southern Kingdom (Judah and Benjamin) and invaded Jerusalem in 701 BC. Under the rule of Sennacherib (c. 705 – 681 BC), the Assyrian ruler wrote letters to King Hezekiah insulting the Lord, and Assyrian officers ridiculed the Lord and spoke against Hezekiah. The Southern Kingdom survived an invasion by the Assyrians through **Divine intervention** (2 Kings 19:20-37; 2 Chronicles 32:20-23). *"And the Lord sent an angel, who annihilated all the fighting men and the leaders and officers in the camp of the Assyrian king. So he withdrew to his own land in disgrace"* (2 Chronicles 32:21, NIV).

Babylonians Conquer the Assyrian Empire and the Southern Kingdom (Judah)
c. 612 BC

In 612 BC a coalition of Babylonians (Babylon, the city of pride and idolatry; Scythians, Iranian equestrian tribes; and Medes, ancient Iranian people of NW Iran and SE Turkey) conquered the Assyrian Empire and destroyed their capital city, Nineveh.

As explained by the prophet **Nahum** (c. 663 BC – 612 BC), **Nineveh was destroyed because of their cruelty, idolatry, pagan superstitions, injustice, and ruthless treatment of the peoples of the Northern Kingdom.** Below is a partial listing of Nahum's prophecies:[2]

- Nahum 1:10 – The people of Nineveh would be drunk from wine.
- Nahum 1:14 – The people of Nineveh would have no descendants.
- Nahum 3:15 – Nineveh would be destroyed by fire and the sword.
- Nahum 3:17 – Nineveh's army officers would desert.
- Nahum 1:15, 3:19 – Nineveh would be totally destroyed and never rebuilt.

The book of Nahum was written before the invasion of Nineveh, and it states that Nineveh would cease to exist—and today it remains just an archaeological site. **In comparison, Israel is once again a nation and prosperous economically and militarily—this should make most people realize there is a God in Heaven. The Lord has kept his promises concerning the perpetual survival of Israel and destruction of wicked, paganistic nations.**

The holiness, justice, and power of the one true God are the basis of Nahum's prophetic book. Nahum proclaims the universal sovereignty of God; that God's commandments and decrees (as asserted in the Mosaic covenant; the Ten Commandments) pertain to the whole world; and that God is in control of history, nations, and their final destinies. Although Nahum writes about the destruction of Nineveh, there is a message of hope:

> God is "*slow to anger and great in power*" (Nahum 1:3); "*is good, a refuge in times of trouble*" (Nahum 1:7); and "*brings good news*" to those who turn to Him (Na. 1:15).

Following the destruction of the Assyrian Empire, the Neo-Babylonians, under the reign of King Nebuchadnezzar, sought to expand their territory by forcing the Southern Kingdom (Judah) into submission and taking Jews captive in surrounding villages. There were three waves of attack against Jerusalem when the Jewish people were taken captive and deported to Babylon (Diaspora)—the first deportation was in 605 BC and the second in 597 BC.

During this time Nebuchadnezzar installed Zedekiah (c. 597 - 586 BC) as king of Judah at the age of twenty-one, but Zedekiah revolted against Babylon and entered into an alliance with Egypt. Nebuchadnezzar responded by invading Judah (2 Kings 25:1) and began a siege of Jerusalem in 589 BC. During this siege, which lasted about thirty months, "*every worst woe befell the city, which drank the cup of God's fury to the dregs*" (2 Kings 25:3; Lamentations 4:4, NIV).

The third deportation occurred in 586 BC when the Babylonians destroyed Jerusalem and the Temple, fulfilling prophecies of **Isaiah, Asaph, Micah, Jeremiah, Ezekiel**, and other prophets of the Bible (see following section, Prophets Who Foresaw These Events). So why did God inflict such punishment on the Jewish people?

Ezra (c. 480 BC – 440 BC), a Jewish scribe and priest, explained: "*The LORD, the God of their ancestors, **sent word to them through his messengers again and again**, because he had pity on his people and on his dwelling place. But **they mocked God's messengers, despised his words and scoffed at his prophets** until the wrath of the LORD was aroused against his people and there was no remedy. He brought up against them the king of the Babylonians...*" (2 Chronicles 36:15-17, NIV). [Bold added]

Zedekiah (ruler of Judah, 597 - 586 BC) "*...did evil in the eyes of the Lord his God and did not humble himself before Jeremiah the prophet.*" (2 Chronicles 36:12, NIV) He and his followers attempted to escape but they were captured on the plains of Jericho. There, after seeing his sons killed, Zedekiah was blinded, bound, and taken captive to Babylon where he remained a prisoner until his death. (See 2 Kings 25:1-7; 2 Chronicles 36:12; Jeremiah 32:4-5, 34:2-3, 39:1-7, 52:4-11; Ezekiel 2:12.)

Destruction of Solomon's Temple and Jerusalem
c. 586 BC

In 586 BC, the eleventh year of Zedekiah's reign, Nebuchadnezzar broke through the great walls of Jerusalem, conquering the city. Ezra continues his account of the destruction of the temple and city (from the previous section):

> "*He brought up against them the king of the Babylonians, who killed their young men with the sword in the sanctuary, and did not spare young men or young women, the elderly or the infirm. God gave them all into the hands of Nebuchadnezzar. He carried to Babylon all the articles from the temple of God, both large and small, and the treasures of the LORD's temple and the treasures of the king and his officials.*

They set fire to God's temple and broke down the wall of Jerusalem; they burned all the palaces and destroyed everything of value there. He carried into exile to Babylon the remnant, who escaped from the sword, and they became servants to him and his successors until the kingdom of Persia came to power" (2 Chronicles 36:17-21, NIV).

After the fall of Jerusalem in 586 BC, Solomon's Temple and the City of Jerusalem were completely destroyed. Most of the people, including temple priests and officials, and all tabernacle furnishings and other sacred objects of the Temple, were carried off to Babylon. Only a small number of people were allowed to remain in Judah to care for the land.

Prophets Who Foresaw These Events

The prophet **Isaiah** (c. 740 BC - 681 BC), who foresaw the destruction of the Northern Kingdom (Israel), also foretold the conquest of Judah. In Isaiah 39:5-7, the prophet informed King Hezekiah of Judah (c. 715 BC – 686 BC), who did what was right in the eyes of the Lord, that a time would come when the Babylonians would invade, overrun and plunder Judah, and take away his descendants.[3]

"Then Isaiah said to Hezekiah, 'Hear the word of the LORD Almighty: The time will surely come when everything in your palace, and all that your predecessors have stored up until this day, will be carried off to Babylon. Nothing will be left, says the LORD. And some of your descendants, your own flesh and blood who will be born to you, will be taken away, and they will become eunuchs in the palace of the king of Babylon'" (Isaiah 39:5-7, NIV).

The prophet **Asaph,** a leader of David's choir who prophesied c. 1000 – 970 BC, also foresaw the destruction of Solomon's Temple (in 586 BC by the Babylonians) which had only just been completed in 957 BC. See Psalms 74 and 79. **And in another prophecy, Asaph foresaw a time when Arab countries would "conspire" to destroy Israel as a nation as** described in Psalm 83—this occurred in 1967. (See chapters 7, The Six Day War, and chapter 8, Israel Surrounded by Hostile Arab Nations.)

The prophet **Micah** (c. 750 BC – 686 BC) foresaw the time when the Lord would expel the Jews from the Promised Land by captivity because of their continual rebellion and idolatry.[4] See Micah 4:9-10. But no one saw the coming destruction with more sorrow, shock, and terror than **Jeremiah** (c. 626 BC – 585 BC) because he foresaw what would befall the people of his day (Jeremiah 25:11-12).[5]

"This whole country will become a desolate wasteland, and these nations [Judah and nations named in v. 19-26] will serve the king of Babylon for **seventy years.*** [c. 586 - 516 BC] 'But when the seventy years are fulfilled, I will punish the king of Babylon and his nation, the land of the Babylonians, for their guilt,' declares the Lord, 'and will make it desolate forever'"* (Jeremiah 25:11-12, NIV).

Jeremiah **warned the people of Judah about their widespread wickedness, corruption,** *turning away* **from God and placing detestable idols in the holy Temple to honor false gods, and building altars to sacrifice their sons and daughters as food to their idols.** (See Jeremiah 32:32-37; Ezekiel 16:20; also see Ezekiel chapters 1-24.)

*"The people of Israel and Judah have provoked me by all the evil they have done—they, their kings and officials, their priests and prophets, the people of Judah and those living in Jerusalem. They **turned their backs to me and not their faces**; though I taught them again and again, **they would not listen or respond to discipline**. They set up their vile images in the house that bears my Name and defiled it. They built high places for Baal in the Valley of Ben Hinnom to **sacrifice their sons and daughters** to Molech, though I never commanded—nor did it enter my mind—that they should do such a detestable thing and so make Judah sin. You are saying about this city, 'By the sword, famine and plague it will be given into the hands of the king of Babylon'; but this is what the LORD, the God of Israel, says: I will **surely gather them from all the lands where I banish them** in my furious anger and great wrath; I will bring them back to this place and let them live in safety"* (Jeremiah 32:32-37, NIV). [Bold added]

The prophet Ezekiel (593-571 BC), who was a captive taken to Babylon, explained that God allowed Babylon to punish Judah **because the people had defiled the Temple, the city, and the land, turned their back on the Lord, and failed to keep the law**. During the first seven years of his ministry, he forewarned the Jewish people of the **harsh reality of Divine judgment**—that Jerusalem would fall and they would be taken captive—but God would eventually restore the exiles to their homeland after a time of punishment (Ezekiel, chapters 4-27).

Medo-Persians (Iran) Conquer the Babylonians
c. 538 BC

In 538 BC a federation of Medes and Persians (Iran) conquered the Babylonians. The captive Jews were freed by Cyrus the Great, first king of the Medo-Persian Empire (c. 550 BC - 529 BC), and they were allowed to return to Judah under the leadership of Zerubbabel with the captured temple treasures and furnishings. Cyrus allowed the Jewish people more cultural and religious freedom than did the Babylonians.

> **Medes** were an ancient Iranian people who lived in northwestern Iran (known as Media) and who spoke the Median language.

Rebuilding the Temple and The Walls of Jerusalem
c. 516 BC

Zerubbabel was the head of the tribe of Judah during their return from Babylonian exile, and upon his return, he began making plans to rebuild the Temple on the old site (Ezra 3:8). Also, Sheshbazzar was appointed governor by Cyrus and told to rebuild the Temple, so he *"laid the foundations of the house of God in Jerusalem"* (Ezra 5:16, NIV).

Sheshbazzar (Ezra 1:8, 11) is likely another name for Zerubbabel (Ezra 2:2, 3:8; Haggai 1:12, 14; Zechariah 4:6, 10)—and so they are likely the same person. For some 20 years Zerubbabel (aka Sheshbazzar) was closely associated with the prophets and priests of that time.

Other individuals who played critical roles in the re-establishment of the Jewish community were **Ezra** (c. 458 BC) and **Nehemiah** (c. 445 BC; contemporary of Ezra).

The Book of Ezra (chapter 6, verses 1 to 11) describes the decree by King Darius I (fourth king of Persia from 522 BC to 486 BC) to continue the reconstruction of the Temple in Jerusalem. Twenty-two years after the Medes conquered Babylon in 538 BC and 70 years after the destruction of Solomon's Temple in 586 BC, the Second Temple was consecrated c. 516 BC during the reign of Darius the Great.[6]

Ezra returned to Jerusalem c. 458 BC and was influential in the spiritual renewal of the Jewish people and helped restore the Torah law within the Jewish community. Although Ezra fought hard against assimilation of beliefs and values and inter-marriage, he was deeply saddened that some of the Jewish people were not obeying God's commands and continued to engage in paganistic practices:

> *"After these things had been done, the leaders came to me and said, "The people of Israel, including the priests and the Levites,* **have not kept themselves separate from the neighboring peoples with their detestable practices**, *like those of the Canaanites, Hittites, Perizzites, Jebusites, Ammonites, Moabites, Egyptians and Amorites....**And the leaders and officials led the way in this unfaithfulness**"* (Ezra 9:1-2, NIV). [Bold added]

The Book of Ezra condemns all the men living in Israel who married foreign women of neighboring countries (Ezra 10:18-44).

Nehemiah was a leader of the Jewish community in Babylon. Nehemiah heard that the Jewish remnant in Jerusalem *"...who survived the exile and are back in the province are in great trouble and disgrace. The wall of Jerusalem is broken down, and its gates have been burned with fire"* (Nehemiah 1:3, NIV).

Nehemiah prayed to God (Nehemiah 1:5-11, NIV) and confessed the sins of Israel. He was concerned that Jerusalem was unwalled and unprotected, and announced: *"Come, let us build the walls of Jerusalem so that we will no longer be an object of scorn"* (Nehemiah 2:17, NIV).

He was then sent to Jerusalem by King Artaxerxes I (fifth king of Persia from 465 BC to 424 BC) in **445 BC, thus beginning Daniel's seventy weeks**. (See Daniel 9:24; also see chapter 11, Daniel's 70th Week.) (Theology scholars generally agree that Nehemiah's first stay in Jerusalem was in 445 BC; Ezra having first arrived in 458 BC.) Despite the efforts of the surrounding peoples to impede its construction, the wall was eventually completed.

In Nehemiah 9:1-37, the Israelites confessed their sins. In verses 33 - 35, in particular, they confess

> *"In all that has happened to us, you have been just; you have acted faithfully, while we did wrong. Our kings, our leaders, our priests and our fathers did not follow your law; they did not pay attention to your commands or the warnings you gave them. Even while they were in their kingdom, enjoying your great goodness...on the spacious and fertile land you gave them, they did not serve you or turn from their evil ways"* (Nehemiah 9:33-35, NIV).

The Second Temple remained unfinished—it was much smaller than the original Temple. The returning Jews were not able to rebuild the Temple as splendid as Solomon's Temple, which was built about 441 years earlier (c. 957 BC). In spite of Ezra's and Nehemiah's efforts to rebuild (including the efforts of other leaders such as Zerubbabel), the Temple remained just "a shadow of its former self."

Disappearance of the Prophets
c. 430 BC

Prophecy disappeared during the early years after building of the Second Temple; the Ark of the Covenant was gone—and although there was a Holy of Holies, it remained empty. What happened to the Ark of the Covenant? One opinion is, the Babylonians took it into captivity. Another opinion is that it was hidden by King Josiah (c. 640 - 609 BC; the last of the good kings in Judah) who had anticipated the Babylonian invasion (c. 605 - 586 BC) through the prophets.

> The **Holy of Holies** refers to the inner tabernacle where God dwelt—defined by four pillars with a veil over the Ark of the Covenant.
>
> The Ark is said to contain the Ten Commandments which were given by God to Moses on Mount Sinai. Some believe that it is located under the Dome of the Rock, but no one knows for sure.
>
> Also, there is an account in the Talmud (central text of Rabbinic Judaism) of a priest who finds a place on the Temple Mount where the Ark is hidden but dies before he can tell others. The point is, the Ark is not supposed to be found—at least not just yet.

Why did prophecy disappear? After the later prophets, Haggai (c. 520 BC), Zechariah (c. 520 BC - 480 BC), and Malachi (c. 440 BC - 430 BC) had died, the gift of prophecy disappeared from the Jewish people. **It disappeared because they continually turned away from the Lord and adopted pagan customs including idolatry.** They were simply unable to achieve the same spiritual insight to receive the gift of prophecy. And today, it is impossible for any individual to achieve this gift in a secular world.

When there were prophets of the Old Testament whose leadership was strong, disagreement with established beliefs (heresy) was unlikely. A prophet talked to God and the Jewish people consulted the prophets on nearly everything in their everyday lives. Even the king consulted the prophets, especially concerning military matters—whether or not to go to war and the use of military tactics. No one could deny the basic

> Prophecy involves Divine inspiration, interpretation, or revelation of future events that is 100% accurate. Old Testament prophecy accurately describes events hundreds or thousands of years in advance.

> **Prophet** of the Old Testament is an individual who actually spoke with God and received Divine understanding and in turn served as a liaison with humanity, delivering knowledge from the Lord God.
>
> Moses may have been the ultimate prophet—reaching the highest level of prophecy that is humanly possible while on Mount Sinai and in the desert. But there were many others; see chapter 1, The Bible's Unity, listing major and minor prophets of the Old Testament.

beliefs (tenets) of Judaism with fulfilled prophecy and open miracles. But when prophecy disappeared, **priests and kings, and people in general, became morally and ethically corrupt,** and it was easier for people to turn away from the Lord.

> Of the 40 kings during the divided kingdom, only 5 kings from the tribe of Judah did what was right in the eyes of the Lord: Asa, Jehoshaphat, Jotham, Hezekiah, and Josiah. The rest did evil in the eyes of the Lord, although a few of the very worst such as Manasseh later humbled himself before the Lord.

Grecian Empire Conquers the Medes and Persians
c. 331 BC

Classical Greece (480 BC to 323 BC) consisted of a group of warring independent city-states, the most famous being Athens and Sparta. Despite constant warfare, this period is also known as the golden age of classical Greek culture—the birthplace of democracy, Western philosophy (Aristotle, Socrates, and Plato), fine art (sculptures and paintings), and renowned architecture, literature, drama, and the Olympic Games.

> Ancient Greece was a civilization belonging to a period of Greek history from about 1200 BC to about 480 BC.

During this period Macedonia was a small kingdom in northern Greece outside the area dominated by the city-states (Athens, Sparta, Corinth, Delphi, Thebes, and others). Macedonia remained detached from the fighting—but this changed under the rule of king Philip (382 - 336 BC) who united Greece by conquering the city-states. After his assassination in 336 BC, his rule was passed on to his son, Alexander the Great.

Alexander the Great united the Greek city-states (Corinthian League) and invaded Persia in 334 BC. After three years of war and three pivotal battles, Alexander destroyed the Persian armies at the Tigris River and defeated the mighty Medo-Persian Empire (331 BC), including the great city of Babylon. This marked the end of the Persian Empire, and the Grecian Empire greatly expanded its territories during the following years. After numerous campaigns, Alexander the Great died in 323 BC.

> In 331 BC Alexander and his army attacked the "island fortress" of the Phoenician city of Tyre. His army built a rubble walkway to the island which eventually allowed Alexander to conquer the city and the Phoenician Empire.[7]

After the death of Alexander the Great, the Grecian Empire divided into several **Hellenistic Kingdoms** (323 BC - 146 BC): southwest Asia (Seleucid Empire, Kingdom of Pergamon), northeast Africa (Ptolemaic Kingdom), and South Asia (Greco-Bactrian Kingdom, Indo-Greek Kingdom). The **Seleucid Empire** (c. 312 BC to 63 BC) was a Hellenistic state that ruled the eastern region of the Greek Empire.

Antiochus Epiphanes was a Greek king of the Seleucid Empire (Syrian-Greeks). He reigned over Judah (c. 175 BC to 164 BC) and tried to eradicate Judaism (the religion, culture, and way of life of the Jewish people) by destroying all copies of the Torah, the first five books of the Bible, and by defiling the Temple in Jerusalem. Today, he is often referred to as the antichrist of the Old Testament.

The **Maccabean Revolt** was a conflict lasting from 167 to 160 BC between a Jewish rebel militia (known as the Maccabees) and the Seleucids—an effort by the Jewish people that gained them some independence and autonomy. **Hanukkah** is an eight-day Jewish holiday commemorating the rededication of the Holy Temple (the Second Temple, consecrated in 516 BC) and the Maccabean uprising against the Seleucid Empire (c. 164 BC)—a time when good overcame evil.

> The **Hellenistic period** of history is between the death of Alexander the Great in 323 BC and the fall of the Grecian Empire c. 146 BC. It is often considered a period of transition—a period of **moral decline and self-indulgence** when compared to the great artistic talent of the Greek classical era (c. 480 BC to 323 BC). The classic Greek culture was absorbed by the Romans, who imitated the Greeks culturally, artistically, religiously, and politically including the idea of democracy.

Roman Republic Conquers the Grecian Empire (c. 146 BC)
Emergence of the Roman Empire (c. 27 BC)

The **Roman Republic** is traditionally dated from c. 509 BC to 27 BC with the creation of the **Roman Empire**. Rome did not expand beyond Italy until the 3rd century (c. 300 BC - 201 BC) when the Hellenistic Kingdoms were eventually absorbed within the Roman Republic during the period c. 323 BC - 146 BC.

In 146 BC the Romans destroyed Corinth (a Greek city known from the two books of the Bible: First Corinthians and Second Corinthians of the New Testament) and then made Greece into a province (see map). Macedonia and the league of Greek cities were defeated—consequently, Greece was brought under Roman control.

In Judea (c. 63 BC) a civil war had broken out between the Pharisees and Sadducees. A Roman general named Pompey arrived and helped the Pharisees (middle-class businessmen and the general population) defeat the Sadducees (aristocrats who held important and powerful positions) in Jerusalem.

> **Sadducees** were primarily aristocrats holding important and powerful positions such as chiefs or high priests.
>
> **They** were self-sufficient, secular, prideful and arrogant, and denied God's involvement in everyday life. Although they believed in the written Law of Moses (primarily the Torah or first five books of the Hebrew Bible), they denied the resurrection of the dead, the afterlife, and the existence of a spiritual world.
>
> **Pharisees** were primarily teachers of the law, elders, and middle-class businessmen. These Jewish sects flourished from 1st century BC to 1st century AD.
>
> **They** believed that God controlled all things, although individuals had freedom of choice. They believed in the resurrection of the dead, in an afterlife (with appropriate reward and punishment on an individual basis), and in a spiritual world.

The Roman Empire (27 BC - AD 476) began to disintegrate when it was no longer able to assimilate the migration of Germanic peoples of "dubious loyalty." The Empire came to an end with the abdication of the last Emperor in AD 476 (Romulus Augustus).[8] For more information see History of the Roman Empire, end note 8.

Roman Empire

The Life and Ministry of Jesus Christ
c. 1 BC - AD 32

Jesus the Messiah (Christ) was born in the town of Bethlehem about 1 BC (the range varies between 5 BC and AD 1 in literature). The Gospel of Matthew (Matthew 2:4-6) explains that the birth of Jesus in Bethlehem was the fulfillment of a prophecy delivered by the prophet Micah (c. 750 to 686 BC) about 700 years earlier (Micah 5:2).

> *"But you, Bethlehem Ephrathah, though you are small among the clans of Judah, out of you will come for me one who will be ruler over Israel, **whose origins are from of old, from ancient times**"* (Micah 5:2, NIV). [Bold added]

Ultimately, Jesus Christ will rule the world and this universe for God the Father—as part of the Trinity, the Father, Son, and Holy Spirit, or "one God in three persons." The beginning of our Lord Jesus Christ was much earlier than His human birth—His beginning was from ancient times beyond eternity.

The Holy Trinity diagram: The Father — Is Not — The Son; Is / Is; God; Is Not / Is Not; Is — The Holy Spirit.

In John 8:58, *"I am"* expresses the eternity of His being and oneness with the Father and Holy Spirit. The three persons are distinct, yet are one "substance, essence or nature." (For more information, see chapter 9, The Big Bang and Its Problems, in the book, *evolution - The Greatest Deception in Modern History*.)

The prophet Zechariah (c. 520 to 480 BC) "foretold Christ's coming in lowliness (6:12), His humanity (6:12, 13:7), His rejection and betrayal for 30 pieces of silver (11:12-13), His crucifixion (struck by the 'sword' [wrath] of the Lord; 13:7), His priesthood (6:13), His kingship (6:13, 9:9, 14:9, 16), His coming in glory (14:4), His building of the Lord's temple (6:12-13), His reign (9:10-14), and His establishment of enduring peace and prosperity (3:10, 9:9-10)."[9]

The Gospel of Matthew (2:1) and Luke (1:5) tells us that Jesus was born during the reign of Herod the Great. Although the "traditional date" for Herod's death is 4 BC (reign c. 37 BC to 1 BC), calculations presented in chapter 11, Daniel's 70th Week, indicate that Jesus was born in 1 BC. So which date is correct—4 BC or 1 BC?

Titus Flavius Josephus, a first-century Roman-Jewish scholar and historian, relates Herod's death to a lunar eclipse (*Jewish Antiquities* 17.6.4). This is traditionally attributed to an eclipse of March 13, 4 BC, but in recent decades the date of 4 BC has been challenged by theology scholars with articles presented in BAR and NCR.

In a letter to *Biblical Archaeology Review* (BAR), physics professor John A. Cramer pointed out that the eclipse of 4 BC was a rather minor, partial eclipse and only visible late that night in Judea and likely not seen by many. There were no other lunar eclipses until 1 BC when there were two—one total lunar eclipse on December 29. "Of the two, the one on December 29, just two days before the change of eras, gets my vote since it was the most likely to be seen and remembered."[10]

The National Catholic Register (NCR) also seems to support the 1 BC date for a number of reasons related to the amount of time Herod served after being appointed king by the Romans, the amount of time he served after conquering Jerusalem, and the full lunar eclipse that occurred in 1 BC before Passover.[11]

Ironically, the tyrant Herod the Great (c. 37 BC to 1 BC), who plotted to kill the baby Jesus, had begun an ambitious rebuilding program which included palaces, citadels, a theatre and an amphitheatre, bridges and public monuments, all done in order to promote his importance in the eyes of Rome.

> How long did Jesus Christ live on earth? Jesus was born in 1 BC (see previous text box). Luke 3:23 tells us that Jesus was about **30 years old** at the start of His ministry and the Gospel tells us that the length of His ministry was about 3 years—so the Lord Jesus Christ would have been about **33 years old at the time of His crucifixion.**
>
> In AD 32 (see time chart and chapter 11, Daniel's 70th Week for a timeline), Jesus was falsely accused of being a heretic and rebel by the Pharisees and was sent to Pontius Pilate, the Roman ruler of Judah. Jesus was placed on trial, beaten, then crucified, and buried in a tomb. On the third day, He was resurrected from the dead—that is, He was restored to life from death.

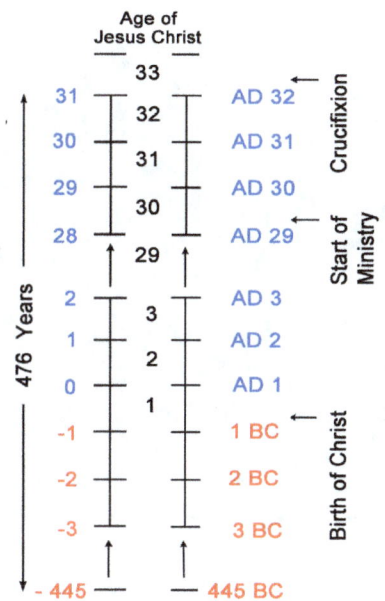

In **AD 29** Jesus began His public ministry when He was about **30 years old** (Luke 3:23). His teachings were recorded by His disciples and apostles who wrote the 27 books of the New Testament, which explain that Jesus is the Savior who was promised by the prophets of the Old Testament. See chapt. 11, Daniel's 70th Week.

Jesus Christ, the promised Messiah, stepped out of Eternity, *"His goings forth are from long ago, From the days of eternity"* (Micah 5:2, NAS), and became a guilt offering for humanity. He offered His life on the Cross as a sacrificial 'Lamb of God' (the ultimate and final sin offering for Israel and the entire world... EXACTLY as the prophets said), and He accepted our iniquities so we can be cleansed of our sins. **The suffering Jesus endured was immeasurable and beyond human understanding—the Creator of the heavens and earth carried the sins of the world.**

> *"He grew up before him like a tender shoot, and like a root out of dry ground.* **He had no beauty or majesty to attract us to him, nothing in his appearance that we should desire him. He was despised and rejected by mankind, a man of suffering, and familiar with pain. Like one from whom people hide their faces he was despised, and we held him in low esteem.** *Surely he took up our pain and bore our suffering, yet we considered him punished by God, stricken by him, and afflicted. But he was pierced for our transgressions, he was crushed for our iniquities; the punishment that brought us peace was on him, and by his wounds we are healed.* **We all, like sheep, have gone astray, each of us has turned to our own way;** *and the LORD has laid on him the iniquity of us all"* (Isaiah 53:2-7, NIV). [Bold added]

> *"...because he poured out his life unto death, and was numbered with the transgressors. For he bore the sin of many, and made intercession for the transgressors"* (Isaiah 53:12, NIV).

> *"Just as there were many who were appalled at him—***his appearance was so disfigured beyond that of any human being and his form marred beyond human likeness***—so he will sprinkle many nations* [sprinkling or cleansing], *and kings will shut their mouths because of him..."* [in astonishment at the suffering and exaltation of the servant] (Isaiah 52:14-15, NIV).

> The apostle Paul "exalts Christ as the very image of God (Colossians 1:15), the Creator (Col. 1:16), the preexistent sustainer of all things (Col. 1:17), the head of the church (Col. 1:18), the first to be resurrected (Col. 1:18), the fullness of deity in bodily form (Col. 1:19; 2:9), and the reconciler (Col. 1:20-22)."[12]

Church of the Holy Sepulchre in 1898
Traditional site of Calvary and the empty tomb

Main denominations sharing church property are Greek Orthodox, Armenian Orthodox, and Roman Catholic.

Inside the Church of the Holy Sepulchre. *Photo by Roger Gallop, March 14, 2016*

Gordon's Calvary, Golgatha, "place of the skull" near the Garden Tomb. *Photo by Roger Gallop, March 15, 2016*

The Garden Tomb near Gordon's Calvary
Photos by Roger Gallop, March 15, 2016

Scripture does not reveal the precise location of Golgatha (Calvary) and the empty tomb of Jesus, although it was outside the City wall (at that time; 32 AD) and on a public road (John 19:20; Hebrews 13:12). There are two possible locations: the Church of the Holy Sepulchre (traditional location) on a hill called Latin Calvary (near the main gate of the 1st century BC walls) and Gordon's Calvary, 100 meters from the Garden Tomb.

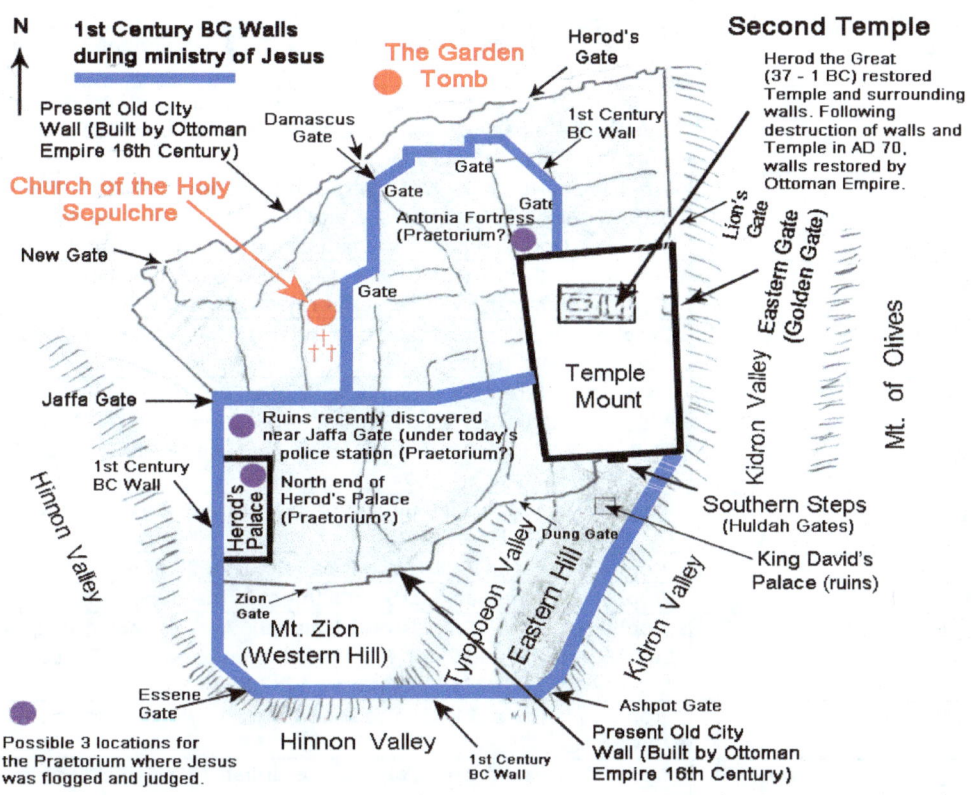

Thick dark blue lines - 1st century BC walls (time of Jesus)
Light blue lines (labeled on map) - Present Day Old City Walls

Sketch by Roger Gallop

Temple Mount is trapezoidal in shape, about 976 ft x 1571 ft, or about 35.2 acres.

Fulfillment of 61 prophecies (New and Old Testament) pertaining to the life of Jesus Christ (e.g., time and manner of birth, betrayal, manner of death, burial, etc.) were beyond anyone's control. These prophecies are presented in the following tables.[13]

If you are interested in a detailed review of these prophecies pertaining to Jesus Christ, please refer to the book by Josh McDowell, *Evidence That Demands a Verdict*. Additionally, McDowell documents 12 specific prophecies regarding cities such as Tyre, Sidon, Samaria, Nineveh, Babylon, Jerusalem, and others not described in this book.[14] Also see the book by Hal Lindsey, *A Prophetical Walk Through the Holy Land,* and many others.

61 Prophecies Fulfilled
Pertaining to Jesus Christ
c. 1 BC - AD 32 [1]

Born of the seed of a woman	Prophecy in Genesis 3:15. Fulfillment in Galatians 4:4 (Also see Matthew 1:20.) This also indicates a struggle between the Messiah of Israel, the Savior of the world, and satan, the adversary of the human soul, and foretells complete victory by the Messiah.
Born of a virgin	Prophecy in Isaiah 7:14. Fulfillment in Mathew 1:18, 24, 25; also see Luke 1:26-35.
Son of God	Prophecy in Psalm 2:7 (Also see 1 Chronicles 17:11-14; 2 Samuel 7:12-16.) Fulfillment in Matthew 3:17; also see Matthew 16:16; Mark 9:7; Luke 9:35, 22:70; Acts 13:30-33; John 1:34, 49.
Seed of Abraham	Prophecy in Genesis 22:18; also see 12:2, 3. Fulfillment in Matthew 1:1 and Galatians 3:16.
Son of Isaac	Prophecy in Genesis 21:12. Fulfillment in Luke 3:23, 34; also see Matthew 1:2. Abraham had two sons, Isaac and Ishmael. Now God eliminates one half of the linage of Abraham.
Son of Jacob	Prophecy in Numbers 24:17; also see Genesis 35:10-12. Fulfillment in Luke 3:23, 33; also see Matthew 1:2 and Luke 1:33. Isaac had two sons, Jacob and Esau. God eliminates one half of the lineage of Isaac.
Tribe of Judah	Prophecy in Genesis 49:10; also see Micah 5:2. Fulfillment in Luke 3:23, 33; also see Matthew 1:2 and Hebrews 7:14.
Family line of Jesse (father of David)	Prophecy in Isaiah 11:1; also see Isaiah 11:10. Fulfillment in Luke 3:23, 32; also see Matthew 1:6.
House of David	Prophecy in Jeremiah 23:5; also see 2 Samuel 7:12-16; Psalm 132:11. Fulfillment in Luke 3:23, 31; also see Matthew 1:1, 9:27, 15:22, 20:30, 31, 21:9, 15; 22:41-46; Mark 9:10, 10:47-48; Luke 18:38-39; Acts 13:22-23; Revelation 22:16.
Born in Bethlehem	Prophecy in Micah 5:2. Fulfillment in Matthew2:1; also see John 7:42; Matthew 2:4-8; Luke 2:4-7.
Presented with gifts	Prophecy in Psalm 72:10; also Isaiah 60:6. Fulfillment in Matthew 2:1, 11.
Herod kills children	Prophecy in Jeremiah 31:15. Fulfillment in Matthew 2:16.
His pre-existence	Prophecy in Micah 5:2; also see Isaiah 9:67, 41:4, 44:6, 48:12; Psalm 102:25; Proverbs 8:22, 23. Fulfillment in Colossians 1:17; also see John 1:1, 2, 8:58, 17:5, 24; Revelation 1:17, 2:8, 22:13.
He shall be called Lord	Prophecy in Psalm 110:1; also see Jeremiah 23:6. Fulfillment in Luke 2:11, 20:41-44.
Shall be Immanuel (God With Us)	Prophecy in Psalm 110:1; also see Jeremiah 23:6. Fulfillment in Luke 2:11, 20:41-44.
Shall be a prophet	Prophecy in Deuteronomy 18:18. Fulfillment in Matthew 21:11; also see Luke 7:16; John 4:19, 6:14, 7:40.
Priest	Prophecy in Psalm 110:4. Fulfillment in Hebrews 3:1 and Hebrews 5:5-6.
Judge	Prophecy in Isaiah 33:22. Fulfillment in John 5:30; also see 2 Timothy 4:1.
King	Prophecy in Psalm 2:6. Fulfillment in Matthew 27:37; also see Matthew 21:5; John 18:33-38.
Special anointment by the Holy Spirit	Prophecy in Isaiah 11:2; also see Psalm 45:7; Isaiah 42:1, 61:1-2. Fulfillment in Mathew 3:16-17; also see Matthew 12:17-21; Mark 1:10-11; Luke 4:15-21, 43; John 1:32.
His zeal for God	Prophecy in Psalm 69:9. Fulfillment in John 2:15-17.
Preceded by messenger	Prophecy in Isaiah 40:3; also see Malachi 3:1. Fulfillment in Matthew 3:1-2; also see Matthew 3:3, 11:10; John 1:23; Luke 1:17.
Ministry to begin in Galilee	Prophecy in Isaiah 9:1. Fulfillment in Matthew 4:12-13, 17.
Ministry of miracles[15]	Prophecy in Isaiah 32:3-4. Fulfillment in Matthew 9:35; also see Matthew 9:32-33, 11:4-6; Mark 7:33-35; John 5:5-9; 9:6-11; 11:43-44, 47.
Teacher of parables	Prophecy in Psalm 78:2. Fulfillment in Matthew 13:34.
He was to enter the Temple	Prophecy in Malachi 3:1. Fulfillment in Matthew 21:12.

(continued)
61 Prophecies Fulfilled
Pertaining to Jesus Christ [1]

He was to enter Jerusalem on a donkey	Prophecy in Zechariah 9:9. Fulfillment in Luke 19:35-37; also see Matthew 21:6-11.
"Stone of Stumbling' to the Jews	Prophecy in Psalm 118:22. Fulfillment in 1 Peter 2:7; also see Romans 9:32-33.
"Light" to the Gentiles	Prophecy in Isaiah 60:3; also see Isaiah 49:6. Fulfillment in Acts 13:47-48; also see Acts 26:23, 28:28.
Resurrection	Prophecy in Psalm 16:10; also see Psalm 30:3, 41:10, 118:17; Hosea 6:2. Fulfillment in Acts 2:31; also see Acts 13:33; Luke 24:46; Mark 16:6; Matthew 28:6.
Ascension	Prophecy in Psalm 68:18. Fulfillment in Acts 1:9.
Seated at the Right Hand of God	Prophecy in Psalm 110:1. Fulfillment in Hebrews 1:3; also see Mark 16:19; Acts 2:34-35.
Betrayed by a Friend	Prophecy in Psalm 41:9; also see Psalm 55:12-14. Fulfillment in Matthew 10:4; also see Matthew 26:49-50; John 13:21.
Sold for 30 Pieces of Silver	Prophecy in Zechariah 11:12. Fulfillment in Matthew 26:15; also see Matthew 27:3.
Money to be thrown In God's House	Prophecy in Zechariah 1:13. Fulfillment in Matthew 27:5.
Price given for Potter's field	Prophecy in Zechariah 1:13. Fulfillment in Matthew 27:7.
Forsaken by His disciples	Prophecy in Zechariah 13:7. Fulfillment in Mark 14:50; also see Matthew 26:31; Mark 14:27.
Accused by false witnesses	Prophecy in Psalm 35:11. Fulfillment in Matthew 29:59-61.
Silent before accusers	Prophecy in Isaiah 53:7. Fulfillment in Matthew 27:12-19.
Wounded and bruised	Prophecy in Isaiah 53:5; also see Zechariah 13:6. Fulfillment in Matthew 27:26.
Struck and spit upon	Prophecy in Isaiah 50:6; also see Micah 5:1. Fulfillment in Matthew 26:67; also see Luke 22:63.
Mocked	Prophecy in Psalm 22:7-8. Fulfillment in Matthew 27:31.
Fell under the Cross	Prophecy in Psalm 109:24-25. Fulfillment in Luke 23:26; also see Matthew 27:31-32.
Hands and feet pierced	Prophecy in Psalm 22:16. Fulfillment in Luke 23:33; also see John 20:25.
Crucified with Thieves	Prophecy in Isaiah 53:12. Fulfillment in Matthew 27:38; also see Mark 15:27-28.
Made intercession for His persecutors	Prophecy in Isaiah 53:12. Fulfillment in Luke 23:34.
Rejected by His own people	Prophecy in Isaiah 53:3; also see Psalm 69:8, 118:22. Fulfillment in John 7:5, 48-49; also see John 1:11; Matthew 21:42-43.
Hated without cause	Prophecy in Psalm 69:4; also see Isaiah 49:7. Fulfillment in John 15:25.
Friends stood far off	Prophecy in Psalm 38:11. Fulfillment in Luke 23:49; also see Mark 15:40; Matthew 27:55-56.
People shook their heads	Prophecy in Psalm 109:25; also see Psalm 22:7. Fulfillment in Mark 27:39.
Stared upon	Prophecy in Psalm 22:17. Fulfillment in Luke 23:35.
Garments parted and lots cast	Prophecy in Psalm 22:18. Fulfillment in John 19:23-24.
Suffered thirst	Prophecy in Psalm 69:21; also see Psalm 22:15. Fulfillment in John 19:28.
Gall and vinegar offered Him	Prophecy in Psalm 69:21. Fulfillment in Matthew 27:34; also see John 19:28-29.
His forsaken cry	Prophecy in Psalm 22:1. Fulfillment in Matthew 27:46.
Committed Himself to go	Prophecy in Psalm 31:5. Fulfillment in Luke 23:46.
Bones not broken	Prophecy in Psalm 34:20. Fulfillment in John 19:33.
Heart broken	Prophecy in Psalm 22:14. Fulfillment in John 19:34.
His side pierced	Prophecy in Zechariah 12:10. Fulfillment in John 19:34.
Darkness over the land	Prophecy in Amos 8:9. Fulfillment in Matthew 27:45.
Buried in rich man's tomb	Prophecy in Isaiah 53:9. Fulfillment in Matthew 27:57-60.

Objection by skeptics: Prophecies were written at the time of Jesus. **Answer:** If skeptics are not satisfied that completion of the Old Testament was 450 BC (historic date for completion of the Hebrew text), then consider that the Greek translation of the Hebrew Scripture, the Septuagint, was completed during the reign of Ptolemy Philadelphus (285 BC - 246 BC). If the Greek translation existed in 250 BC, then the Hebrew text is on or before 250 BC.[16]

Objection by skeptics: Fulfillment was deliberate. **Answer:** This might seem plausible until we realize that these prophecies were beyond human control. These prophecies (see tables, 61 Prophecies Fulfilled Pertaining to Jesus Christ) include: 1) He would be betrayed by one of His 12 disciples (Matthew 26:21), 2) Peter would deny Him three times before the cock crowed (Matthew 26:34), 3) He would go to Jerusalem, people would spit, strike, mock, and stare, and He would be killed (Mark 10:33-34), 4) His disciples would abandon Him (Mark 14:27), 5) He would rise from the dead (Luke 24:45-46), 6) His disciples would perform miracles (Mark 16:17-18), 7) the Temple in Jerusalem would be destroyed and that "...*not one stone here will be left on another, every one will be thrown down.*" (Matthew 24:2, NIV), 8) the gospel would go out to the whole world (Mark 16:15), and 9) Christians would be persecuted (John 15:20).[17]

Objection by Skeptics: Fulfillment of prophecy was coincidental (by accident). **Answer:** There could possibly be a few prophecies fulfilled in other men, but not all 61 major prophecies. The probability of 8 prophecies being fulfilled (place of birth; time of birth; manner of birth; betrayal; manner of death; peoples' reaction such as mocking, spitting, striking, and staring; piercing; and burial) in any one man is 1 in 1×10^{17} (this would be 1 in 100,000,000,000,000,000) and the chance of any 48 prophecies is 1 in 1×10^{157}—**or the chance is Zero.**[18]

> According to the laws of probability, anything smaller than 1 in 1×10^{50}, the chance of an event occurring is zero—so this is our threshold. See book, *evolution – The Greatest Deception in Modern History*, chapter 3, Evolution – A Statistical Impossibility.

Jesus Christ Teaches About Sin and Repentance

Does Christ by His death save all humanity? Sadly, the answer is no. Scripture speaks of an eternal Hell and makes clear that only believers are saved. (Personally, this is a **terrifying thought** and at the very least, it should compel everyone with any ounce of sense to take the time to pause and evaluate what's really important in this life—family, truth (science and theological), and most importantly, faith in the Creator God.)

Jesus said, *"Unless you repent, you too will all perish"* (Luke 13:3, NIV). [Bold added] Jesus tells the Parable of the Fig Tree found in Luke 13:6-9—a parable about the vineyard owner and the gardener who took care of the vineyard. **The vineyard owner represents God the Father and the gardener represents Jesus**, the Son of God, who feeds His people and gives them living water. The tree itself has two symbolic meanings: the **State of Israel** and the **individual** (both Jew and Gentile).

As the parable begins, the vineyard owner is expressing his disappointment with the **fruitless tree—that is, the lack of *repentance* by the Jewish people.** The owner (God the Father) looked for fruit for three years, but found none. **The three-year period is significant because for three years**

Ancient Olive trees from the time of Christ at the Garden of Gethsemane, Jerusalem. *Photos by Roger Gallop*

John the Baptist and Jesus preached the message of *repentance* throughout Israel but repentance was not a priority to the people. John the Baptist warned the people about the impending Messiah and told them to repent because *"...the ax is already laid at the root of the trees and every tree that does not produce fruit [show evidence of repentance] will be cut down..."* (Luke 3:8-9, NIV).

The **Jews were offended by the idea of repentance because of their reliance on Judaic laws and decrees,** and therefore rejected the Messiah because He demanded repentance. **(Most unfortunately, this is true of many people today and throughout all of history—*that repentance is not considered necessary*.)** The Jews had it all—the law, the prophets, the Scriptures, the covenants, and the adoption as God's chosen people (Romans 9:4-5; Deuteronomy 7:6)—after all, they were the descendants of Abraham, Isaac, and Jacob. The Jews had departed from the true faith and created a 'system of works and earthly position' (i.e., *social status* that they equated or compared to righteousness as many do today.)

The apostle Paul states, *"For it is by grace you have been saved, through faith—and this not from yourselves, it is the gift of God—not by works, so that no one can boast"* (Ephesians 2:8-9, NIV). The vineyard owner was justified in tearing down the tree that had **no fruit—that showed no repentance.** The Lord's ax was already laid at the root of the tree—the State of Israel (worldwide exile in AD 70) and the individual (Jew and Gentile).

However, the gardener (Jesus, the Son) asked the owner (God the Father) for more time. It was still several months before the crucifixion and more miracles yet to come for many to witness first hand (with their own eyes). Especially the miracle of the raising of Lazarus from the dead astonished many and word of mouth caused many to repent. As it turned out, Israel as a nation (as a whole) still did not believe (John 12:37-40), but many individuals who witnessed the miracles repented and believed in the Deity of Jesus.

Just like in the days of Noah, and in the days of the Canaanites (see chapter 2, The Ethical Question of War, and chapter 3, Israel's Triumph in the Land of Canaan), and in the last days (see chapters 8 – 12), there will be a time when the **"measure of sin is full" and there will be no time left. The lesson to be learned for the individual is that time is short, and God's patience has a limit.**

In the parable, the vineyard owner grants another year of life for the tree. **In the same way, God in His mercy grants us another day, another hour, and even another minute. Christ stands at the door of each man's heart knocking and seeking to gain entrance and *requiring repentance from sin*.** Jesus said, *"Here I am! I stand at the door and knock. If anyone hears my voice and opens the door, I will come in and eat with him, and he with me"* (Revelation 3:20, NIV). But **if there is no repentance, the unrepentant individual will be cut down. We all live on borrowed time, and judgment is much closer than we think.**

That is why the defiant prophet Isaiah wrote, *"Seek the LORD while he may be found; call on him while he is near. Let the wicked forsake his way and the evil man his thoughts. Let him turn to the LORD, and **he will have mercy on him, and to our God, for he will freely pardon**"* (Isaiah 55:6-7, NIV). [Bold added]

Rejection of Jesus Christ by the Jewish People
c. AD 30 - AD 70

In AD 29 Jesus explains to Nicodemus what a person must do to be saved and have eternal life. Jesus says: *"For God so loved the world that he gave his one and only Son, that whoever believes in him shall not perish but have eternal life. For God did not send his Son into the world to condemn the world, but to save the world through him. Whoever believes in him is not condemned, but whoever does not believe stands condemned already because he has not believed in the name of God's one and only Son"* (John 3:16-18, NIV).

When the Lord Jesus Christ came to earth 2,000 years ago, the religious leaders (Pharisees) were looking for a 'warrior king' who would deliver them from Rome's oppression. Although the message of a suffering Messiah and crucifixion (see Isaiah 53) was predicted in the Old Testament (see section/table, 61 Prophecies Pertaining to Jesus Christ), **the Pharisees did not know Him and would not accept Him as the Messiah.**

> In Colossians, the apostle Paul exalts Christ as the very image of God (1:15), the Creator (1:16), the preexistent sustainer of all things (1:17), the head of the church (1:18), the first to be resurrected (1:18), the fullness of deity in bodily form (1:19; 2:9), and the reconciler (1:20-22).[19]

As explained in the previous section, the religious leaders believed that **approval by God was based on observance of Judaic laws and decrees—*and so they believed there was no need for repentance.*** When Jesus began preaching about sin and repentance (see previous section, Jesus Teaches About Sin and Repentance), they rejected the message (as Isaiah had predicted) and ultimately forced His crucifixion.[20]

Also the Jewish people (as a whole) did not want to hear the message of repentance. They too were very familiar with Old Testament Scripture and the prophecies of a coming Messiah, but they continued in their unbelief that Jesus Christ was the prophesied Messiah because of His message of sin and repentance (John 10:25-39, 12:37-50) and His claim as the Messiah. Although many Jews chose to believe, many more rejected Jesus (the man who was the incarnation of God the Father, the Creator of all that exists). **They hated Jesus *without cause,*** all foretold throughout the Old Testament and fulfilled in the New Testament.

> The result is expressed in some of the saddest verses in Scripture. **"He came to that which was his own, but his own did not receive him"** (John 1:11, NIV). [Bold Added]

> The Pharisees did not distinguish between the two returns of the Messiah (first and second coming) as described in Isaiah 7:14, 9:6-7, and Zechariah 14:4, but rather they were looking for a conquering Messiah. They did not understand the need for a suffering Messiah as described in Isaiah 53—the need for repentance. Ultimately, Jesus fulfilled the role of the suffering servant in His First Coming and will fullfill the role of Israel's deliverer and conquering King in His Second Coming.
>
> Zechariah 12:10 and Revelation 1:7, in describing the second coming, explain that Israel and much of the world will grieve bitterly for not having accepted the Messiah the first time He came and for turning their backs on the Lord (although, unbelievably, many will continue to wage war against Christ Jesus and His angelic army). See chapter 12, The Second Coming of Jesus Christ.

In Luke 8:10-12 (NIV), Jesus described it as *"though seeing, they may not see; though hearing, they may not understand."* And in Matthew 13:14 (NIV), *"You will be ever hearing but never understanding; you will be ever seeing but never perceiving."* They did not accept Jesus Christ as the Messiah—*just like many in the world today* **who will be unable to discern between the false Messiah (the antichrist; chapter 11) and the true Messiah (chapter 12).** Even after Jesus raised Lazarus from the dead and performed miracles for all to see, many of the **chief priests and Pharisees plotted to kill Jesus and Lazarus.** (See John 5:18, 11: 53, 12:10.)

> **Prophecy of Rejection** in Isaiah 53:3; also see Psalm 69:8, 118:22, and its **fulfillment** in John 7:5, 48-49; also see John 1:11; Matthew 21:42-43. **Prophecy of Hatred of Jesus** in Psalm 69:4; also see Isaiah 49:7 and its **fulfillment** in John 15:25.

And when He [Jesus] drew near and saw the city [Jerusalem], He wept over it and explained why Jerusalem would be destroyed (in AD 70).

> *"As he approached Jerusalem and saw the city, he wept over it and said, 'If you, even you, had only known on this day what would bring you peace—**but now it is hidden from your eyes** [the people did **not recognize the time of God's return].** The days will come upon you when your enemies will build an embankment against you and encircle you and hem you in on every side. They will dash you to the ground, you and the children within your walls. They will not leave one stone on another, because you did not recognize the time of God's coming to you'"* (Luke 19:41-44, NIV). [Bold added]

> Peter speaks in Solomon's Colonnade by stating that the **Jews killed the Author of Life**—*"...You handed him [Jesus] over to be killed, and you disowned him before Pilate, though he had decided to let him go. You disowned the Holy and Righteous One and asked that a murderer be released to you. You killed the **author of life**, but God raised him from the dead. We are witnesses of this"* (Acts 3:13-15, NIV). [Bold added]

Thus, **Israel's rejection of Jesus of Nazareth as the coming Messiah** foretold in Isaiah 53:2-7 (fulfilled in John 7:5, 48-49; also see John 1:11; Matthew 21:42-43) **was the cause of the Jewish worldwide Diaspora.** As a result, the Jews lost their "Promised Land" for nearly two thousand years, and they lost their status as *"a people holy to the LORD."*

> The word **"Diaspora"** means scattering of a people away from an established or ancestral homeland. The word is most often used in reference to the Jewish dispersion or exile. The Jewish exile worldwide occurred in AD 70 when the Second Jewish Temple was destroyed.

notes: **Chapter 4**

1. Konig, G. and Konig, R. (1984; 3rd Revised Edition). *100 prophecies.* George and Ray Konig, 26. See www.100prophecies.org.

2. Konig, op. cit, 107-112.

3. Ibid., 27.

4. Personal notes, p. 21.

5. Konig, op. cit., 28.

6. Personal notes; Second Temple, Wikipedia. Retrieved from https://en.wikipedia.org/wiki/Second_Temple.

7. About Bible Prophecy, Timeline, 331 BC: Alexander conquers Tyre (Phoenician Empire). Retrieved from http://www.aboutbibleprophecy.com/timeline.htm#top.

8. History of the Roman Empire, Wikipedia, The Free Encyclopedia. Retrieved from http://en.wikipedia.org/wiki/History_of_the_Roman_Empire and http://en.wikipedia.org/wiki/Roman_Republic.

9. NIV Study Bible, New International Version, Introduction to the Book of Zechariah, Theological Teaching, Grand Rapids, MI: Zondervan Publishing House.

10. Biblical Archaeology Society Staff (November 29, 2015). Herod's Death, Jesus Birth and a Lunar Eclipse. *Biblical Archaeological Society*; as cited in http://www.biblicalarchaeology.org/daily/people-cultures-in-the-bible/jesus-historical-jesus/herods-death-jesus-birth-and-a-lunar-eclipse/.

11. Adkin, J. (April 2013). Jesus' birth and when Herod the Great really died. *National Catholic Register*; as cited in http://www.ncregister.com/blog/jimmy-akin/jesus-birth-and-when-herod-the-great-really-died.

12. NIV Study Bible, New International Version, Introduction to the Book of Colossians, Purpose and Theme, op. cit.

13. McDowell, J. (1972). *Evidence that Demands a Verdict.* San Bernardino, CA: Campus Crusade for Christ, 147-183.

14. Ibid., 277-336.

15. The disciples and apostles of Jesus record more than 30 miracles in the New Testament—miracles that Jesus performed during his public ministry. The miracles include healing people of blindness (Matthew 9:27-31), deafness (Mark 7:31-37), muteness (Luke 11:14), and lameness (John 5:5-17), as well as calming a storm (Luke 8:22-25), walking on water (Matthew 14:22-33), miraculously feeding thousands of people (John 6:5-14), and bringing Lazarus back to life (John 11:1-44).

16. McDowell, J., op. cit., 61, 150.

17. Ibid., 174.

18. Stoner, Peter W. (1963). *Science Speaks.* Chicago: Moody Press; as cited in McDowell, 175.

19. NIV Study Bible, New International Version, Introduction to the Book of Colossians, Purpose and Theme, op. cit.

20. Morrisson, J.L. (2002). "A Perspective About the End Times." Retrieved from http://www.scriptureinsights.com/EndTimes.html.

Chapter 5

Worldwide Dispersion of the Jewish People

> *"Then the Lord will scatter you among all nations, from one end of the earth to the other."* —Deuteronomy 28:64, NIV

In a quest for an independent state, the Jewish people attempted to overthrow the Roman occupation of Judah and Israel. This rebellion, called the Jewish-Roman War, began in AD 66 and ended in AD 70 with the total destruction of the City of Jerusalem and the Jewish Temple. The Roman army, under the command of Titus (Titus Flavius Vespasianus who later became the Emperor of Rome from AD 79 to AD 81), began a siege of the City in AD 68, and the walls of the City were breached in AD 70. The Romans plundered, pillaged, and burned nearly the entire City including the Temple—and as prophesied by Jesus, *"...not one stone here will be left on another; every one will be thrown down"* (Matthew 24:2, NIV).

According to the historian Titus Flavius Josephus (see chapter 4, The Life and Ministry of Jesus Christ), about 1.1 million Jews were killed, and about 97,000 were captured and enslaved, and many more fled into surrounding Arab countries and North Africa. They eventually dispersed throughout Europe, Eastern European countries, and Russia over a period of many centuries.[1] The Romans crushed a second Jewish rebellion

> "After the Jewish revolt of AD 135, the Romans replaced the Latin name *Judea* with the Latin *Palaestina* as their name for this province." Following the revolt the name **Palestine** was used instead of the "land of Israel" as a slur or insult to the Jewish people. "Those living there became known as Palestinians."[2]

> In Luke 21:20-24, Jesus foretold the fall of Jerusalem with the destruction of the Temple, the scattering of the Jews into all nations, and their remarkable growth and survival.
>
> Unlike the Babylonian captivity in 586 BC which lasted 70 years (see chapter 4, Prophets Who Foresaw These Events), this worldwide dispersion was to continue for a long length of time. (Lev. 26:31-33; Deut. 28:64-68, 30:1-5)

> **Palestine** is identified today as a geographic region between the Mediterranean Sea and the Jordan River. But interestingly, the name "Palestine" is not found in the Bible. The name was identified with the "Philistines," a war-like tribe to the SW along the coast but an older name is synonymous with "Canaan," a name most frequently used in the Old Testament. See glossary for definitions.

for independence (AD 132 - AD 135). See chapter 4, Rejection of Jesus Christ by the Jewish People.

The Jewish people were forewarned of **an exile in which they would be scattered from one end of the earth to another. Moses first prophesied this great dispersion** in Leviticus 26:31-33 and then in Deuteronomy 28:64-68, 30:15. (See chapter 3, Punishment for Disobedience and Moses Predicts the Future.) The contents of Leviticus and Deuteronomy were given to Moses by God at Mount Sinai.[3]

Beginning AD 70, Gentiles (non-Jews) have been in control of Palestine until the State of Israel was miraculously restored on May 14, 1948, in direct fulfillment of end time prophecy (see chapter 6, Miraculous Rebirth of the State of Israel)—also Gentiles were in complete control of Jerusalem until this ancient City fell into the hands of Israel during the 1967 Six Day War. (See chapter 7, The Six Day War.) Although the land has often changed hands (as described in this chapter), the occupiers had two primary characteristics: they were Gentiles, and they had an enmity of the Jews.

Why This Fierce Punishment for Disobedience?

In Deuteronomy 29:24-29 (NIV), *"All the nations will ask: 'Why has the LORD done this to this land? Why this fierce, burning anger?' And the answer will be:*

"It is because this people abandoned the covenant of the LORD, the God of their ancestors, the covenant he made with them when he brought them out of Egypt. They went off and worshiped other gods and bowed down to them, gods they did not know, gods he had not given them. **Therefore the LORD's anger burned against this land, so that he brought on it all the curses written in this book.** *In furious anger and in great wrath the LORD uprooted them from their land and thrust them into another land, as it is now"* (Deuteronomy 29:24-28, NIV).

It is not just the disobedience, but it is the continuous, willful disobedience over many centuries since the time of Moses (1526 – 1406 BC). **Despite witnessing first-hand the reality of God and the many miracles for all to see** (e.g., their release from Egyptian bondage, the miraculous crossing of the Red Sea, being told that they [the Jewish people] will be *'a kingdom of priests and a holy nation'* (Exodus 19:5-6, NIV), God leading them in a cloud by day and fire by night, and then allowing them to see God in a dense

> The reason for worldwide exile of the Jews and their condition of humiliation while in exile was
> 1) their rejection of the 'author of life'—the Messiah Jesus Christ,
> 2) their persistence in breaking the Mosaic covenant (decrees and commandments), and
> 3) their adoption of pagan religious practices including idolatry. After much patience, God imposed the curses of the covenant (a long exile and humiliation), which stood as a warning to them from the beginning. (See chapter 3, and Leviticus 26:27-45; Deuteronomy 28:15-68.)

cloud and to hear God speaking with Moses), **the Jewish people chose to disobey and turn their backs on the Lord.**

Over the many generations, the Jews continued to do evil in the eyes of the Lord including the **rejection of Jesus of Nazareth as the coming Messiah** (foretold in Isaiah 53:2-7; Psalm 69:8, 118:22; and fulfilled in John 1:11, 7:5, 48-49; Matthew 21:42-43) which led, ultimately, to His crucifixion. Also see Acts 3:13-15.

> **Punishment** (discipline) is the imposition of an unpleasant outcome upon an individual or group in response to behavior that an authority (in this case, the Lord God) deems unacceptable or in violation of His commandments and decrees (Mosaic covenant). Obviously, punishment means some measure of suffering. (For example, in today's judicial system, incarceration for a certain length of time for being found guilty of some felony is a form of punishment.)
>
> In the eyes of God, sin demands punishment. Sin is breaking the moral law, or any one of the Ten Commandments, or a departure from goodness. (See chapter 3, Human Nature and the Moral Law in the book, *evolution – The Greatest Deception in Modern History*.)

> **Disobedience** is the **tendency of humanity throughout history to do evil and to turn away from their Creator** (turning their backs on God, mocking, scoffing, and worshiping material things of this world)—**a downhill tendency** that began at the time of Adam and Eve, and Cain and Abel; then continually increased during the antediluvian days; during post-flood Mesopotamia (Tower of Babel); and then during the paganistic, idolatrous culture of the Canaanites and surrounding countries (the Gentiles); and finally the rebellion of the Jewish people toward their Divine King, God the Father, following their Exodus (1446 BC) from captivity in Egypt. **This defiant, rebellious nature of humanity, both Jew and Gentile, has existed throughout history and continues in today's world.**

Hebrews 12:3-11 (NIV) explains that God disciplines His children.

> *"Consider him who endured such opposition from sinners, so that you will not grow weary and lose heart.*
>
> *In your struggle against sin, you have not yet resisted to the point of shedding your blood. And have you completely forgotten this word of encouragement that addresses you as a father addresses his son?*
>
> *It says, 'My son, do not make light of the Lord's discipline, and do not lose heart when he rebukes you, because the Lord disciplines the one he loves, and he chastens everyone he accepts as his son.'*
>
> *Endure hardship as discipline; God is treating you as his children. For what children are not disciplined by their father? If you are not disciplined—and everyone undergoes discipline—then you are not legitimate, not true sons and daughters at all. Moreover, we have all had human fathers who disciplined us and we respected them for it. How much more should we submit to the Father of spirits and live! They disciplined us for a little while as they thought best; but God disciplines us for our good, in order that we may share in his holiness. No discipline seems pleasant at the time, but painful. Later on, however, it produces a harvest of righteousness and peace for those who have been trained by it"* (Hebrews 12:3-11, NIV).

Persecution is Not from God

Persecution is the systematic mistreatment (without cause) of an individual or group by another individual or group **motivated by intense hatred or hostility**. The most common forms are religious persecution, ethnic persecution, and political persecution, though there is some overlap among these terms. **Persecution comes from evil within the hearts of mankind.**

One type involves verbal attack: harassment, ridicule, belittlement, mocking, scoffing, and showing contempt for an individual or group of people. Another type involves personal physical attack: acts of violence, and in severe cases, it would include oppression (abusiveness), beating (striking), scourging, flogging, and any type of torture (including crucifixion) and death. Both types occur in the world today, especially towards Christians and Jews.

> **Sin** is breaking the moral law or any one of the Ten Commandments, or a departure from goodness. (See chapter 3, Human Nature and the Moral Law in the book, *evolution – The Greatest Deception in Modern History*.)
>
> **Evil** is sin, iniquity, wickedness, immorality, or corruption. "Evil, in its essence, refuses to accept God as God and puts someone or something else [idolatry] in His place... For this reason, the Bible treats idolatry as the ultimate sin, since it worships as God what is not God."[4]

> The apostle Paul warned that *"everyone who wants to live a godly life in Christ Jesus will be persecuted"* (2 Timothy 3:12, NIV). Jesus said, *"If they persecuted me, they will persecute you also"* (John 15:20, NIV).

As described in the previous chapter there were times during the destruction of their homeland and exile by foreign nations (721 BC, 586 BC, and AD 70) when the Jewish people found themselves the victims of persecution and anti-Semitism. The Jews in the Northern Kingdom (Israel) were killed and persecuted (most severely including torture), and enslaved by the Assyrians (721 BC); the Jews in the Southern Kingdom (Judah) were also killed and persecuted and taken captive by the Babylonians (between 605 BC – 586 BC).

> The Bible tells us that God is holy, righteous, and merciful; in Habakkuk 1:13, God is *"too pure to look on evil"*; in John 4:8 *"...God is love"*; and in John 3:16, the word "love" is agape or a self-sacrificing love. Then the question must be asked...
>
> **Why does God tolerate evil and persecution and allow evil empires such as the Assyrian, Babylonian, and Roman to execute punishment on the Jewish people?** This question is addressed in the epilogue (question 17).

The Jews in Judea were killed and persecuted by the Greek ruler Antiochus Epiphanes (c. 175 BC to 164 BC) who tried to eradicate Judaic culture and destroy all copies of the Torah. In AD 70 the Jewish people were killed, enslaved, and exiled worldwide by the Romans—and then during 1,878 years of worldwide dispersion (Diaspora), the Jews endured terrible persecution at the hands of various nations and groups until they were miraculously restored to their homeland on May 14, 1948.

In the 13th century, Jews and non-Christians were questioned and tortured by Catholics because of their unorthodox beliefs during the "Inquisition" (including those who had already converted to Christianity). And during the 14th century, Jews were blamed for the Black Death (the Bubonic plague), a bacterial epidemic that killed almost half of Europe during the years 1346-1353.

There were "Pogroms" (anti-Jewish riots and violence) in Russia, Poland, Lithuania, Romania, the Ukraine, and even Ireland. The Jews were called "Christ killers," and as we know, **they have been persecuted by Muslims throughout their history.**

> **Inquisition** was a period of intense questioning involving extreme forms of persecution and torture. It was a court established by the Roman Catholic Church (c. 1231 to early 1800s) to try cases of heresy and other offenses against the church. **Pogrom** is a Russian word meaning "to wreak havoc, to demolish violently." Historically, the term refers to violent attacks on Jews.

During World War II the Jews faced genocide at the hands of the Nazis in what has come to be called the "**Holocaust**." **The Holocaust is a term that describes the systematic extermination of 6 million European Jews (including 1.5 million children) by Nazi Germany or the Third Reich in what they called their "final solution of the Jewish question."** Jews were identified, stripped of their possessions, separated from family members, and then shipped to concentration camps where they were starved, shot, hung, buried alive, put to death in gas chambers and ovens, injected with drugs and chemicals, and subjected to horrific experiments. This is the **face of demonic evil.**

And more recently, unspeakable atrocities include beheadings (shown live on television) and massacres of children and their families in the Middle East by Islamic extremists; the massacre of 148 school children in Peshawar, Pakistan; enslavement of women; and horrifying slaughter of captives. **This is the face of evil in the world today.**

Such motivation and behavior is a supernatural evil that permeates the world—an evil that "steals, kills, and destroys" with the ultimate goal of eliminating the church and seizing control of God's authority. (See section, Nazi Germany and the Holocaust; chapter 6, Anti-Semitism and Wholesale Attempts to Eradicate the Jewish People, and Appendix C, Satan's Attempts to Seize Total Control.)

Further discussion is found in the prologue of this book and in the book by Roger Gallop, *Defeating Evil - God's Plan Before the Beginning of TIme*, specifically chapter 8 and the epilogue.

> Paul knew that false doctrine (false religion or ideology, fanaticism, and terror) ultimately leads to destroying the witness of the church and the believer. The enemy's goal is to **"steal, kill, and destroy!"** Paul instructed Timothy to "stand firm and have a wartime mentality... [and] to pray!" [5] See 1 Timothy 2:1-8.

The problem of evil and suffering has been addressed by theologians and authors throughout the centuries; more prominently by C. S. Lewis in *The Problem of Pain* (1940, restored 1996, NY: Harper Collins Publishers); by best-selling author Randy Alcorn in his book, *If God Is Good – Faith in the Midst of Suffering and Evil* (2009), Colorado Springs, CO: Multnomah Books; by Dr. Carl Wieland in his book, *Beyond the Shadows - Making Sense of Personal Tragedy* (2011, Atlanta, GA: Creation Book Publishers); and by Dr. N. L. Geisler in his book, *If God, Why Evil?* (2011, Minneapolis, MN: Bethany House Publishers).

Also see articles by Dr. T. Mitchell (December 2011). Death and Steve Jobs. *Answers Update*, 18 (12), Hebron, KY: Answers in Genesis, 1-2 (answersingenesis.org), and Dr. J. Johnson (November 2011). Human suffering: Why this isn't the "best of all possible worlds." *Acts & Facts*, 40 (11), Dallas, TX: Institute for Creation Research, 8-10 (ICR.org).

Scripture about Persecution

The following is relevant Scripture about the persecution of Christians and Jews:

Matthew 5:10-12, NIV, *"Blessed are those who are persecuted because of righteousness, for theirs is the kingdom of heaven. Blessed are you when people insult you, persecute you and falsely say all kinds of evil against you because of me. Rejoice and be glad, because great is your reward in heaven, for in the same way they persecuted the prophets who were before you."*

1 Peter 4:13-16, NIV, *"But rejoice inasmuch as you participate in the sufferings of Christ, so that you may be overjoyed when his glory is revealed. If you are insulted because of the name of Christ, you are blessed, for the Spirit of glory and of God rests on you. If you suffer, it should not be as a murderer or thief or any other kind of criminal, or even as a meddler. However, if you suffer as a Christian, do not be ashamed, but praise God that you bear that name."*

Luke 21:12, NIV, *"But before all this, they will seize you and persecute you. They will hand you over to synagogues and put you in prison, and you will be brought before kings and governors, and all on account of my name."*

Persecution of Jews and Christians throughout history and in today's world is humanity **at its very worst**. Through all the world's hate and injustice, there is a God who knows love and justice and, ultimately, He will wipe out the hate, persecution, and injustice of this world; in short, **there is a righteous and holy God who will make things right**. And that God is the God of the Holy Bible.[6]

Jesus Christ suffered persecution infinitely more than any of us are asked to suffer—a great encouragement for Christians who are weary and discouraged by the trials and tribulations of this life.

2 Timothy 3:12-13, NIV, *"In fact, everyone who wants to live a godly life in Christ Jesus will be persecuted,* **while evil men and imposters will go from bad to worse, deceiving and being deceived."** [Bold added]

This is what we are witnessing in the world today—lying, deception, corruption, and persecution are a way of life for many people.

John 15:20, NIV, *"If they persecuted me, they will persecute you also."*

For those who have accepted the Lord Jesus Christ as their Savior, Jesus has already suffered the full penalty of all our sins; hence it is written *"...the blood of Jesus Christ his Son cleanseth us from all sin"* (1 John 1:7, KJV). This does not mean the Christian will not continue to sin and suffer in this present age. **A sinful nature is found in the hearts of all God's people until the Lord returns**, and discipline (punishment from God the Father) is necessary to rebuke, subdue, and humble.

For those who have never accepted Jesus as their Lord and Savior, guilt for sins will fall directly on that person, and God will act as Judge. But punishment for sins can never fall upon the child of God in a "judicial sense because guilt was all transferred directly to Christ." Relevant Scripture: *"He himself bore our sins in his body on the tree..."* (1 Peter 2:24, NIV).[7]

What Became of the Land of Palestine?
AD 70 - 1948

In AD 70 the Romans destroyed Jerusalem and the Temple, and the Jews were scattered to the four corners of the world and persecuted for the next 1,878 years. During this time the land of Judea (Palestine) and surrounding lands were occupied by various countries. Interestingly, the name "Palestine" is not found in the Bible. How did Palestine get its Name? See text boxes at start of chapter.

> **Judea** is the biblical, Roman, and modern name of the mountainous southern part of the historic Land of Israel. **Palestine** is a geographic region between the Mediterranean Sea and the Jordan River. This region is also known as the Land of Israel, the Holy Land, or Promised Land.

Roman Occupation and Parthians in the East
27 BC - AD 500

During the period 27 BC – AD 476, the Middle East was controlled by the **Western Roman Empire.** Rome controlled much of southern Europe including modern day France, Spain, Portugal, Italy, and North Africa along the Mediterranenan Coast. See map, The Roman Empire, in chapter 4.

From AD 200 the **Eastern Roman Empire** (or Byzantine Empire) was the continuation of the Roman Empire with its capital in Constantinople (modern day Istanbul). The Eastern empire controlled modern day Egypt, Libya, the Levant (eastern Mediterranean including Palesine), Turkey, Greece, and parts of eastern Europe. The Eastern empire survived the breakup and fall of the Western empire and continued to exist for an additional thousand years until it fell to the Ottoman Turks in 1453.

Between 247 BC – AD 224, the **Parthians** (closely related to the Persians) controlled the area of Mesopotamia, the region of today's modern day Iran and Iraq and eastern Turkey. A new Persian empire replaced the Parthians.

> The **Byzantine Empire,** sometimes known as the **Eastern Roman Empire**, was a predominantly Greek-speaking eastern extension of the Roman Empire during the Middle Ages. Its capital city was Constantinople (modern-day Istanbul), originally founded as Byzantium.
>
> **Constantinople** was located on the Bosporus Strait, the waterway that connects the Black Sea to the Sea of Mamara, then to the Aegean Sea, an embayment of the Mediterranean. This city was strategically placed, being both defended by water on three sides and well positioned to demand taxes from ships traveling through this waterway.

Arab Occupation
AD 500 - AD 979

Between AD 500 and AD 750, Arab tribes united under "Islam" (a vast empire called the Caliphate that moved into Iraq and Iran, Syria and Palestine, Egypt and North Africa, Spain, France, central Asia and western India). The Caliphate initially ruled from Damascus but Baghdad eventually replaced Damascus as its capital (AD 750 – AD 979). In a short while, the empire began to disintegrate.

A **caliphate** is a form of Islamic government led by a **caliph**—a political and religious successor to the Islamic prophet, Muhammad, the original leader of the Muslim community.

Umayyad Caliphate was the second of the four major Islamic caliphates established after the death of Muhammad (AD 570 - AD 632).

Dome of the Rock. See chapter 10, Rebuilding the Third Temple, for location map of these existing structures and the possible site of the Third Temple.
Photo by Roger Gallop, March 14, 2016

The Temple Mount is one of the most important religious sites in the City of Jerusalem. This site has been used for thousands of years by the three primary religions: Judaism, Christianity, and Islam. The present site is dominated by three structures from the early Umayyad period (AD 661 – 750): Dome of the Rock (AD 685 – 691), Dome of the Chain (AD 691), and al-Aqsa Mosque (AD 705; rebuilt AD 754, 780). The Dome of the Rock and Dome of the Chain were built on or near the site of the Second Jewish Temple.

Turko-Persian Empire
(aka Seljuk Empire)
AD 979 - AD 1215

During the period AD 979 – AD 1215, Turko-Persians (a group of Muslim Turks from central Asia) overran Iran, Iraq, Syria, Palestine, and much of Asia Minor, but this empire soon became "regional states" ruled by Turkish sultans. This occupation led to a series of "crusades" from Europe which attempted to establish Christian states in Syria—but this was met with very strong resistance from the Arabs and eventually failed.

The **Seljuk Empire**, a medieval Turko-Persian empire, controlled a vast area stretching from the Hindu Kush (mountain range between Pakistan and Afghanistan) to eastern Anatolia (eastern region of Turkey) and from Central Asia to the Persian Gulf.

Crusades were military campaigns authorized by the Latin Roman Catholic Church during the Middle Ages. In AD 1095 Pope Urban II proclaimed the **First Crusade** with the goal of restoring Christian access to holy places in and around Jerusalem. The crusades were not about restoring the Jewish homeland—land given to the Jews through the Abrahamic and Mosaic covenants—but rather, **crusades were military campaigns to reclaim "Christian lands" captured by the Muslims.**

Inquisition was a period of intense questioning by the Roman Catholic Church (c. 1221 to early 1800s). See previous section, Persecution is Not from God. Also, defintions are found in the glossary.

Mongol Empire of Asia
AD 1215 - AD 1453

During the period AD 1215 – AD 1453, the Mongol Empire emerged with the alliance of nomadic tribes in the Mongolian homeland under the leadership of Genghis Khan who was proclaimed ruler of all Mongols in 1206. The empire grew rapidly under his rule—they invaded in every direction and became one of the largest empires in human history.

The Mongols of Asia invaded the Levant (eastern Mediterranean) including Iraq, Iran, Syria, Palestine and much of Asia minor, and in 1258 they captured Baghdad, eliminating the last of the Caliphs (Muslim rulers).

The Mongols were stopped by the Mamluk Turks, a group of slave-soldiers who seized control of Egypt, Syria, and western Arabia. The Mamluks were a military caste system spanning Egypt, the Levant (eastern Mediterranean), and Hejaz (today's western Arabia along the eastern side of the Red Sea).

Meanwhile, Asia Minor (primarily Turkey) came under the control of the Ottoman Empire. In 1453, the Ottomans (Turkish Empire or Turkey) captured the great Byzantine capital of Constantinople of the Eastern Roman Empire.

Ottoman Empire
AD 1453 - AD 1917

During the period AD 1453 – AD 1917, most of the Middle East was under the rule of the Ottoman Empire which brought peace, stability, and economic progress to the general region. Military outposts in the western region of the Middle East began to govern as independent states. The opening of the Suez Canal in 1869 soon changed the Middle East into an area of vital military and economic importance to Europe and the U.S.—and British and French influence grew throughout that general region.

During World War I (1914 - 1918), the Ottoman Empire made the strategic mistake of siding with Germany and Austria. The Battle of Jerusalem occurred during the British "Jerusalem Operations" against the Ottoman Empire. When

> The **Ottoman Empire**, historically referred to as the Turkish Empire or Turkey, was a Sunni Islamic state founded in AD 1299. During the late 1800s, many Jews returned to their ancient homeland of Israel. Between 1882 and 1903 about 35,000 Jews, primarily from Russia and Yemen, moved to Palestine.

British forces took Jerusalem in December 1917, a Jewish Legion with Jews representing many nations was part of the retaking of Palestine. The entire region (except Turkey and Saudi Arabia) was now under British or French military and administrative control. Britain had control over Egypt, Sudan, Jordan, and Iraq, and France had control over Syria and Lebanon.

> During World War I (1914 - 1918) Britain, France, Serbia, and Imperial Russia (joined later by Italy, Greece, Portugal, Romania, and the United States) fought the Central Powers—Germany and Austria-Hungary (joined later by Ottoman Turkey and Bulgaria). During this time the Ottoman government (in collusion with Germany) exterminated 1.5 million Christian Armenians and other ethnic groups, and it is the second most-studied case of genocide after the WWII Holocaust by the Germans. (See following section, Nazi Germany and the Holocaust, 1933 - 1945).

World in Denial - Defiant Nature of Mankind

Looking west toward the Eastern Gate, or Golden Gate (see photo below). In right center of panorama photo, Kidron Valley in foreground and Dome of the Rock left of center. *Photos by Roger Gallop, March 12, 2016*

Prophecy: He was to enter Jerusalem on a donkey. Prophecy in Zechariah 9:9. **Fulfillment** in Luke 19:35-37; also see Matthew 21:6-11. See chapter 4, second table, 61 Prophecies Fulfilled Pertaining to Jesus Christ.

Ottomans Rebuilt the City and Temple Walls:

The Eastern Gate was the main entrance into the Temple area, and it was the gate that Jesus entered on a humble donkey in His triumphal entry in AD 32. After Jerusalem was destroyed and the walls demolished by the Romans in AD 70, the City and Temple walls were rebuilt by the Ottoman Empire in the 16th century. The East Gate was walled up in AD 1530 and a cemetery was placed in front—although unclear, many believe this was done to prevent the entrance of the Jewish Messiah through this gate as prophesied by Ezekiel around 600 BC (Ezekiel 43:1-9). The Muslims consider the sealed gate their exclusive property but by sealing the gate, they unwittingly fulfilled the first part of the prophecy of Ezekiel 44:1-4. The rest of the prophecy will be fulfilled with the Second Coming (see chapter 12, The Second Coming of Jesus Christ).

British and French Control
1917 - 1948

On November 2, 1917, Britain issued the famous Balfour Declaration announcing British support for the establishment of a Jewish Homeland in Palestine. Under a Mandate from the League of Nations in 1922, Britain continued to govern Palestine (Land of Israel, the Holy Land or Promised Land), and the Jews continued their return to the region under strict immigration guidelines of Britain. See start of chapters 6 and 7 for more information.

Nazi Germany and the Holocaust
1933 - 1945

During the period 1933 – 1945, Jews in Germany endured intense persecution. In an effort to completely eradicate the Jews as God's chosen people, Hitler's Nazi Germany sought to murder the entire Jewish population of Europe by coordinating the identification, confinement, and organized slaughter of 6 million Jews (including 1.5 million children) in gas chambers and ovens. The slaughter of over 6 million Jews in Nazi concentration camps during World War II is known as the **Holocaust**.

> **Holocaust** is a term that describes the systematic extermination of 6 million European Jews by **Nazi Germany or the Third Reich in what they called their "final solution of the Jewish question." Why?**
>
> Because Nazi Germany had an intense hatred of the Jewish people (and God) for *"...you are a people holy to the LORD your God. The LORD your God has chosen you out of all the peoples on the face of the earth to be his people, his treasured possession"* (Deuteronomy 7:6, NIV).
>
> Hitler and the Nazi Third Reich were the face of evil in the world at that time.

Jewish fathers, mothers, children, and entire families (primarily in Germany and throughout Europe and eastern Europe) were identified, confined, stripped of their possessions, separated from family members, and then shipped to concentration camps where they were starved, shot, hung, buried alive, put to death in gas chambers and ovens, injected with drugs and chemicals, and subjected to horrific unspeakable medical experiments.

Such horrific demonic behavior by human beings is a supernatural, repugnant evil that still permeates much of the world today—an evil with the ultimate goal of eliminating the Jewish people, the church, and seizing control of God's authority. It took World War II to stop this **demonic madness** and keep end time prophecy on course. **The rise of Hitler was due to economic instability in Germany which resulted in WW II—and similar to the rise of Hitler, the future rise of the antichrist will be due to worldwide economic instability.**

> The world's tenuous economic system today is facing impending collapse which will spark a global panic and rise of the antichrist (similar to the rise of Hitler in Germany during WW II). For more information on economic instability and the future rise of the antichrist, see chapter 9, Economic Decline, and chapter 11, Rise of the Antichrist.

As a result of this dehumanizing cruelty, and methods used to exterminate the Jewish people, the pressure to re-establish a Jewish homeland greatly escalated. Enough Jews survived the Holocaust to see the formation of the State of Israel on May 14, 1948. Indeed, the **Bible proved once again to be a book of true prophecy—100 percent accurate.** (See chapter 6, Anti-Semitism and Wholesale Attempts to Eradicate the Jewish People, and Appendix C, Satan's Attempts to Seize Total Control.)

> Hitler's book, "Mein Kampf" ('my struggle' in German) may soon be re-published after being hidden away for 70 years—a book deemed "too dangerous for the general public." Why? This demonic manifesto espouses warped political ideas and hatred of the Jews. Old copies of the book are kept in what is called a secured "poison cabinet"—described as a "literary danger zone in the dark recesses of the vast Bavarian State Library." It is said by Jewish groups and Holocaust survivors that "the book espouses an evil and violent ideology that must be kept from spreading."[8]

notes: Chapter 5

1. Josephus, *The Wars Of The Jews,* Book VI.9.3. Retrieved from https://en.wikipedia.org/wiki/Siege_of_Jerusalem_(70_CE); and Konig, G. and Konig, R. (1984; 3rd Revised Edition), *100 prophecies*. 95. See www.100prophecies.org.

2. Nelson's Bible Dictionary; as cited in Let Us Reason Ministries; retrieved May 2016, from www.letusreason.org/juda14.htm.

3. McDowell, J. (1972). *Evidence that Demands a Verdict.* San Bernardino, CA: Campus Crusade for Christ, 327. (Josh McDowell is a Christian apologist, evangelist, and writer. He is within the Evangelical tradition of Protestant Christianity. His best-known book is *Evidence That Demands a Verdict*, which was ranked 13th in Christianity Today as one of the most influential evangelical books. This book is highly recommended.)

4. Alcorn, R. (2009). *If God Is Good – Faith in the Midst of Suffering and Evil.* Colorado Springs. CO: Multnomah Books, 24-25.

5. Spiritual Warriors Advancing Truth (SWAT) (October 12, 2015). Doug McCary <tim@pvpctide.ccsend.com> on behalf of Doug McCary dmccary@hislight.org.

6. McDowell, op. cit., 330.

7. Young, E. (March 24, 2012) "The Difference Between God's Punishment and God's Discipline" – A.W. Pink. Retrieved January 25, 2016, from http://www.erictyoung.com/2012/03/24/the-difference-between-gods-punishment-and-gods-discipline-a-w-pink/.

8. Chokshi, N. (December 3, 2015). "Too Dangerous for the general public." The Washington Post article in The Florida Times-Union, Jacksonville, Florida, A-4.

Chapter 6

Miraculous Rebirth of the State of Israel
May 14, 1948

> *"...and gather you again from all the nations where he scattered you. Even if you have been banished to the most distant land under the heavens, from there the LORD your God will gather you and bring you back. He will bring you to the land that belonged to your ancestors, and you will take possession of it."* —Deuteronomy 30:1-5, NIV

Immediately following World War II, the United Nations met to vote for or against partitioning of **Palestine** as a homeland for the Jews as mandated by the Balfour Declaration on November 2, 1917. (See Appendix A, glossary, and adjacent text box for more information about Transjordan.)

Many in the U.N. were horrified by Hitler's mass murder of more than 6 million Jews during the war, so despite fierce opposition by most of the Arab countries, the **U.N. received the necessary 2/3 majority to divide Palestine into 7 parts: 3 parts for the Jews, 3 parts for the Palestinian Arabs, and Jerusalem to be internationalized.** The U.N. gave Britain 8 months to conclude their occupation of the land, and **Israel was born in one day—on May 14, 1948**, the State of Israel was officially proclaimed.

When did other countries in the Middle East gain independence? Egypt (independence from Britain) on February 28, 1922; Sudan (independence from Britain) on January 1, 1956; Jordan (independence from Britain) on May 2, 1946; Syria (independence from France) in 1941 (but not recognized until January 1, 1944); Lebanon (independence from France) on November 26, 1941; Saudi Arabia (never colonized, so independence day is actually the day when the kingdom was created) on May 20, 1927; and Iraq (independence from Britain) on October 3, 1932.

On November 2, 1917, Britain issued the famous Balfour Declaration announcing British support for the establishment of a Jewish homeland in **Palestine**—a homeland that would include lands east and west of the Jordan River (as it was during the Period of Judges, c. 1400 to 1050 BC, and the Jewish United Kingdom, c. 1050 to 930 BC; chapter 3). So what happened?

In 1921 Britain unilaterally granted Emir Abdullah the territory east of the river known as **Transjordan** (see map on next page) which **overturned the purpose of the original mandate.** This angered the Jewish people because **this secret negotiation separated land east of the river from land west of the river—and it did not account for using some of this land (east of the river) as possible resettlement for Palestinian Arabs.**[1]

Britain continued to govern the territory and the Jews continued their return to the region under strict immigration guidelines. Immediately following WW II, the United Nations met to vote for or against partitioning of Palestine as a homeland for the Jews as mandated by the Balfour Declaration. Despite fierce opposition from the Arabs, the Partition Plan called for the division of Palestine west of the Jordan River into 7 parts: 3 parts for the Jews, 3 parts for the Palestinian Arabs, and 1 part to be internationalized (Jerusalem).

In 1946 **Transjordan** officially gained its independence from Britain, and in 1949 the land was renamed Jordan. **Palestinian Arabs could have been (should have been) easily absorbed into Transjordan—but they were slated to remain in Palestine west of the Jordan River as a thorn or source of conflict for Israel. See start of chapter 7 for more information.**

About 2,900 years after the reign of King Solomon (970 BC – 930 BC) and 1,878 years after the Romans destroyed the City of Jerusalem and the Second Temple (AD 70), the Jews declared an independent state of Israel on May 14, 1948, a miraculous rebirth in just one day. The prophet Isaiah said, *"Who has heard of such a thing? Who has seen such things? Shall a land be born in one day? Shall a nation be brought forth in one moment?"* (Isaiah 66:7-8) [Bold added]

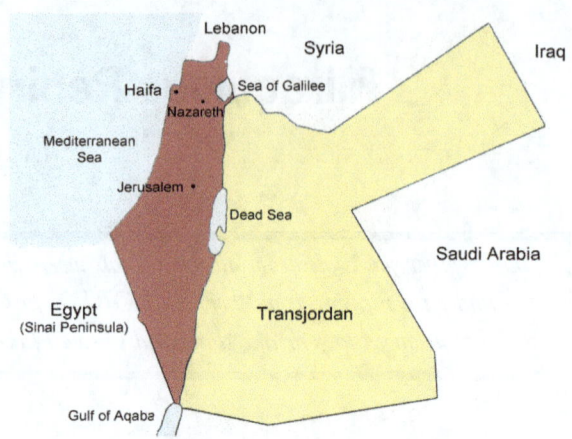

Palestine and Transjordan

Old Testament Scripture Pertaining to the Rebirth of Israel

Even after pronouncing the judgments for disobedience in advance (Deuteronomy 28:15-68), **Moses predicts the restoration of the Jewish people and renewal of the Abrahamic covenant** in Deuteronomy 30:1-5 (NIV).

> *"When all these blessings and curses I have set before you come on you and you take them to heart wherever the LORD your God disperses you **among the nations**, and when you and your children return to the LORD your God and obey him with all your heart and with all your soul according to everything I command you today, then the LORD your **God will restore your fortunes** and have compassion on you and **gather you again from all the nations where he scattered you. Even if you have been banished to the most distant land under the heavens, from there the LORD your God will gather you and bring you back. He will bring you to the land that belonged to your ancestors, and you will take possession of it.** He will make you more prosperous and numerous than your ancestors"* Deuteronomy 30:1-5 (NIV). [Bold added]

After nearly 2,000 years of worldwide exile beginning AD 70 (see chapter 5), the Jews were miraculously restored to their ancient homeland on May 14, 1948, **in direct fulfillment of end times prophecy foretold about 2,500 years ago** by the prophets Ezekiel (c. 593 - 571 BC), Amos (c. 760 - 750 BC), Isaiah (c. 740 - 681 BC), Jeremiah (c. 626 - 585 BC), and Hosea (c. 750 - 715 BC). (See the following Scripture in this section: Ezekiel 28:25-26, 34:13, 36:22-24, 33-36, 37:1-6, 11-14, 21-22, 39:27-29; Amos 9:14-15; and Isaiah 11:11-12, 43:5-7.)

To any open minded person, this is prophetic proof of God of the Holy Bible. God promised to search all the nations to which He had driven the Jews and, from among these, return a sufficient number to rebuild the uninhabited lands of Judea. "**The return of more than a million Jews to the land of Israel [the Promised Land]...is one of the most amazing and remarkable miracles of all time.**"[2] [Bold added]

> *"'This is what the Sovereign Lord says: **When I gather the people of Israel from the nations where they have been scattered, I will be proved holy through them in the sight of the nations.** Then they*

will live in their own land, which I gave to my servant Jacob. They will live there in safety and will build houses and plant vineyards; **they will live in safety when I inflict punishment on all their neighbors who maligned them.** Then they will know that I am the Lord their God'" (Ezekiel 28:25-26, NIV). [Bold added]

"I will bring them out from the nations and gather them from the countries, and I will bring them into their own land. I will pasture them on the mountains of Israel, in the ravines and in all the settlements in the land" (Ezekiel 34:13). [Bold added]

"Therefore say to the Israelites, 'This is what the Sovereign LORD says: **It is not for your sake, people of Israel, that I am going to do these things, but for the sake of my holy name, which you have profaned among the nations where you have gone.** I will show the holiness of my great name, which has been profaned among the nations, the name you have profaned among them. Then the nations will know that I am the LORD, declares the Sovereign LORD, when I am proved holy through you before their eyes. **For I will take you out of the nations; I will gather you from all the countries and bring you back into your own land**'" (Ezekiel 36:22-24, NIV). [Bold added]

"'This is what the Sovereign LORD says: On the day I cleanse you from all your sins, **I will resettle your towns, and the ruins will be rebuilt.** The desolate land will be cultivated instead of lying desolate in the sight of all who pass through it.' They will say, 'This land that was laid waste has become like the garden of Eden; the cities that were lying in ruins, desolate and destroyed, are now fortified and inhabited. **Then the nations around you that remain will know that I the LORD have rebuilt what was destroyed and have replanted what was desolate. I the LORD have spoken, and I will do it**'" (Ezekiel 36:33-36, NIV). [Bold added]

"The hand of the LORD was on me, and he brought me out by the Spirit of the LORD and set me in the middle of a valley; it was full of bones. He led me back and forth among them, and I saw a great many bones on the floor of the valley, bones that were very dry. He asked me, 'Son of man, can these bones live?' I said, 'Sovereign LORD, you alone know.' Then he said to me, 'Prophesy to these bones and say to them, Dry bones, hear the word of the LORD! **This is what the Sovereign LORD says to these bones: I will make breath enter you, and you will come to life. I will attach tendons to you and make flesh come upon you and cover you with skin; I will put breath in you, and you will come to life. Then you will know that I am the LORD**'" (Ezekiel 37:1-6, NIV). [Bold added]

"Then he said to me: **Son of man, these bones are the people of Israel.** They say, 'Our bones are dried up and our hope is gone; we are cut off.' Therefore prophesy and say to them: 'This is what the Sovereign LORD says: **My people, I am going to open your graves and bring you up from them; I will bring you back to the land of Israel. Then you, my people, will know that I am the LORD, when I open your graves and bring you up from them. I will put my Spirit in you and you will live, and I will settle you in your own land. Then you will know that I the LORD have spoken,** and I have done it, declares the LORD'" (Ezekiel 37:11-14, NIV). [Bold added]

"...and say to them, 'This is what the Sovereign LORD says: **I will take the Israelites out of the nations where they have gone. I will gather them from all around and bring them back into their own land. I will make them one nation in the land, on the mountains of Israel. There will be one king over all of them and they will never again be two nations or be divided into two kingdoms** [as in the days following the reign of King Solomon]'" (Ezekiel 37:21-22, NIV). [Bold added]

"When I have brought them back from the nations and have gathered them from the countries of their enemies, I will be proved holy through them in the sight of many nations. **Then they will know that I am the LORD their God, for though I sent them into exile among the nations** [AD 70] **I will gather them to their own land, not leaving any behind.** *I will no longer hide my face from them, for I will pour out my Spirit on the people of Israel, declares the Sovereign LORD"* (Ezekiel 39:27-29, NIV). [Bold added]

"'I will bring back my exiled people Israel; *they will rebuild the ruined cities and live in them. They will plant vineyards and drink their wine; they will make gardens and eat their fruit.* **I will plant Israel in their own land, never again to be uprooted from the land I have given them,' says the LORD your God"** (Amos 9:14-15, NIV). [Bold added]

"In that day the Lord will reach out his hand a second time to reclaim the surviving remnant of his people from Assyria, from Lower Egypt, from Upper Egypt, from Cush....He will raise a banner for the nations and **gather the exiles of Israel; he will assemble the scattered people of Judah from the four quarters of the earth"** (Isaiah 11:11-12, NIV). [Bold added]

"Do not be afraid, for I am with you; **I will bring your children from the east and gather you from the west. I will say to the north, 'Give them up!' and to the south, 'Do not hold them back.' Bring my sons from afar and my daughters from the ends of the earth**—*everyone who is called by my name, whom I created for my glory, whom I formed and made"* (Isaiah 43:5-7, NIV). [Bold added].

Not only did God promise to search all the countries and return a sufficient number to rebuild the land, **but also to defend Israel against its enemies.** (See Hosea 3:4-5 and Jeremiah 31:10, 35-36.)

"For the **Israelites will live many days without king or prince**, *without sacrifice or sacred stones, without ephod or household gods. Afterward* **the Israelites will return and seek the LORD their God** *and David their king. They will come trembling to the LORD and to his blessings in the* **last days**" (Hosea 3:4-5, NIV). [Bold added]

"Hear the word of the LORD, you nations; proclaim it in distant coastlands: **'He who scattered Israel will gather them and will watch over his flock like a shepherd'"** (Jeremiah 31:10, NIV). [Bold added]

"This is what the LORD says, he who appoints the sun to shine by day, who decrees the moon and stars to shine by night, who stirs up the sea so that its waves roar—the LORD Almighty is his name: **'Only if these decrees vanish from my sight,'** *declares the LORD,* **'will Israel ever cease being a nation before me'"** (Jeremiah 31:35-36, NIV). [Bold added]

The prophet Isaiah said, *"Who has heard of such a thing? Who has seen such things?* **Shall a land be born in one day? Shall a nation be brought forth in one moment?"** (Isaiah 66:7-8) [Bold added]

This prophecy was fulfilled on May 14, 1948, after 1,878 years of worldwide exile. During the Six Day War, Israel reclaimed the ancient City of Jerusalem on June 5–10, 1967, in fulfillment of Psalm 83:2-18, all necessary prerequisites for the fulfillment of prophetic end time (last days) events. The chance of such events occurring without Divine intervention is Zero—these events are prophetic proof of God of the Holy Bible, Creator of the heavens and earth and all that exists. Bible prophecy enjoys 100% accuracy and it is wise to believe future end time prophetic events as described in chapters 11 and 12.

New Testament Scripture Pertaining to the Rebirth of Israel

The **Olivet Discourse** is the teaching of the end time by Jesus Christ on the Mount of Olives (also see introduction to chapter 11). Christ was speaking of the rebirth of the State of Israel (**Budding of the Fig Tree**) found in Matthew 24:32-35 and Luke 21:29-33 and the **rapture of the church** which is found in 1 Corinthians 15:51-52, 1 Thessalonians 4:13-18, and in Matthew 24:36-44. The discourse is recorded in Matthew 24:1–25:46. Parallel passages are found in Mark 13:1-37 and Luke 21:5-36. Other passages to consider when studying the **Olivet Discourse** are Daniel 9:24-27 and Revelation 6:1–19:21 which refer to the **future seven year period called the tribulation** (see chapters 11 and 12).

> The **fig tree** represents the State of Israel reestablished as a nation in their land. Israel did not exist as a self-governing country for 2,534 years from the time it was conquered by Babylon in 586 BC to May 14, 1948.

> **Olivet Discourse** is the teaching of the end times by Jesus Christ on the Mount of Olives. This discourse is recorded in Matthew, chapters 24 and 25. Parallel passages are found in Mark 13:1-37 and Luke 21:5-36.
>
> Jesus discusses pre-tribulation signs in Matthew 24:4-8, the first 3 ½ years of the tribulation in Matthew 24:9-14, the second 3 ½ years of the tribulation in Matthew 24:15-26, the **Budding of the Fig Tree** in Matthew 24:32-35, and the **rapture of the church** in Matthew 24:36-44.
>
> The record in Matthew is the most extensive, so reference here is to Matthew's gospel. It is important to recognize that Jesus' teaching in this discourse is in reference to Israel and not the church.

Now Jesus spoke of a parable of the fig tree (Matthew 24:32-35, NIV).

*"Now learn this **lesson from the fig tree:** As soon as its twigs get tender and its leaves come out, you know that summer is near. Even so, when you see all these things, you know that the end is near, **right at the door.** [Door is a passageway between heaven and earth; Revelation 4:1.] Truly I tell you, **this generation will certainly not pass away** until all these things have happened. Heaven and earth will pass away, but my words will never pass away"* (Matthew 24:32-35, NIV). [Bold added]

*"Look at the fig tree, and all the trees. When they sprout leaves, you can see for yourselves and know **that summer is near.** Even so, when you see these things happening, you **know that the Kingdom of God is near.** I tell you the truth, **this generation will certainly not pass away** until all things have happened. Heaven and earth will pass away, but my words will never pass away"* (Luke 21:29-33, NIV).

After the Jewish people were exiled worldwide in AD 70, the State of Israel was miraculously restored as a sovereign nation on May 14, 1948. What does this mean? It means we can expect an increase in pretribulation signs (Matthew 24:4-8) and the soon return of Jesus Christ through the rapture of the church (Matthew 24:36-44).

Jesus said: *"**No one knows about that day or hour, not even the angels in heaven, nor the Son, but only the Father**"* (Matthew 24:36, NIV). [Bold added] In other words, God has not revealed to anyone exactly when Jesus is coming back (via the rapture), although we have been given physical signs foreshadowing the coming seven year tribulation following the rapture of the church. (See chapter 11, Rapture of the Church and linear timeline.)

Concerning the term '**generation**' in the previous Scripture, many have tried to determine the length of one generation in this day and age (about 30 to 40 years) and apply this to the rebirth of Israel, but strictly within the context of the sentence, the Scripture is simply stating that those who witness these things (pre-tribulation super signs including rebirth of Israel; see chapter 8) will see the rapture of the church followed by the tribulation and the Second Coming of Christ. As Scripture indicates, *"No one knows about that day or hour* [rapture of the church], *not even the angels in heaven, nor the Son, but only the Father"* (Matthew 24:36, NIV). [Bold added] (See generation in glossary; strictly by the numbers, time is possibly between 2008 and 2028: 1948 + 60 [30 + 30 for those born at the beginning and end] = 2008 and 1948 + 80 [40 + 40 for those born at the beginning and end] = 2028.)

Jerusalem panorama early twentieth century

Jerusalem panorama looking west from Mount of Olives.
Photo by Roger Gallop, March 12, 2016

Mount of Olives; looking east from the Temple Mount. Orthodox Church of Maria Magdalene in left foreground (golden spire) and Church of Dominus Flevit in mid-upper right (small, gray spire). *Photo by Roger Gallop, March 14, 2016*

Prophecies Fulfilled on May 14, 1948[3]

Description	Biblical Passage	Date Written	Date Fulfilled
Jacob's descendants to regain control of Israel	Amos 9:14-15	c. 750 BC	Since May 14, 1948
Israel to be brought back to life	Ezekiel 37:10-14	c. 593-571 BC	May 14, 1948
Israel to be reborn in one day	Isaiah 66:7-8	c. 701-681 BC	May 14, 1948
Israel to be re-established as a united nation	Ezekiel 37:21-22	c. 593-571 BC	May 14, 1948
The second Israel to be more impressive than the first	Jeremiah 16:14-15	c. 626-586 BC	1948
Ezekiel predicted when Israel to be revived	Ezekiel 4:3-6	c. 593-571 BC	1948
The people of Israel to return to "their own land"	Ezekiel 34:13	c. 593-571 BC	After May 14, 1948
God to watch over the people of Israel	Jeremiah 31:10	c. 626-586 BC	1948
Israel's army to be more powerful but fewer in number	Leviticus 26:7-8	c. 1400 BC	1948-49, 1967, etc.
The fortunes of the people of Israel to be restored	Deuteronomy 30:3-5	c. 1400 BC	1948

God's Chosen People and Prophecy Fulfilled

There is no other example in recorded history of a people who have preserved their unique, unprecedented national identity after almost 2,000 years of worldwide exile. The historian Arnold Toynbee wrote, "As for long life, the Jews live on—the same peculiar people—today, long ages after the Phoenicians and the Philistines have lost their identity. Their ancient Syriac neighbors have gone into the melting pot and have been reminted, with new images and superscriptions, while Israel has proved impervious to this alchemy."[4]

Even though the Jews were scattered among all the nations of the world, and without territory or government, and harshly persecuted, hunted and murdered without mercy, they survived as a distinct people "making them one of the **truly great wonders of the ages.**"[5] [Bold added] This is further proof of **Divine intervention**.

> God describes the Jewish people: *"For you are a people holy to the LORD your God. The LORD your God has chosen you out of all the peoples on the face of the earth to be his people, his treasured possession.* ***The LORD did not set his affection on you and choose you because you were more numerous than other peoples, for you were the fewest of all peoples. But it was because the LORD loved you and kept the oath he swore to your ancestors*** *that he brought you out with a mighty hand and redeemed you from the land of slavery, from the power of Pharaoh king of Egypt. Know therefore that the LORD your God is God; he is the faithful God, keeping his covenant of love to a thousand generations of those who love him and keep his commandments"* (Deuteronomy 7:6-9, NIV). [Bold added]

How did the prophets of the Old Testament Bible foresee thousands of years into mankind's future? How did they know, in advance, that pagan nations (the Kenites, Kenizzites, Kadmonites, Hittites, Perizzites, Rephaites, Amorites, Canaanites, Girgashites, and Jebusites in Genesis 15:16, 18-21; and Assyrian and Babylonian Empires; and cities such as Ninevah and Babylon, and many others) would fade away while Israel's God (the God of Abraham, Isaac, Jacob, and Moses) would be worshiped in every nation throughout time? How did they know the Temple and ancient City of Jerusalem would be destroyed (twice) and its people ultimately scattered to the four corners of the world, only to be restored (in one day) almost 2,000 years later?

They simply wrote down exactly what they were told by God—the message was God-breathed as described in 2 Timothy 3:16, and the prophets knew the veracity and certainty of what they were being told. (Also see 2 Peter 1:21; Genesis 2:7; Exodus 24:3, 4, 7; Jeremiah 36:1-4; 1 Corinthians 14:37; Revelation 1:1, 2, 10, 11, 19; and Ephesians 3:3-5.)

> **Why did prophecy disappear?** After the later prophets, Haggai (c. 520 BC), Zechariah (c. 520 BC – 480 BC), and Malachi (c. 440 BC – 430 BC), had died, the gift of prophecy disappeared from the Jewish people. **It disappeared because the Jews broke their covenant (their relationship) with God by** *turning away* **and adopting pagan customs of surrounding nations.** They were unable to achieve the same spiritual insight and understanding to receive the gift of prophecy. And even today, it is almost impossible for any individual to achieve this gift in such a secular, materialistic world. See prologue and chapter 4, Disappearance of the Prophets.

In 2 Peter 1:21 (NIV) [Bold added], *"For prophecy never had its origin in the will of man, but **men spoke from God as they were carried along by the Holy Spirit.**"* God, in turn, knew the future, being omnipresent, omnipotent, and omniscient (Romans 8:29; Ephesians 1:4-5; 1 Corinthians 2:7; Jeremiah 23:24, 32:27)—He foreknew the future from ancient times. He could make it happen simply by whispering in someone's ear.

Indisputable Evidence

Regardless of what men choose to do (using the 'free will' that He granted them), the **Lord intervenes in human affairs to affect or produce fulfillment of prophecies.** These prophecies, undeniably fulfilled thousands of years later, **offer indisputable evidence of the truthfulness, inspiration, and reliability of the Bible.**

Fallacy of Replacement Theology

During the period between AD 70 and May 14, 1948, many Christians and theologians firmly believed the restoration of the Jewish homeland (Land of Israel, the Holy Land, or Promised Land) was absolutely impossible. As a result many believed the Covenant between God and the Jewish people was forfeited because of the rejection of Jesus Christ which led to His crucifixion in AD 32.

As a result many Christians believed there was no possibility for a future State of Israel, and it appeared that the Jews relinquished their claim as God's chosen people. But all that changed following World War II with the restoration of Israel in 1948. Since that time, the idea of replacement theology has been discarded by mainstream Christian theologians and denominations although some radical (most often, anti-Semitic) Christians incorrectly cling to this assumption.

Most mainstream theologians such as Hal Lindsey and Jack Van Impe denounce replacement theology because God made certain **"unconditional promises"** to the descendants of Abraham, Isaac, and Jacob (see chapter 2, The Abrahamic Covenant and The Mosaic Covenant) and reaffirmed these promises to Moses and other prophets. These **covenants are binding forever** despite the disobedience and failings of Jews of the Old and New Testaments and modern Israelis today.

Consider the following Scriptures where God makes certain **promises of blessings, and forever means forever and everlasting means everlasting. The restoration of Israel validates that the Lord will keep His covenant with the Jewish people forever, and we are in the last days.**

Replacement Theology states that Old Covenants made with the descendants of Abraham, Isaac, Jacob, and Moses were forfeited when they rejected Jesus as the Messiah and forced His execution. Those today still clinging to this assumption believe the church has replaced the Israelites as God's representatives on earth and the church inherited a New Covenant. (See Appendix B, Establishment of a New Covenant.)

Those holding to replacement theology now believe that Old Testament prophecies have already been fulfilled and conclude that the present State of Israel is destined to destruction which, in turn, fosters an anti-Semitic attitude toward the Jews which we see today. And unbelievably, such people in the Christian community are profanely and irreverently rooting for the destruction of Israel.

In Genesis 12:2-3 (NIV) [Bold added], God makes promises of blessings to the Jewish people: *"I will make you into a great nation, and I will bless you; I will make your name great, and you will be a blessing.* **I will bless those who bless you, and whoever curses you I will curse; and all peoples on earth will be blessed through you.***"* Other blessings are described in Deuteronomy 28:1-14 (NIV).

A title deed of the land was given to the Jewish people by the Creator—a deed that will last **forever.** In Genesis 13:14-15 (NIV) [Bold added], *"The LORD said to Abram after Lot had parted from him, 'Look around from where you are, to the north and south, to the east and west. All the land that you see I will give to you and your offspring* **forever.***'"* Genesis 15:18-21 even defines the boundaries of the land.

Abraham reminded God (as if God needed reminding) that he already had a son, Ishmael, but God **reaffirmed the original covenant** by stating, *"Yes, but your wife Sarah will bear you a son, and you will call him Isaac. I will establish my covenant with him as an* **everlasting covenan***t for his descendants after him. And as for Ishmael, I have heard you: I will surely bless him; I will make him fruitful and will greatly increase his numbers. He will be the father of twelve rulers, and I will make him into a great nation"* (Genesis 17:19-20, NIV). [Bold added]

"They will be a sign and a wonder to you and your descendants **forever***"* (Deuteronomy 28:46, NIV). [Bold added]

"The secret things belong to the LORD our God, but the things revealed belong to us and to our children **forever,** *that we may follow all the words of this law"* (Deuteronomy 29:29, NIV). [Bold added]

In Leviticus 20:26 (NIV), *"You are to be holy to me and because I, the Lord, am holy, and I have set you apart from the nations to be my own."* In Hebrews 8:10 (NIV), *"This is the covenant* [New Covenant] *I will make with the house of Israel after that time* [end times], *declares the Lord. I will put my laws in their minds and write them on their hearts. I will be their God, and they will be my people."*

God **reaffirmed the covenant** to Abraham's son, Isaac, in Genesis 26:2-4 and to Isaac's son, Jacob, it was **again reaffirmed** in Genesis 28:4, 13, and then to the prophet Moses (Deuteronomy 5:1-5, NIV). The covenant was **again reaffirmed** to King David (1,000 years after Abraham) in Psalm 105:8-10 (NIV), *"He remembers his covenant* **forever,** *the word he commanded, for a* **thousand generations,** *the covenant he made with Abraham...to Isaac...to Jacob...to Israel as an* **everlasting covenant***"* [Bold added] and to the prophet Jeremiah (1,400 years after Abraham) in Jeremiah 31:35-37.

The Jews remained disobedient and stubborn, *"But concerning Israel he says, 'All day long I have held out my hands to a* **disobedient and obstinate people.***'"* In Romans 10:21 (NIV), *"I ask then:* **Did God reject his people? By no means!** *I am an Israelite myself, a descendant of Abraham, from the tribe of Benjamin.* **God did not reject his people that he foreknew.** *Don't you know what the Scripture says in the passage about Elijah— how he appealed to God against Israel... And what was God's answer to him? 'I have reserved for myself seven thousand who have not bowed the knee to Baal.'* **So too, at the present time there is a remnant chosen by grace. And if by grace, then it is no longer by works; if it were, grace would no longer be grace***"* (Romans 11:1-6, NIV). [Bold added]

But despite worldwide exile for almost 2,000 years, the Jewish people endured—and the reason for their existence was not because of their good works but only by the grace of God.

"Therefore say to the Israelites, This is what the Sovereign LORD says: **'It is not for your sake, people of Israel, that I am going to do these things, but for the sake of my holy name, which you have profaned among the nations where you have gone.** *I will show the holiness of my great name, which has been profaned among the nations, the name you have profaned among them. Then the nations will know that I am the LORD, declares the Sovereign LORD, when I am proved holy through you before their eyes.* **For I will take you out of the nations; I will gather you from all the countries and bring you back into your own land'"** (Ezekiel 36:22-24, NIV). [Bold added] Also see Isaiah 14:1 and Amos 9:14-15.

God has a great end time plan for salvation of the Jewish nation. See Appendix B, Establishment of a New Covenant. All Israel will be saved. *"...Israel has experienced a hardening in part until the full number of the Gentiles has come in* [**the total number of the Gentiles to be saved**]. *And so all Israel will be saved, as it is written: "The deliverer will come from Zion; he will turn godlessness away from Jacob. And this is my covenant* [New Covenant] *with them when I take away their sins"* (Romans 11:25-27, NIV). [Bold added] "Then he will save, not just a minority of the Jewish people, but a large majority....At present, God is saving a remnant but the time is coming when God will save the vast majority of Israel."[6] (See Appendix B, Establishment of a New Covenant.)

In 1948, Israel was recognized as a sovereign state for the first time since AD 70. God promised Abraham and his descendants would have the land of Canaan as *"an everlasting possession"* (Genesis 17:8, NIV) [Bold added], and Ezekiel prophesied a physical and spiritual revival of Israel (Ezekiel 37). Israel's rebirth as a sovereign nation in its own land is essential because of Israel's role in eschatology (see Daniel 10:14, 11:41, and Revelation 11:8). These **facts alone disprove man-made assumptions** regarding replacement theology.

Anti-Semitism and Wholesale Attempts to Eradicate the Jewish People

In Genesis 12:2-3 (NIV), God makes certain promises to the Jewish people (see Scripture in previous section). In verse 3, the Lord states *"...I will bless those who bless you, and whoever curses you I will curse...."* God knew that the Jews would be subject to attack and persecution, **so He warns these peoples and nations, especially those who are trying to eliminate Israel as a people and as a nation. Today, many countries of the world (including many liberal minded U.S. congressional and presidential leaders) have turned their backs on Israel with anti-Semitic attitudes—this is a very grave strategic mistake of the U.S.**

What exactly were the attempts to eradicate the Jews as a people? Such attempts to eliminate God's plan for redemption of human kind began at the Garden of Eden; then during the rebellion at the Tower of Babel; then trying to deter Jesus Christ in the wilderness (Matthew 4:1-11, Mark 1:12-13; Luke 4:1-13); then attempts to destroy the Jewish people during the Holocaust of WW II; and finally, attempts to destroy the

Church. This question is described in detail in Appendix C, Satan's Attempts to Seize Total Control.

In an attempt to impede the fulfillment of prophecy, Hitler's Nazi government (1933 – 1944) began the systematic slaughter of 6 million Jews (including 1.5 million children). The Jewish people in Europe and Eastern Europe were identified, stripped of their possessions, separated from family members, and then shipped to concentration camps where they were starved, shot, hung, put to death in gas chambers, and subjected to horrific unspeakable medical experiments. It took WW II to stop this demonic madness and to keep the prophecy of a revised Israeli State on track to fulfillment in 1948. The Bible is a book of true prophecy.

What was Satan's motive in eradicating the Jews as a people? If these attempts or threats to eradicate the Jews ever succeeded, or if the Jewish people were never given the opportunity to form a new State of Israel in Palestine (the Holy Land), prophecy and the word of God (Hosea 3:4-5; Jeremiah 31:10, 35-36) **would have become completely worthless — fulfillment of Bible prophecy requires the Jews' survival as a nation**. The Lord is Sovereign and He assured the survival of the Jewish people as a nation.

> Fulfillment of these Old Testament prophecies and the restoration of Israel provide *indisputable evidence* of the truthfulness and reliability of the Bible and a Divine Creator.

The Jews are a gifted people and have played leading roles in the fields of art, literature, science, and medicine—but worldwide, anti-Semitism has resulted in **humiliation, persecution, and death.** But the Jewish people were not without some comfort—Scripture that speaks of the restoration of the Jews from the four corners of the world in the end times.[7] (See Scripture in chapter 6, Miraculous Rebirth of the State of Israel.)

How could Bible prophets forecast such events thousands of years into the future? We know for sure that no one in recent history—no one in the last few thousand years—could forecast such a thing. Without Divine help, the Jewish state would never have been restored after worldwide banishment. **Only a Divine miracle could bring about the restoration of Israel,** and this miracle was promised in Bible prophecy. **Although it took two world wars, the miracle occurred after 1,878 years as the hand of God guided world events with the restoration of Israel on May 14, 1948—within the lifetime of many people living today. *Yet most people are oblivious to the significance of such events.***

> God knows the future—He knew you (that is, all human beings) in ancient times (Romans 8:29; Ephesians 1:4-5; 1 Corinthians 2:7) and foreknew all the choices you will make in your lifetime (to choose either good or evil; to live a righteous life or a sinful life, and to believe that Jesus Christ is Savior).
>
> **Don't make the most terrible mistake by turning away from God. God is holy, righteous, and merciful,** and through our Lord Jesus Christ offers the gift of eternal salvation (John 3:16, 5:24, 14:6; Romans 10:9, 13; and Ephesians 2:8-9) to those who do not turn away and are willing to accept the free gift of pardon through faith and repentance—so by grace [mercy] you are saved through faith (Ephesians 2:8-9).
>
> People lest not forget the Lord is **omnipresent, omnipotent, and omniscient** (Romans 8:29; Ephesians 1:4-5; 1 Corinthians 2:7) and *"the Lord is a warrior"* (Exodus 15:3)—*"He does whatever pleases Him"* (Psalms 115:3, 135:6; Job 23:13; Daniel 4:35, NIV), and *"He is to be feared."* (1 Chronicles 16:25; Psalm 96:4; Isaiah 8:13, NIV) [Bold added] See Preface, Who is God?

notes: **Chapter 6**

1. Creation of Transjordan. Retrieved January 26, 2016, from http://www.palestinefacts.org/pf_mandate_transjordan.php; and The Making of Transjordan. Retrieved January 26, 2016, from http://www.kinghussein.gov.jo/his_transjordan.html.

2. McDowell, J. (1972). *Evidence that Demands a Verdict.* San Bernardino, CA: Campus Crusade for Christ, 328. (Josh McDowell is a Christian apologist, evangelist, and writer. He is within the Evangelical tradition of Protestant Christianity. His best-known book is *Evidence That Demands a Verdict*, which was ranked 13th in Christianity Today as one of the most influential evangelical books. This book is highly recommended.)

3. Watchman Bible Study, 10 Prophecies Fulfilled in 1948. Retrieved from http://watchmanbiblestudy.com/Articles/1948PropheciesFulfilled.htm and http://www.100prophecies.org/.

4. Toynbee, A. (1957). *A Study of History.* Oxford University Press, Vol. 1, 194; as cited in DeLoach, C. (1974). *Seeds of Conflict.* NJ: Logos International, 10.

5. DeLoach, C. (1974). op. cit., 10.

6. Mathew, P.G. (May 29, 2011). "The Salvation of the Jews." Grace Valley Christian Center. Retrieved on January 26, 2016, from http://www.gracevalley.org/sermon_trans/2011/Salvation_of_Jews.html.

7. DeLoach, C. (1974), op. cit., chapter 4.

Chapter 7

Renewal of the Ancient Conflict Between Isaac and Ishmael

> [4] *'Come,' they say, 'let us destroy them as a nation, so that Israel's name is remembered no more.* [Israel's very existence is at stake.] [5]*With one mind they plot together; they form an alliance against you."* —Psalm 83:4-5, NIV

War of Independence
1948 and 1949

On May 14, 1948, at 4 pm, David Ben-Gurion, the primary founder of the State of Israel and the first Prime Minister of Israel, announced the rebirth of the State of Israel before a special session of the Provisional State Council in Tel Aviv, Israel. This event renewed the ancient quarrel between the sons of Isaac and the sons of Ishmael.[1] A state of undeclared war now existed between the Arabs and the Jews.

Immediately following Israel's declaration of independence and the departure of British troops from Palestine, armies of Egypt, Syria, Transjordan, and forces from Lebanon and Iraq, on the pretense of restoring peace and stability, initiated an invasion and takeover of Israel (1st attack). Although outnumbered 20:1, the tiny State of Israel fought and outflanked the invading Arab armies, and the Israelis captured more of their ancient Jewish homeland, expanding its partitioned size by about 50%.

On June 11, 1948, the Arabs accepted a cease fire, but the Arabs broke the truce with yet another attack on Israel (2nd attack). As a result, the Israelis gained control over almost half of Galilee. Cease fire was once again agreed to, but the Arabs initiated yet another attack (3rd attack) in January, 1949, and Israel captured the remaining portion of the Negev (the southern portion of Israel), essentially a desert wilderness. Around 700,000 Palestinian

---

Six countries formed an Arab League in Cairo on March 22, 1945: Egypt, Iraq, Transjordan (gained independence from Britain in 1946 and renamed Jordan in 1949), Lebanon, Saudi Arabia, and Syria. (Yemen joined as a member on May 5, 1945.) These countries bitterly opposed a Jewish state and when the UN Partition Plan was adopted on November 29, 1947, it was unanimously rejected by the Arab League. Ultimately, a united and strong Israeli effort and over-confident speech-making (bravado), disunity, and confusion among Arab countries led to an Israeli victory.[2]

Following the 1917 Balfour Declaration, in 1921 Britain granted Emir Abdullah the territory known as **Transjordan**. (See start of chapter 6 for more information.) **This unilateral deal excluded the land east of the Jordan River thereby eliminating the use of this land as rightful Jewish homeland and potential resettlement for Palestinian Arabs. Palestinian Arabs could have been (and should have been) easily absorbed into Transjordan but were not—they remained in Palestine west of the Jordan River as a preconceived source of contention (conflict) with Israel.**

Arabs fled or were expelled from these areas that Israel now controlled, and they became what is known today as Palestinian refugees.

> See the film, Israel – Birth of a Nation (History Channel 1996); https://www.youtube.com/watch?v=dXCdwrO09wA for a documentary of the war.

Result of these wars: Israeli victory, a Palestinian Arab defeat, and an Arab League strategic failure. Territorial changes: Israel keeps area allotted to it by the Partition Plan and captures 50% of the area allotted to Arab Palestinians, Jordan occupies the West Bank, and Egypt takes control of the Gaza Strip.

1956 Sinai and Suez Crisis[3]

In October 1956, Egypt blocked Israeli shipping through the Straits of Tiran, a narrow passage of water connecting the southernmost Israeli port of Eilat through the Gulf of Aqaba to the Red Sea—and also closed Israeli shipping through the Suez Canal, an international waterway. Closure of the Straits damaged Israel's trade with Asia because ships carrying essential cargo (food, medicine, building materials, etc.) were forced to travel an exceedingly long and dangerous route around South Africa (Cape of Good Hope) to Israel's Mediterranean ports.

> **Suez Canal** is an artificial waterway in Egypt extending from Port Said to Suez and connecting the Mediterranean Sea with the Red Sea. The **Straits of Tiran** is the narrow sea passage, about 13 km (7 nautical miles) wide, between the Sinai and Arabian peninsulas which separate the Gulf of Aqaba from the Red Sea. **Eilat** is Israel's southernmost city, a busy port and popular resort located at the northern tip of the Gulf of Aqaba.

During the Egyptian blockade, Palestinian Arab fedayeen (Palestine Arab insurgents or guerillas) launched cross-border attacks on Israeli civilian areas and military outposts from Egypt, Jordan, and Syria. **Arab incursions and Israeli reprisals became a routine military operation.** In one year alone (1955)

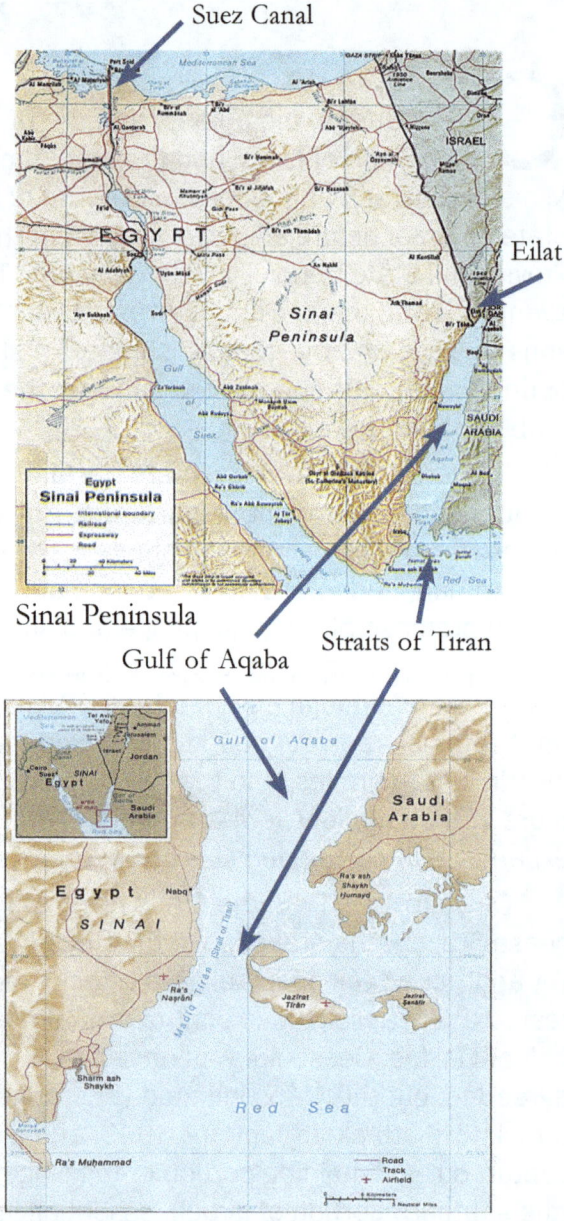

Sinai Peninsula

Straits of Tiran and Gulf of Aqaba

approximately 260 Israeli citizens were killed or wounded by the fedayeen. In July 1956, Egypt nationalized the Suez Canal jeopardizing shipping interests of Britain, France, and the U.S.

On October 29, 1956, Israel attacked Egyptian military positions, capturing the **Gaza Strip** and the **Sinai Peninsula**. On October 31, France and Britain joined the conflict and the fighting ended on November 5.

Results of the crisis: The U.S. pressured Israel to withdraw from captured Egyptian territory. United Nations (UN) forces were positioned along the Gulf of Aqaba and the Egyptian-Israeli border to prevent an Egyptian blockade and cross-border incursions by the fedayeen. In the following years, Egyptians and other surrounding Arab countries maintained a fragile truce.

> **Fedayeen** are Palestinian Arab guerillas who operate mainly against Israel. This guerilla group is not normally connected to an organized government or military and frequently operates in areas with little or no government control.

The Six Day War[4]
June 5-10, 1967

The **Six Day War**, also known as the **1967 Arab-Israeli War**, or **Third Arab-Israeli War**, was fought by Israel and surrounding Arab nations of Egypt, Jordan, and Syria. Following the 1956 conflict, relations between Israel and its Arab neighbors never stabilized and tensions only increased. In June 1967, Syria mobilized forces along the Golan Heights; Jordan mobilized along the east bank of the Jordan River; and Egypt mobilized along the Sinai border with Israel. **This was a united military confederacy of Egypt, Syria, and Jordan to drive Israel into the sea.**

On June 5, following a massive buildup of Arab forces along Israeli borders, Israel launched preemptive airstrikes against Egyptian airfields to the south and Syrian airfields to the north, giving the Israelis air superiority. Nasser of Egypt tried to convince Syria and Jordan to begin attacks on Israel to take some pressure off Egypt but it was too late. The Israelis launched a ground offensive into the Gaza strip which again caught the Egyptians by surprise—and the Egyptian leader, Gamal Abdel Nasser, ordered a retreat from the Sinai.

That same afternoon of June 5, Israel retaliated against Jordanian incursions into the west bank by surrounding East Jerusalem under command of Minister of Defense, Moshe Dayan. Israeli forces seized West Bank cities of Nablus and Bethlehem,

> A **preemptive airstrike** is an attempt to repel a perceived or impending invasion (based on military intelligence) in order to gain a strategic advantage.

> East Jerusalem came under Israeli control and includes the Old City and some of the holiest sites of Judaism, Christianity, and Islam, such as the Temple Mount, the Western Wall, Al-Aqsa Mosque, Dome of the Rock, and the Church of the Holy Sepulcher (traditional site of the crucifixion and the tomb of Jesus). The Palestinian Authority, the European Union, and the United Nations considered the West Bank and Jerusalem to be "occupied" by Israel.

and Jordanian forces were ordered by king Hussein to retreat back across the Jordan River. Israeli forces now occupied the entire West Bank without resistance.

Then on June 6 and 7, Israeli forces along the Sinai border continued westward in pursuit of retreating Egyptian forces. By June 7 the Israelis had reached the Suez Canal and control of the Sinai was achieved by June 8. On June 9, Dayan ordered a ground assault of the Golan Heights (northern front) against Syrian forces. Despite strong reinforcements, the Israelis overran the Syrian military and by June 10, Israeli forces had taken the Golan plateau and the Syrians retreated east.

On June 11 these Arab nations signed a ceasefire with Israel. Arab casualties were far heavier—less than a thousand Israelis killed compared to over 20,000 Arabs. Israel now had control of the Gaza Strip and the Sinai Peninsula (taken from Egypt), the West Bank and East Jerusalem (taken from Jordan), and the Golan Heights (taken from Syria). Areas of Israeli control had increased significantly (nearly tripled in size) which, in turn, enhanced Israel's overall defense.

The Arab world was humiliated by the "lightning-fast" rout of the Egyptian–Syrian–Jordanian alliance, and Israeli morale and international prestige dramatically increased, but the displacement of Arab civilians had long-term undesirable consequences. About 300,000 Palestinians fled the West Bank as refugees, about 110,000 Syrians left the Golan Heights, and about 10,000 Egyptians fled the Gaza Strip. These newly acquired territories became yet another cause of bitter conflict between Israel and the Arab world.

> The 1967 Six Day War was the fourth offensive, unprovoked attack on Israel by surrounding Arab nations: 1948 (2), 1949 (1) and 1967 (1).

Results of the war: Decisive Israeli victory. Territorial Changes: Israel captured the Gaza Strip and the Sinai Peninsula from Egypt, the entire West Bank (including East Jerusalem) from Jordan, and the Golan Heights from Syria.

Israel (West Bank, Golan Heights, and the Gaza Strip)

Golan Heights, *Photos by Roger Gallop, March 10, 2016*

Fulfillment of Bible Prophecy

Asaph, a prophet and leader (director) of King David's choir (1000 to 970 BC), told the Temple congregation of a time when Arab countries would conspire (form an alliance or confederation) to destroy Israel as a nation—see Psalm 83:1-18. He spoke of the conspiracy of nations, identifying the countries aligned against Israel, Israel's "lightning-fast" victory, and the humiliation of the proud Arabs.

" O God, do not remain silent; do not turn a deaf ear, do not stand aloof, O God. ²See how your enemies growl, how your foes rear their heads. ³With cunning they conspire against your people; they plot against those you cherish.

*[Arabs speaking] ⁴'Come,' they say, **'let us destroy them as a nation, so that Israel's name is remembered no more.*** [Israel's very existence is at stake] ⁵**With one mind they plot together; they form an alliance against you**— ⁶the tents of Edom and the Ishmaelites, of Moab and the Hagrites, ⁷Gebal, Ammon and Amalek, Philistia, with the people of Tyre. ⁸Even Assyria has joined them to reinforce Lot's descendants.*

[Jewish people pleading with God] ⁹Do to them as you did to Midian, as you did to Sisera and Jabin at the river Kishon, ¹⁰who perished at Endor and became like dung on the ground. ¹¹Make their nobles like Oreb and Zeeb, all their princes like Zebah and Zalmunna, ¹²who said, 'Let us take possession of the pasturelands of God.'

¹³Make them like tumbleweed, my God, like chaff before the wind. ¹⁴As fire consumes the forest or a flame sets the mountains ablaze, ¹⁵so pursue them with your tempest and terrify them with your storm. ¹⁶Cover their faces with shame, LORD, so that they will seek your name. ¹⁷May they ever be ashamed and dismayed; may they perish in disgrace. ¹⁸Let them know that you, whose name is the LORD—that you alone are the Most High over all the earth" (Psalm 83:2-18, NIV). [Bold added]

A. F. Kirkpatrick, a Bible scholar of the 19th century said, "History records no single occasion upon which the nations and tribes mentioned in the Psalms were united as a confederacy against Israel."⁵ This prophecy was fulfilled June 5-10, 1967.

Until June 1967 there were always disunity and different ethnic factions amongst the Arabs. Even during the War of Independence, unprovoked attacks by Arab countries (May 1948, June 1948, and January 1949) were with dissention and disagreement. Disunity goes all the way back to Genesis 16:12, when an angel of the Lord described Ishmael to Hagar (Egyptian handmaiden of Sari and concubine to Abram; see chapter 2, Abraham and His Sons Isaac and Ishmael): *"He will be a **wild donkey of a man; his hand will be against everyone and everyone's hand against him, and he will live in hostility toward all his brothers"*** (Genesis 16:12, NIV). This is exactly what we see today—continual ethnic fighting and conflicts amongst the Arabs and between the Arabs and Israel.

In Psalm 83 the prophet Asaph (1000 to 970 BC) predicted a confederacy of Arab nations and a swift, dramatic Israeli victory which included occupation of the Old City, Jerusalem. About 2,900 years after the United Kingdom and the construction of the

First Temple by King Solomon (970 BC – 930 BC); about 2,553 years after the destruction of the City and the First Temple; and 1,897 years after the Romans destroyed the City of Jerusalem and the Second Temple (AD 70), the ancient City was once again in the hands of the Jewish people. Prior to the 1967 war, the beloved and ancient Jerusalem seemed unattainable to the Jewish people.

> During the war, the population of the Arabs was about 110 million, compared to Israel's 2.5 million (44:1 ratio), and the Arabs had a significant superiority of weapons. Egypt lost approximately 20,000 men, Jordan 6,000, Syria 800, and Israel 700.
>
> This quick and devastating defeat of the Arabs by the vastly fewer Israeli soldiers, while the world looked on, greatly shamed the Arab confederacy as foretold in Psalm 83:16-18. The war lasted only 6 days, and it is one of Israel's most celebrated victories.

Israelis Are Aware of Bible Prophecy

Yes, most Jewish people in Israel and throughout much of the world are aware of Old Testament prophecies and end time events being fulfilled this day in history (1948 and 1967), and **they await the most significant event promised in Scriptures—the coming of their Messiah**—a conquering King who will rule the world from Jerusalem. During the wars of 1956 and 1967, Israeli radio broadcasted the words of the Lord through Amos:

> *"...and I will bring my people Israel back from exile. They will rebuild the ruined cities and live in them. They will plant vineyards and drink their wine; they will make gardens and eat their fruit. I will plant Israel in their own land, never again to be uprooted from the land I have given them, says the LORD your God"* (Amos 9:14-15, NIV).

Devout Jews (and many within the Christian church) recognize that certain significant events (those that occurred on May 14, 1948, and during June 5-10, 1967) are **necessary before the appearance of the Messiah**. (Jerusalem became the capital of Israel on January 23, 1950, under a resolution passed by the Israeli Knesset although Jerusalem was not under Israeli control at that time.)

While scattered throughout the world for almost 2,000 years, the Jews knew **the coming of the Messiah could not occur until the State of Israel occupied their homeland** (Land of Israel, the Holy Land, the Promised Land) **and possessed their ancient City and the Temple site as God's chosen people** (Deuteronomy 7:6-9, NIV)[6]—events that seemed utterly hopeless and impossible prior to 1948. (See Scripture in chapter 6, God's Chosen People and Prophecy Fulfilled.)

The City of Jerusalem
The Temple Mount and the Western Wall

How old is **Jerusalem** and how did the City become holy? We know that Jerusalem is at least as old as Abraham (2166 BC to 1991 BC). The Bible mentions that for a brief time there was a connection between the City and Abraham through his meeting with Melchizedek, the king of Salem (shortened name for Jerusalem). (See Genesis 14:18-20; Psalm 76:2; Hebrews 7:1-2.)

> **Melchizedek** (translated as "my king is righteous") was a **king and priest** who blessed Abram in chapter 14 of Genesis (c. 2000 BC). In Christianity, according to Hebrews 2, Christ is identified as a priest forever in the order of Melchizedek—so Jesus assumes the role of High Priest forever.

Later in the time of Joshua and Judges (c. 1406 BC), we see that Jerusalem was strongly defended by Jebusites, a Canaanite tribe who fortified and inhabited Jerusalem prior to its conquest by King David. The area was considered inhospitable, and Israelites did not want to stay overnight (Judges 19:10-12). Jebusites maintained control of Jerusalem until David overran the hilltop fortress (c. 1003 BC). Jerusalem's sanctification (dedication) began with David (c. 1010 BC – 970 BC). See maps at the end of this section.

The **Temple Mount** is one of the most important religious sites in the City of Jerusalem. This site has been used for thousands of years by the three primary religions: Judaism (c. 1003 BC), Christianity (c. 32 AD), and Islam (c. 500 AD). The present site is dominated by three Muslim buildings from the early Umayyad period (AD 661 – AD 750): Dome of the Rock (AD 685 – AD 691), Dome of the Chain (AD 691), and al-Aqsa Mosque (AD 705, rebuilt AD 754, 780).[7] See maps at the end of section.

With the return of the Jewish people from the four corners of the world following the national restoration of Israel on May 14, 1948, the Jews made their first pilgrimage to Jerusalem to view the Western Wall and the Temple Mount exactly a week following its capture on June 11, 1967. Just a few weeks later, Israel's parliament (the Knesset) passed legislation placing **Jerusalem under permanent Israeli military control**. The Jews then converged on the Wailing Wall and the Temple Mount, the site of the Second Temple (516 BC) and Solomon's Temple (957 BC).[8]

> The **Western Wall** or **Wailing Wall** is located in the Old City of Jerusalem at the the west side (south end of Temple site) of the area known as the Temple Mount (known to Muslims as Haram al-Sharif). The Temple site is the holiest site in Judaism and is the place where Jews turn during their daily prayer—and the Western Wall is the second most sacred site.
>
> The wall that surrounded the Temple Mount and the Second Temple was restored by Herod the Great (c. 37 BC - 1 BC). (See chapter 4, The Life and Ministry of Jesus Christ.) Later, it was Herod Antipas (c. 4 BC - 39 BC) who ruled Galilee during the time of John the Baptist and the ministry and crucifixion of Jesus.
>
> The Western Wall was all that was left after the destruction of Jerusalem by the Romans in AD 70. The City and Temple walls were rebuilt by the Ottoman Empire in the 16th century. See chapter 5, Ottoman Empire, for more information.
>
> **Today, Jerusalem and the Temple Mount are under Israeli military control, but the Temple site is policed by the Islamic Wakf (Waqf), a joint Palestinian-Jordanian religious body.** The area attracts daily crowds of worshipers of all faiths.

Muslim al-Aqsa Mosque
Photo by Roger Gallop, March 14, 2016

Eastern Wall and Dome of the Rock

Muslim Dome of the Rock
Photos by Roger Gallop, March 14, 2016

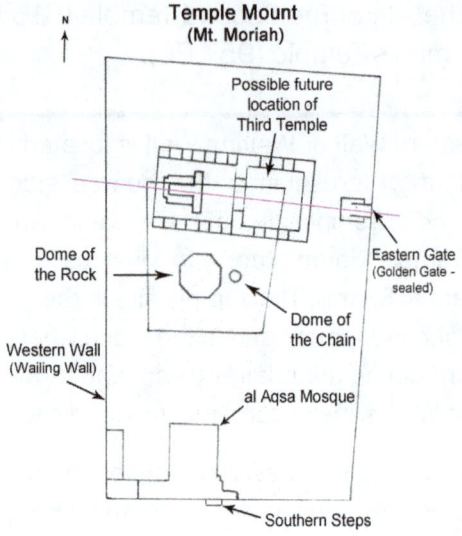

Sketch of approximate future location of Third Temple in relation to Dome of the Rock. Note the temple is directly in line with the Eastern Gate (Golden Gate). See maps at end of section.
Sketch by Roger Gallop

Western Wall (Wailing Wall)
Photo by Roger Gallop, March 14, 2016

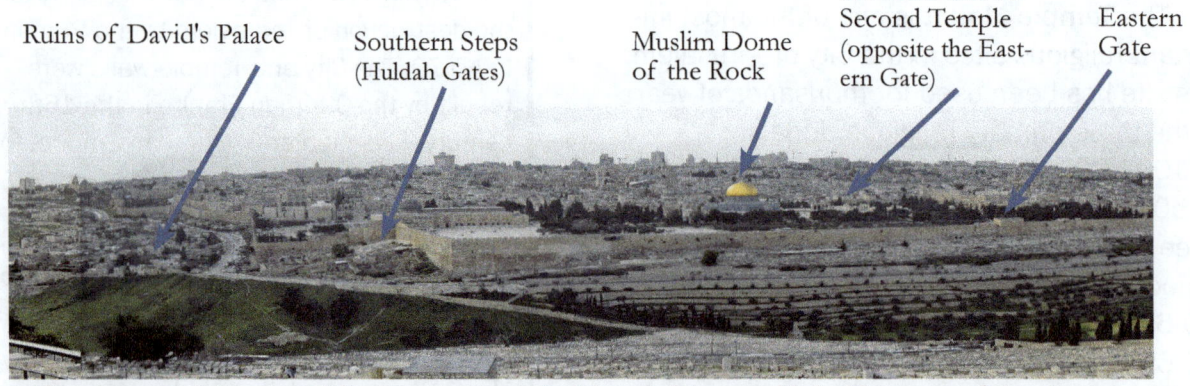

Looking from the Mount of Olives west across the Temple Mount with its Eastern and Southern Walls, Dome of the Rock to right center, al-Asqa mosque just right of the Huldah Gates, Kidron Valley in the foreground, and ruins of King David's palace to the left. *Photo by Roger Gallop, March 14, 2016*

Jerusalem is located 14 miles west of the Dead Sea, 33 miles east of the Mediterranean, and is situated on a rocky plateau at an elevation of 2,550 feet and about 3,800 feet above the level of the Dead Sea (1,250 feet below sea level).

As shown on the maps (following page), Mount Zion is a hill in Jerusalem just outside the walls of the Old City. The term Mount Zion has been used in the Hebrew Bible for the City of David (2 Samuel 5:7; 1 Chronicles 11:5; 1 Kings 8:1; 2 Chronicles 5:2), but more commonly it refers successively to three locations:

1) Lower Eastern Hill was the name of the "Jebusite fortress" that was conquered by King David c. 1003 BC, then renamed the "City of David" where he built his palace,

2) later expanded northward to the top of the Eastern Hill where King Solomon built the First Temple, The Temple Mount, and

3) then later, it again expanded to the Western Hill separated from the lower Eastern Hill by the Tyropoeon Valley. The Western Hill became more dominate by the first century because of population growth and (by that time) the lost palace of King David. The Western Hill is what today is called Mount Zion.

> **Jerusalem was totally destroyed two times:**
>
> The Babylonians under King Nebuchadnezzar destroyed the city almost completely in 586 BC. Upon the return of the Jews from Babylonian captivity 70 years later (516 BC), they began a rebuilding program of Jerusalem and the Temple.
>
> Ironically, the tyrant Herod the Great (c. 37 BC - 1 BC), the person who plotted to kill the baby Jesus, had begun a rebuilding program which included palaces, citadels, a theatre and an amphitheatre, bridges and public monuments to elevate his importance in the eyes of Rome.
>
> For more on the reign of Herod and the timing of his death of 1 BC, see chapter 4, The Life and Ministry of Jesus Christ.
>
> Following the rejection and crucifixion of the Messiah Jesus (AD 32), Jerusalem's second total destruction was by the Roman Empire in AD 70. This terrible devastation included the brutal killing of men, women, and children, and worldwide exile of the remaining Jewish people.

Southern Steps, 1st Century Stairs of Ascent. The primary entrance to the Temple Mount through the Huldah Gates, now blocked by al-Aqsa Mosque. Jesus once walked and taught on these steps. *Photo by Roger Gallop, March 14, 2016*

Model of the Second Temple located at Israel Museum, Jerusalem

World in Denial - Defiant Nature of Mankind

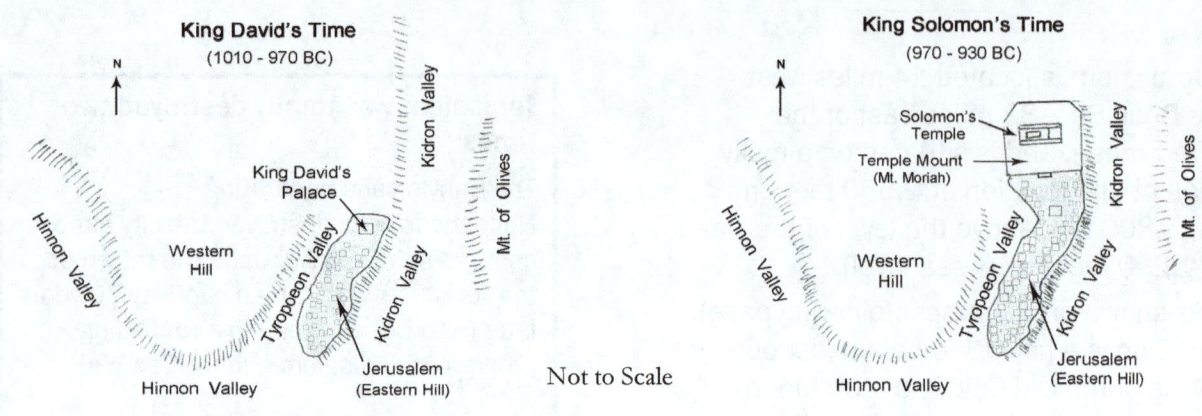

City of Jerusalem - 1st Century BC and Present Day

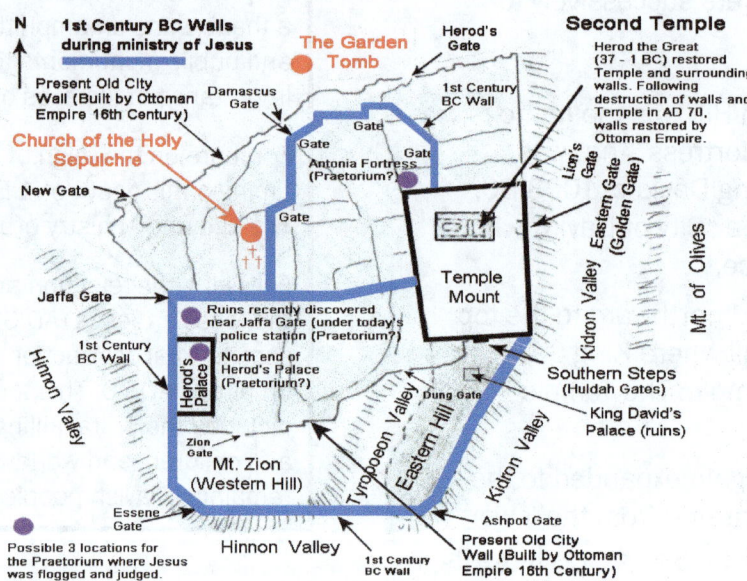

Dark blue lines - 1st century BC walls (time of Jesus)
Light blue lines - Present Day Old City Walls

Temple Mount is trapezoidal in shape, about 976 ft x 1571 ft, or about 35.2 acres.

City of Jerusalem - Present Day

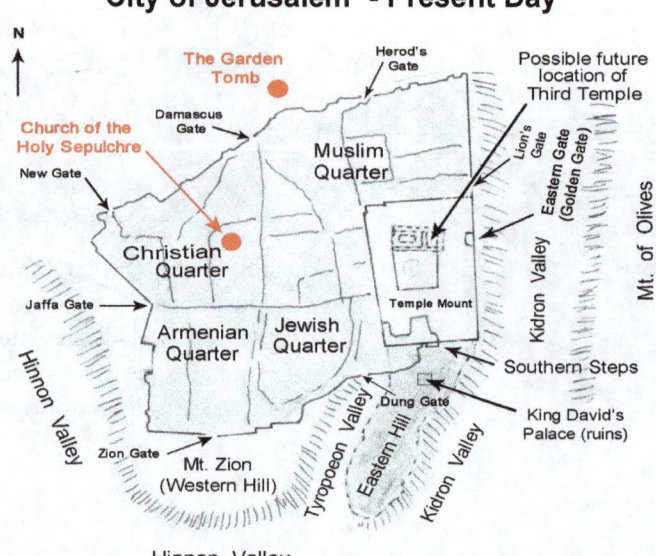

Sketches by Roger Gallop

1973 Yom Kippur War[9]
October 6 - 25, 1973

On October 6, 1973, Syria and Egypt (see text box) launched yet another **unprovoked attack** (sixth since 1948) on Israeli positions in the Golan Heights and the Sinai Peninsula, land occupied by Israel since the 1967 Six Day War. The attack began on Yom Kippur, the holiest day in Judaism (which coincided that year with the Muslim holy month of Ramadan). This conflict is known as the **Yom Kippur War, Ramadan War** (also known as the 1973 Arab–Israeli War).

> At least ten other Arab states (Iraq, Saudi Arabia, Kuwait, Libya, Algeria, Tunisia, Sudan, Morocco, Lebanon, and Jordan including Palestinian Arabs) supported the Egyptian-Syrian forces with military personnel, equipment, and financial backing.

> **Yom Kippur**, also known as Day of Atonement, is probably the most important day of the year for the Jewish people. Central themes are centered on **atonement and repentance** because, according to custom, it is during this time that God decides the fate of each person, so Jews ask for forgiveness of sins, and they are encouraged to make amends. **Ramadan** is the ninth month of the Islamic calendar; Muslims observe this as a month of fasting.

Egyptian and Syrian forces crossed the 1967 ceasefire lines into the Sinai Peninsula and Golan Heights, respectively. The purpose of the invasion was to regain territory lost to Israel in the 1967 Six Day War. In the Golan Heights the Syrians initially made headway into Israeli territory, but within just a few days Israeli forces pushed the Syrians back to the original ceasefire lines, and in the Sinai Israeli forces stopped the advancing Egyptian forces in days.

The Egyptian army tried another offensive but the Israelis counter-attacked, crossed the Suez Canal into Egypt, and advanced south and west during a week of fighting. On October 22 a UN brokered ceasefire failed, and by October 24 the Israelis had surrounded Egypt's army and the city of Suez. Another UN ceasefire was imposed on October 25 that ended the war.

Results of the war: Israeli military victory. Territorial Changes: The Egyptian army occupied the eastern coast of the Suez Canal, the Israeli army occupied the Sinai and territory along the southwestern coast of the Suez within 100 km of Cairo, and the Israeli army occupied five hundred square kilometers atop the Golan Heights.

Golan Heights, Valley of Tears
Photos by Roger Gallop, March 10, 2016

Camp David Accords and Return of the Sinai to Egypt
1978 and 1982

Israel captured the Gaza Strip and Sinai Peninsula from Egypt in the 1967 Six Day War. Military victories by Israel in 1973 resulted in the subsequent peace process—the 1978 Camp David Accords that led to the return of the Sinai to Egypt in 1982 and, in turn, Egypt recognized Israel as a sovereign nation.

> The Camp David Accords were signed by Egyptian President Anwar El Sadat and Israeli Prime Minister Menachem Begin on September 17, 1978, following twelve days of negotiations at Camp David.

But other occupied territories (Gaza Strip, West Bank, and Golan Heights) remained a cause for continued conflict between Israel and Palestinian Arabs and the rest of the Arab world.

While at Mount Sinai, God told Moses and the Jewish people: *"I will fix your boundary from the Red Sea to the sea of the Philistines, and from the wilderness to the River Euphrates: for I will deliver the inhabitants of the land into your hand, and **you will drive them out before you. You shall make no covenant with them or with their gods.** They shall not live in your land...."* (Exodus 23:31-33, NIV). [Bold added]

In Exodus 23:31-33 (NIV), **God commanded Israel not to surrender its 'land of promise' to other people or nations, but now it appears that Israel has violated the long-standing Mosaic covenant.** See section, **Surrendering Land for Peace**, for more information.

1982 Lebanon Crisis
1982 - 2000

The **1982 Lebanon Crisis**, called **Operation Peace for Galilee** by Israel, and later known in Israel as the Lebanon War, began on June 6, 1982. Following attacks and counter-attacks between the **Palestine Liberation Organization (PLO)** in southern Lebanon and the Israeli Defense Forces (IDF) with civilian casualties on both sides, and the attempted assassination of the Israeli ambassador to Britain (UK), the IDF invaded southern Lebanon on June 6, 1982.[10] See next section, Oslo Accords, and glossary for more information about the PLO.

The offensive by the IDF was supposed to be a short-term operation to eliminate the continual unprovoked attacks by the PLO on northern Israel.[11] The operation was meant

> Israel invaded Lebanon because of an attempt to assassinate Israel's ambassador to Britain (UK). Prime Minister Menachem Begin blamed the PLO, and the Israelis treated the incident as *casus belli*—**an act that provokes or justifies war.**

to destroy PLO infrastructure (suspected terrorist strongholds, tunnels, and entry points into Israel) and artillery positions used to attack Israeli communities and IDF defensive positions.

After the 1982 incursion, Israel occupied a strip of south Lebanon with the help of the Maronite-Christian dominated South Lebanon Army (SLA), an ally of Israel.

The PLO was eventually expelled from Lebanon with diplomatic support from the United States.

Hezbollah, a paramilitary force funded by Iran, waged a guerilla campaign against the SLA and the Israeli occupation of south Lebanon. The SLA eventually collapsed, and Israel had to withdraw from Lebanon in May 2000.

> **Maronites** are an ethno-religious group located in the Levant (eastern Mediterranean). They derive their name from the Syriac Christian Saint Maron whose followers migrated to the area of Mount Lebanon from the area of Antioch, establishing the Maronite Church. Maronites maintained their Christian religion and their distinctive Aramaic language.

Results of the crisis: Israeli strategic failure. The PLO was expelled from Lebanon, collapse of the Maronite-Israeli alliance, failure to achieve Lebanese-Israeli peace, increased Syrian political influence in Lebanon, and continued conflict between Israel and PLO/Hezbollah over South Lebanon.

> **South Lebanon Army** or **South Lebanese Army (SLA)** was a Maronite-Christian dominated Lebanese militia during the Lebanese Civil War (1975 - 1990) which split from the Army of Free Lebanon. After 1979, the SLA operated in southern Lebanon and was supported by Israel during the 1982–2000 South Lebanon conflict to fight against the Palestine Liberation Organization (PLO) and Hezbollah.

> **Palestine Liberation Organization (PLO)**—see defintion in next section and in the glossary.
>
> **Hezbollah** is a Shi'a Islamist paramilitary group and political party based in Lebanon. It was conceived by Muslim Iranian clerics and funded by Iran following the Israeli invasion of Lebanon in 1982 and was primarily formed to oppose or resist Israel.
>
> **Paramilitary** is a semi-military force similar to those of a professional military but not included as part of the state's formal armed forces. Hezbollah's leaders were followers of Ayatollah Khomeini, and its forces were trained and organized by Iranian Revolutionary Guards with consent of the Syrian government.

The Oslo Accords
1993 - 1995

Oslo Accords are a set of agreements between Israel and the **Palestine Liberation Organization (PLO)**: the Oslo I Accord, signed in Washington, D.C., on September 13, 1993; follow-up was completed with the Gaza-Jericho agreement of May 4, 1994; and the Oslo II Accord, signed in Taba (small Egyptian town near the northern tip of the Gulf of Aqaba) in 1995.

This was the start of a peace process with the goal of achieving peace based on UN Security Council Resolutions 242 and 338. The PLO recognized Israel's right to exist in peace and rejected "violence and terrorism"—and in response, Israel officially recognized the PLO as the representative of the Palestinian people.[12]

Pursuant to the **Oslo Accords** signed in 1993 and 1994, the **Palestinian Authority (PA)** became the "provisional administrative body" of Arab Palestinian population centers while Israel controlled the airspace, territorial waters, and border crossings (with the exception of the border with Egypt).

In 1994, despite continuous Arab Palestinian aggression toward Israel, Israel granted Palestinians living in the Gaza Strip the "right to self-govern through the PA." But instead of creating a peace-time commercial and residential infrastructure designed for economic prosperity, the Gaza strip became the staging ground for continued terrorist incursions and rocket attacks on Israel by the PLO.

Palestine Liberation Organization (PLO) was founded in 1964 with the purpose of "liberating Palestine" through armed struggle. It is headquartered in Ramallah, West Bank, and recognized as the "sole legitimate representative of the Palestinian people" by over 100 countries with which the PLO has diplomatic relations, and has had "observer status" at the United Nations since 1974.[13]

The PLO was considered by the United States and Israel to be a terrorist group until the **Madrid Conference in 1991**. This was a peace conference hosted by Spain and supported by the United States and the Soviet Union in an attempt by the international community to revive the Israeli-Palestinian peace process, involving Israel, the Palestinian Arabs, as well as Arab countries such as Jordan, Lebanon, and Syria.[14]

In 1993, the PLO recognized Israel's right to exist in peace, accepted UN Security Council Resolutions 242 and 338, and rejected "violence and terrorism"; and in response, Israel recognized the PLO as the representative of the Palestinian people.

What is the difference between the PLO and the PA? The PLO is recognized internationally as the "representative of the [Arab] Palestinian people." The **Palestinian Authority** (PA) is a "temporary (provisional) administrative body" of Arab population centers established as a result of the Gaza-Jericho Agreement of May 4, 1994 (follow-up treaty to the Oslo I Accord detailing Palestinian autonomy). The PA was only supposed to have lasted for 5 years—and its leaders were mostly **Fatah** members, the largest faction of the PLO. (See section, The Gaza Wars, for the difference between **Hamas and Fatah**.)

Israel Disengages from Gaza and Parts of the West Bank
2005

The Gaza Strip

In 2003 Prime Minister Ariel Sharon proposed complete disengagement from the Gaza Strip. This was adopted by the Israeli government in June 2004, approved by the Knesset (legislative branch of the Israeli government) in February 2005, and enacted in August 2005.

Disengagement meant withdrawal of the Israeli army and the dismantling of all Israeli settlements. Why did the Israelis disengage from Gaza? They disengaged as **an act of appeasement and reconciliation in hopes of bringing about a lasting peace.**

Israeli residents in Gaza who refused to accept government reimbursement by voluntarily vacating their homes prior to the deadline of August 15, 2005, were summarily evicted by Israeli security forces in just a few days. The eviction of Israeli residents and evacuation of security personnel was completed by September 12, 2005. This land had been occupied by Israel since the Six Day War (June 5–10, 1967).[15]

> Gaza Strip is a region on the eastern coast of the Mediterranean Sea that borders Egypt on the southwest for 11 kilometers (6.8 mi) and Israel on the east and north along a 51 km (32 mi) border. Gaza is part of the current Palestinian territory.[16] (Palestinian territory also includes parts of the West Bank.)

The West Bank and Golan Heights

In August 2005, Israel handed over the Gaza Strip and four settlements in northern West Bank to the Arab Palestinians, again as an act of appeasement and reconciliation.

Although these settlements were evacuated, Israel considers all of Jerusalem to be its capital and sovereign territory. Israel kept the Golan Heights for security reasons.

Surrendering Land for Peace
1982 and 2005

Israel disengaged from the Sinai Peninsula in 1982 and then handed over all of the Gaza Strip and part of the West Bank to the Palestinians in 2005—as acts of appeasement to the Arabs in hopes of bringing about a lasting peace. But with such concessions, Israel became the **first country in modern history to surrender territory acquired in a "defensive war." Ultimately, the Arabs viewed such concessions as weakness by the Israelis—and so they continued their aggression.**

Consider the following verses given to Moses (as previously mentioned). While at Mount Sinai, God told Moses and the Jewish people: *"I will fix your boundary from the Red Sea to the sea of the Philistines, and from the wilderness to the River Euphrates: for I will deliver the inhabitants of the land into your hand, and **you will drive them out before you. You shall make no covenant with them or with their gods.** They shall not live in your land...."* (Exodus 23:31-33, NIV). [Bold added]

> All previous wars (1948 (2), 1949 (1), 1967 (1), and 1973 (1)) were initiated by Arabs in an effort to destroy Israel—to drive Israel and the Jewish people into the (Mediterranean) Sea because of their everlasting hatred. For information on this subject, see chapter 2, The Seed of Everlasting Hatred.
>
> Between 1948 and 1997, 20,093 Israeli soldiers were killed in combat, 75,000 Israelis were wounded, and nearly 100,000 Israelis were considered disabled army veterans.[17]

In these verses, **God commanded Israel not to surrender its promised land to other people or nations**, but now it appears that Israel has once again violated the long-standing Mosaic covenant, and Israel continues to suffer the consequences of their decision of appeasement and ignoring God's command.[18]

2006 Lebanon War[19]
July 12 - August 14, 2006

The **2006 Lebanon War** (also called the **2006 Israel – Hezbollah War**) was a military conflict between Hezbollah paramilitary forces and the Israeli military in Lebanon, northern Israel, and the Golan Heights. The Iranians provided Hezbollah with military and financial support before and during the war.

On July 12, 2006, Hezbollah militants based in Lebanon conducted a cross-border raid on an Israeli military patrol in Israel. Using rockets fired into several Israeli towns as a diversion, Hezbollah militants crossed from Lebanon into Israel and ambushed two Israeli Army vehicles, killing three soldiers and abducting two others. In a failed rescue attempt of the two abducted soldiers another five Israeli soldiers were killed inside Lebanese territory.

> **Hezbollah** is a Shi'a Islamist paramilitary group and political party based in Lebanon. It was conceived by Muslim Iranian clerics and funded by Iran following the Israeli invasion of Lebanon in 1982 and was primarily formed to oppose Israel. See section, 1982 Lebanon War, for more information.

Hezbollah demanded the release of Lebanese militants held by Israel in exchange for the release of the two abducted soldiers. Israel refused and the IDF launched a large-scale military campaign into southern Lebanon. Israel attacked Hezbollah strongholds imbedded in Lebanese civilian infrastructure, including Beirut's Rafic Hariri International Airport. Israel also imposed an air and naval blockade but Hezbollah continued to launch more rockets into Israel and engage in guerrilla warfare with the IDF.

The conflict continued until a United Nations brokered ceasefire went into effect on August 14, 2006, though Israel did not lift its naval blockade until September 8. The conflict is believed to have killed about 1,200 Lebanese people and 165 Israelis. It severely damaged Lebanese residential and commercial infrastructure and displaced about one million Lebanese and at least 300,000 Israelis.

> Two years later, on July 16, 2008, the bodies of the two abducted soldiers were returned to Israel by Hezbollah in exchange for a convicted, notorious terrorist, murderer, and kidnapper and four other Hezbollah prisoners.

Results of the war: Military stalemate. A ceasefire was enacted through UN Resolution 1701. The Lebanese Army was introduced into South Lebanon, and UNIFIL (United Nations Interim Force in Lebanon) was reinforced.

The Gaza Wars

In 2006 Hamas won a majority in the Palestinian Authority (PA) legislative elections and then refused to accept any previous agreements the PA made with Israel, leading Hamas to withdraw from the PA and govern Gaza independently of the PA. In November 2012, Fatah controlled the PA which was renamed the State of Palestine after the UN voted to recognize Palestine as a non-member UN observer state.[20] In recent years these rival Palestinian factions, Fatah and Hamas, have tried some form of reconciliation and unity government with little success. (See text box for information about Palestinian Authority, Fatah, and Hamas; see glossary.)

The Gaza Wars are three conflicts between **Israel and Hamas.** Hamas controls Palestinian territory in the Gaza Strip, located on the Mediterranean Sea that borders Egypt and Israel.

The **Palestinian Authority (PA)** is a provisional administrative body of Arab population centers. For background information, see section, The Oslo Accords (1993 - 1995).

Fatah is the political and military organization of the PLO founded in the late 1950s by Yasser Arafat and Khalīl al-Wazīr with the mission of overthrowing the state of Israel using guerrilla warfare and forming a Palestine Arab state. Fatah is a more moderate party (as compared with Hamas) and currently controls parts of the West Bank.

Hamas is a Palestinian Islamist political organization and militant group that has waged war on Israel since 1987 through suicide bombings and rocket attacks. Hamas seeks the destruction of Israel and replacing Israel with a Palestinian state. **Hamas governs Gaza** (independent of the Fatah-controlled PA), and it is the **primary catalyst for aggression against Israel.**[21]

First Gaza Conflict
2008 - 2009

The Gaza conflict of **Operation Cast Lead** was in response to **Hamas continually launching rockets into Israel from Gaza**. Israeli forces attacked police stations, military targets including weapons stockpiles and rocket-launch positions, but unfortunately, these targets were located by Hamas in densely populated areas resulting in heavy civilian Palestinian casualties. The conflict ended in a unilateral ceasefire. Israel's stated goal was to stop rocket fire into Israel and weapons smuggling.

Second Gaza Conflict
2012

The Gaza conflict of **Operation Pillar of Defense** was an eight-day Israeli Defense Force (IDF) operation which began in response to **Hamas launching hundreds of rockets into Israel** during a 24-hour period in November 2012. The operation commenced with the targeted killing of the commander of Hamas's military-terrorist faction followed by air strikes on stockpiles of Iranian-supplied long range rockets. The Israeli government stated that the goal of the military operation was to stop rocket attacks against civilian targets and to disrupt the capabilities of militant organizations. Hamas cited the blockade (land, sea, and air) of the Gaza Strip and occupation of the East and West Banks as reasons for their attacks.[22]

Third Gaza Conflict
2014

The Gaza conflict of **Operation Protective Edge** was an effort to stop **continual, escalating bombardment of rockets into Israeli cities**. After 10 days of airstrikes against Hamas strongholds, Israel failed to curb the rocket attacks. Consequently, Israeli tanks moved into northern Gaza on July 8, 2014. This seven-week ground operation (July 8, 2014 – August 26, 2014) **focused on destroying Hamas strongholds and miles of concrete reinforced tunnels constructed deep inside Israeli territory**. Although Israel considered reoccupation of the coastal territory, they withdrew after completing their objective.

Blame for this conflict is placed directly on Hamas—and on Iran for providing Hamas with funding and military supplies (as they did with Hezbollah in Lebanon; see section 1982 Lebanon War and 2006 Lebanon War). **This conflict was due to the avowed commitment of Hamas to destroy Israel; the unending rocket and missile barrages into Israel** (numbering in tens of thousands of rockets over two years); **the construction of dozens of fortified concrete 'terror tunnels' from Gaza into Israel; maniacal use of innocent families and their children to shield its rocket launchers, arsenals, and command centers**—all of which has caused untold misery and sorrow in Gaza and Israel.[23]

Conclusion

Since 1948 the tiny nation of Israel has defended itself each time it was attacked, and Israel won each and every time. This included 1948-1949 (3), 1967 (1), 1973 (1), 2006 (1), and the Gaza Wars of 2008-2009, 2012, and 2014 (3), or a total of nine. (The 1956 Sinai and Suez Crisis and 1982 Lebanon War are not included in this tally.)

While fighting for its very survival against an overwhelming number of Arabs, the Israeli army withdrew from most of the areas it captured (Sinai Peninsula, Gaza, and parts of the West Bank) as acts of appeasement and reconciliation in hopes of a lasting peace. The return of land acquired in a "defensive war" is unprecedented in world history. The Golan Heights remains in Israeli hands because it is needed for Israeli safety and security.

> In attempts at a peace plan between Israel and the Arabs, **the United States administration failed to understand or comprehend that the sons of Ishmael (Arabs) do not want compromise—they want Israel completely eliminated.** See chapters 9 and 10, Decline of the United States.

The fact of the matter is, the Sovereign God of the Holy Bible is protecting Israel. The hand of God is on the Jewish people and the State of Israel through a Divine irrevocable covenant with Abraham and reaffirmed with Issac, Jacob, and Moses. The true, Sovereign God exiled the Jewish people worldwide for their continual disobedience, contempt, and idolatry (for continual defiance and turning away from the true God) during Old Testament times and for rejecting the Messiah and Savior, Jesus Christ (AD 29 – AD 32). But the Lord God, Creator of the heavens and the earth, miraculously restored the State of Israel in just one day following worldwide exile as foretold in Bible prophecy (see chapter 6, Miraculous Rebirth of the State of Israel).

What are the odds of a Jewish state and control of the City of Jerusalem after worldwide exile for almost 2,000 years? **The answer is Zero without Divine intervention. If a person does not believe this, then that person simply chooses not to believe.** The world and its world leaders, especially many in the United States, do not seem to understand, comprehend or believe the reality of God of the Holy Bible.

Only a Divine miracle could bring about the restoration of the State of Israel (May 14, 1948) and the repossession of the ancient City of Jerusalem **(June 5–10, 1967), their ancient capital.** It is obvious the hand of God is on Israel, so the question people should be asking, "are we fast approaching the End Times as foretold in the Bible?" **The answer is Yes, but *much of the world seems oblivious and uncaring—many denying the truth of Jesus Christ and the signs of the times.***

notes: **Chapter 7**

1. DeLoach, C. (1974). *Seeds of Conflict.* NJ: Plainfield, Logos International, 18-20; and personal notes, 7.

2. Arab League and the Arab-Israeli Conflict; as cited in https://en.wikipedia.org/wiki/Arab_League_and_the_Arab%E2%80%93Israeli_conflict.

3. Anti-Defamation League. Retrieved from The 1956 Sinai Campaign, http://archive.adl.org/israel/record/sinai.html.

4. Six Day War. Retrieved from http://en.wikipedia.org/wiki/Six-Day_War.

5. Kirkpatrick, A.F., *The Book of Psalms.* The University Press, 1897, Vol. I, p. 499; as cited in DeLoach, C. (1974), op. cit., chapter 8; and personal notes, p. 13.

6. Personal notes, 25.

7. Temple Mount. Retrieved January 2016, from https://en.wikipedia.org/wiki/Temple_Mount.

8. Personal notes, 17.

9. Yom Kippur War. Retrieved January 2016, from https://en.wikipedia.org/wiki/Yom_Kippur_War.

10. 1982 Lebanon War. Retrieved January 2016, from https://en.wikipedia.org/wiki/1982_Lebanon_War.

11. The Lebanon War (1982). Retrieved January 2016, from http://www.ynetnews.com/articles/0,7340,L-3631005,00.html.

12. Oslo Accords. Retrieved January 2016, from https://en.wikipedia.org/wiki/Oslo_Accords.

13. Palestine Liberation Organization. Retrieved January 2016, from https://en.wikipedia.org/wiki/Palestine_Liberation_Organization.

14. Madrid Conference of 1991. Retrieved January 2016, from https://en.wikipedia.org/wiki/Madrid_Conference_of_1991.

15. Israeli Disengagement from Gaza. Retrieved January 2016, from https://en.wikipedia.org/wiki/Israeli_disengagement_from_Gaza.

16. Gaza Strip. Retrieved January 2016, from https://en.wikipedia.org/wiki/Gaza_Strip.

17. Israeli Casualties of War. Retrieved January 2016, from https://en.wikipedia.org/wiki/Israeli_casualties_of_war.

18. The PBI, 1425 Lachman Lane, Pacific Palisades, CA 90272; as cited in http://www.heraldmag.org/2006/06nd_13.htm.

19. 2006 Lebanon War. Retrieved January 2016, from http://en.wikipedia.org/wiki/2006_Lebanon_War.

20. Palestinian National Authority. Retrieved January 2016, from http://en.wikipedia.org/wiki/Palestinian_National_Authority; and http://www.vox.com/cards/israel-palestine/hamas; and Hamas. Retrieved January 2016, from https://en.wikipedia.org/wiki/Hamas; and Fatah. Retrieved January 2016, from https://en.wikipedia.org/wiki/Fatah.

21. Ibid.

22. Operation Pillar of Defense. Retrieved January 2016, from http://en.wikipedia.org/wiki/Operation_Pillar_of_Defense.

23. Hal Lindsey (August 1, 2014). The Hal Lindsey Report, News from Hal Lindsey Media Ministries. (www.hallindsey.org); and Coughlin, Con (April 21, 2015). Iran Rekindles Relations with Hamas, The Wall Street Journal; as cited in http://www.wsj.com/articles/iran-rekindles-relations-with-hamas-1429658562.

Chapter 8

Prophetic Super Signs Before the Seven Year Tribulation

> *"I will make you into a great nation, and I will bless you; I will make your name great, and you will be a blessing. I will bless those who bless you, and whoever curses you I will curse; and all peoples on earth will be blessed through you."* —Genesis 12:2-3, NIV

This chapter provides a summary of significant end time prophetic events found in the Bible—but it does not attempt to list and describe in detail all such events. There are **six super signs** indicating we are in the times just before the start of the seven year tribulation:

- Rebirth of the State of Israel (1948) after the Jewish people endured almost 2,000 years of worldwide dispersion;

- Repossession of the City of Jerusalem (1967) by the State of Israel;

- State of Israel surrounded by hostile Arab nations;

- Increase in arrogance, immorality and lawlessness worldwide (with no normal sense of right or wrong);

- Rise of Russia and its alliance with Iran and other Muslim states; and

- Modern transportation and increase in knowledge and technology (travel to and fro and use of supercomputers).

The first two are essential prerequisites to end time Bible prophecy (eschatology) and point to the soon coming of the rapture of the church and seven year tribulation. These are perhaps the most amazing of these super signs.

There are many excellent books by Bible scholars on the subject of eschatology and signs of the end time. Some of these authors include Jack Van Impe, Hal Lindsey, Tim LaHaye and Thomas Ice, John C. Hagee, David Jeremiah, Mark Hitchcock, and Chuck Missler, just to name a few.

> **End time** (also called **end times, end of time, end of days, last days, final days**) is a period described in eschatology (study of Bible prophecy)—in Christianity, it traditionally depicts the period just prior to and including the **seven year period preceding the Second Coming of Christ.**
>
> In Judaism, the term "end of days" refers to the Messianic Age that includes the return of the exiled Jewish people (Diaspora) to the Promised Land and the coming of the Messiah.
>
> A Sovereign God, Creator of the heavens and the earth and all that exists, has His hands on Israel and the entire world.

Rebirth of the State of Israel
May 14, 1948

The most prominent sign of the end times is the rebirth of the State of Israel on May 14, 1948. After being scattered throughout the world for 1,878 years (AD 70 – 1948) with no territory, homeland or nation of their own, Israel was recognized as a sovereign state in 1948 for the first time since AD 70. After nearly 2,000 years the Jews were **miraculously** restored to their ancient homeland (in just one day) in direct fulfillment of Bible prophecy (Deuteronomy 30:1-5; Isaiah 43:5-7, 66:7-8; Ezekiel 34:13, 36:22-24, 37:1-6, 11-14, 21-23, 39:27-29; Hosea 3:4-5; Jeremiah 31:10, 31:35-36; and Amos 9:14-15).

In an irrevocable covenant (see chapter 2) God promised Abraham that his descendants would have the land of Canaan as *"an everlasting possession"* (Genesis 17:8), and Ezekiel prophesied a physical and spiritual revival of Israel (Ezekiel 37). And how do we know we are in pre-tribulation times? <u>Because Israel must be in the land of Canaan as a nation and in possession of the ancient City of Jerusalem before the start of the seven year tribulation</u>. This is fundamental or essential to end time Bible prophecy. See chapter 6 for more information about the Miraculous Rebirth of the State of Israel.

During the period between AD 70 and May 14, 1948, many Christians and theologians believed the restoration of the Jewish people as a nation in the land of Canaan was unattainable (impossible), and the Covenant between God and the Jewish people was forfeited because the Jews rejected the Messiah, Jesus Christ, and forced His crucifixion in AD 32. Many early Christians taught that the Old Covenant (Abrahamic and Mosaic) was fulfilled and replaced (superseded) by the New Covenant in Jesus Christ—this belief was given the name **replacement theology**. This is not official Roman Catholic doctrine and, supposedly, it does not appear in church documents, but the Catholic Church taught varying doctrines of replacement theology prior to 1948.

> **Replacement Theology** is a man-made assumption that the Christian church has replaced the Jews as God's 'chosen people' and that the Mosaic covenant (law; commandments and decrees) has been replaced by the New Covenant. This theology states that the Old Covenant made with the descendants of Abraham, Isaac, and Jacob was forfeited when the Jews rejected Jesus as the Messiah and forced His execution. (For more information, see chapter 6, The Fallacy of Replacement Theology; Appendix A, Replacement Theology; and Appendix B, Establishment of a New Covenant.)

This assumption by Bible skeptics provided an explanation for the worldwide dispersion with no possibility of a future State of Israel. But all this dramatically changed following World War II and the Nazi Holocaust with the restoration of Israel in 1948. Immediately following this miraculous event, replacement theology was discarded by most mainstream Christian theologians although some people with anti-Semitic bias held tightly to this false doctrine.

Repossession of Jerusalem
By the State of Israel
June 5–10, 1967

Similar to the rebirth of the State of Israel, **the second most prominent sign is the possession of the ancient City of Jerusalem—a fundamental event before the seven year tribulation and return of the Messiah.** Taking possession of the ancient City in the 1967 Six Day War was the **outcome of a war initiated by an Arab alliance** of Egypt, Syria, and Jordan—an aggressive confederation of Arab nations with the sole intent of completely destroying the State of Israel. The Arab world was humiliated by the "lightning-fast" victory of the Israelis, and Israeli morale and international prestige was greatly enhanced—but the resulting displacement of Arab civilian populations had long-term consequences.

> **Result of the 1967 Six Day War:** Decisive Israeli victory. Territorial Changes: Israel captured the Gaza Strip and the Sinai Peninsula from Egypt, the West Bank (including East Jerusalem) from Jordan, and the Golan Heights from Syria. See chapter 7, The Six Day War.

In Psalm 83:9-15, the prophet **Asaph** describes a swift and dramatic victory which included occupation of Jerusalem. About 2,900 years after the United Kingdom (the first State of Israel with a political government and bureaucracy) under King Saul (1050 BC – 1010 BC), King David (1010 BC - 970 BC), and King Solomon (970 BC - 930 BC); about 2,553 years after the Babylonians destroyed the City and the First Temple, and exiled the people for 70 years; and about 1,897 years after the Romans destroyed the City and the Second Temple (AD 70), the ancient City of Jerusalem was once again in the hands of the Jewish people. Prior to the 1967 war, the beloved and ancient City of Jerusalem was utterly unattainable to the Jewish people.

Devout Jews recognized the events of May 14, 1948, and June 5-10, 1967, as **essential prerequisites before the appearance of the Messiah.** While the Jews were scattered worldwide, they knew the return of the Messiah could not occur until the ancient City of Jerusalem and Temple Mount were again in the hands of God's chosen people. (See chapter 7, sections Fulfillment of Bible Prophecy and Israelis Are Aware of Bible Prophecy.)

> Although Jerusalem became the capital of **Israel** on January 23, 1950, under a resolution passed by the Israeli Knesset, the City was not under Israeli control until June 10, 1967.

Sign Reads:
"This Road Leads To Area A
Under The Palestinian Authority.
The Entrance For Israeli
Citizens Is Forbidden,
Dangerous To Your Lives
And Is Against The Israeli Law."
Photo by Roger Gallop, March 13, 2016

Israel Surrounded By Hostile Arab Nations

Today, the tiny country of Israel (shown in red on the map below) is surrounded by at least 20 Arab countries that were unable to defeat them after nine attempts in which the Arabs were the aggressor! What makes such a tiny country so great? How did they return as a nation after almost 2,000 years? *It is because the hand of God is on Israel. This one fact alone alludes to the unbelieving mind-set of Arab leaders as well as leaders of the European Union and United States.*

Why this fervent, everlasting hatred of the Arabs toward the Jews? (See chapter 2, The Seed of Everlasting Hatred.) It is about the lost birthright of Ishmael to his half-brother Isaac about 4,100 years ago—a feud that initiated this everlasting hatred of the Arabs toward the Jews with a relentless motivation by the Arabs to take the land of Israel by force. Such unrestrained, unbridled hatred over thousands of years is a '**supernatural phenomenon.**' Throughout history and certainly in today's world, the Islamic faith has been used to keep the Arab's ancient hatred of the Jews in a highly agitated state.

Since 1948 Israel has had full support from the U.S. but this changed under the 2009-2016 administration. The U.S. Secretary of State

> **God's hand is on Israel as stated in the Covenant Scriptures.** After all, God brought Israel back to the land of Canaan according to Scripture—and **He will not let Israel be defeated.** Second, Israel's nuclear capability is not just a deterrent, but there would be a quick and fierce reaction to any attempt to attack Israel. Israel is a very staunch adherent of the policy of "offense being the best form of defense."

travelled around the world making unilateral concessions with Iran and other nations without Israel's blessings (see chapter 10, Decline of the United States, Part 2). This cool and disdainful policy toward Israel will ultimately have dire strategic and economic consequences for the U.S. and the world.

Arab nations are represented below in dark green, other Muslim countries in light green; and there is only one Jewish nation—the tiny State of Israel in red that can be barely seen. Israel is the only democracy in the Middle East. Arab countries are primarily monarchies with some military regimes such as Syria, Libya, and the Sudan and republics

Map of Israel (red) surrounded by Arab countries (dark green) and other Muslim countries (light green).

Israel is like a tiny island (red) in a sea of Arab countries.

It is easy to understand that the conflict between Israel and Arabs is not about land but about the everlasting hatred described in chapter 2, The Seed of Everlasting Hatred.

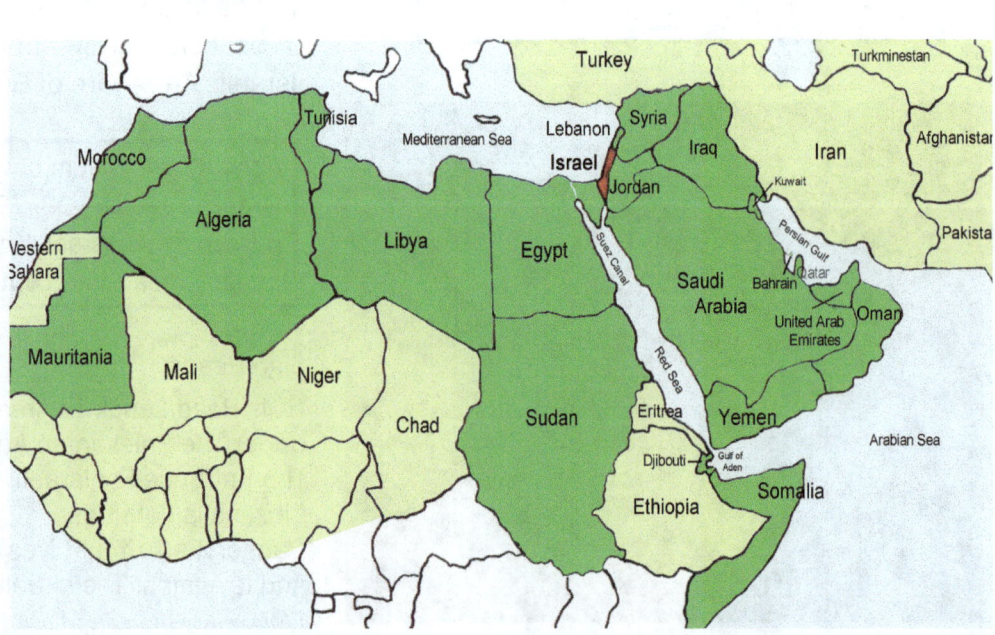

such as Algeria, Egypt, Djibouti, Lebanon, Mauritania, Tunisia, and Yemen.

Israel is only 2.5 times the size of Rhode Island, and 1/19th the size of California, and only slightly larger than the Canary Islands. **The combined territories of Arab countries are 640 times greater in size than Israel** (see map on facing page of Israel surrounded by Arab and Muslim countries). **Arab countries have huge oil reserves**, and **Arab population is 60 times greater than Israel's**.[1] Yet Israel is the most disputed piece of land on the planet—and do you wonder why? It is the Promised Land of the Holy Bible.

Israel has only sought peaceful coexistence with its neighbors who are fiercely dedicated to its destruction. **The conflict between Israel and surrounding Arab countries is not about land or oil but about the everlasting (supernatural) hatred of the descendants of Ishmael with the descendants of Isaac! This reality needs to be understood by the United States, the European Union, and other nations of the world.**

> In 2006, Israel's Jewish population was 5.6 million, surpassing 5.2 million in the U.S. For the first time since c. AD 135, there are more Jews in Israel than any other country on earth.

Fallacy of an Arab Palestinian State

As the Jews continued to re-inhabit their historic homeland of Judea and Samaria (see glossary, Appendix A) following WW II (after almost 2,000 years of exile and persecution at the hands of Hitler's Nazi Germany and other nations), the Palestinian Arabs began to market a plan to create a Palestinian state.

Are there any historical facts that support the legitimacy of an Arab Palestinian state?

No—there has never been a nation known as Palestine governed by Palestinians.

Islam was a religion founded in the 7th Century AD by Muhammad (AD 580 – AD 632), an Arabian merchant from the city of Mecca. In the centuries leading up to the birth of Muhammad, Christianity had become the predominant faith of the Levant (eastern Mediterranean region) with its message of salvation *"by grace you have been saved through faith"* (Ephesians 2:8, NIV).

> "After the Jewish revolt of AD 135 [see start of chapter 5], the Romans replaced the Latin name *Judea* with the Latin *Palaestina* as their name for this province." Following the revolt the name "Palestine" was used instead of the "land of Israel" as a slur or insult to the Jewish people. "Those living there became known as Palestinians."[2] It is interesting to note that Palestine is not found in the Holy Bible.
>
> The name Palestine was identified with the "Philistines" (1200 to 600 BC) along the coast to the SW but the name is most synonymous with "the land of Canaan," a term more frequently used in the Old Testament. See glossary for definitions.

Who possessed the land between AD 70 and May 14, 1948: Jerusalem remained under Roman control from c. AD 70 – AD 500; Arab jihadists from AD 500 – AD 979 (Mohammed never came to Jerusalem; Dome of the Rock was built c. AD 685 to AD 691 only as a shrine for Muslim pilgrims; it was built near or over the site of the Second Temple as an affront to Judaism and the Jewish people); Turks-Persians ruled from c. AD 979 – AD 1215; Mongols of Asia from AD 1215 to AD 1453; Turkish Ottoman Empire from AD 1453 to 1917 (who rebuilt the walls of Jerusalem); and Britain from 1917 to 1948.

During the period from 1948 to 1967, the City of Jerusalem was supposed to be internationalized (according to the UN partition plan; see introduction to chapter 6), but the City was occupied and controlled by the Jordanians. Also, Jerusalem has never been the capital of any Arab or Muslim nation and Arab leaders never visited the City. Further, Jerusalem is not mentioned once in the Koran (Quran).

There is no historical covenant granting Palestinian Arabs the right to the Holy Land or any portion of the land; there is no language known as Palestinian or any Palestinian culture that is uniquely different from other Arabs in the general region; and Palestinian Arabs are indistinguishable from their Arab brothers in Jordan, Syria, and throughout the Middle East.

What are the facts that support the legitimacy of the State of Israel?

1. Israel was a United Kingdom under Kings Saul, David, and Solomon (1050 BC to 930 BC), and the **City of Jerusalem has been the Jewish capital beginning with King David** (1010 BC – 970 BC) until AD 70 when the Romans completely destroyed Jerusalem and the Second Temple. Many thousands of Jews were exiled by God of the Holy Bible to the four corners of the world because of their continual disobedience and rejection of the Messiah Jesus Christ. In fulfillment of Bible prophecy, the State of Israel was miraculously restored on May 14, 1948. See chapter 6.

In the Old Testament, Jerusalem is mentioned over 660 times and Zion (which usually means Jerusalem, sometimes the Land of Israel) 150 times, and in the New Testament, Jerusalem is mentioned 146 times and Zion 7 times—and as previously mentioned, Jersualem is not mentioned once in the Koran (Quran), and the word Palestine is not found in the Bible.

2. God granted the Jewish people right of possession of the Holy Land through an unconditional covenant—commonly known as the **Abrahamic Covenant** (Genesis 12:1-3, 13:14-15). See chapter 2 for more information.

God **reaffirmed the covenant** with Abram with boundaries of the promised *"land of Canaan"* (Genesis 15:16, 18-21, 17:2, NIV). This Promised Land (Holy Land or Land of Israel) stretched from the Sinai Desert north and east to the Euphrates River which would include present-day Israel, Lebanon, and Jordan plus substantial portions of Syria, Iraq, and Saudi Arabia.

God reaffirmed the covenant to Abraham's son, Isaac, in Genesis 26:2-4; and to Isaac's son, Jacob, it was again reaffirmed in Genesis 28:4, 13; and to the prophet Moses in Deuteronomy 5:1-5.

The covenant was again reaffirmed to King David (1,000 years after Abraham) in Psalm 105:8-10 (NIV), *"He remembers his covenant **forever**, the word he commanded, for a thousand generations, the covenant he made with Abraham...to Isaac...to Jacob...to Israel as an **everlasting covenant**,"* and to the prophet Jeremiah (c. 1,450 years after Abraham) in Jeremiah 31:35-37.

Consider Scriptures where God makes certain **promises of blessings**, and **forever means forever, and everlasting means everlasting**. See chapter 6, The Fallacy of Replacement Theology. **The rebirth of**

Israel on May 14, 1948, **validates that the Lord will keep His covenant with the Jews forever, and we are in the last days just prior to the return of Christ** as described in chapters 11 and 12.

3. Hebrew was the language of the Jewish people in Biblical times, and most of the Old Testament was written in Hebrew. Prior to the restoration of Israel in 1948, Hebrew was a dead language. Although the language died out over time, it was revived in the 1900s, and Hebrew and Arabic are currently official languages of Israel, and Hebrew is spoken today throughout Israel. In Zephaniah 3:9 (NIV), *"For then I will return to the people a pure language, that they may all call upon the name of the Lord, to serve him with one consent."*

The people of modern day Israel share the same language and Jewish heritage and religion passed from one generation to another (even through almost 2,000 years of exile) beginning with their founding patriarch, Abraham (c. 2166 BC to 1991 BC).

4. In Deuteronomy 7:6-9 (NIV), God uniquely describes the Jewish people:

*"For you are a people holy to the LORD your God. The LORD your God has **chosen you out of all the peoples on the face of the earth to be his people, his treasured possession. The LORD did not set his affection on you and choose you because you were more numerous than other peoples, for you were the fewest of all peoples. But it was because the LORD loved you and kept the oath he swore to your ancestors** that he brought you out with a mighty hand and redeemed you from the land of slavery, from the power of Pharaoh king of Egypt. Know therefore that the LORD your God is God; he is the faithful God, **keeping his covenant of love to a thousand generations** of those who love him and keep his commandments"* (Deuteronomy 7:6-9, NIV). [Bold added]

And how old are the Arab countries that surround and harbor so much animosity and hostility toward tiny Israel? When did they gain their independence?

Egypt gained independence from Britain on February 28, 1922; Sudan gained independence from Britain on January 1, 1956; Jordan gained independence from Britain on May 25, 1946 **(land known as Transjordan which was originally set aside as a portion of the Jewish homeland)**; Syria gained independence from France in 1941 (but not recognized until January 1, 1944); Lebanon gained independence from France on November 26, 1941; Saudi Arabia gained independence from Britain on May 20, 1927; and Iraq gained independence from Britain on October 3, 1932.

Discarded Solution to the Palestinian Dilemma

On November 2, 1917, Britain issued the famous Balfour Declaration announcing British support for the establishment of a Jewish Homeland in Palestine—and the **homeland would include lands east and west of the Jordan River** (as it was during the Period of Judges, 1400 BC to 1050 BC, and the United Kingdom, 1050 BC to 930 BC; see chapter 3). What happened?

In 1921 Britain unilaterally granted Emir Abdullah all the land east of the Jordan River known as Transjordan and side-stepped terms of the original mandate. This angered the Jewish people because this secret negotiation separated land east of the river from land west of the river—and it did not account for using some of this land (east of the river) as possible resettlement for Palestinian Arabs.³ See beginning of chapter 6.

Britain continued to govern the territory, and the Jews continued their return to the region under strict immigration guidelines. Immediately following WW II, the United Nations met to vote for or against partitioning of Palestine as a homeland for the Jews as mandated by the Balfour Declaration. Despite fierce opposition from the Arabs, the UN Partition Plan called for the **division of Palestine west of the Jordan River** into 7 parts: 3 parts for the Jews, 3 parts for the Palestinian Arabs, and 1 part (Jerusalem) to be internationalized.

In 1946, Transjordan officially gained its independence from Britain, and in 1949 the land was renamed Jordan. The **Palestinian Arabs could have been (and should have been) easily absorbed into Transjordan—but they were slated to remain in Palestine west of the Jordan River as a thorn or source of conflict for Israel.**

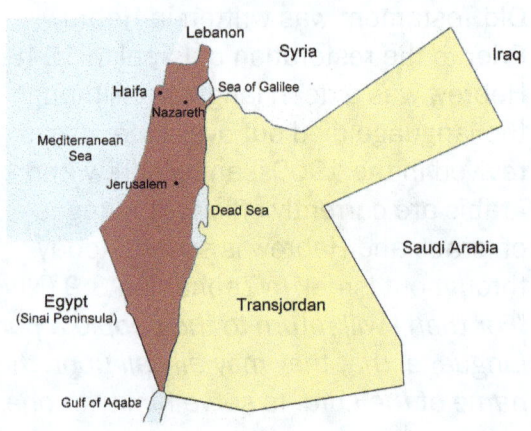

Stated Goals of Arab Nations

One of the stated goals of Arab countries, including the nation of Iran (ancient Persia), is to eliminate the State of Israel. This stems from an "everlasting hatred" of the sons of Ishmael with the sons of Isaac as described in Genesis 21:8-10; 26:2-4. (See chapter 2, The Seed of Everlasting Hatred, and chapter 7, Renewal of the Ancient Conflict Between Isaac and Ishmael.)

Israel is cast in the eyes of the world as an aggressor (which is unequivocally false), but it **should be obvious to most that Israel's intention is not about conquering foreign land—it is about defending itself and surviving as a nation.**⁴ **Israel's only goal is to live in peace and security, and the Arabs' only goal is to drive Israel into the Sea**—but it seems the world and world leaders, including some in the United States, are blind to the truth and do not understand Bible history.

The Arab nations initiated nine unprovoked attacks against Israel: 1948 -1949 War of Independence (3), 1967 Six Day War (1), 1973

> Anonymous quote: "If the Arabs (Muslims) put down their weapons today, there would be no more violence. If the Israelis put down their weapons today, there would be no more Israel."⁵

Yom Kippur War (1), 2006 Lebanon War (1), and the Gaza Wars of 2008, 2012, 2014 (3). Israel defended itself each time and won. (The 1956 Sinai and Suez Crisis and 1982 Lebanon War are not included; see chapter 7.) After each war the Israeli army withdrew from most of the areas it captured (except the Golan Heights for security reasons and parts of the West Bank). **Withdrawal from captured lands in defensive wars is unprecedented in world history and shows Israel's motivation to reach peace even at the risk of fighting for its very existence each time.**⁶

Proposed UN resolution (December 2014) to establish a Palestinian state by requiring the Israelis to withdraw to June 1967 borders is ludicrous and completely ignores Israel's

security. Who could rationally conceive of such a proposal?[7] Attack the tiny State of Israel nine times (see section, Israel Surrounded By Hostile Arab Nations) with a history dating from Kings Saul, David, and Solomon (1050 BC to 930 BC) to AD 70 with a Divine irrevocable covenant with God of the Holy Bible, and then demand that land be returned to Arab aggressors who have no legitimate religious or historical rights to the land—and including the fact there has never been an Arab Palestinian State!

God Blesses Israel
With A Warning to Other Nations

As declared in Genesis 12:2-3, God's hand will bless Israel, and **He conveys a dire warning to those people who do not support Israel:**

> *"I will make you into a great nation, and I will bless you; I will make your name great, and you will be a blessing.* **I will bless those who bless you, and whoever curses you I will curse;** *and all peoples on earth will be blessed through you"* (Genesis 12:2-3, NIV). [Bold added]

"God promises to punish the nations that come against Israel. America, the Arabs, the European Union, the United Nations, Russia, China—indeed, all nations....Every nation that presumes to interfere with God's plan for Israel, including the United States, stands not only against Israel but also ultimately against God. God is rising to judge the nations of the world based on their treatment of the State of Israel."[8]

Nations that have blessed the descendants of Abraham have been blessed, and nations that have cursed the descendants of Abraham have been cursed (Genesis 12:3). One needs only to step back and ask the question—where are the following empires: Assyrian, Babylonian, Medo-Persian, Grecians, and Roman—and where are the Turko-Persians and Ottomans—and in modern times, where is Adolf Hitler and his Nazi military? "They are merely footnotes in the graveyard of human history" because they all attacked and persecuted the Jewish people, and God brought these nations to ruin.[9]

At the turn of the 20th century no one would have dreamed that Israel would be back in her Promised Land (The Holy Land) and possess the ancient City of Jerusalem. **But make no mistake, Israel and the City of Jerusalem are at the center of world geopolitics, and Israel seemingly stands alone and isolated against its enemies.**

> *"This is the word of the Lord concerning Israel. The Lord, who stretches out the heavens, who lays the foundation of the earth, and who forms the spirit of man within him, declares:* **I am going to make Jerusalem a cup that sends all the surrounding peoples reeling.** *Judah will be besieged as well as Jerusalem.* **On that day, when all the nations of the earth are gathered against her, I will make Jerusalem an immovable rock for all the nations. All who try to move it will injure themselves"** (Zechariah 12:1-3, NIV). [Bold added]

We have seen this Scripture fulfilled in all the various wars against Israel since May 14, 1948—and with many failed attempts by the U.S. to find a peaceful solution to the Arab Palestinian problem. **Again, it must be reemphasized that the United States, especially its leaders and those who**

The United States has supported Israel since 1948 and has been blessed—but U.S. politicians and citizens should take note **that turning their back on Israel (as the 2009 – 2016 U.S. administration did) will bring great economic calamity to this nation.**

have their hearts set against Israel, should understand that turning their back on Israel is the same as turning their back on the Creator God, and such actions will bring misfortune to these nations (Genesis 12:3; Zechariah 12:1-3).

God will never again let His people be removed from the Land He gave them! Ezekiel 38-39:1-20 says that **Gog** and **Magog** (an authoritarian leader and the land of Russia), **Meshech** (Turkmenistan and Uzbekistan east of the Caspian Sea), **Tubal** (the southern tip of Russia east of Ukraine), **Beth Togarmiah** and **Gomer** (Turkey), and **Persia** (Iran) will rise up against Israel in the last days.

Isn't this what we are beginning to witness with the alliance between Russia and Iran and the initial, preparatory incursion of Russia into Syria with military personnel, armament, and jet aircraft? We will witness the hand of the Lord stand by and defend Israel as He did in the Old Testament! (See section, Rise of Russia and Its Alliance with Muslim States, and chapter 12 for more information.)

Psalm 83

Psalm 83:1-18 (previously cited in chapter 7, Fulfillment of Bible Prophecy) describes the continuous conflict between Israel and the Arabs. Since 1948, the Arab nations have attempted nine times to eliminate Israel. (See previous section, Israel Surrounded by Hostile Arab Nations; section, Stated Goals of Arabs, and chapter 7.) Each time Israel has prevailed. **However, one Arab leader after another has clearly stated that the only way of gaining peace in the Middle East is through the total annihilation of Israel.**

A psalm of Asaph: Psalm 83:1-18, NIV

"O God, do not remain silent; do not turn a deaf ear, do not stand aloof, O God. ²See how your enemies growl, how your foes rear their heads. ³With cunning they conspire against your people; they plot against those you cherish.

[Arabs speaking] ⁴'Come,' they say, 'let us destroy them as a nation, so that Israel's name is remembered no more. [Israel's very existence is at stake] *⁵With one mind they plot together; they form an alliance against you—⁶the tents of Edom and the Ishmaelites, of Moab and the Hagrites, ⁷Gebal, Ammon and Amalek, Philistia, with the people of Tyre. ⁸Even Assyria has joined them to reinforce Lot's descendants.*

[Jewish people pleading with God] ⁹Do to them as you did to Midian, as you did to Sisera and Jabin at the river Kishon, ¹⁰who perished at Endor and became like dung on the ground. ¹¹Make their nobles like Oreb and Zeeb, all their princes like Zebah and Zalmunna, ¹²who said, 'Let us take possession of the pasturelands of God.'

¹³Make them like tumbleweed, my God, like chaff before the wind. ¹⁴As fire consumes the forest or a flame sets the mountains ablaze, ¹⁵so pursue them with your tempest and terrify them with your storm. ¹⁶Cover their faces with shame, LORD, so that they will seek your name. ¹⁷May they ever be ashamed and dismayed; may they perish in disgrace. ¹⁸Let them know that you, whose name is the LORD—that you alone are the Most High over all the earth" (Psalm 83:1-18, NIV). [Bold added]

Since 1948 to current day, nations such as Iran and Syria and terrorist groups such as Hamas, Hezbollah, Fatah, Fedayeen, al-Qaeda, ISIS (Iraq Syria Islamic State) and the Taliban (Afghanistan) are described beginning in verse 4 of this psalm. Arab nations say, "...**let us destroy them as a nation, so that Israel's name is remembered no more.**" Isn't this the same hate-filled mantra arising from Iran, Syria, and surrounding Arab countries today?

In these last days the common bond that unites these nations and groups is their hatred of Israel and their Islamic doctrine. The Islamic religion has only existed since the 7th Century beginning with Muhammad (AD 580 – AD 632), a relatively recent period of time and long after this Psalm was written.

Increase in Arrogance, Immorality, and Lawlessness Worldwide

The last days are described as "terrible times" because of the increasingly evil nature of man and because of those who actively and fiercely *"oppose the truth"* (2 Timothy 3:1-5, 13; and Isaiah 5:20). There will be an increase in wickedness, and the love of many will grow cold. As we already see in today's world, this is how people will think and act in the last days:

> *"But mark this: There will be **terrible times** in the last days. **People will be lovers of themselves, lovers of money, boastful, proud, abusive, disobedient to their parents, ungrateful, unholy, without love, unforgiving, slanderous, without self-control, brutal, not lovers of the good, treacherous, rash, conceited, lovers of pleasure rather than lovers of God**—having a form of godliness but denying its power. Have nothing to do with such people"* (2 Timothy 3:1-5, NIV). [Bold added]

And then just a few verses later in verse 13, Paul warned, *"...evil men and impostors will go from bad to worse, deceiving and being deceived"* (2 Timothy 1:13, NIV). [Bold added]

Those days are here today and it will only grow worse. Isaiah 5:20 says, *"Woe to those who call evil good, and good evil."* (Also see 2 Thessalonians 2:3.)

We see these traits in many people today, especially those who teach the false doctrine of evolution (see the book, *evolution – The Greatest Deception in Modern History*) and

> **Last days** (also called **end times, end of time, end of days, final days**) is a time period described in eschatology (study of Bible prophecy). Christianity traditionally depicts the "last days" just prior to and including the seven year tribulation period preceding the Second Coming of Christ (see chapter 12 for more information). In Judaism, the term "end of days" refers to the Messianic Age that includes an in-gathering of the exiled Diaspora and the coming of the Messiah.

hold fast to atheistic ideas. All those who teach this false doctrine have entrenched themselves in a demonic mindset—and there is no escape for them. All this fits our modern age exactly.

Arrogance (including scoffing and mocking) is a sign of the last days as described in 2 Peter 3. Denial of God's Word (the Holy Bible) is prevalent worldwide—most especially in the media, on television, and **especially in movies when they ridicule God and continually take the Lord's name in vain. There is apathy in this secular world with no true sense of belief or understanding.**

> *In 2 Timothy 3:2, at start of section, "People will be...**boastful, proud...conceited...**"* [Bold added] *And in Romans 1: 30, "They are gossips, slanderers, God-haters, insolent, **arrogant and boastful**; they invent ways of doing evil..."* (Romans 1:30, NIV). [Bold added]

*"Above all, you must understand that in the last days **scoffers will come, scoffing and following their own evil desires**. They will say, 'Where is this 'coming' he promised? Ever since our ancestors died, everything goes on as it has since the beginning of creation.' But **they deliberately forget** that long ago by God's word the heavens came into being and the earth was formed out of water and by water. By these waters also the world of that time was deluged and destroyed. By the same word the present heavens and earth are reserved for fire [nuclear war], being kept for the day of judgment and destruction of the ungodly"* (2 Peter 3:3-7, NIV). [Bold added]

In Luke 8:10-12 (NIV), Jesus described such people as **"though seeing, they may not see; though hearing, they may not understand."** [Bold added] Also see Matthew 13:14. For whatever reason, if a person's mind is closed to Scripture, no amount of evidence will change him. This *"hardening of their hearts"* (see Ephesians 4:18) against God is a **supernatural phenomenon, an unseen battle between good and evil we witness in the news and in our everyday lives.** Many people dismiss such claims because they have "an enormous predisposition against the supernatural."[10]

Immorality is another sign of the last days—a downhill slippery slope that will only get worse. In 2 Timothy 3:1-5 (NIV) (see start of section) in the last days, *"...People will be... **unholy, without love, unforgiving...lovers of pleasure....**"*

The world is filled with crime of all types: shootings and murder, and drugs, pornography and XXX businesses which proclaim our godless, paganistic, immoral nature. Just read the newspaper in any city or listen to national or world news or go to the movies. Or watch television with the broad array of edgy, gun-toting, crime-ridden, violent, sexually explicit programs for anyone to watch, and the sexual oriented advertisements on television (certainly not available 30 years ago), or see the selection of pornographic magazines in bookstores. We know that the U.S. and world are in dire trouble and, unfortunately, it will only get worse. For more information, see chapter 9, Arrogance, Immorality, Violence, and Lawlessness.

Will man change his own heart? No. The downhill slide of immorality began more than several decades ago, and only God's wrath and punishment (like in the days of the Old Testament when people turned away from God to paganistic cultures) will change men's hearts and set a new course. See chapter 12 and epilogue.

The moral degeneration of man is portrayed by the repugnant and exceedingly evil behavior of some clergymen over the ages—physical cruelty, collusion with political dictators, and abhorrent sexual abuses—behavior that has alienated many from the Christian faith. The problem has never been with the God of the Holy Bible but with deliberate turning away, corruption, and moral depravity of humankind. The Bible speaks of it in Romans 1:18-32—it reads like a commentary of today's world.

"The wrath of God is being revealed from heaven against all the godlessness and wickedness of men who suppress the truth by their wickedness, since what may be known about God is plain to them, because God has made it plain to them. For since the creation of the world God's invisible qualities—His eternal power and divine nature—have been clearly seen, being understood from what has been made, so that men are <u>without excuse</u>. For although they knew God, they neither glorified Him as God nor gave thanks to Him, but their thinking became futile and their foolish hearts were darkened" (Romans 1:18-21, NIV). [Bold added]

*"Although **they claimed to be wise, they became fools** and exchanged the glory of the immortal God for images made to look like mortal man and birds and animals*

and reptiles. Therefore God gave them over in the sinful desires of their hearts to sexual impurity for the degrading of their bodies with one another. **They exchanged the truth of God for a lie,** *and worshiped and served created things rather than the Creator—who is forever praised. Amen. Because of this, God gave them over to* **shameful lusts [e.g., homosexuality, transgenderism].** *Even their women exchanged natural relations for unnatural ones. In the same way the* **men also abandoned natural relations with women and were inflamed with lust for one another. Men committed indecent acts with other men,** *and received in themselves the due penalty for their perversion"* (Romans 1:22-27, NIV). [Bold added]

"*Furthermore, since they did not think it worthwhile to retain the knowledge of God, He gave them over to a depraved mind, to do what ought not to be done.* **They have become filled with every kind of wickedness, evil, greed and depravity. They are full of envy, murder, strife, deceit and malice. They are gossips, slanderers, God-haters, insolent, arrogant and boastful; they invent ways of doing evil; they disobey their parents; they are senseless, faithless, heartless, ruthless.** *Although they know God's righteous decree that those who do such things deserve death, they not only continue to do these very things but also approve of those who practice them"* (Romans 1:28-32, NIV). [Bold added]

Lawlessness (terrorism) has significantly increased worldwide over the last few decades. Let's review Scripture concerning the last days:

"*And because* **lawlessness** [wickedness, NIV] *will be increased, the* **love of many will grow cold**" (Matthew 24:12, ESV). [Bold added] And many will commit acts of terrorism as if they are offering a service to God: "*...Indeed the hour is coming when* **whoever kills** *...*[**e.g., while detonating bombs strapped to their bodies**] *will think he is offering service to God*" (John 16:2, NIV). [Bold added]

Depravity cannot get much worse than the atrocities committed by Islamic extremists such as ISIS. Over the last few years the world has been horrified by the barbarism and brutality of this Islamic terror group. This includes mass murder and torture including crucifixion, burning people alive, beheading, mass rape, plunder, and enslavement.

And we are talking about innocent families—men, women, and children of all ages—subjected to such savagery. Women are often taken as sex slaves. Christians (entire families) are being rounded up and murdered in the worst ways in front of other family members. The father of pure evil—Satan—is working his deceit and treachery through Islamic extremism.[11]

> "The news is but the latest in a litany of horrors perpetrated by the Islamic State group, which has beheaded, burned [alive] and crucified male captives while passing around women as sex slaves." This is pure evil—a supernatural, satanic phenomenon.[12]

Where did ISIS come from? ISIS is the Sunni radical hardline Islamist terrorist army that filled a vacuum by a retreating U.S. military in Iraq under the 2009-2016 administration—an army that has swept across Lebanon, Syria, Libya, and Iraq, destroying everything in its path. This has led to millions of innocent families (men, women, and young children) being brutally slaughtered, and then fleeing for their lives from Syria and Iraq into neighboring countries: Greece, Croatia, Serbia, and Europe including Germany, Sweden, Britain, France, and Belgium, and the U.S.

The U.S. did nothing in the way of coordinating with other countries to eliminate the growing terrorist threat and to provide a temporary "safe haven" for migrating refugees in Arab lands (e.g., Jordan and Saudi Arabia). The U.S. opened the door to ISIS by abandoning Iraq (2009–2016) and then abandoning Afghanistan (2001-2021) (see pp. 135, 139, and 196) —all this, leading **to Russia's (and China's) direct involvement in Syria and the entire region.**

> Today, ISIS and al-Qaeda are active in Libya, Egypt, Algeria, Saudi Arabia, Tunisia, Yemen, Gaza, Syria, Iraq, Afghanistan, Pakistan, Bahrain, Lebanon, Jordan, and the Philippines. The U.S. does not know who exactly the enemy is, and we will never defeat a terrorist enemy whose existence we cannot define.[13] Eventually the U.S. defined the enemy as "Islamic terrorists."

> Islam's two major factions are Sunnis and Shiites. The Sunni faction (85% of Muslims) is being led by either al-Qaeda or ISIS. But America has aligned itself with the Shiites (represented by Iran who is on the verge of developing a nuclear bomb), which comprise 15% of the world's Muslims. This has become a recruiting tool for ISIS and al-Qaeda.[14]

Islamic terrorists are responsible for most of the attacks throughout the world. We have seen terrorist attacks in Munich, Germany (9 killed and 16 wounded on July 22, 2016); Nice, France (84 killed including 10 children on July 14, 2016); at least seven attacks in Instanbul, Turkey (43 killed and 230 wounded on June 23, 2016; 51 killed and 70 wounded on August 20, 2016); several attacks in Brussels, Belgium (35 killed in March 2016); several more attacks in Paris, France (17 killed in January 2015; 130 killed and 299 wounded in November 2015), and attacks in London in the first half of 2017.

There have been horrific killings throughout the Middle East, Afghanistan, Iraq, Pakistan and many other countries of the world. Since 2012, the brutal slaughter of hundreds of thousands of innocent Syrian families (fathers, mothers, children) in Aleppo, Syria during fighting between Syrian opposition (Sunni rebels including ISIS) and the Shite Syrian government aligned with Russia; the slaughter of innocent families in Mosul, Iraq and in other cities of that region. And since 2009, the slaughter of nearly 20,000 West African men, women, and children at the hands of Nigerian-based Islamic (Sunni) ISIS terrorists, Boko Haram. The list is too numerous to recount.

These terrorists are committed to destroying anything that stands in the way of an Islamic worldwide **Caliphate—an orchestrated worldwide Islamic movement with Sharia Law without national boundaries with the goal of taking over the world. Most westerners have no idea what this religion demands—submission, acceptance, and surrender.** "The apologists [those who appease Islam] can't continue to ignore the clear terrorism link [Islamic ideology]."[15]

Methods to achieve their goals includes the killing of all secular or apostate Muslims, all Christians and Jews, and the annihilation of Israel and the United States. Muslims will not tolerate Christianity in their homelands—but the **United States and Europe, under the guise of political correctness and freedom of expression, openly tolerate Islamic ideology and Sharia law. Have people lost their minds, especially those in the U.S. and Europe who are trying to appease Muslims and Sharia law by allowing mass immigration of people with such ideology?**

The Islamic religion is a totalitarian ideology that will not assimilate into the host country. This is the primary reason Britain has exited the EU because that country is losing its British identity. The EU has fallen into the trap of Political Correctness (PC); that is, **appeasing** Muslims and allowing massive immigration into EU countries. (See chapter 10, Political Correctness, for more information as to why this is such a bad idea.) In Luke 8:10-12 (NIV), Jesus described such mindless people *"though seeing, they may not see; though hearing, they may not understand."* [Bold added] And in Matthew 13:14, NIV, *"You will be **ever hearing but never understanding**; you will be **ever seeing but never perceiving**."* [Bold added]

In the last days prior to the seven year tribulation, there will be an unusual increase in Satanic influence in the world. We've already seen terrible depravity this past century: Hitler murdering 6 million Jews (the Holocaust) during WW II; Stalin's purges; Mao Tse Tung's murdering of 65 million Chinese; Pol Pot's Khmer Rouge and the Cambodian killing fields; and now the continued horrific mass killings throughout Africa, and the horrific killing and torture by Islamic extremists in the Middle East and worldwide. The Bible tells us that in the last days evil will grow stronger—it will become a terrible reality. Such things only confirm to us that our time on this earth is very short.[16]

Rise of Russia and Its Alliance with Muslim States

The rise of Russia as a superpower after WWII (1950 to 2015) is fulfillment of Bible prophecy, notably in Ezekiel 38 and 39. For hundreds of years Russia was a regressive, inwardly focused nation that rarely strayed beyond its own borders. The Bolshevik Revolution of 1917 (headed by Vladimir Lenin) led to the Bolshevik (communist) government which ultimately gave rise to the Soviet Union, a coalition of multiple Soviet republics. The country underwent a time of rapid industrialization, and then following WWII, this growth propelled the Soviet Union toward superpower status.

But in 1989 these Soviet republics or satellite countries in Eastern Europe overthrew their communist governments which eventually led to the collapse of the Soviet Union. At the time of the Soviet Union's collapse, critics of Bible prophecy thought it was impossible Russia could play a role in the end times. They confused the disintegration of the Soviet Union (12/26/1991) with **'alive and well' mother Russia, known as Magog in the Bible and its leader, Gog.** Although the Soviet Union (1922-1991) no longer exists, Russia retained all its political and military power including nuclear weaponry and reemerged as one of the world's leading superpowers.[17]

Russia has invested heavily in military weaponry and close alliances, most particularly Arab Muslim nations hostile to Israel. Not only has Gog (and Magog) established strategic bases of operations in these countries, but has actively and publically (in the news) established itself as the partner and protector of Iran and Syria. Is this significant? Yes, and right under the nose of world leaders (including the United States) who do not seem to have a clue what's going on from a prophetic Biblical standpoint. If you recall, about 2,600 years ago the prophet Ezekiel (Ezekiel 38 and 39) said that one day

> Ezekiel's ministry (593 BC - 571 BC) was during the time of the Babylonian invasion and fall of Jerusalem in 586 BC. He was among the Jews exiled to Babylon by Nebuchadnezzar in 597 BC and received the call to become a prophet.

Magog and Persia—modern day Russia and Iran, as well as other surrounding Arab countries—would form an alliance that would attack Israel in the first battle of the seven year tribulation.[18]

Russia dissolved its diplomatic relations with Israel following the 1967 Six Day War (Israel was in a defensive war of survival against a confederacy of Arab nations bent on destroying Israel) and then formed an alliance with Iran, Syria, Lebanon, and Turkey, and gave support to Palestinian militants (Hamas in Gaza and Hezbollah in Lebanon, and others).

> **End times** (also called **end of time, end of days, last days, final days**) is a period described in eschatology (study of Bible prophecy). Christianity traditionally depicts the "last days" as a time just prior to and including the seven year tribulation period preceding the Second Coming of Christ.
>
> In Judaism, the term "end of days" refers to the Messianic Age that includes an in-gathering of the exiled Jews (Diaspora) and the coming of the Messiah.

Alliances of the end times are being formed today—at this very time in history! We are very close to the 'tipping point' of the seven year tribulation but **the world seems oblivious and unconcerned about such events,** *"though seeing, they may not see; though hearing, they may not understand"* (Luke 8:10-12, NIV). Russia is building a new axis of power with Iran, Syria, and Turkey—Israel's enemies—and actively asserting itself into the Middle East via these countries.

Russia is now perfectly situated geographically, politically, and militarily to fulfill its prophetic role in the end times. Ezekiel 38 clearly describes an **end time military superpower** which will *"come from the remotest parts of the north"* being directly *"north"* of Israel (Ezekiel 38:15). The capital of Russia is directly "north" of Israel as the Scriptures describe in the last days, specifically during the seven year tribulation. **The primary event fulfilled by Russia during these times will be a military attack on Israel as described in Ezekiel 38 and 39.**

According to Ezekiel, other countries that will join with **Russia** [Gog, Magog; Rosh, Tubal] (including Kazakhstan) (see p. 189) in the invasion of Israel include: **Turkey** [Gomer; Beth Togarmiah], **Turkmenistan** and **Uzbekistan** east of the Caspian Sea [Meschech], **Iran** [Persia], **Sudan** [Cush] and **Libya** [Put]. Like Russia, these countries will also be crushed by Israel (Ezekiel 38:4-8). Incredibly, **the tiny State of Israel** (with the "hand of God" like in the days of Joshua of the Old Testament) will decimate the military force of Russia on the mountains of Israel as Ezekiel predicts (Ezekiel 39:1-6). And caution to the readers of this book: **Such events are not far off—a matter of years.** For more information about this Russian invasion, see chapter 12, Invasion by Russia and Its Allies and map.

All this has been brought on by the power vacuum left by a retreating U.S. presence in Iraq and the Middle East (see chapter 9, Decline of the Unites States, Signs of the End Times)—consequently, Russia is now (today) sending troops, heavy armor (tanks, military transport vehicles, artillery, anti-aircraft batteries, missiles), fighter jets, and Navy ships into Syria and the region. It has essentially established a strategic base of operations in Syria, Iran, Turkey and other parts of the Middle East. Also, Russia continues to strengthen its ties with Iran by supplying it with nuclear technologies (nuclear weapons programs, parts and supplies) and military support under the nose of the U.S., Europe, and the IAEA (International Atomic Energy Agency).

Russia is following in the same footsteps of Germany before World War II. National pride and the memory of the empire they once had is now motivating them to rebuild a strong military under an authoritative leader, Vladimir Putin. The goal of Putin is to restore Russia's greatness and fill the vacuum in the Middle East left by the disastrous U.S. foreign policy of withdrawal and appeasement—abandoning Iraq (2009-2016) and then abandoning Afghanistan after 20 years of occupation (2001-2021). (See pp. 135, 139, and 196.)

The annexation of Crimea from Ukraine (2014) and the movement of Russian personnel and military hardware into Syria (2015) was unprecedented and far "beyond anything Russia has ever done in the Middle East."[20] And then comes the botched, humiliating Russian invasion of Ukraine (February, 2022) which, ultimately, will lead to future escalation in the Middle East (not reckless aggression into NATO countries to the west and north). See p. 188.

Russia is allied with Israel's enemies and strengthening an axis of power with Turkey, Iran, and Syria. Russia has increased military and diplomatic cooperation with Syria and Iran. What is Russia's ultimate goal? Control over the entire region of the Middle East. And what is Russia's motivation? **It is warm water ports, Arabian oil, and mineral deposits in the Dead Sea.**[19]

With the collapse of the Soviet Union in 1991 and Russia's reemergence as a world superpower in today's world, alliances of opposing countries that seemed impossible just 30 years ago are now falling into place as the prophets predicted.[21]

Syria is immediately northeast of Israel! This movement of Russian personnel and weaponry into Syria is not the fulfillment of Ezekiel 38 but **it is a prelude to the coming invasion of Israel by Russia and its allies.** Russia's hostility toward the Jews will finally lead to her (Russia's) destruction and shame as God will supernaturally destroy her military on the mountains of Israel. The collapse of Russia and her allies will be for the purpose of exalting and honoring God among the nations and making it clear to the world that the God of Israel is Sovereign.

Modern Transportation and Increase in Knowledge

The fulfillment of end times prophecies seemed impossible before the advent of modern technology such as computers, automobiles, airplanes, and medical diagnostics and pharmaceuticals—even space travel and DNA research are all examples of the rapid increase in knowledge in our generation. Daniel 12:4 foretold of **continuous travel from one place to another (in automobiles and commercial airplanes) and an unprecedented increase in knowledge which could only apply to the advent of today's modern 'supercomputer age' and science advancements.**

*"But you, Daniel, **shut up the words and seal the book**, until the time of the end. **Many shall run to and fro, and knowledge shall increase**"* (Daniel 12:4, NIV). [Bold added]

Daniel was told that his visions were prophetic in nature, and **fulfillment would not be understood by him or anyone of his day until the end of the age. Today, however, this prophecy is obvious to those reading it.** The angel also informed Daniel that as the end of this era approaches, knowledge about prophecy would greatly increase because so much would be seen (e.g., TV, the internet, smart phones, books, eBooks, newspapers, magazines, etc.) but **only a few would understand.** Then the angel informed Daniel that the outcome will be sealed until the time of the end—the days in which we are currently living.

> *"I heard, but I did not understand. So I asked, 'My lord, what will the outcome of all this be?' He replied, 'Go your way, Daniel, because the **words are rolled up and sealed until the time of the end.** Many will be purified, made spotless and refined, but the wicked will continue to be wicked. **None of the wicked will understand, but those who are wise will understand'"*** (Daniel 12:8-10, NIV). [Bold added]

God told Daniel that **at the end of the age the wise would understand. In Biblical terminology the 'wise' are people who study and read the Bible and become open-minded to its meaning through the Holy Spirit. We are living in the end times.** The next great event, the removal ('snatching-up'; rapture) of the church from the earth (described in chapter 11), could occur at any moment. There are books available about Bible prophecy and the rapture (books by Hal Lindsey, Jack Van Impe, Tim LaHaye and Thomas Ice, and many other theology scholars).

notes: Chapter 8

1. The World Bank; retrieved from http://data.worldbank.org/country; Geography, Maps Don't Lie. Retrieved from http://www.mefacts.com/cached.asp?x_id=10190; Economy of the Middle East, https://en.wikipedia.org/wiki/Economy_of_the_Middle_East; and Israel, https://en.wikipedia.org/wiki/Israel.

2. Nelson's Illustrated Bible Dictionary (Youngblood, R. F., General Editor). Thomas Nelson, 842; and Let Us Reason Ministries. Retrieved May 2016, from www.letusreason.org/juda14.htm.

3. Creation of Transjordan. Retrieved January 26, 2016, from http://www.palestinefacts.org/pf_mandate_transjordan.php; and The Making of Transjordan. Retrieved January 26, 2016, from http://www.kinghussein.gov.jo/his_transjordan.html.

4. Estrich, S. (July 26, 2014). Israel only wants peace, not territory. The Florida Times-Union, Jacksonville, Florida, B-9.

5. The PBI, 1425 Lachman Lane, Pacific Palisades, CA 90272; as cited in http://www.heraldmag.org/2006/06nd_13.htm.

6. Ibid.

7. Lederer, E.M. (December 30, 2014). U.S. against Palestinian resolution. The Florida Times-Union, Jacksonville, Florida, A-7.

8. John Hagee (2006). *Jerusalem Countdown – A Warning to the World.* Lake Mary, FL: FrontLine, A Strang Company, 201.

9. Ibid.

10. Burrows, M. (1956). *What Mean These Stones?* New York: Meridian Books; as cited in McDowell, J. (1972). *Evidence That Demands a Verdict.* San Bernardino, CA: Campus Crusade for Christ, 69.

11. Hal Lindsey (November 7, 2014). The Hal Lindsey Report, News from Hal Lindsey Media Ministries. (www.hallindsey.org)

12. Dilanian, K. (August 15, 2015). Islamic State leader sexually abused U.S. hostage. The Florida Times-Union, Jacksonville, Florida, A-4; Hal Lindsey (July 24, 2016), op. cit.

13. Hal Lindsey (July 24, 2015); op. cit.

14. Hal Lindsey (July 10, 2015), op. cit.

15. Coulter, Ann (July 2, 2016). Many terrorists have Islam in common. The Florida Times-Union, Jacksonville, Florida, B-9.

16. Hal Lindsey (May 22, 2015 and June 5, 2015), op. cit.; Boko Haram. Retrieved from https://en.wikipedia.org/wiki/Boko_Haram

17. LaHaye, T. and Ice, T. (2001). *Charting the End Times.* Eugene, OR: Harvest House Publishers, 119; and Russian Revolution; as cited in https://en.wikipedia.org/wiki/Russian_Revolution

18. Hal Lindsey (April 24, 2015), op. cit.

19. Hal Lindsey (April 22, 2016), op. cit.; and John Hagee (2006), op. cit., 104-105.

20. Hal Lindsey (September 18, 2015), op. cit.

21. Hal Lindsey (July 11, 2014, September 18, 2015, October 21, 2016), op. cit.; Missler, C. (August, 2006). Magog Revisited. Retrieved February 2016, from http://www.khouse.org/articles/2006/663/; LaHaye, T. and Ice, T. (2001), op. cit., 119.

Chapter 9

Decline of the United States
Part 1

> *"Because of the increase in wickedness, the love of most will grow cold, but he who stands firm to the end will be saved."* —Matthew 24:12, NIV *"Woe to those who call evil good and good evil, who put darkness for light and light for darkness, who put bitter for sweet and sweet for bitter."* —Isaiah 5:20, NIV

There is no mention of America in the Bible as an essential country in the last days—but many Bible prophecy scholars believe that America fits the profile of 'political Babylon' aligned with the Antichrist in the last 3½ years of the 7-year tribulation period (as described in Revelation 18, Isaiah 18:1-2, Jeremiah 50-51). (See chapter 12, p. 195 for more information.)

Over the last several decades the U.S. has been losing its role as the military leader of the free world—and it is no longer the same vibrant, morally upright country as it was following WW II. Although the 2017-2020 administration had a pragmatic foreign policy (e.g., trade and foreign policies, and border security, etc.) and understood the importance of Israel in the Middle East, the slogan "Make America Great Again" **did not happen**—there was too much political opposition.

Exactly how or even if the U.S. is removed from its position as a world power is speculation but there are a few possibilities: societal collapse with a **continuing increase in immorality, violence and lawlessness, and economic debt collapse** with no solution in sight. Other possiblities are a nuclear attack, a cyber (computer generated) attack, or an EMP (electromagnetic pulse) disabling computer networks. (See glossary for definition of terms.) Other possibilities are described in chapter 10 (Part 2).

Is America experiencing prophetic signs of the last days? The answer is Yes. The U.S. military was utterly demoralized after 20 years in Afghanistan with an incompetent chaotic withdrawal (exit) on August 31, 2021, resulting in the loss of credibility with foreign allies and other world leaders. The lying, deceit, and corruption by many of our politicians are epidemic—and many people today have difficulty discerning between the truth and a lie. Our national debt is soaring over 30.4 trillion (May, 2022; total debt of 90.2 trillion)—and inevitably, there is a coming economic debt collapse. Most people have a knowing (realization) that something is wrong in our society and the world with no apparent solution.

The next chapter (Part 2) focuses on political correctness; the lack of empathy and understanding by the current U.S. administration (2021--2024) and many in the U.S. concerning Israel's role in end time Bible prophecy; appeasement of evil political ideologies and all religions (except Christians and Jews); and the decline in the quality of the learning environment in public schools (due to no moral code, chronic misbehavior without consequences, teaching of socialism and marxism, and acceptance of transgenderism).

> *"...There will be **terrible times** in the last days. **People will be lovers of themselves, lovers of money, boastful, proud, abusive, disobedient to their parents, ungrateful, unholy, without love, unforgiving, slanderous, without self-control, brutal, not lovers of the good, treacherous, rash, conceited, lovers of pleasure rather than lovers of God**—having a form of godliness but denying its power. Have nothing to do with such people"* (2 Timothy 3:1-5, NIV). [Bold added] And then just a few verses later in verse 13, Paul warned, *"...**evil men and impostors will go from bad to worse, deceiving and being deceived**"* (2 Timothy 13, NIV). [Bold added]

Arrogance, Immorality, Violence, and Lawlessness

These signs were described in chapter 8, Increase in Arrogance, Immorality, and Lawlessness, as it relates to the world. Although much of the previous section is restated herein, this section pertains more specifically to the United States.

Arrogance is one of the great signs of the last days. Take a moment to review chapter 8, Increase in Arrogance, Immorality, and Lawlessness and the Scripture presented in that section: 2 Peter 3:3-7, 2 Timothy 3:2, and 1 Romans: 1:1-32. It is directly relevant to today's world.

It is one of the spritual forces of evil that **causes people to turn away without reason—to willfully forget!** In Luke 8:10-12 (NIV), **Jesus described such people as** *"though seeing, they may not see; though hearing, they may not understand."* [Bold added] Also see Matthew 13:14. For whatever reason, if a person's mind is closed to Scripture, no amount of evidence will change him. This "hardening of the heart" against God is a supernatural phenomenon, an unseen battle between good and evil we witness in the news and in our everyday lives. Many people dismiss such claims because they have "an enormous predisposition against the supernatural."[1]

Arrogance in the U.S. can be seen in many of our secular, atheistic university professors who teach the false doctrine of evolution as 'proven fact' (read the book, *evolution - The Greatest Deception in Modern History* by Roger Gallop) based on false, unproven assumptions. Evolution is a myth—yet despite overwhelming evidence in favor of Creation, many in the academic scientific community hold tight to the false doctrine of evolution because the concept of Divine Creation is outside the realm of known science—thus, evolution is the only "naturalistic" way to explain our existence.

Immorality is a downhill slippery slope that will only get worse as time goes on. Once the door is cracked open to such behavior, there is no turning back. In the last days, as stated in 2 Timothy 3:1-5 (see full Scripture at the start of chapter 8), "*...People will be... unholy, without love, unforgiving...lovers of pleasure...*" The Bible speaks of turning away, corruption, and moral depravity in Romans 1:18-32—it reads like a commentary of today's world.

The immorality rampant in society today is a symptom of mankind's rebellion against God—whether we want to admit this or not. In every city, town, and neighborhood in the U.S. and world, abortion, homosexuality, drug abuse, trafficking of child prostititutes, and child molestation are proof that "*evildoers and impostors will go from bad to worse*" (2 Timothy 3:13, NIV). [Bold added]

Since 2000 there has been an **abrupt shift in 'what is considered normal'** toward a shocking abnormality—what was considered normal is now **upside down**.[2] We live in a society where a white NAACP leader claims to be black; a white senator from Massachusetts claims to be an American Indian; men claim to be women and women claim to be men (transgenderism); and a lie is claimed to be the truth and truth is claimed to be a lie. We are living at a time when police are called 'racist pigs' and instigators of criminal activity are called 'innocent victims.'

Our society today is **redefining morality of what is right and what is wrong,** and year by year it has gotten significantly worse. Here are just a few examples.

- The '**new normal**' in America today is depicted in a newspaper article which reads: "Hustler Hollywood... is coming to St. Augustine. The store, which calls itself 'an upscale, modern

World In Denial - Defiant Nature of Mankind

erotic boutique dedicated to providing a sophisticated shopping experience for the sexually curious...' Among items featured on its website is...an entire section devoted to BDSM [a lifestyle that involves Bondage and Discipline/Dominance and Submission/Sadism and Masochism], which...involve whips [and] chains... [with] 14 stores around the country." This is certainly one of the signs of a paganistic, hedonistic society.[3]

- In 2014 the Florida Capitol was adorned with a Nativity scene and a protest display from a satanic temple. In 2015 visitors may likely see "an irreverent disco ball-topped, multi-colored gay pride festivus pole—built of beer cans."[4] These types of irreverent displays and activities are increasing throughout the U.S. It seems that **people today cannot discern between the truth and a lie—between what is good and what is evil.**

- Parents and their children throughout the U.S. celebrate Halloween (October 31) each year with glee while wearing zombie and ghoulish costumes as if there was nothing wrong with this activity. This festival is an old pagan holiday, masquerading as if it were one of the customs of the church. And yet, unbelievably, professing Christians today naively allow their children to revel in the spirit of this paganistic celebration![5]

- The satanic temple, a national group in Salem, Massechusetts...has asked schools to start satan clubs in nine public school districts across the country including school districts in Missouri, Georgia, Florida, Oregon, Washington, Arizona, and California.[6]

- And as previously stated at the beginning of this section, all states and cities throughout America, (including many of our neighborhoods and schools) are filled with crime of all types, shootings and murder, and drugs, pornography and XXX businesses which proclaim our godless, paganistic, immoral nature.

> While watching television or reading the newspaper, one cannot help but be overwhelmed by the evil that is flooding our society and world. From mass shootings in public schools (see chapter 10, Moral Decline of Public Schools and Universities); continuing year-by-year increase in violence in our cities; depravity and immorality; corruption in business, government, and politics; and unceasing release of vile and sadistic hollywood movies—the disappearance of moral standards in our society is commonplace.
>
> We are becoming **"normalized"** (desensitized) to lawlessness and moral decay—just like it was in the pre-Flood 'days of Noah' when the **'tipping point' (the measure of sin)** was reached and God saved a righteous family. Jesus said in the last days, *"...iniquity* [lawlessness] *shall abound, the love of many shall wax cold"* (Matthew 24:12, KJV) [Bold] and it is abounding exponentially.[7] 2 Peter 3:3-7 is Scripture that everyone in the world should read and understand.

Does all of this sound familiar? It is what we see every day in the news and on the streets, and in movies and television—it is rapidly infiltrating our society and the world and getting worse by the day. We are now living in a hedonistic, materialistic, paganistic society where Pagan Pride Day is a common event in America.[8]

When the foundations of normal, decent behavior are challenged, when the "doors are cracked open," the tendency is for evil to infiltrate society which changes our sense of normality. People are lovers of themselves—and there is the tendency to do what is right in their own eyes "as it was in the times of Noah." All these things, and much more, can be seen around us every day.

The cause of increasing immorality is simply an increase in pride (arrogance, superiority) and sinfulness, and a decrease in righteousness—that is, turning away from a Sovereign God.

> "If Americal falls, it will be the result of moral decay from within." (Hal LIndsey, Hal Lindsey Report, February 17, 2017) [Bold added]
>
> "Remember the drug craze of the late 60's? In 1968 we were horrified that 5,000 Americans died of drug overdoses. In 2015, 52,000 Americans died of drug overdoes...[but] no media outcry...only yawns...."
> (Hal Lindsey Report, April 21, 2017)

<u>Violence</u> is raging all across our globe, and most notably, the **indiscriminate shootings** in every country, state, city, and neighborhood in the U.S. Scripture states that in the last days, violence will increase.

*"And because **lawlessness** [wickedness, NIV] will be increased, the love of many will grow cold, but he who stands firm to the end will be saved"* (Matthew 24:12-13, ESV). [Bold added]

And "...here in America we embrace violence as one of our biggest sources of entertainment. The most successful prime time TV shows and movies are those with violent, bloody plot lines....I just wonder why we are so fascinated by violence. [One reader writes], 'We put entertainment industry people on pedestals and expect that just because someone sings a popular song or makes a good movie, then their voice carries authority'... What we don't talk about...is all the violence we—and especially our children—consume under the guise of entertainment and the lasting effect it...[has] on us."[9]

Murder rates and other violent crimes have risen dramatically from 2014 to 2016 in more than 30 cities throughout the U.S. including New York, Chicago, New Orleans, Baltimore, St. Louis, Milwaukee, Cincinnati, and Los Angeles. Chicago's murder rate soared 72% in 2016, and the city had more murders this year than New York and Los Angeles combined.[10]

The numbers are shocking, compared to 2014: homicide is up 76% in Milwaukee; 60% in St. Louis; 56% in Baltimore; 44% in Washington, D.C.; 75% in Denver; 83% in Austin Texas; 27% in Cleveland; 29% in Houston; 23% in Dallas; and many other large cities have had at least a 15% increase in violent crimes.[11] Murder rates spiked in every major city across the U.S in 2020, and most major cities are infested with homelessness and drug use. The Justice Department commonly releases hundreds of inmates from penitentiaries due to overcrowding, many of whom are drug dealers—and drug gangs in larger cities are primarily responsible for this incredible amount of violence.

Also, the explosive migration of hundreds of thousands of unvetted illegal aliens across the U.S. southern border from Central and South America, Mexico, Haiti, and Africa has added many thousands of drug dealers and child sex traffickers to the U.S. population. Expect violence to increase (exponentially) in future years.

Police sometimes make bad decisions (and they should be held accountable and the police department should also be held accountable for **deficient training of its officers**), but too often good police find themselves in very difficult and stressful situations, often make poor choices, and are unjustly punished for defending themselves while instigators are celebrated. Without a fair and deliberate police force that is allowed to do its job without fear of reprisal, **anarchy (disorder and chaos) will prevail in our society**—but it seems that many city leaders of this country cannot understand this reality.

> The title of a newspaper article read, "Relationship violence must be ended" and the sub-title read, "What exactly is love? That question is the focus of a campaign to help people distinguish between love and abuse." The article states that "nearly six out of every 10 college students has difficulty distinguishing when relationships cross into the gray area between the two [love and abuse]." Further, "One in every three women and one in every four men will face violence within a relationship sometime during their lives." **Incredibly, this is the deteriorated state of morals and values of the world today.**[12]

Many argue that one of the great signs of America's decline is the disintegration of the core foundation of any society—**marriage and the family.** The violence and racial conflicts we have witnessed in Chicago, Illinois; Ferguson, Missouri; Baltimore, Maryland; and in every major city throughout the U.S. have more to do with the breakdown of the American family and the absence of a Christian father— 'love and caring' in the family, teaching sons and daughters Christian moral values and the absolute truth and importance of understanding the saving grace of our Lord Jesus Christ.

<u>**Lawlessness**</u> (terrorism) has been on the increase during the past ten years, as described in chapter 8. Around the world we have seen horrific killings by Islamic terrorists in the Middle East, Iraq, Afghanistan, and Pakistan; in Munich, Germany; in Nice, France; in Istanbul, Turkey; in Brussels, Belgium; and in London, England (March and June 2017); and since 2012, the brutal slaughter of hundreds of thousands of innocent families (fathers, mothers, children) in Aleppo, Syria and Mosul, Iraq and other cities in that region, and since 2009, the slaughter of thousands of West African men, women, and children at the hands of Nigerian-based Islamic (Sunni) ISIS terrorists. The list goes on and is too numerous to recount.

In the U.S. we witnessed the attack by two airliners on the World Trade Center in New York City on September 11, 2001, and one airliner on the Pentagon, and the unsuccessful attempt by yet another airliner that was thwarted by heroic crew and passengers—all of which led to the invasion of Afghanistan by U.S. military in search of Al-Queda and Taliban terrorists; the Boston Marathon bombings by Islamic terrorists on April 15, 2013; on December 20, 2014, the assassination of two New York City police officers; on April 13, 2014, the killing of three (man, woman, and child) by a neo-Nazi sympathizer at the Overland Park Jewish Community Center in Kansas CIty, Missouri; on July 16, 2015, the shootings by an Islamic terrorist on two military installations where four Marines and a Navy sailor died and a Marine recruiter and a police officer were wounded in Chattanooga, TN; on December 2, 2015, the killing of 14 and injuring of 22 by Islamic terrorists in San Bernardino, California; on June 12, 2016, the killing of more than 49 (most in their 20s and 30s) and wounding of more than 50 by a lone Islamic terrorist at a 'gay' nightclub in Orlando, Florida; on July 7, 2016, the killing of 9 Dallas police officers (wounding 7 officers and wounding 2 civilians), and the list of terror goes on and on to present day (2021).

The following "last days" Scripture applies aptly to increased violence and terrorism:

> *"And because **lawlessness** [wickedness, NIV] will be increased, the love of many will grow cold"* (Matthew 24:12, ESV). [Bold added]

> And many will commit acts of terrorism as if they are offering a service to God. *"...in fact, a time is coming when anyone who kills you* [while committing suicide] *will think he is offering a service to God"* (John 16:2, NIV).

As mentioned in the previous chapter, ISIS is the Sunni radical hardline Islamist terrorist army that filled a vacuum by a retreating U.S. military in Iraq—a terrorist army that is sweeping across Lebanon, Syria, and Iraq, destroying everything in its path. This has led to millions of innocent families being brutally slaughtered, or fleeing for their lives from Syria and Iraq into neighboring countries including Greece, Turkey, and Germany.

The U.S. administration did nothing in the way of coordinating with other countries to eliminate the growing ISIS threat and to provide temporary "safe havens" for migrating refugees in Arab lands. Previous U.S. leadership opened the door to ISIS by abandoning Iraq—and all this, in turn, has opened the door to Russia's direct involvement in Syria and the region, and even more bloodshed. In an attempt to curb the flood of immigrants into Europe and U.S., the U.S. proposed "safe havens" in the Middle East—but such non-sensical solutions will not be successful due to lack of cooperation by host countries and terrorist infiltration of these safe zones.

> The Islamic religion is a totalitarian ideology that will not assimilate into the host country. It is a religion that demands submission, acceptance, and surrender. **Wake up America!** The goal of Islam is **Caliphate**—an orchestrated worldwide Muslim movement with Sharia Law without national boundaries with the goal of taking over the world.

Islamic terrorists are committed to destroying anything that stands in the way of an Islamic worldwide **Caliphate**—an orchestrated worldwide Islamic movement of Sharia Law without national boundaries with the goal of taking over the world. It seems that U.S. leadership and many Americans have no idea what this religion demands—that is, submission, acceptance, and surrender.

As previously mentioned, methods to achieve their goals include the killing of all secular or apostate Muslims, all Christians and all Jews, and the annihilation of Israel and the United States. **Muslims will not tolerate Christianity in their homelands—but the United States and Europe, under the pretext of political correctness and freedom of expression, openly tolerate Islamic ideology and Sharia law.** This irrational, senseless mindset has opened the doors to an Islamic worldwide Caliphate.

Today, many of our congressional leaders turn away from Israel and try to appease Islam—a totalitarian ideology that will not assimilate into the host country. These liberal-minded congressmen and too many of our citizens do not understand Caliphate and the dangers of the Islamic ideology and mass migration of Muslims to this country. Mass immigration of Muslims into Britain (at the request of the EU) is the primary reason Britain exited the EU because that county is losing its British identity. The EU has fallen into the trap of Political Correctness (PC); that is, appeasing Muslims and allowing massive immigration. More on political correctness and appeasement in the next section!

> In 2017-2020 the U.S. proposed "extreme vetting" of immigrants from seven Middle East countries who harbor and train "Islamic terrorists." This certainly seems like a rational, prudent, and common sense effort to protect this country. **But why not Afghanistan?? And why not Mexico, Central and South America where drug smuggling is a major industry?**
>
> These seven countries are Iraq, Iran, Libya, Somalia, Sudan, Syria, and Yemen. (See map, chapter 12, Invasion by Russia and Its Allies.) This is not a Muslim ban because the 5 largest Muslim countries, including Indonesia, are not on the list (comprising 90% of Muslims). This is a terrorist ban to protect America!!

Another example of international appeasement is the disastrous Joint Comprehensive Plan of Action (adopted October 18, 2015). The U.S. **surrendered every concession possible to Iran**—lifting more than $100 billion in sanctions ("all based on empty promises from a nation whose leaders brag about deceiving its enemies, namely us!"); thus, clearing a path for Iran to complete its nuclear weapons program and continue its secret funding of Hamas and Hezbollah, and other terrorist organizations—**and what did the U.S. get in return? Nothing and Israel got even less than nothing—a more dangerous Middle East.**

For the U.S. it seems to be all about politics, political correctness, and appeasement (just like in the days of Neville Chamberlin, best known for his disastrous appeasement foreign policy with Hitler's Nazi Germany) but to the jihadists (including ISIS, Hezbollah, Hamas, and Fatah), it's a fanatical Holy War. In Luke 8:10-12 (NIV), **Jesus described such mindless people *"though seeing, they may not see; though hearing, they may not understand."*** [Bold added] And in Matthew 13:14, NIV, ***"You will be ever hearing but never understanding; you will be ever seeing but never perceiving."*** [Bold added]

Economic Decline

With a national debt of over 28.80 trillion dollars and total debt of 86 trillion dollars as of September 2021 (and in February 2017, national debt of 19.97 trillion and total debt of 66.88 trillion) and an entitlement mindset (welfare, disability, **bloated pensions for the top managers and executives** in almost every city and county), the United States is clearly in an advanced state of decline and is heading down the same path as Greece and other socialist countries. The American economy is being eroded from within by liberal-minded, greedy, inept politicians and bureaucrats and ever-increasing massive government handouts. (See glossary for definitions of national and total debt.)

Our economic foundation is decaying and our nation is collapsing under the weight of entitlement debt. But let's make it clear—entitlement programs such as **social security and Medicare require employees to pay monies *in advance* from their paycheck (matched by their employers) into these programs for future compensation**. (The employer must also pay a payroll tax for unemployment insurance which provides income for workers whose jobs have been terminated through no fault of their own.) **These are entitlement programs because they have been paid *in advance*** in accordance with state and federal regulations, and **workers are entitled to future compensation**. Unfortunately, these monies **are being siphoned into non-entitlement government handout programs** such as welfare, food stamps, Medicaid, social services, etc., etc.

Social security liability of 21.4 trillion in September 2021 (19.83 trillion dollars in June 2019; 15.7 trillion in February 2016) is climbing because of the ineptitude of government management. **See common sense solution in text box.** In this progressive politically correct society, non-working healthy adults and illegal aliens often receive better government treatment and seem to have more advantages than the average working American.

> It is important to make a distinction between social security (SS), Medicare, and unemployment compensation, and other "so-called" entitlement programs. For social security and Medicare, the employee and employer pay **in advance** into the entitlement program. Also, the employer pays **in advance** an unemployment tax. These are entitlement programs because the recipients have paid **in advance** over many years according to a contract with the government, and they are **entitled** to future compensation.
>
> However, programs such as welfare, food stamps, and Medicaid are "handout programs" that are funded by all taxpayers. Please do not misunderstand: **there are individuals with medical issues and families with children that need government help to survive and get a new start in life.** But unfortunately, there are those who are healthy and can work but choose not to, but prefer to defraud the system (which hurts all of us, especially those in real financial need).
>
> **Common Sense Solution**: Eliminate Medicare and SS fraud with law enforcement; stop siphoning monies from SS to other government programs; provide welfare, housing, and medical help for those in REAL financial need; and **tax 100% of wage earnings for SS, thus eliminating the wage cap of $118,500 (2016) which is a huge, gigantic loophole for the rich.**

We are not the same country that we were prior to 1980. For those of us born before 1950, the world we grew up in was relatively innocent. Today, Americans are "proud, selfish, greedy, arrogant, ungrateful, treacherous [deceitful], and completely addicted to entertainment and pleasure... Our country is literally falling apart around us..."—economically, politically, morally, socially, spiritually, and structurally (referring to deteriorating roads, bridges, sewer lines, and public buildings). Most people are so plugged into their smart phones and music (iPods and MP3 players) that they are completely unaware what is really happening to our economy and the world.[13]

World in Denial - Defiant Nature of Mankind

> The **Federal Reserve** (enacted December 23, 1913) is the central banking system of the United States. It is a private, non-government agency which was created by an Act of Congress (signed by President Woodrow Wilson) to control the nation's money supply. This non-government agency, administered by non-elected privileged financial elite, has control over every investment in America, and whatever they decide has a direct effect on the value of the dollar. Action by the Federal Reserve by creating trillions of dollars "out of thin air" in hopes of stimulating economic activity not only puts America's economy in jeopardy (on a "bubble" that will eventually burst), but it puts other economies in jeopardy as well.[14]

Investment companies which deal primarily in stocks want you to assume that we will have endless prosperity—just talk to any stockbroker who will give you good news no matter what. "We inherited the greatest economic machine the world has ever seen and we [this progressive, self-absorbed welfare generation] have wrecked it"—and a day of judgment will soon be coming upon the earth. But most people will not see it coming—they will not have a clue until it is too late.[15]

Most Americans think that if the Dow sets new all-time highs (e.g, surge in early 2018), then the American economy is in great shape. Right now the U.S. economy is exhibiting all of the classic symptoms of what is described by elite economists as a "bubble economy." But most Americans show little concern that the national debt has soared from less than 8 trillion dollars in 2005 to over 22 trillion dollars in June 2019 and to over 28.8 trillion dollars in September 2021. Since 2005 the U.S. has added nearly 21 trillion dollars in just 16 years (2005–2021). And the government seems **oblivious and incapable** of solving the problem—the problem of government expenditures continuing to grossly exceed revenue.[16]

Why? Why can't the U.S. administration recognize and solve the problem of government debt, bloated pensions and welfare? Why is the U.S. walking down the path of other socialist countries such as Greece and Venezuela (knowing full well that economic disaster is just around the corner)? In a newspaper column by Robert Ringer, he writes:[17]

> "Once someone gets something without paying for it, human nature takes over and that person not only wants to continue getting the product or service for free, he wants more and more of it. At that point, free stuff becomes, in the mind of the recipient, a "need."
>
> It gets worse. As a person gets more free stuff, he starts demanding that it be given to him in ever-increasing amounts. So what was originally a desire is now elevated from a "need" to a "right."
>
> In order to give anyone free stuff, the money to pay for it has to be taken from someone else, which means violating another person's property rights."

> The State government of California is flat broke (very much analogous to the country of Greece)—and they will have to continue begging for more money (in the form of loans) for years to come. This, of course, is not sustainable and will eventually lead California careening off a financial cliff (along with the U.S. with a national debt of 28.8 trillion dollars).
>
> Californians already pay some of the highest taxes in the nation, but it is not enough to cover the state's expenditures. This is exactly what's happening on the federal level. Also, the U.S. Department of Agriculture has recently said that 1 in 7 Americans is enrolled in the food stamp program (see item #15 this section).

Madness rules when the Federal Reserve prints trillions of dollars to keep the American financial system afloat in an effort to fund an over-bloated economy and a non-entitlement welfare system. Recently the Feds printed and then flooded the U.S. financial system with $1.2 trillion. The money was used to introduce government bonds.

The Fed does not explain that these monetary infusions are printed currency with nothing to back it up, and such quantitative easing (QE) not only reduces the purchasing power of Americans by devaluing the dollar, but **it virtually eliminates retirement income (due to record low interest rates) for those who have placed their savings into bank certificates of deposits. The Fed virtually takes from the middle class and senior citizens and gives to the wealthy on Wall Street and the largest corporations**.

> Economic investment companies are delusional when they proclaim an "economic recovery"—we are racing toward a "total economic collapse and our leaders are doing nothing to stop it."[18]

Meanwhile, Wall Street has now become the "biggest gambling house" on the planet, and **most of the new money that the Federal Reserve has printed (out of thin air—called "quantitative easing" by the Federal Reserve) has gone directly into stocks**, further enriching corporate managers and executives on Wall Street, all sitting on an inflated stock market and economic bubble ready to collapse.

This is what happened at the start of the Great Depression of 1929—and when a stock market crash finally happens, it will be catastrophic to our economy and the world. It is said that "the top 25 U.S. banks have over 212 trillion dollars of exposure" (total amount of unsecured loans; debt exceeds revenue)—and "when that house of cards comes crashing down there is no way that anyone will be able to prop it back up."[19]

The United States is in the middle of a long-term economic decline, although financial stock market types (stockbrokers) continue to be over-optimistic (because they are the ones who are reaping the monetary benefits of "quantitative easing"—again, paper money with no security or anything to back it up), and most Americans don't seem to understand the enormous debt problem and the non-entitlement welfare dilemma. Until the American people truly understand how bad our economic problems are, we will never accept the austere solutions needed to correct the problems.

The truth is that our political leaders (city, state, and federal) have absolutely wrecked our once greatest economy. As previously mentioned, most Americans just assume that we will always experience great prosperity, but that is not the case. Many of our manufacturers have moved overseas where goods are cheaper to produce. More Americans are dependent on government non-entitlement handouts than ever before—in other words, America is going the way of Greece, our dollar is dying (devalued due to quantitative easing), and as a nation we are absolutely drowning in debt (19.97 trillion dollars national debt and 66.88 trillion dollars total debt as of February 2017, and climbing to 28.8 trillion and 84.8 trillion, respectively, in September 2021).[20]

The American people have been deliberately deceived by a very liberal, progressive-minded government, and they need to come to their senses—but they won't—they want their share of the bloated financial pie. We will all soon experience painful economic turmoil and suffering that exists in much of Europe and the world.

Consider the following signs that the United States is in economic decline (statistics cited are dated 2011-2012 with a few noted exceptions):[21]

> #1 U.S. Gross Domestic Product (GDP) accounted for about 32% of global economic activity in 2001, but that number dropped to about 22% in 2011.
>
> #2 In 1988 the U.S. was the best country to live in but by 2012 it was tied for 16th.
>
> #3 The U.S. has fallen in global economic rankings four years in a row.

#4 The U.S. was home to the greatest manufacturing cities in the world but most have become "festering hellholes." Many manufacturing cities such as Detroit are on the brink of financial collapse, and this declining economy is causing "ghost towns" to appear across the U.S.

How can anyone say that "things are getting better" when manufacturing is in massive decline? Manufacturers are **shipping jobs overseas** because it is simply cheaper. See item #9 for more information. More than 56,000 manufacturing facilities have shut down since 2001.

#5 We are told that the unemployment rate is 5.6% (5.2%). But the problem is, the unemployment rate touted by the government is a "rigged computation" and does not include those who gave up looking for work. The real unemployment rate in January 2017 was 9.4 percent which is double the widely reported unemployment rate of 4.8 percent, but the rate is actually much higher. Donald Trump (U.S. President, 2017–2020) said the following in an interview with Time magazine:[22] (posted 2015)

"Don't forget in the meantime we have a real unemployment rate that's probably 21%. It's not 6. [It's] not 5.2 and 5.5... you have ninety million people that aren't working. Ninety-three million to be exact." That's about 28%.

The "official...unemployment rate is a **big lie.**" What is the real reality: only 44% of U.S. adults are employed for 30 or more hours per week. "It has been hovering between 42% and 45% since the end of 2009."[23] (posted 2015)

#6 In 1950 more than 80% of men in the U.S. had jobs, but by 2012 less than 65% had jobs.

#7. According to the Debt Clock (USDebtClock.org), the median household income has risen from $28,579 in year 2000 to just $30,438 in September 2016 to just $33,095 in June 2019, and $35,636 in September 2021— **very meager** over a span of 21 years.

#8 The U.S. trade deficit with China in 2011 was 28 times larger than it was in 1990, and it is much higher today. (Trade deficit: the cost of imports exceeds the value of exports; that is, we are buying much more than we are selling.) China's recent devaluation of their currency is "going to be devastating...." to the U.S. and the world. Also, both the Japanese yen and the Euro have been devalued relative to the dollar.

When a nation lowers the value of its money, it cuts into the buying power of the people in the country where devaluation is occurring— so China's exported goods (as well as those of other nations mentioned) will be cheaper (which is good for the Chinese), and the imports from the U.S. will be more expensive (not so good for the U.S.). The devaluation of currency means more consumers in China, Japan, and Europe who will Not be able to afford Buicks and Cadillacs. (Keep in mind that GM sells more cars in China than it does in the U.S.)

Solution: How do we end these money games and pending global economic collapse—**a global currency compliments of the future antichrist!!**[24] (See chapter 11.)

#9 The poverty rate for children in the U.S. is about 22% (2012)

#10 In 1983 income earners in the U.S. had about 62 cents of debt for every dollar earned but by 2007, that figure skyrocketed to $1.48. Part of the reason is that student loan debt rose to a stunning 1.61 trillion dollars in June 2019 and 1.77 trillion in September 2021 (USDebtClock.og), contributing to the slowdown of the economy.

#11 The value of the dollar has declined by more than 96% since the Federal Reserve was created on December 23, 1913. Through their quantitative easing program (printing currency out of thin air and giving the money to money managers and executives on Wall Street; see commentary at beginning of section), the **Federal Reserve is robbing from the poor and older retirees and giving to the rich.**

#12 About 29% of Americans age 25 to 34 years old are still living with their parents.

#13 In 1950 about 78% of households in the U.S. were a married couple, but by 2012 this number declined to 48%.

#14 About 35.4% of people live on welfare (more than 1 in 3, or 109.6 million people).[25]

Back in 1965, only 1 in 50 Americans was on Medicaid (a social health care program for families and individuals with low income and limited resources). In 2012 about 1 in 6 Americans were on Medicaid and this continues to escalate.

#15 About 45.7 million people are on food stamps, or more than 1 in 7. The number of Americans on food stamps exceeds the combined populations of "Alaska, Arkansas, Connecticut, Delaware, District of Columbia, Hawaii, Idaho, Iowa, Kansas, Maine, Mississippi, Montana, Nebraska, Nevada, New Hampshire, New Mexico, North Dakota, Oklahoma, Oregon, Rhode Island, South Dakota, Utah, Vermont, West Virginia, and Wyoming."

#16 In 2001 the U.S. national debt was less than 6 trillion dollars (5.8 trillion). Today, it is over 22 trillion dollars (June 2019) and increasing by more than 100 million dollars every hour. Approximately one out of every four dollars the U.S. government borrows is used to pay interest on the national debt.

#17 As the U.S. economy declines, the American people have been "gobbling up" more antidepressants and antianxiety medication than ever before. That's for sure.

#18 The U.S. lost its Standard & Poor's AAA rating (August 6, 2011)—the outlook on U.S. government debt was altered from "stable" to "negative." This is another sign that the world no longer has faith in the U.S. dollar.

#19 About 80% of American men had a job in 1950, but by 2012 less than 65% had jobs. That was the lowest level that has ever been recorded in U.S. history.

#20 The average CEO made 343 times more money than the average American worker. Through quantitative easing (printing money out of thin air), **the Federal Reserve has assured the fat cats of Wall Street and CEOs of large corporations continued exorbitant salaries on our money. See start of this section.**

#21 Average household debt in the U.S. is about 136% of average household income, but in China average household debt is only 17% of average household income.

#22 As the economy continues to decline, we will see more "random acts of violence." See previous section, Arrogance, Immorality, Violence, and Lawlessness.

So what do government leaders do to solve these economic failures? <u>**Nothing**</u>. They continue to insist that everything is "just fine." The mainstream media tells us over and over that a "recovery" has already begun but this is a fabricated 'talking point'—the U.S. economy is in much worse shape than most Americans realize. Although there will be economic "ups and downs" as we move along, people must realize that we are in the middle of a long-term economic decline.[26]

"While professing to care for the interests of the average person, the underlying motivation for the vast majority of government leadership is first and foremost self-aggrandizement and the acquisition of wealth. While some may be motivated by noble and decent ideology, the preponderance are not."[27]

A Deep Knowing Something Is Wrong

In recent years the theme of many action shows on television, movies, and video games is the depiction of imminent global apocalypse and take-over by alien creatures. And these movies are being shown worldwide. People of all nationalities and religions have an unrelenting fixation on "end of the world" themes. These shows "depict an evil humanity facing judgment for its sins"—though the judgment is not by God. They visualize judgment coming from extreme climate change, great earthquakes, tornadoes, gigantic tsunamis, and hurricanes, meteors, animals that have gone beserk, alien invasion from outer space, the walking dead, and angry zombies.[28]

> There is a sense that strange, unexplainable things are happening, and even secular newshounds seem to understand that **things are not quite right and there is a sense of impending doom**. Apocalyptic themes have invaded television and movie theaters. People have a sense that something Big is about to happen in the world—but very few people seem to understand the truth.[29]

Another interesting phenomenon is that animals tend to detect something wrong long before humans. Today, we are witnessing an unusual rise in the number of animal attacks on humans around the world—such as coyotes killing two girls in New York to an unusual number of shark attacks on the beaches of North and South Carolina, Florida, and elsewhere in the world. And then there are aggressive feral hogs in Texas; hostile monkeys overrunning New Delhi, India; the first death by alligator in Texas and an alligator snatching a little boy at Disney World, Orlando; to a lioness grabbing a special effects editor from her car while on a photo safari in Africa; bison attacks in Yellowstone to dingo attacks in Australia; and the list seems to go on and on.[30]

Does anyone remember the days when most Americans enjoyed living the American Dream in a land filled with happy, healthy, and prosperous people? As previously mentioned, if you were born before 1950, everything was "relatively innocent." And people were much the same way in the 20s, late 40s and 50s and early 60s. But these days it seems to be continual news stories of tragedy and despair almost daily—pollution, extreme weather events, violence, and increasingly bizarre behavior of human beings. Here are a just few examples:

The massive Gulf of Mexico Deepwater Horizon Oil Spill (April 20 – July 15, 2010) when oil wells flowed for 87 days before being capped;

The Environmental Protection Agency (a federal environmental watch dog) causing the discharge of deadly chemicals from the Gold King mine in San Juan County, Colorado, into the largest source of drinking water in the West (August 5, 2015);

Lead contamination of drinking water in Flint, Michigan (April 2014) after the city changed its water source from treated water (which was sourced from Lake Huron as well as the Detroit River) to the Flint River with a serious contamination problem;

Disastrous weather events on the national news just about every night for the last several years: terrible flooding in the east and northeast; tornadoes ripping through the midwest; severe drought and fires scorching thousands upon thousands of acres throughout California and the west; and on July 30, 2016, the 1-in-1,000 year flash flood event devastating the main street of Ellocott, Maryland, killing two people; and the recent massive flooding across Lousiana (August 2016) killing 11 people and 20,000 requiring rescue. And most recently, Hurricane Matthew (category 4) battered the Carribbean, the Bahamas, and the east coast of Florida, Georgia and the Carolinas (Sept. 29 - Oct. 9, 2016) with historic flooding and devastation killing at least 14 people in 3 states and over 800 people in Haiti;

Increased shootings of police officers (which, by the way, leads to anarchy and even more violence) and violent crime including daily gang related shootings in Chicago, Detroit, New York, Baltimore, Milwaukee, Los Angeles, San Francisco, and elsewhere through the U.S.;

Economic despair in cities like Detroit, Chicago, and many other cities throughout the U.S.

And in Washington, D.C., there is so much political division (spewing vitriol and fake news) that it is extremely unlikely anything will ever improve (including violence and lawlessness).

Lawmakers in Illinois are so alarmed by the violence in **Chicago** that they have considered help from the National Guard. These lawmakers have no idea what to do.

There are over 2.2 million people in prison in the U.S., yet violent crime continues to soar. In **New York City, Chicago, Detroit, Baltimore, Milwaukee, and many other cities throughout the U.S.**, parts of these cities are like war zones, and violent crime is flourishing.

This pattern of violence is also found across the Midwest where unemployment is widespread, primarily because we have allowed manufacturing jobs to be moved to China, India, Mexico, and elsewhere.

The reality is that America is a nation ravaged by crime. There are about 12 million crimes committed in the U.S. each year which is the **worst in the world.**

If you read the newspapers and listen to the local and national news, you cannot help but get the feeling that a whole lot of terrible things are happening in America. So why is all of this happening in the U.S. right now? Why does it seem like there is no place in the United States that is untouched by a major crisis? Many believe that such events are **pre-apocalyptic—Biblical last days**—a warning to America and the world that something big is going to happen, and people need to get their lives in order.

There is a **deep knowing** in the human psyche, a realization that something is wrong in the world. To the average American it is obvious that **something is WRONG**—what I refer to as the "gray veil." Romans 8:22 (NIV) says that *"the whole creation groans and labors with birth pangs...."* Many believe the world is going through something akin to childbirth. That means that the labor pangs are growing in frequency and intensity as we move toward a specific event.

The whole Creation groans and travails. God has been long-suffering and tolerant in his judgment of the U.S. and the world, but the time is coming that the *"measure of sin is now full."* (See Genesis 15:16.) **We are very close to the 'tipping point' of the seven year tribulation but the world seems oblivious to such events**, *"though seeing, they may not see; though hearing, they may not understand"* (Luke 8:10-12, NIV).

All of these events seem to be a warm-up of things to come—many believe they are pre-apocalyptic warnings.

notes: Chapter 9

1. Burrows, M. (1956). *What Mean These Stones?* New York: Meridian Books; as cited in McDowell, J., 69.

2. DePetris, L. (June 25, 2015). Up is down in today's contrary Orwellian world. The Florida Times-Union, Jacksonville, Florida, lead editorial letter.

3. Bull, R. (August 14, 2015). Hustler to open St. Augustine store. The Florida Times-Union, Jacksonville, Florida, C-1.

4. Turner, J. (December 7, 2015). No Nativity or Satanic displays in Capital, but Festivus endures, Orlando Sentinel, The News Service of Florida. Retrieved January 2016, from http://www.orlandosentinel.com/news/politics/os-holiday-display-tallahassee-nativity-festivus-20151207-story.html. Also see Turner, J. (December 8, 2015). Menorah, Festivus take place of Nativity. The Florida Times-Union. The News Service of Florida.

5. Where Did Halloween Come From? Retrieved from http://www.cgom.org/Publications/Booklets/Halloween.htm.

6. Hollingsworth, H., Associated Press (August 5, 2016). Satanic Temple asks schools to start club. The Florida Times-Union, Jacksonville, Florida, B-3.

7. Hal Lindsey (November 6, 2015), op. cit. Also see http://z3news.com/w/warning-sexual-immorality-increase-2013/.

8. Pagans take pride in their day (September 14, 2015). The Florida Times-Union, Jacksonville, Florida, B-6.

9. Dimond, D., Creators Syndicate (November 10, 2015). Our love for violence is a scary thing, The Florida Times-Union, Jacksonville, Florida, A-7.

10. Madhani, A., USA Today (April 1, 2016). Chicago's murder rate soars 72% in 2016; shootings up more than 88%. Retrieved September 2016, from http://www.usatoday.com/story/news/2016/04/01/murders-shootings-soar-chicago-through-first-three-months-2016/82507210/; and Berman, M., The Washington Post. (September 1, 2016). Chicago has had more homicides this year than New York and Los Angeles combined. Retrieved September 2016, from https://www.washingtonpost.com/news/post-nation/wp/2016/09/01/chicago-has-seen-more-homicides-this-year-than-new-york-and-los-angeles-combined/?utm_term=.f4013ad4299e.

11. Fox News, The Factor by Bill O'Reilly, October 7, 2015; ABC Nightly News, October 8, 2015; and Kay Anderson (September 1, 2015). Murder rates rise steeply in US cities: Experts can't agree on the reasons why. Inquisitr. Retrieved January 2016, from http://www.inquisitr.com/2383822/murder-rates-rise-steeply-in-us-cities-experts-cant-agree-on-the-reasons-why/#5vproVr5ElfsbF4y.99. Read more at Monica Davey and Mitch Smith (August 31, 2015). Murder rates rising sharply in many U.S. cities. The New York Times. Retrieved January 2016, from http://www.nytimes.com/2015/09/01/us/murder-rates-rising-sharply-in-many-us-cities.html?_r=0.

12. Relationship violence must be ended. (November 25, 2015). The Florida Times-Union, Jacksonville, Florida, A-8.

13. Snyder, M. (2012). 34 Signs That America is in Decline. Retrieved January 2016, from http://theeconomiccollapseblog.com/archives/34-signs-that-america-is-in-decline; and http://endoftheamericandream.com/archives/tag/economic-decline. (Michael T. Snyder is an attorney, a Christian, an author, a speaker and an activist, and publisher of The Economic Collapse Blog.)

14. James, T. (2015). Antichrist: Where is He? Retrieved January 2016, from http://www.raptureready.com/terry/where.html.

15. Snyder, M. (2012), op. cit.

16. Treasury Direct, Historical Debt Outstanding (2000 – 2015). Retrieved January 2016, from http://www.treasurydirect.gov/govt/reports/pd/histdebt/histdebt_histo5.htm.

17. Ringer, R., Guest Columnist (June 5, 2017).Creating new rights is the road to socialism. The Florida Times Union, Jacksonville, Florida, A-8.

18. Snyder, M. (2011). 24 Signs of Economic Decline in America. Retrieved January 2016, from http://theeconomiccollapseblog.com/archives/24-signs-of-economic-decline-in-america.

19. Snyder, M. (May 21, 2013). America's Bubble Economy is Going to Become an Economic Black Hole. Retrieved January 2016, from http://theeconomiccollapseblog.com/archives/americas-bubble-economy-is-going-to-become-an-economic-black-hole and Snyder, M. (March 20, 2013). Why Is The World Economy Doomed? The Global Financial Pyramid Scheme by the Numbers. Retrieved January 2016, from http://theeconomiccollapseblog.com/archives/why-is-the-world-economy-doomed-the-global-financial-pyramid-scheme-by-the-numbers.

20. U.S. Debt Clock. Retrieved Sept. 2016; June 2019, and Sept. 2021 from http://www.usdebtclock.org/.

21. Snyder, M. (2011), op. cit.; Snyder, M. (2012), op. cit.; Snyder, M. (November 9, 2011). 35 Statistics That Show The Average American Family Has Been Broke Down, Tore Down, Beat Down, Busted And Disgusted By This Economy. Retrieved January 2016, from http://endoftheamericandream.com/archives/tag/economic-decline. (Statistics were from surveys, the Gallup organization, U.S. Debt Clock, World Bank, AFL-CIO, the World Economic Forum, Pew Research Center, The Economist, The Wall Street Journal, U.S. Census Bureau, Standard & Poors, U.S. Bureau of Labor Statistics, and a variety of other reliable sources.)

22. Bruenig, M. (posted on August 21, 2015). What is the Real Unemployment Rate? Retrieved February 2016, from http://www.demos.org/blog/8/21/15/what-real-unemployment-rate. Also see Amadeo, K. (posted on February 3, 2017). What Is the Real Unemployment Rate? Retrieved February 2017, from https://www.thebalance.com/what-is-the-real-unemployment-rate-3306198.

23. Snyder, M. (2015). Only 44 Percent of U.S. Adults Are Employed for 30 or More Hours per Week. Retrieved February 2016, from http://theeconomiccollapseblog.com/archives/44-percent-u-s-adults-employed-30-hours-per-week.

24. Hal Lindsey (August 21, 2015), op. cit.

25. Jeffrey, T.P. (August 20, 2014). The 35.4 Percent: 109,631,000 on Welfare, cnsnews.com. Retrieved January 2016, from http://cnsnews.com/commentary/terence-p-jeffrey/354-percent-109631000-welfare.

26. Snyder, M. (November 9, 2011), op. cit.

27. McCann, S. (November 29, 2012). The Governing Class and Decline of America. American Thinker. Retrieved February 2016, from http://www.americanthinker.com/articles/2012/11/the_governing_class_and_the_decline_of_america.html#ixzz2DdCUjIsK.

28. Hal Lindsey (July 10, 2015), op. cit.

29. Hal Lindsey (January 29, 2016), op. cit.

30. Hal Lindsey (July 10, 2015), op. cit.

Chapter 10

Decline of the United States
Part 2

> *"Woe to those who call evil good and good evil, who put darkness for light and light for darkness, who put bitter for sweet and sweet for bitter."* —Isaiah 5:20, NIV

As mentioned in the previous chapter, there is no reference to America in the Bible as an essential country in the last days. The U.S. has been losing its role as the leader of the free world over the last several decades—and it is no longer the same vibrant, morally upright country as it was following WW II (the relatively innocent times of the 50s).

We can only speculate how the U.S. is finally removed from its political and military position as world leader. A few possibilities mentioned in the previous chapter include the increase in immorality, violence, and lawlessness (anarchy), economic debt collapse, and perhaps even a cyber (computer generated) attack, an EMP attack or nuclear attack.

Other possibilities described in this chapter include Divine judgment for 1) the U.S. role in dividing Jerusalem and advocating the return of ancient Jewish homeland in "defensive wars" (chapter 7), 2) appeasement and nuclear/monetary giveaway with Iran (see next section), and 3) appeasement of all religions (except Christianity and Judaism); and finally, 4) removal of the church (millions of people) from the world scene (see chapter 11, Rapture of the Church).

Today, America is experiencing a significant moral decline in the family, in the workplace, and in pubic schools; and most certainly there is the lack of worldwide leadership, empathy, and understanding of the history of Israel and the Middle East, especially the role that Israel will play in the last days according to the Bible. **This lack of understanding and insight** (by many U.S. citizens and liberal-minded leaders) is clear and resounding to those who know and study Bible history and prophecy.

The U.S. (much of its leadership and a large percentage of its population) does not realize the sheer truth and reality of Bible history and prophecy—that God made **an irrevocable, unconditional covenant** with the Jews to return them to the land of Israel in the years just prior to the return of Jesus Christ for His church and the seven year tribulation.

Additionally, **God promised to bless all those who bless and protect His chosen people (the Jews)—the descendants of Abraham, Isaac, and Jacob. Conversely, God promised to curse, harm, or abandon all those who do not** (Genesis 12:2-3). Throughout history, nations that have blessed the descendants of Abraham have been blessed, and the nations that have cursed the sons of Abraham have been or will be cursed.[1]

Not only did the previous U.S. administration (2009–2016) make the egregious mistake of criticizing Prime Minister Netanyahu for his unwavering defense of Israel's sovereignty (its independence as a nation and its right to defend itself), but blatantly inferred that Netanyahu was a coward. The administration showed no empathy or understanding of Israel's security predicament and ancient Bible history. This outward blatant distain and arrogance was inconceivable—but the following administration (2017–2020) renewed closer ties with Israel.

The reason Netanyahu would not cave to American and UN demands to return territory to the Palestinians is because Israel is already a "tiny" nation (as compared to surrounding hostile Arabs) making Israel completely indefensible— see chapter 8, Israel Surrounded by Hostile Arab Nations. Also, Israel has historical and divine rights to the land—see chapter 8, The Fallacy of an Arab Palestinian State. Certainly, one might think the U.S. administration (2009-2016) would have understood this—but apparently not. They had trouble comprehending the political courage of Mr. Netanyahu and believing the Divine position of the State of Israel. See Final Message in the epilogue.

Political Correctness

Political correctness (PC) is a term primarily used to describe language, actions, or policies intended not to offend any particular group of people in society (except Christians and Jews); that is, to appease, tolerate, and fully embrace so as not to offend. If you say "something wrong" in America today, you can be fired, fined, or even taken to court in some states. PC has run amuck in our society, and it is literally destroying the constitution (fabric) of this nation. In his novel *1984*, George Orwell imagined a future world where speech was greatly restricted.

The problem is, PC does not take into account a "moral standard" of behavior. Some language, actions, or policies 'deemed appropriate' by our government are inherently "evil" (morally corrupt, depraved, and decadent) and contrary to a moral standard—a law of "right and wrong" behavior. (For more information, see Human Nature and the Moral Law in chapter 3 of the book by Roger Gallop, *evolution - The Greatest Deception in Modern History*). But, unfortunately, **in today's world there is no longer any moral standard.**

The policy of appeasement leads to a shift in moral values, including rejection of God of the Holy Bible and a moral code, and ultimately leads to a debased (immoral, corrupt, excessive) society. Empires throughout history such as the Canaanites, Assyrians, Babylonians, Medes-Persians, and Romans (see chapters 2 - 5) became extremely paganistic and immoral and collapsed under the weight of moral depravity. **This is exactly what's happening to America today.**

> A **moral code** of conduct such as The Ten Commandments of the Bible has seemed to evaporate over the last several decades. If immoral behavior or evil is tolerated in the name of political correctness, the U.S. will crumble under the weight of excessiveness and immorality. Sadly, our leaders and many of our citizens have no moral compass or understanding of the Holy Bible.

> God of the Bible is sovereign and "governs all nations, bringing them into being (Amos 9:7, NIV) and **calling them into account** (Amos 1:3-2:3). He is the Great King who rules the whole universe (Amos 4:13, 5:8, 9:5-6). Because He is all-sovereign, the God of Israel holds the history and destiny of all peoples and the world in His hands. ...He is Lord over all." (Introduction to the Book of Amos, The NIV Study Bible, 1985. Bold added)

Appeasement of Evil Political Ideologies

The actions of Arthur Neville Chamberlain, who served as Prime Minister of the United Kingdom from May 1937 to May 1940, is best known for his appeasement foreign policy of Nazi Germany and, in particular, for his signing of the Munich Agreement in 1938. Later Adolf Hitler invaded Poland and surrounding countries beginning World War II in Europe. This led to millions of deaths and the Jewish Holocaust when over 6 million Jews perished at the hands of Nazi Germany. Appeasement of an evil political ideology is "immoral" and "wicked."

The recent agreement (Joint Comprehensive Plan of Action, adopted October 18, 2015) between the U.S. administration (i.e., then U.S. President and Secretary of State) and Iran concerning nuclear compliance completely excluded Israel. **The agreement surrendered every concession to Iran** – bestowing billions of dollars in cash and lifting more than $100 billion in sanctions (based on empty promises whose leaders brag about eliminating its enemies, namely the U.S. and Israel); thus, clearing a path for Iran to complete its nuclear weapons program and to continue its secret funding of Hamas and Hezbollah, and other terrorist organizations—**and what did the U.S. get in return?** Nothing—the U.S. got nothing in return and Israel got less than nothing.

> Iran is a country whose universal chant is "death to America." No Republicans voted for the nuclear deal with Iran—it was all democrats.[2] Why would the President and the democrats support this awful deal with Iran? Did the administration [2009 - 2016] have any understanding of Bible history? It appeared to ignore Israel's position (a tiny nation trying to survive) and completely empathized with Iran and Islamic ideology.

> Of course, it doesn't help to have our national political leaders look at all the major crises enveloping the world (including our own nation) and then decide that the primary issue that needs urgent attention is Israel's decision to build 2,500 residential apartments in Jewish neighborhoods of East Jerusalem and do what it must to protect itself. **The U.S. and E.U. nations seem disconnected from reality**—either intentionally or out of arrogance, ignorance, incompetence, and **political correctness.**

The U.S. administration just wanted "a deal" no matter the cost. The agreement is obscure, and "we can never be certain what America actually agreed to...Iran operates under a cloud of secrecy and deception that we can never trust that they are complying with the agreement...this deal will not prevent Iran from getting nuclear weapons and that it openly declares its intent to destroy the state of Israel."[3]

"So here's a country [Iran] whose universal chant is 'death to America'" and to Israel—but in the meantime, the U.S. made sure that Iran gets to keep their nuclear technology, facilities, and ballistic missiles; they get no surprise inspections and ample warnings (24 days, ample time to hide anything); and after 10 years all restrictions are lifted.[4] What a deal for Israel and the U.S. And since the deal, the Iran agreement (JCPA) is mysteriously no longer in the news.

Just a few years ago the U.S. promised never to let Iran have a nuclear weapons program but **in the end, the U.S. agreed to permit, protect, and defend the very nuclear weapons program it vowed to eliminate through sanctions and military options.** Further, the agreement skillfully "disguises the clear path...left open for Iran" and virtually **makes it impossible for any future Israeli or U.S. military strike against Iran.**[5]

The 2009-2016 administration seemed to believe and empathize that all Islamic jihadists (see glossary) want a 'just life' with greater economic opportunity—and this is why they are terrorists. But this type of illusionary rationale is absurd and shows an extreme lack of understanding of fanaticism associated with a false religion. This **unfathomable naiveté** (or delusion) will make possible the catastrophic events of the last days.

For the U.S. it seems to be about political correctness and appeasement but to the jihadists (including ISIS, al-Qaeda, Hezbollah, Hamas, Fatah, and the fedayeen), it's a fanatical Holy War. Fanatical islamists have been so deluded by their beliefs that they do not fear death but think that murdering the infidel and apostate (American, Israeli, Christian, and Jew) "will gain them [immediate] entry into paradise with limitless sexual pleasure." Is this not a paganistic and evil mindset similar to the Canaanites of the Old Testament?[6]

For more information about extreme social decay in America, see the website: The Last Days of America? 25 Signs of Extreme Social Decay. http://theeconomiccollapseblog.com/archives/the-last-days-of-america-25-signs-of-extreme-social-decay.

Why did the administration seem to make excuses for the jihadist—either intentionally or unintentionally? A young Muslim man with jihadist leanings drove his car to an armed forces recruitment center and fired an assault rifle through the front window of the center—fortunately no one was killed but then he drove across town to a Naval Reserve Center where he killed four Marines and a sailor. Ultimately, the assailant was shot and killed by police.

The assailant had a degree in electrical engineering, lived in a comfortable neighborhood, had an outgoing social life, and even drove a new car. It is not about finding a 'normal, just, and happy life' but it is about a 'supernatural' evil obsession to eliminate the Jewish people and all who oppose their (the jihadist's) ideology.

> "...we also know that we will never defeat an enemy whose very existence we deny....But apparently this Administration [2009 - 2016] has determined that not only do we not need to identify the enemy, as long as we deny it exists, we can live side-by-side with it."[7]

Because the U.S. administration backed away from dealing directly with ISIS on the battlefield and coordinating with nations in the Middle East to provide a temporary safe haven in that general region, the U.S. is now partly to blame for the flood of refugees (hundreds of thousands) from Syria into Europe and other parts of the world.

Appeasement of All Religions
(except Christianity and Judaism)

Political correctness is also a tool used to appease or promote all religions "together as one" as depicted in the text box below. Today, this misconceived idea is fully displayed on automobile bumper stickers with symbols of many religions (spelling 'COEXIST')—the idea that there is one God for all religions, in turn promoting a one world religion and the false idea that there are many ways to heaven. Contrary to this sacrilegious

> Religions of the world include: Judaism, Christianity, Islam, Hinduism, Buddhism, Shintoism, Atheism, Taoism, Jainism, Candomble, Bahai, Paganism, Santeria, Zoroastrianism, Rastafari, Mormonism, Unitarianism, Animism, Asatru, Aladura, Greek Mythology, and the list goes on.

ideology, the Bible teaches that there is only one way to salvation through Jesus Christ who says in John 14:6 (NIV), *"I am the way, the truth, and the life. No one comes to the Father except through me."* See an expanded explanation in the epilogue—the Bible Warns: There is Only One Way to Heaven.

> God will deal with sin either by grace or by wrath. John 3:36 (NIV) says, *"Whoever believes in the Son has eternal life, but whoever rejects the Son will not see life, for God's wrath remains on him."* Those who do not accept Jesus Christ as their Savior will remain under the Lord's wrath.

The far left New Age movement has lured people into believing that tolerance of all religions including Islam is a good thing—all the while the Muslim faith is the most "intolerant" of all major religions. Tolerance used to mean "agree to disagree" but in today's politically correct world it means "endorsement" or "acceptance" of all religions, ideologies, life-styles, and behavior except, of course, Christianity and Judaism.

Political correctness has also been applied to those that prefer perverse or radical lifestyles. Today, people are besieged by society that it's okay to have promiscuous sex anytime and anyplace, and for men to have sex with men and for women to have sex with women, or men to become women and women to become men (transgenderism), and that such lifestyles are perfectly normal. We see this type of activity graphically portrayed in movies, television and TV advertisements, and in books and magazines on full display. **Our society is racing towards all levels of deviant behavior.**

> **Those who advocate alternative lifestyles, evolutionary-atheistic ideas, and appeasement of all religions, demand that we tolerate their behavior and beliefs but they, in turn, will not tolerate conservative beliefs and moral values based on the Holy Bible.**

It seems that just about every day the mainstream media inundates us with messages about 'what we should believe,' 'how we should act,' and 'what we should say' so as not to offend those with different lifestyles and ideologies, and most Americans silently comply. The following are just a few examples of PC:[8]

> #1 Chaplains in the U.S. military are required to perform gay marriages regardless of their religious beliefs. Refusing such an order means an end to their military careers.

#2 In America today there are many atheistic groups that are fiercely obsessed with eradicating every trace of God from the public arena. For example, an elementary school teacher demanded that a six-year-old girl remove the word "God" from a poem that she wrote honoring her two grandfathers who served in Vietnam.

#3 A high school track team was disqualified (2013) because a runner "made a gesture thanking God" upon crossing the finish line.

#4 In 2013 a university student was banned from class because the student refused to stomp on a poster bearing the name 'Jesus.'

#5 A female student at a university was told to remove a Cross that she was wearing because someone "could be offended."

#6 A teacher was fired for offering a Bible to a student.

#7 Volunteer chaplains for a city police department were banned from using the name of Jesus on government premises.

#8 The military has seemed to embrace social and political issues and ideologies of the left.

#9 A professor was recently banned from mentioning 'intelligent design' (a Divine Creator) because it would "violate the academic integrity" of the course.

#10 A state bill was signed into law which allows transgender students to use any gym facility (bathroom or shower). Transgender students will have access to any facilities that are "consistent with his or her gender identity" rather than the student's actual gender biology.

"**Islamophobia**" is a word we have heard often over the last 10 years or so. It is saying or doing anything that any Muslim anywhere might find offensive. It can include criticizing Muslim behavior and history that any Muslim might disapprove. For example, if you say Islamic terrorism is wrong, you can be accused of "Islamophobia."[9]

Islamophiles are non-Islamists who have only good things to say about the actions of Muslims or their culture. Influential people on this list of Islamophiles include European and American politicians and, unbelievably, high ranking military officers of the U.S. including the Joint Chiefs of Staff (likely as a direct result of political pressure).

On June 24, 2016, Britain voted to withdraw from the EU (aka Briexit) primarily because they were being forced to accept Muslim immigrants who would not assimilate into British society or culture—part of a worldwide Muslim movement (without national boundaries) known as **Caliphate**. **Non-assimilation is "just another name for invasion! Islam wants to control every aspect of life—the definition of a totalitarian ideology."**[10]

Integration of Islamic ideologies into a democratic society is extremely dangerous—so why do leaders in the U.S. (both democrat and republican, but especially liberal democrats) naively want to embrace an ideology that opposes a free society? Progressive, liberal leaders do so in the name of **"political correctness"—or appeasement.**

A true Muslim lives by the Quran (Koran) which advocates hostility against infidels (who do not accept the Islamic religion). **Can we be so naïve and foolish as a people to allow this type of thinking to infiltrate our society, government, and military—and ultimately subvert everything our forefathers stood for?**[11]

In a major city, an "equal rights ordinance" has a stipulation that allows access to restrooms and showers based on how a student "feels" about their gender (rather their actual biological gender).

This ridiculous idea is spreading to other places around the country, and if a school doesn't comply, it may lose its federal funding. Transgender activists in the U.S. are frantically promoting the idea of "gender fluidity"—people can be either male or female at will, and such aberrant ideas will certainly damage the psychological health of our young people.

> What does the Bible say about such ideas: *"Woe to those who call evil good and good evil, who put darkness for light and light for darkness, who put bitter for sweet and sweet for bitter"* (Isaiah 5:20, NIV). [Bold added]

This insane idea "is being perpetuated on 99.7% of the American public by a paltry **0.3% of the population.**"[12] [Bold added] Has the world gone utterly mad?

#11 In a major city authorities have installed plastic "privacy screens" on library computers so that people can exercise their "right" to watch pornography at the public library.

#12 In a new military manual, U.S. service personnel are instructed to avoid criticizing "anything related to Islam."

#13 Applicants that do not advocate "climate change" are not hired by a federal agency.

The truth is that PC ideology that originates from government, the media, and the public education system is a non-stop atheistic indoctrination system. The way that we all see the world (religion, the origin of man, the earth and the universe, etc.) has been "shaped" by many thousands of hours of "thought training" (brain-washing) we have all received over the years from public schools, mainstream media, and the government.

Countries such as Great Britain and the United States, where people once honored God, experienced unprecedented security and prosperity for their faithfulness. **These same countries today are morally bankrupt and collapsing economically as people turn away from God and toward political correctness.** *"Righteousness exalts up a nation, but sin is a disgrace to any people"* (Proverbs 14:34, NIV).

When nations turn their backs on God and live as if He does not exist, then corruption and wickedness abound. This is exactly what is happening in America today. Economic woes follow as taxes increase and governments print and borrow money to pay for larger police forces, prisons, and social services to repair the myriad of social maladies. Does this sound familiar?

The controlling nature of "PC" is entrenched in all areas in our society. Defining issues include abortion, same sex marriage, gender rights, parental rights, and the role of God in our schools and in our personal lives. Our militaries, schools (**public schools and the entertainment industry were lost decades ago**), courts, media, and governments (state and federal) are in a race to eliminate every last trace of Christianity while Islam, humanism (see glossary), evolution, and other secular ideologies are being celebrated and encouraged. It will eventually come down to making a personal stand for the truth—for Jesus Christ and not upholding the atheistic doctrine of political correctness.[13]

Political Correctness Is Mind Control
Wake Up America!

Sketch by Anton Zakharov

Moral Decline of Public Schools and Universities

Public Middle Schools and High Schools

This section briefly discusses the decline of our public education system and the lack of progress due to political correctness.

Government leaders and school administrators continue to wonder and speculate why the public school system (specifically, middle schools and often high schools) has failed to educate its students. The following are a few unsettling statistics:[14]

1. Recent NAEP (National Assesment of Education Progress) reviews indicate less than 33% of U.S. fourth graders are proficient in reading, mathematics, science, and American history.

2. More than 50% of low income students cannot demonstrate a basic proficiency in science, reading, and history.

3. U.S. eighth graders ranked 19th in mathematics and 18th in science out of 38 countries.

4. U.S. twelfth graders ranked 18th in combined mathematics and science out of 38 countries.

The school system comes up with many 'reasons and excuses' for this failure which typically include:

1. unqualified teachers,

2. no accountability for underachieving schools,

3. wasted funds by the school system,

4. non-effective, exotic education plans devised by state judiciaries, legislatures, and bureaucracies,

5. one class level for all students holds the best and brightest back, and

6. too much emphasis on test scores.

So let's briefly address these 'reasons and excuses':

#1 is a false assumption. Most teachers (the vast majority) are over-qualified and highly motivated. Also, teachers with graduate degrees (teaching classes in their degree subject) are made to take certification exams to get hired. This is a waste of funds in an already highly stressful occupation. **Stop testing teachers with graduate degrees who are teaching classes in their degree subject, or teachers with 5 + years of professional experience.**

#2 is both true and false. Today, there is some accountability based on student test scores, but there is zero accountability of the "quality of the classroom learning environment." Why is this a problem? This refers to the level of daily disruption in the classroom due to chronic misbehavior (primarily in middle school).[15]

The "quality of the learning environment" (maintaining a non-disruptive environment) is absolutely essential to learning, but the learning environment is undercut by chronic student misbehavior. This issue is not seriously addressed by the school system primarily due to "political correctness"—fear of offending the parent and the student.

#3 is a true assumption. There are wasted funds which can be remedied with a good CPA, competent accounting staff, and leadership at the top, but more money does not solve the real problem which is chronic classroom misbehavior.

#4 is a true assumption. Well intended exotic plans do more harm than good. Common Core, for example, is a scheme to rewrite education. "If something is not done soon, the vast majority of American K-12 school children will be taught using dubious, federally backed national education 'standards' that have come under fire from across the political spectrum."[16]

#5 is a false assumption. Teach all students at the same level—the best and the brightest will excel anyway and these students will help motivate others. Often, the underachievers are late bloomers and many go on to graduate school and turn out to be the great innovators and entrepreneurs in our society. Keep it simple—one size fits all fits perfectly well. (Of course, advanced mathematics or science classes should be open to all.)

#6 is a true assumption. The No Child Left Behind Act was created to 'fix' our public schools, but it has done more damage by placing extreme emphasis on excessive testing and test scores. Schools spend more time training students to take tests rather than offering basic, essential education—reading, writing, mathematics, science, and history—in a quality learning environment without disruptive behavior.

Can government leaders and school administrators (including the school board) be this naïve? Yes, absolutely, they can and are. They do not recognize that chronic misbehavior and lack of moral standards and consequences for chronic misbehavior are the primary problems.

Also, school board members and the superintendent often have petty childish feuds and extreme differences of opinion and, ultimately, little gets accomplished. When the chairwoman of the school board has to layout the ground rules for common courtesy amongst school board members and administrators (for example, "address each other respectfully, listen with the intent of moving forward productively," etc.), something is fundamentally wrong with these people.[17]

Also, school administrators make the quick, 'knee-jerk" assumption that underachieving schools must be the teachers' fault and so teachers are held directly accountable, or they come up with other unconvincing, vague reasons that have nothing to do with the real problem.

What is the underlying cause of violence (including mass school shootings), chronic misbehavior, and academic failure?

1. **Liberalized textbooks and school curricula** have utterly abandoned the Moral Code (Ten Commandments) and acknowledgment of God—which, in turn, leaves our schools teaching a worldview of "nihilism"—that is, "...the rejection of all religious and moral principles, often in the belief that life is meaningless."[18]

Such teaching dehumanizes students resulting in failure of the school system and, ultimately, in violence, moral depravity, and mass shootings. (See p. 45 of the book by Roger Gallop, *Defeating Evil - God's Plan Before the Beginning of Time*.) Without the moral code the world has become "normalized" (desensitized) to lawlessness, depravity, moral decay, transgenderism, political corruption, and violence (e.g., massacre of 17 students at Marjory Stoneman Douglas H.S in Parkland, Florida, in 2018).

For example, the public education system today teaches the false doctrine of evolution "as proven fact"—which is an absolute deception. See the book by Roger Gallop, *evolution – The Greatest Deception in Modern History (Scientific Evidence for Divine Creation)* and websites such as ICR (ICR.org), CMI (Creation.com), Answers In Genesis (AIG.org), Creation Research Society (creationresearch.org), and CST (creationsciencetoday.com), etc.

Solution: Return to school prayer, teach the Ten Commandments (the Moral Code), and teach real 'science'; that is, the overwhelming 'scientific' evidences that support creation, not evolution.

2. <u>**Overworked and overwhelmed teachers do practically everything**</u>: teach the curriculum, prepare daily lesson plans; create and grade tests and written papers; assign grades; continually discipline and manage disruptive students (which has become the greatest challenge for most teachers); monitor students in the hallways, cafeteria, and at school bus stops (primarily elementary and middle school); meet with parents; attend seminars and teacher meetings; plus the principal's expectation of the teacher getting involved in extra-curricular school activities.

Solution: The fact is, most teachers are highly skilled and dedicated but vastly overworked in a very stressful environment; consequently, **most teachers do not last long in their careers. Teachers must be given more authority and held in higher esteem in the school system.** Further, teachers in critical core subjects (math and

> Why do administrators (school board, superintendent, principal) have no realistic idea how bad the classroom environment is? Parents and even school administrators rarely enter the classroom during teaching hours, and if they decide to monitor a class, it is for a very limited time period and students are always on their best behavior.

science, English, reading and writing, history, etc.) should be provided with a "teaching assistant" (an apprentice) with specific mandated tasks: help with classroom discipline and escort disruptive students from the class room, monitor hallways and cafeteria, help the teacher grade exams, and act as a substitute teacher as needed, etc. **Teachers should just teach. Period.**

Expecting teachers to do more than "teach" is partly what's wrong with the school system. There is a lot of wasted funds in the system—so take money used for exotic,

> When the teacher is "reprimanded" by the principal or school board for being too harsh with a student or a police officer is actually "fired" for having to physically remove an obstinate, unruly student from the classroom, **students know they "rule the roost" and anarchy in the classroom eventually ensues.** "How many times must a student be told to leave a room [for misbehavior]? They are not 'home-schooled' to respect family, teachers, and police...Students get a slap on the hand and [the] officer [or teacher in most cases] gets fired [or reprimanded]." **The lack of moral standards and swift discipline for chronic misbehavior is a major component of what's wrong with our school system.**[19]
>
> When a teacher "used reasonable force to restrain a combative seventh-grade student," the Department of Education sought to revoke the teacher's state certificate. A judge ruled that the teacher used reasonable force, but the school board fired the teacher anyway at the recommendation of the superintendent. Power and authority has been taken out of the hands of the teacher and placed in the hands of the student.[20]

wasteful programs (including testing of teachers with graduate degrees) and **hire permanent teacher assistants.**

3. Chronic disruptive behavior in the classroom absolutely destroys the learning environment. School administrators must come to grips with this reality and solve the problem with an effective disciplinary protocol.

In today's schools, school administrators and the school board have no realistic idea how bad the situation is in the classroom, especially in middle school. It takes just one chronic misbehaving student to destroy the learning environment—and if there are 3 or 4 (and often this is the case), it is much worse. Currently, the problem of misbehaving students is laid at the feet of the teacher—administrators and parents often take the attitude that teachers are at fault and unable to manage the classroom, and teachers routinely become the scapegoat.

The classroom is a revolving door (in and out of the classroom) for disruptive students with no real consequences for misbehavior—thus, *the learning environment is severely compromised on a daily basis.* Due primarily to **political correctness**, school administrators are afraid to discipline defiant students for fear of antagonizing parents. This has opened the door to continued chronic misbehavior and **severe degradation of the learning process.**

When a student is disrespectful to the teacher, or does not obey instruction, or is chronically disruptive, the teacher is often held responsible and reprimanded (in the name of **political correctness**) for either being too harsh or for lacking the skills to manage the students. Please explain how a teacher is supposed to effectively teach when a student or students are continually disrupting the class because there is no fear of discipline or corporal punishment?
In today's public school, there is no effective, administrative protocol to enact fair, swift, and effective discipline for bad behavior.

Solution: There must be swift, harsh punishment for chronic disruptive behavior in the classroom—otherwise, the school system will continue to fail to teach its students. Chronic misbehavior is not the teacher's fault but rather, the fault of school administrators and the school system for not adopting standard, efficient protocol.

First and foremost, there must be a strict 'moral and behavioral standard' and 'dress code', including no cross-dressing (transgenderism), and the standard must be strictly enforced by the school. Students should be given no more than two warnings.

> Part of the solution has been removed from the classroom with the progressive idea of separation of church and state. When moral standards (the Ten Commandments) were removed from the classroom, and when immoral behavior in America became the norm (students emulating uncaring immoral parents), classroom misbehavior increased.

If misbehavior continues, here are a few non-politically correct suggestions to consider:

1) swiftly remove the student from the classroom and place the student in punitive detention monitored by school administrative officials, facing a wall with no talking, sleeping, or use of smart phones (all students at least 20 feet apart). Each student should be assigned school work by the teaching assistant for each class missed that day,

2) parents should be called by the school administrator (not the teacher) advising parents that the student has been placed in detention for misbehavior,

3) corporal punishment for middle school students with parents' approval,

4) in some cases, chronically disruptive students should be required to remain an additional one hour after school to write a paper (to be graded) on "moral and ethical behavior."

Rationale: If students are allowed to stay after school for sports (e.g., football, baseball, basketball, swimming, tennis, music, drama, and other activities), then students who chronically misbehave can do the same as a form of punishment for classroom misbehavior. This type of punishment would be dreaded by most students, especially those who participate in after school activities.

But unfortunately, school administrators continue to ponder the cause and solutions for failing schools while devising exotic solutions that have nothing to do with classroom misbehavior.

Public Colleges and Universities

Prior to the 1950s (post WW II), America was a nation where sexual morality was based on the norms of the church, and in the 1960s and 70s the idea of coed dorms in universities was unthinkable. Women's dorms had a front desk where men were not allowed to venture past, and usually there was a "house mother" to oversee the dorm. But in today's world, men and women share the same dorms and even the same dorm rooms. Some 20 universities and colleges, or more, have decided to allow undergraduates of the opposite sex to share an on-campus room. This is the decades-long downhill drift away from gender separation in college dorms, hallways, and even bathrooms.[21]

One university in Florida, for example, is offering "a place to call home for transgender students" with inclusive dorms—and this college is the fourth in Florida to offer this option.[22] Also, neo-Marxism, a political-philosophical system based on the ideas of Karl Marx and Friedrich Engels, what would later become communism, is being taught in many of our colleges and universities. Again, it must be restated that when foundations are challenged, **when the doors are cracked open, the tendency is for evil to creep in, and this ultimately has an impact on our sense of normality—our ability to decipher between good and evil.** If the foundations of the church were challenged all at once in a major way, people would reject the proposed change, but **when the challenge comes slowly (little by little), people eventually accept the change as normal.** This sense of normality has eroded our educational system on all levels.

The enormous volume of sexual assault on U.S. college campuses is not only a reflection of "campus culture awash in sexual immorality" but a reflection of the wickedness in an assailant's heart.[23] This illustrates the truth of Jeremiah 17:9 (NIV) that *"the heart is more deceitful than anything else, and incurable -- who can understand it?"*

Will man change his heart? The answer is No. The downhill slide of immorality began several decades ago, and ultimately, only God's wrath and punishment will change men's hearts and set a new course.

This must again be restated because it applies to our world today. What does the Bible say about such ideas: *"Woe to those who call evil good and good evil, who put darkness for light and light for darkness, who put bitter for sweet and sweet for bitter."* (Isaiah 5:20, NIV)

One would be naïve to think there is no crisis of morality in the United States and throughout the world. Sexual morals are being challenged at every turn. If you look at television programs, commercials, and movies, **you cannot find a program without a sexual scene or constant, sadistic violence and lawlessness.** Young people can turn on the television at almost any time or use the internet and get exposed to sexual images, perversion, violence, and pornography.

Compromised Teaching of the Bible

The seven churches described in Revelation 2-3 were seven literal churches in Asia-Minor (Western Anatolia; Turkey) described by John the apostle. The literal churches of that time have a spiritual connection to the churches of today.[24]

1. Ephesus (Revelation 2:1-7) is the church that had forsaken its first love (2:4).

2. Smyrna (Revelation 2:8-11) is the church that would suffer persecution (2:10).

3. Pergamum (Revelation 2:12-17) is the church that needed to repent (2:16).

4. Thyatira (Revelation 2:18-29) is the church that had a false prophetess (2:20).

5. Sardis (Revelation 3:1-6) is the church that had fallen asleep (3:2).

6. Philadelphia (Revelation 3:7-13) is the church that had endured patiently (3:10) and is still present in the world today—holding fast to the truth of Jesus Christ. It will be here until the end, but it is not the dominant church. We can certainly see these churches today.

7. Laodicea (Revelation 3:14-22) is the church with lukewarm faith (3:16) and **a focus on material wealth as the standard for success. Doesn't this sound like the attitude of many people today?** This church has been caught up in scientific and philosophical rationalism (i.e., evolution and humanism)—and although it calls itself Christian, "Christ sits in the back row."

Christian churches in America have lost many of their members over the last several decades, and this trend is especially obvious among young people. According to a recent survey by America's Research Group, of the 95% of 20 to 29 year olds of the protestant faith who attended church regularly with their families as young children, only 55% attended church regularly during high school, and only 11% attended church regularly when in college.[25] Why?

1. The church has compromised the teaching of the Bible. It is not teaching 1) end time prophecy (prophecy that is directly relevant to today's world), 2) eternal consequences of not believing in the saving grace of Jesus Christ. Many churches today are "feel good" churches; that is, they are the Laodicea church with a lukewarm faith and secular mindset, and 3) the truth of Genesis; the overwhelming scientific evidence supporting Creation.

2. The public education system today teaches the false doctrine of evolution "as proven fact"—which is an absolute deception. See the book by Roger Gallop, *evolution – The Greatest Deception in Modern History* and websites such as ICR (ICR.org), CMI (Creation.com), Answers In Genesis (AIG.org), Creation Research Society (creationresearch.org), and CST (creationsciencetoday.com), etc.

3. The church is not talking about God's plan of redemption available to every human being and the terrible consequences of rejecting the free gift of pardon (Revelation 20:11-15). See epilogue, The Bible Warns: There is Only One Way to Heaven.

According to a survey, "87 percent of Americans say they believe in God and 52 percent say they believe the Bible is God's authoritative word. But only 36 percent believe people should live by God's principles; 15 percent say they will live by their own principles even if they conflict with God's principles; and 45 percent prefer to combine God's teachings and their own values."[26]

A major finding is that America is losing its fear of God. "America no longer enjoys cultural consensus on God, religion, and what constitutes right and wrong, stated the report."[27] This finding directly correlates with the decline of morality and our declining public educational system and the increase in violence in cities across America. **The reality is that a record number of young Americans are leaving the church—and they have rejected the Christian faith in favor of a paganistic, hedonistic lifestyle.** This has got to be incredibly sobering to Christian theologians in the United States.

Along this same tendency (that is, the church drifting away from the Bible), there is a dangerous movement among those on the left, including some mainline churches, to punish Israel for not surrendering to the Palestinian Arabs. (See chapter 8, The Fallacy of an Arab Palestinian State.) It is commonly referred to as BDS (Boycott, Divest, Sanction Israel). This is the same demonic, false thinking of Replacement Theology (see chapter 6, The Fallacy of Replacement Theology).[28]

Remember that Genesis 12:3, NIV [Bold added] states, *"I will bless those who bless you, and whoever curses you I will curse; and all peoples on earth will be blessed through you."* God said that He will bless those who bless and protect Israel, and He will curse those who curse or abandon Israel. The United States, by turning its back on Israel, will bring disaster to America.

> God will deal with sin either by grace or by wrath. John 3:36 (NIV) says, *"Whoever believes in the Son has eternal life, but whoever rejects the Son will not see life, for God's wrath remains on him."* Those who do not accept Jesus Christ as their Savior will remain under the Lord's wrath.

---

notes: Chapter 10

1. Hal Lindsey (November 7, 2014). The Hal Lindsey Report, News from Hal Lindsey Media Ministries. (www.hallindsey.org)

2. The O'Reilly Factor, Memo; September 14, 2015.

3. Hal Lindsey (September 9, 2016), op. cit.

4. Iran Deal is Dangerous and Makes No Sense (September 15, 2015). The Florida Times-Union, Jacksonville, Florida (source: Wall Street Journal; IAEA report; Global Security-Washington Post; and Hal Lindsey (January 29, 2016; January 25, 2015), op. cit.

5. Hal Lindsey (July 24, 2015; July 31, 2015), op. cit.

6. Hal Lindsey (August 15, 2014), op. cit.

7. Hal Lindsey (July 24, 2015), op. cit.

8. Snyder, M. (August 14, 2013). 19 Shocking Examples of How Political Correctness is Destroying America. Retrieved January 2016, from http://www.infowars.com/19-shocking-examples-of-how-political-correctness-is-destroying-america/.

9. Murray, D. (June 12, 2013). The Middle Eastern Hornets' Nest. Retrieved January 2016, from http://www.gatestoneinstitute.org/3759/middle-eastern-hornets-nest; and Hal Lindsey (January 8, 2016), op. cit. Also see Hal Lindsey (June 3, 2016), op. cit.

10. Hal Lindsey (June 3, 2016; June 10, 2016), op. cit.

11. Tolerance? Not now. (February 8, 2011). The Florida Times-Union, Jacksonville, Florida, B-3. Also see Hal Lindsey (January 8, 2016), op. cit.

12. Hal Lindsey (June 3, 2016), op. cit.

13. Hal Lindsey (March 20, 2015; March 27, 2015; September 4, 2015), op. cit.

14. Top 5 Reasons Why Public Schools Are Failing Our Children (August 23, 2007). Retrieved January 2016, from http://study.com/articles/Top_5_Reasons_Why_Public_Schools_Are_Failing_Our_Children.html.

15. Support the teachers (December 21, 2015). The Florida Times-Union, Jacksonville, Florida, A-6.

16. Newman, Alex (August 2013). New American. Retrieved January 2016, from http://www.thenewamerican.com/culture/education/item/16192-common-core-a-scheme-to-rewrite-education.

17. Pantazi, A. (February 13, 2016). Dissention's depth.... The Florida Times-Union, Jacksonville, Florida, A-1; and Amos, D. S. (February 16, 2016). Ousters sought after texts.... The Florida Times-Union, A-1; and Amos, D.S. (February 28, 2016) Can...board learn to get along? The Florida Times-Union, A-1.

18. Hal Lindsey (May 25, 2018), op. cit.

19. Officer fired while student gets a slap (November 6, 2015). The Florida Times Union, Jacksonville, Florida, B-5. Also see Franke, K. (August 22, 2016). Increase in violent school threats causes learning disruptions, Schools in vexing spot as number of incidents increase, The Florida Times Union, Jacksonville, Florida, A-1.

20. Stepzinski, T. (November 7, 2015). Judge sides with teacher who restrained student, The Florida Times-Union, Jacksonville, Florida, B-2.

21. Arnoldy, B. (December 28, 2006). In dorms, men and women now room together. The Science Christian Monitor. Retrieved January 2016, from http://www.csmonitor.com/2006/1228/p02s01-legn.html.

22. Thompson, R. (September 14, 2015). A place to call home for transgender students, The Florida Times-Union, Jacksonville, Florida, A-1.

23. Roach, D. (February 2, 2015). "Analysis: Rape on college campuses." Baptist Press. Retrieved January 2016, from http://bpnews.net/44146/analysis-rape-on-college-campuses.

24. What do the seven churches in Revelation stand for? Retrieved January 2016, from http://www.gotquestions.org/seven-churches-Revelation.html.

25. The Decline of Christianity in America. (June 2009). The Last Days. Retrieved January 2016, from http://signsofthelastdays.com/archives/the-decline-of-christianity-in-america. Also see Kwon, Lillian (June 29, 2009). Survey: Churches Losing Youths Long Before College, Christian Post. Retrieved January 2016, from http://www.christianpost.com/news/survey-churches-losing-youths-long-before-college-39433/.

26. Departure from God is Cause of America's Moral Decline. Retrieved January 2016, from http://www.christianpost.com/news/survey-departure-from-god-is-cause-of-america-s-moral-decline-26212/. Also see http://endoftheamericandream.com/archives/why-are-so-many-horrible-things-happening-to-america-all-of-a-sudden.

27. Ibid.

28. Hal Lindsey (August 14, 2015), op. cit.

Chapter 11

What Can We Expect in the Near Future?

> *"Know this first of all, that in the last days mockers will come with their mocking, following after their own lusts, and saying, 'Where is the promise of His coming? For ever since the fathers fell asleep, all continues just as it was from the beginning of creation.' For when they maintain this, it escapes their notice ["deliberately forget" NIV] that by the word of God the heavens existed long ago and the earth was formed out of water and by water, through which the world at that time was destroyed, being flooded with water. But by His word the present heavens and earth are being reserved for fire [nuclear war], kept for the day of judgment and destruction of ungodly men."* —2 Peter 3:3-7, NAS

The Olivet Discourse is the end time teaching of Jesus Christ on the Mount of Olives. This discourse is recorded in Matthew 24:1 – 25:46. Parallel passages are found in Mark 13:1-37 and Luke 21:5-36. The Scripture discusses pre-tribulation signs (v. 4-8), rapture of the church (v. 36-44), and signs of the seven year tribulation period including the first 3 ½ years (v. 9-14) and second 3 ½ years (v. 15-26). Matthew is perhaps the most extensive discourse, so reference is primarily to Matthew's and sometimes to Luke's Gospel. It is important to recognize that Jesus' teaching in this discourse is in reference to Israel and not the church.

> **End time** (also called end times, end of time, end of days, last days, final days) is a time period described in **eschatology** (study of Bible prophecy)—in Christianity, it traditionally depicts the period prior to and including the seven year period preceding the Second Coming of Christ. In Judaism, the term "end of days" references the Messianic Age that includes an in-gathering of the exiled Jews and the coming of the Messiah.

> The **Olivet Discourse** includes a description of the events prior to and during the end times and Jesus' warning to His followers (Christians and Jews) that they will suffer tribulation and persecution before the ultimate triumph of the Kingdom of God.

In Matthew 24:1-2, NIV, Jesus was leaving the Temple when the disciples called His attention to the magnificent buildings on the Temple Mount. Jesus says, *"Do you see all these things?' he asked. 'Truly I tell you, not one stone here will be left on another; every one will be thrown down.'"* This prophecy was fulfilled in AD 70 when the Romans destroyed Jerusalem and the Temple.

In Christianity, last days events go like this: **Rebirth of Israel** (this happened on May 14, 1948) → **Israel acquired the City of Jerusalem** (this occurred on June 5–10, 1967) → **Increase in Intensity of Signs of the End Times** (currently happening) → **Rapture of the church** (next great future event) → **Rise of the antichrist** (after the rapture) → **Seven Year Tribulation** (beginning with a peace covenant and ending with Armageddon) → **the Day of the Lord** (Second Coming of Christ with His Saints) → **the Millennium Period** → **the Last Judgment** → **Eternity** → **New Heaven and New Earth**. For information concerning the pretribulation rapture, see section, Rapture of the Church (p. 171).

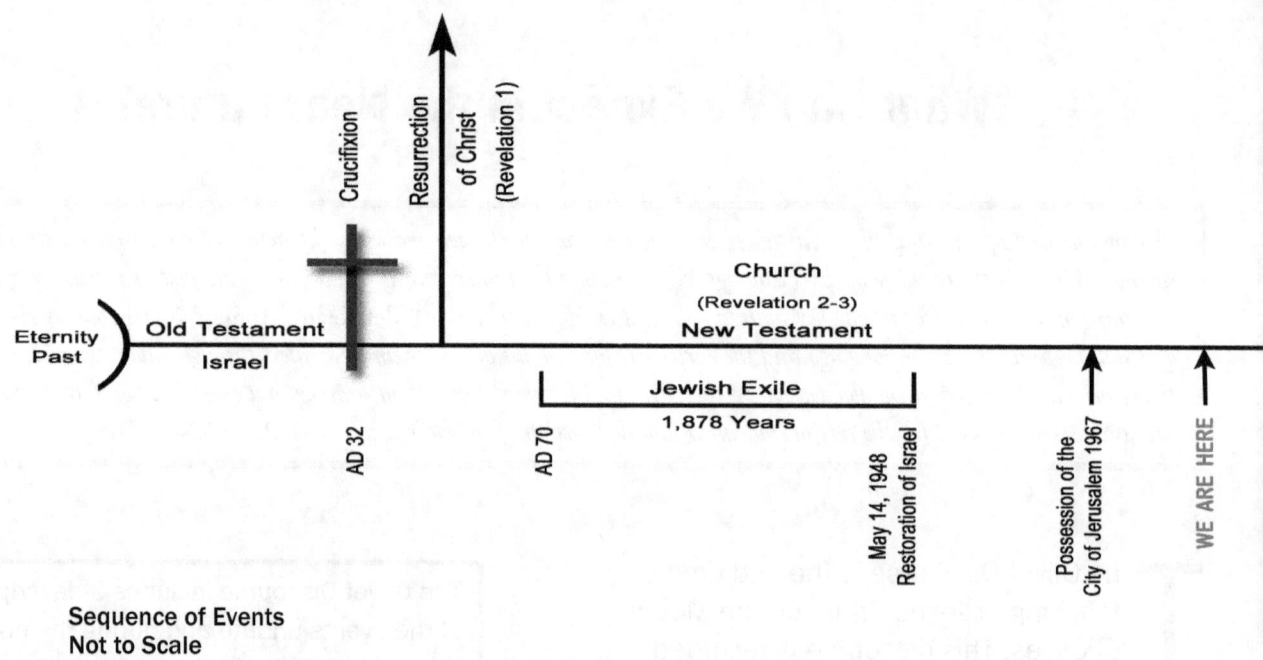

Sequence of Events
Not to Scale

Pre-Tribulation Prophetic Signs

Jesus' prophecy of disaster got the disciples curious, and they were likely very concerned about the near future. When they were alone with Jesus on the Mount of Olives, they asked Him, *"Tell us, when will these things be, and what will be the sign of Your coming, and of the end of the age?"* (Matthew 24:3, NIV; see Luke 21:7.) Matthew 21:4-8 and Luke 21:8-11 refer to signs (birth pangs) **during a period before** the seven year tribulation period. These signs are the *"beginnings of sorrows"* (KJV) or **"the beginning of birth pangs"** (NIV). These verses are setting the stage for the coming tribulation.

> *"Jesus answered: 'Watch out that no one deceives you. **For many will come in my name, claiming, 'I am the Messiah,' and will deceive many.** You will hear of **wars and rumors of wars**, but see to it that you are not alarmed. Such things must happen, but the end is still to come. **Nation will rise against nation, and kingdom against kingdom.** There will be **famines and earthquakes** in various places. All these are the **beginning of birth pains'"** (Matthew 24:4-8, NIV). [Bold added]*

*"There will be **great earthquakes, famines and pestilences** in various places, and fearful events and great signs from heaven"* (Luke 21:11, NIV). [Bold added]

"For many will come in my name, claiming, 'I am the Messiah,' and will deceive many" (verse 5) describes anyone who is a spiritual leader who claims to be God or a direct representative of God. A list of Jewish, Christian, and Muslim messiah claimants is found on the following website: http://en.wikipedia.org/wiki/List_of_messiah_claimants. There are at least five false messiahs in the world today.[1] Also, "Islamic figures wreaking havoc in the world today" include Iran's Ayatollah Ali Khamenei, Abu Bakr al-Baghdadi, the former leader of ISIS (reportedly killed by a U.S. airstrike), and Abubakar Shekau, the leader of Boko Haram.[2]

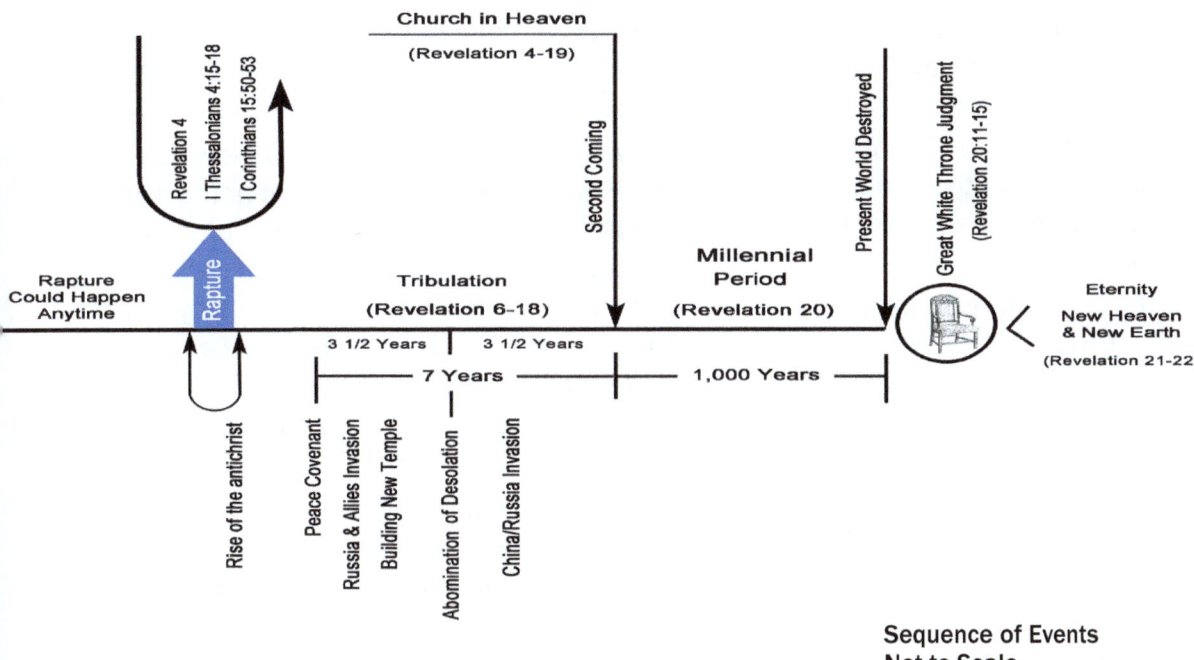

Sequence of Events
Not to Scale

"Wars and rumors of wars....Nation will rise against nation, and kingdom against kingdom" indicate that wars and rumors of wars will be unequaled in the last days—there will be continual ethnic conflicts and rumors of wars worldwide. Although there have been wars and rumors of wars throughout history, in recent times there has been an escalation of wars and ethnic conflicts (African conflicts; eastern European conflicts; and Korean conflicts), especially in the Middle East (Syria; Iraq; Afghanistan [Taliban]; Sunni-Shiite conflicts; and wars between Israel and Arab neighbors). Jesus reminded the disciples *"see to it that you are not alarmed. Such things must happen, but the end is still to come."*

Wars include the following: World War I (The Great War) and World War II (U.S. and its allies fighting Imperial Japan and Nazi Germany), the Korean War, the Vietnam War, Iraq and Afghanistan Wars, and wars and rumors of wars throughout the Middle East, 1948 and 1949 Israeli War of Independence, 1956 Sinai War, 1967 Six Day War, 1973 Yom Kippur War, 2006 Lebanon War, and the Gaza Wars of 2008-2009, 2012, 2014. When the Bible speaks of the end times, it describes increased intensity of these things. Whether it is the recent civil war in Syria, or terrorist activity of ISIS, al-Qaeda, or other groups throughout the world, no single conflict today is necessarily a sign that the end times are imminent.

Examples of ethnic wars since the 1990s are the Yugoslav Wars, the First Chechen War, the Nagorno-Karabakh War, the Rwandan Civil War, the War in Darfur, and the 2014 pro-Russian unrest in Ukraine, among many others. "The 20th century has sometimes been called **the 'Killing Century.' The latter half of that century saw more wanton death and murder than many previous centuries combined**."[3] [Bold added]

List of Conflicts in Africa: Egypt, Sudan, Libya, Tunisia, Algeria, Morocco, Somalia, Uganda, Mali, Mauritania, Niger, Nigeria, Western Sahara, Democratic Republic of Congo and Chad. https://en.wikipedia.org/wiki/List_of_conflicts_in_Africa.

More people have been killed in warfare during this past century than at any other time in history—the "Killing Century." (See text box previous page.) The death toll continues to rise in the Middle East, and other countries (Iran, North Korea, and many others in secret) work to develop devastating weapons of mass destruction (chemical, biological, and nuclear).

Add to all of this the expanding threat of terrorism by ISIS, al-Qaeda, and other terrorist groups (Hezbollah, Hamas, Fatah, the Fedayeen, the Taliban, and Boko Haram); unpredictable dictators in Iran, Iraq, Syria, and other nations in that region; the direct involvement of Russia in Iran's nuclear program and establishing bases of operation in Syria under the nose of the U.S.; and the potential for a devastating nuclear and chemical war in that region and in the U.S. continues to escalate. (See chapter 12, Invasion by Russia and Its Allies, and text box about the prophetic Demise of Damascus, p. 191.)

Earthquakes, famines and pestilences (Luke 21:11) will increase during the last days. In the last decade the world has experienced numerous earthquakes and tsunamis along and near the Pacific Rim (outer rim of the Pacific Ocean). The annual number of major earthquakes (with a magnitude >6.99) **nearly tripled over the past ten years**. "Apart from the 'long-term' trends...which show an on-going persistent increase...earthquakes across the planet show a marked increase in activity since 1997. There are more major earthquakes occurring now, and this on an ever more frequent basis."[4] Additionally, "A new study finds there were more than twice as many major earthquakes in the first quarter of 2014 as compared with the average since 1979."[6] Recent earthquakes in Japan and Ecuador (magnitude > 7.0 in April 2016) were massive and ominous.[7]

And there continues to be a growing worry about super volcanoes with continuing signs of inflation—that is, an increase in pressure from magma activity building from below. (For more information, see the book by Roger Gallop, *evolution - The Greatest Deception in Modern History*; chapter 4, section Beginnings of Catastrophic Volcanoes; and Appendix D, Earthquakes and Tsunamis.)

Farmers are forced out of Zimbabwe in growing numbers as life-sustaining food crops are being replaced with poppies that now supply 25% of the world's heroin. There are over 870 million people who suffer from food shortage, primarily in Africa. The top 10 worst affected countries are Burundi, Eritrea, Comoros, Sudan, Chad, Yemen Republic, Ethiopia, Madagascar, and Zambia. Some countries, particularly in sub-Sahara Africa, and also Mali, Niger, and Nigeria, continue to have extreme cases of famine.

The undernourished and starving are not just limited to Africa but also in Asia (North Korea, Timor Leste, India, Pakistan, Iraq, Afghanistan, and Armenia) and Central America (El Salvador, Guatemala, Haiti, Nicaragua, and Honduras). Nearly every continent in the world has experienced a period of famine in recent history.[8] Such on-going tragedies are rarely reported in the U.S.

Famine and pestilence will become major problems during the tribulation period. Virulent plagues (antibiotic resistant superbugs) and pests will afflict the world as food supplies dwindle during this time. It fits a variety of outbreaks we've seen throughout the world in recent years, including the bizarre monkey infestation in New Delhi, India, AIDS and Coronavirus (COVID-19) pandemic, Ebola and Zika virus, and the Bubonic plague. Today we are facing a whole host of new virulent, drug resistant diseases.[9] (For information about superbugs, see the book *evolution - The Greatest Deception in Modern History*, chapter 3, Are There Beneficial Mutations?)

> "Between 2004 and 2014, 18 earthquakes with magnitudes of 8.0 or more rattled subduction zones around the globe. That's an increase of 265 percent over the average rate of the previous century, which saw 71 great quakes, according to a report to the annual meeting of the Geological Society of America... in Vancouver, British Columbia."[5]

Rapture of the Church

The church, made up of all who have placed their trust in the Lord Jesus Christ (see epilogue, The Bible Warns: There Is Only One Way to Heaven), will not be present during the seven year tribulation. The church will be removed from the earth—snatched away in an event known as the rapture (Revelation 4:1-11; Thessalonians 4:13-18; 1 Corinthians 15:50-54).

Following the rapture, the Holy Spirit will no longer restrain the "lawless one" (the antichrist) and the increase of evil in the world (2 Thessalonians 2:6-7), but the Holy Spirit will continue to indwell and minister to those being saved following the rapture. The church is saved from the wrath that is to come (1 Thessalonians 5:9)—like in the days of Noah when only eight righteous people were saved from the Flood. Most theology scholars believe the rapture will occur immediately before the tribulation period.

> The **rapture** is when Jesus Christ returns to remove the church (all believers in Christ) from the earth as described in 1 Thess. 4:13-18 and 1 Cor. 15:50-54. This event occurs before the seven year tribulation period. How do we know? Before the tribulation (Rev. 1-3) the church is mentioned 7 times, but during the tribulation (Rev. 6-18) the **church is not mentioned once**.
>
> Chapters 2-3 of Revelation speak of the churches, *"He who has an ear, let him hear what the Spirit says to the churches"* (Rev. 2:7, 11, 17, 29, 3:6, 13, 22) while in chapter 13:9 it states, *"If anyone has an ear, let him hear."* This is the same warning **except the church is absent**. God would not have omitted the church if it was still on earth.

> At the judgment seat of Christ, believers (those who have repented of sins and accepted Jesus Christ as their Lord and Savior) will be rewarded for good works and faithful service during their time on earth or may actually lose rewards for lack of service and obedience but not eternal life (1 Corinthians 3:11-15; 2 Corinthians 5:10).

During the tribulation—also called "the time of Jacob's trouble" (Jeremiah 30:7)—God will again turn His attention to Israel (Romans 11:17-31). When believers died in the past (throughout the history of mankind), their souls and spirits entered the presence of God, but the body remained in the grave. **How do we know?** In 2 Corinthians 5:8 (NIV), *"...would prefer to be away from the body and at home with the Lord."* The spirit and soul, absent from the body, are with Christ.

In verse 16 of 1 Thessalonians, the body of those who already died will rise first and then in verse 17, **the body, soul, and spirit of those who have already died are reunited with those who are raptured—and they will all meet the Lord in the air.** This great reunion will all occur in a moment, in a "twinkling of an eye."

*"Brothers and sisters, **we do not want you to be uninformed about those who sleep in death, so that you do not grieve like the rest of mankind, who have no hope.** [14]For we believe that Jesus died and rose again, and so we believe that **God will bring with Jesus those who have fallen asleep in him.** [15]According to the Lord's word, we tell you that we who are still alive, who are left until the coming of the Lord, will certainly not precede those who have fallen asleep. [16]For the Lord himself will come down from heaven, with a loud command, with the voice of the archangel and with the trumpet call of God, **and the dead in Christ will rise first.** [17]After that, we who are still alive and are left will be caught up together* [rapture of the church; Greek is harpazo 'to catch away; to snatch'] *with them in the clouds to meet the Lord in the air. And so we will be with the Lord forever.* [18]*Therefore encourage one another with these words"* (1 Thessalonians 4:13-18, NIV). [Bold added]

> **Rapture of the church**—In Christian eschatology the rapture refers to the belief that Christians will be raised from the earth (in body and in spirit) to meet Christ in the air prior to the seven year tribulation period. This has its basis in various interpretations of 1 Thessalonians 4:13-18, 1 Corinthians 15:51-53, and Revelation 4:1-11. The church, comprising all who have trusted in the Messiah, Jesus Christ, will not be present during the tribulation.
>
> **Pretribulation rapture** is the belief that the rapture will occur before the tribulation; midtribulation rapture is the belief the rapture will occur at the midpoint of the tribulation; and posttribulation rapture is the belief the rapture will occur at the end of the tribulation. For more information supporting the validity of pretribulation rapture, see Glossary – Appendix A.[10]
>
> See http://www.soundchristian.com/prophecy/who/#TOP for a listing of authors of end times. **Those authors highlighted in green teach a pretribulation rapture of the church, a future seven year tribulation period, and a 1,000-year reign of Jesus Christ on earth which is considered sound doctrine.**

The Lord Jesus Christ talks about the rapture in the **Olivet Discourse** mentioned at the start of this chapter.

> "But about that **day or hour no one knows**, not even the angels in heaven, nor the Son, but only the Father. [37]**As it was in the days of Noah, so it will be at the coming of the Son of Man.** [38]**For in the days before the flood, people were eating and drinking, marrying and giving in marriage, up to the day Noah entered the ark;** [39]**and they knew nothing about what would happen until the flood came and took them all away. That is how it will be at the coming of the Son of Man.** [40]Two men will be in the field; one will be taken and the other left. [41]Two women will be grinding with a hand mill; one will be taken and the other left.
>
> [42]"Therefore keep watch, because you do not know on what day your Lord will come. [43]But understand this: If the owner of the house had known at what time of night the thief was coming, he would have kept watch and would not have let his house be broken into. [44]So you also must be ready, because the Son of Man will come **at an hour when you do not expect**" (Matthew 24:36-44, NIV). [Bold added]

Luke 17:26-27 (NIV) states, *"**Just as it was in the days of Noah**, so also will it be in the days of the Son of Man. People were eating, drinking, marrying and being given in marriage up to the day Noah entered the ark. Then the flood came and destroyed them all."* [Bold added] The essential elements of Jesus' warning are that no one knows when He will return, and we should always be discerning, mindful, and watching for that time.

> In today's world, while watching television or reading the newspaper, one can easily be "overwhelmed by the evil that is flooding our world"—from continual violence and moral decay in every major city and town in America to chronic misbehavior in public schools and the moral decline in our public universities, and the general flouting of Christian norms across society in the name of political correctness. **So much that we are becoming "normalized" to violence and moral degeneration—especially in the minds of many of our young people, it is perfectly normal.** Jesus said in the last days, *"...iniquity [lawlessness] shall abound, the love of many shall wax cold"* (Matthew 24:2, KJV), and it is "abounding exponentially."[11]

Like it was in the days of Noah, today's world is filled with political corruption, lying, deceit, slander, public displays of depravity, immoral behavior, violent crimes (lawlessness), abortion, theft, adultery, use of illegal drugs, drunkenness, gambling, and greed of all kinds, not to mention wars, rumors of wars, and terrorism. (Refer to Romans 1:18-22—it reads like today's headlines.) **Just like in the days of Noah** (antediluvian period—Age of Conscience), *"The Lord saw how great man's wickedness on the earth had become, and that every inclination of the thoughts of his heart was only evil all the time"* (Genesis 6:5, NIV).

> Paul wrote to Timothy that *"There will be **terrible times** in the last days."* [Bold added] And then just a few verses later he warned, *"...evil men and impostors will go from **bad to worse, deceiving and being deceived"*** (2 Timothy 3:1, 13, NIV; also see 2 Thessalonians 2:3). Those days are here, and with the removal of the church and the Holy Spirit (the restrainer of evil and the antichrist; see second paragraph this section), times will only grow worse.

The parallels between the days of Noah and the rapture (return of the Son of Man) are described by the apostle Peter as well:

*"Know this first of all, that in the last days **mockers will come with their mocking,** following after their own lusts, and saying, **'Where is the promise of His coming?** For ever since the fathers fell asleep, all continues just as it was from the beginning of creation.' For when they maintain this, it **escapes their notice** ["deliberately forget" NIV] that by the word of God the heavens existed long ago and the earth was formed out of water and by water, through which **the world at that time was destroyed, being flooded with water. But by His word the present heavens and earth are being reserved for fire** [nuclear war], **kept for the day of judgment and destruction of ungodly men"** (2 Peter 3:3-7, NAS). [Bold added]

Just like in the days of Noah when 8 righteous people (4 men and 4 women) were saved by the ark from the worldwide flood, the church (believing Christians) in today's world *"will be caught up together"* (1 Thessalonians 4:13-18) and *"will be raised imperishable"* (1 Corinthians 15:51-53) and escape judgment.

In this passage of Scripture the apostle Peter spoke of a day in the future when men would scoff and mock at the possibility of Christ's return during a pretribulation rapture and at the possiblity of the Second Coming. And the reason for this skeptical attitude is because of man's cynicism and unbelief in God and blind obedience to atheistic, evolutionary doctrine, and humanism taught in our public schools and universities, and proclaimed by our government and the national media, and in movies and television. Just like in the Old Testament, *such people choose not to believe*.

Essentially, it is the belief that God has never judged the world through a worldwide flood and the belief the earth is billions of years old. Because we are told by atheistic academia and evolutionists that this is so, even in the face of contrary and irrefutable "scientific evidence" to the contrary (see book, *evolution – The Greatest Deception in Modern History*), most people unbelievably show little or no concern for God's future judgment as foretold in the Bible. Don't make this terrible mistake.

Imagine being "left behind" while millions of Christians all over the world suddenly vanish without explanation (including young children of unbelieving parents). We have been sufficiently warned by the Bible and the testimony of God's own Son to be ready. We must be ever watchful of world events, and we must be knowledgeable of the promises of God (Ephesians 6:13-18). Today, the devil and his legion of demons roam the earth **looking for those who are open to deception, primarily Christians.**

Do not be fooled into thinking the devil only focuses on pagans (non-believers). He already has non-believers in his grasp unless they spiritually awaken to the truth of Christ Jesus. **Christians are the ones the devil wants to corrupt and destroy, and that is why Christians must be diligent, discerning, and perseverant** and ready for the Lord's return. For the Christian, the rapture will be a joyous, momentous event—and for those left behind, it will be earth-shattering.

The spiritual forces of evil cause people to turn away—to *willfully forget without reason! (See 2 Peter 3:5-6, ASV.)* In Luke 8:10-12, NIV, Jesus described such people as *"though seeing, they may not see; though hearing, they may not understand."* Also see Matthew 13:14. If a person's mind is closed to Scripture (often without any apparent reason), no amount of evidence will change him. This *"hardening of their hearts"* (Ephesians 4:18) against God is a supernatural phenomenon, part of the unseen battle between good and evil around us every day—in the news and in our everyday lives. Many people dismiss such claims because they have **"an enormous predisposition against the supernatural."** But the reality is, the battle between good and evil is very real.

> We are to watch for signs of the last days because Jesus told us that He would return for His own (the rapture prior to the seven year tribulation period which ends with the Second Coming of Jesus Christ). The Lord will come like a thief in the night (2 Peter 3:10). *"Be always on the watch, and pray that you may be able to escape [via the rapture] all that is about to happen, and that you may be able to stand before the Son of Man"* (Luke 21:36, NIV).

The Bible claims all men (including atheists and skeptics) have a knowledge of God.

> "For since the creation of the world God's invisible qualities—his eternal power and divine nature—have been clearly seen, being understood from what has been made, so that people are **without excuse**.
>
> ²¹*For although they knew God, they neither glorified him as God nor gave thanks to him, but their thinking became futile and their foolish hearts were darkened"* Romans 1:20-21, NIV. [Bold added]

There will always be a time when people know in their heart there is a sovereign God, Creator of the heavens and earth and all that exists. Their choice, whether to believe or reject what they know to be true, determines their eternal destiny. They either choose to follow and obey God or they choose to turn away. <u>Everyone makes this choice sometime during their lifetime</u>.

Even atheists know in their heart the reality of God. If they continue to turn away, it is because their heart is so 'hardened' that they are no longer able to acknowledge the sin in their life and the truth of God and Creation.

Rise of the Antichrist

The European debt crisis is a debt upheaval in the European Union (EU) that began near the end of 2009. "Several eurozone member states (Greece, Portugal, Spain, Ireland, and Cyprus) were unable to repay or refinance their government debt" without the assistance of other EU countries, the ECB (European Central Bank), or the IMF (International Monetary Fund).[12] Such debt was (is) due to excessive welfare spending and inability to bail out overly indebted banks due to liberal lending practices similar to the current socialist policies in the U.S. (See chapter 9, Economic Decline, for more information.)

In addition to the economic problems in Europe, the U.S. has a national debt of 28.8 trillion dollars and a total debt of 86 trillion dollars as of September 14, 2021 (previously, 22.4 trillion dollars and total debt of 73.58 trillion dollars as of June 2019, and 19.97 trillion and a total debt of 66.88 trillion as of February 2017), liberal non-entitlement handout government programs (welfare, food stamps, and Medicaid), and bloated pensions for the top managers and executives in almost every city and county. See text box in chapter 9, Economic Decline (p. 141).

Despite inflated optimism by U.S. administrations during the last two decades, the United States is clearly in a state of decline and heading down the same path as Greece and other socialist countries, but most people are not aware of the situation. The actions of debtor nations (i.e., EU nation states, the U.S., and others that spend more than they receive; or deficit spending) **will set off a chain reaction that leads directly to a "global debt implosion" and military conflict across the globe.**

In these last days economic conditions will become so grim that **people will literally turn to anyone who is charismatic and who they think has the answer to their economic woes. Do you think this is a possibility? Yes—without question.** *This is exactly what happened to Germany just prior to WW II. The economic situation became so grim that the people propelled Adolph Hitler into the role of dictator*. And like Hitler, the antichrist will charismatically (and supernaturally) convince practically everyone he has the answer and can solve their economic woes. True believers will not be here to suffer through the agony and chaos the **"man of lawlessness"** will bring upon this world.[15]

> The **International Monetary Fund (IMF)** is an international organization headquartered in Washington, DC, comprising "188 countries working to foster global monetary cooperation, secure financial stability, facilitate international trade, promote high employment and sustainable economic growth, and reduce poverty around the world."[13]

> In today's world, we are seeing economic instability in the EU and the rest of the world including the U.S. and China. Both the yen and the euro were made intentionally lower relative to the dollar. When a nation lowers the value of its currency, it cuts into the buying power of the people of that country (where devaluation is occurring)—so China's exported goods will be cheaper (they can sell more overseas which is good for the Chinese) and U.S. exported goods will be more expensive (we sell less overseas which is not so good for the U.S.)[14]

> The devaluation of the yuan in China (including the devaluation of the yen in Japan and euro in Europe) means fewer overseas consumers will be able to afford U.S. automobiles. Buying more overseas and selling less overseas means **increased trade debt for the U.S.** (Keep in mind that GM sells more cars in China than it does in the U.S.)

Will the rapture of the church, as described in the previous section, encourage the rise of the antichrist? Yes! With the removal of perhaps 25 to 30% of people in the U.S. (a lesser percentage throughout the rest of the world), this earth-shattering event will completely unhinge an already chaotic and fragile economy and will have severe aftershocks on the social fabric of the U.S. and the world. World chaos will occur and economic chaos will ensue which, in turn, will assure the meteoric rise of the antichrist (2 Thessalonians 2; Revelation 6:1-16).

The lack of any credible solutions by debtor nations to solve the economic problems will set the stage for collapse of the world economy and initiate the rapid rise of a world leader—the antichrist—and ultimately lead to global currency and monetary controls.

The word antichrist is only found in 1 John 2:18, 2:22, 4:3, and 2 John 7. Many antichrists have appeared between the time of Christ (c. 1 BC - AD 32) and present day—but there will be **one great antichrist** who will rise to power during the end times, or "last hour," as stated in 1 John 2:18. He will deny that Jesus is the Christ, the Messiah; he will deny both God the Father and God the Son; and he will be a liar and a great deceiver (unfortunately, like many of our politicians today).

The world is primed to place the blame on 'alien abduction' but some will recognize what has really happened. During the past 10 or more years much of the movie and television programming has been based on 'alien invasions' and 'alien abductions.' The ancient Roman Empire revives as the political antichrist arises out of the EU and its economic difficulties. (See p. 135 and p. 195 for more information concerning U.S. connection to political Babylon.)

The Coming Seven Year Tribulation

The term 'Latter Days' in the Old Testament and in the book of Daniel refers to the latter days of the state of Israel. In Daniel chapter nine, in particular, *"seventy weeks"* is mentioned which includes a 69 week period and then the final 70th week, or the time of tribulation following the rapture of the church. This is a seven year period of unprecedented war and nuclear catastrophe—the **first 3 ½ years begins with a 7-year peace covenant between the antichrist and Israel**, and the **second 3 ½ years is called the great tribulation** (last 42 months or 1,260 days as described in Revelation 6 - 22). The tribulation period is described in the following sections.

Revelation 6 through 22 (see chapter 12, Seals, Trumpets, and Bowls) gives us a detailed description of the tribulation—also known as the **Time of Jacob's Trouble** (Jeremiah 30:7). *"How awful that day will be! No other will be like it. It will be a time of trouble for Jacob, but he [they; the church] will be saved out of it"* (Jeremiah 30:7, NIV).

Daniel's 70th Week

Most Christians theologians agree that the proper name for the final seven years is **Daniel's 70th Week**.

²⁴"Seventy 'sevens' [**70 weeks of years**] *are **decreed for your people** and your holy city to finish transgression, to put an end to sin, to atone for wickedness, to bring in everlasting righteousness, to seal up vision and prophecy and to anoint the Most Holy.*

²⁵Know and understand this: From the issuing of the decree to restore and rebuild Jerusalem [decree of Artaxerxes to restore the walls of Jerusalem in 445 BC; see chapter 4, Rebuilding the Temple and the Walls of Jerusalem] *until the Anointed One* [the Messiah], *the ruler, comes, there will be seven 'sevens,' and sixty-two 'sevens.'* [**69 weeks of years**] *It will be rebuilt with streets and a trench, but in times of trouble"* (Daniel 9:24-25, NIV). [Bold added]

When Jesus was crucified on the cross, the 69th week of Daniel's prophecy ended. The prophetic time clock *stopped* for Israel and will not resume again until the seven year tribulation (Daniel 9:26-27) **which begins with the peace covenant.**

²⁶"After the sixty-two 'sevens,' [**7 weeks + 62 weeks = total 69 weeks**] *the Anointed One will be put to death* [**cut off; crucified on the cross**] *and will have nothing. The people of the ruler who will come will destroy the city and the sanctuary. The end will come like a flood: War will continue until the end, and desolations have been decreed. ²⁷He* [the antichrist] *will **confirm a covenant** with many for **one 'seven'*** [**1 week of years**]. *In the middle of the 'seven'* [**after the first 3 ½ years**] *he will put an end to sacrifice and offering. And at the temple he will set up an **abomination** that causes desolation, until the end that is decreed is poured out on him"* (Daniel 9:26-27, NIV). [Bold added] (See the timeline at the beginning of this chapter.)

Daniel 9:24-27 speaks of 70 weeks that have been "decreed for *your people.*" Daniel's people are the Jews and the State of Israel. Daniel 9:24 speaks of a period of time that God has given *"to finish transgression, to put an end to sin, to atone for wickedness, to bring in everlasting righteousness, to seal up vision and prophecy and to anoint the most holy"* (Daniel 9:24, NIV).

God declares that "seventy sevens" will fulfill all these things. This is 70 sevens of years, or 490 years. (Some translations refer to 70 weeks of years.) This is confirmed by another part of this passage in Daniel. In verses 25 and 26, Daniel is told that the Messiah will be cut off (crucified on the cross) after *"seven sevens and sixty-two sevens"* (69 weeks of years), beginning with the decree of Artaxerxes to restore the walls of Jerusalem in **445 BC** (see Daniel 9:25 and chapter 4, Rebuilding the Temple and the Walls of Jerusalem) and ending with the rejection and crucifixion of Jesus, exactly **483 years**.

> What is the **seven sevens and sixty-two sevens?** It took 49 years to rebuild Jerusalem [1 week of years, or 7 sevens], which occurred in troublesome times according to the book of Nehemiah, and then after another 434 years [62 weeks of years, or 62 sevens], the Messiah was cut off. 49 years [rebuilding the temple] plus 434 years [time of the crucifixion] = **483 years.**

In the Book of Genesis and in the Book of Revelation, the Bible was written on a 360 days per year calendar. When calculating the coming of the Messiah from 445 BC (decree to restore the walls), it is critical to count the time according to the Bible's calendar of 360 days per year and not by today's 365.25 day solar calendar. From Nisan 445 BC, where does the 483 years end based on the Bible's calendar? With the establishment of 360 days per year, the exact time can be determined.

To identify the exact time, the 360 days per year has to be reconciled with the 365.25 solar days per year. We know the total number of years in the 69 weeks of years: 69 weeks of years x 7 years per week totals **483 years**; then multiplying this number by 360 days for each year, the total is exactly **173,880 days** based on the Bible's calendar until the crucifixion. Then dividing 173,880 days by 365.25 solar days per year equals 476 years based on the current solar calendar. There are exactly **173,880 days, or 476 solar years, from the month of Nisan in 445 BC to the month of Nisan in AD 32 (the time of the crucifixion).**

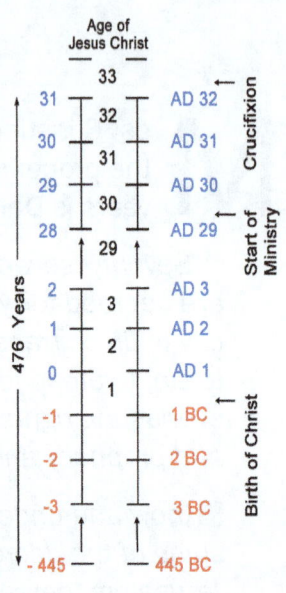

Starting from the month of Nisan in 445 BC and working forward 476 years to the crucifixion would be the month of Nisan AD 32. There are a total of 476 years minus the 445 BC years which leaves 31 years in AD. Doing the simple math leaves us one year short because it does not account for the extra year zero when doing the linear conversion from BC to AD. The 31 years plus one year for year zero comes to Nisan AD 32. The countdown which began in Nisan 445 BC with the decree to rebuild Jerusalem by the Persian King Artaxerxes ended in Nisan AD 32. Most Christian theology scholars, regardless of their view of eschatology (future events), have this understanding of Daniel's 70 sevens.[16]

Increase in the Severity of Signs

Matthew 24:4-8 refers to "birth pangs" or increased intensity of signs **before** the beginning of the last week—the seven year tribulation period. Then Matthew 24:9-14 (see Luke 21) refers to further intensity and severity of signs (birth pangs) **during** the first 3 ½ years. These signs will increase in intensity and severity as the Great Tribulation approaches (the last 3 ½ years of Daniel's 70th Week), much like the birth pangs or contractions of a woman in labor. The world is experiencing these signs today. See chapters 8 - 10.

> First 3 ½ years of the great tribulation: *"Then you will be handed over to be **persecuted and put to death**, and you will be **hated by all nations because of me** [Jesus Christ]. At that time **many will turn away from the faith and will betray and hate each other**, and **many false prophets will appear and deceive many people**. Because of the **increase of wickedness, the love of most will grow cold**, but he who stands firm to the end will be saved. And this **gospel of the kingdom will be preached in the whole world** as a testimony to all nations, and **then the end will come"** (Matthew 24:9-14, NIV). [Bold added]*

> Revelation 6 is a parallel passage. The apostle John writes of the seal judgments (see chapter 12, section Seals, Trumpets, and Bowls). Revelation 6:2 speaks of a rider on a white horse, which refers to the antichrist or the beast. Revelation 6:4 says that peace is taken from the earth, and Revelation 6:6-8 speaks of famine and death.
>
> Revelation 4–22 is a description of the coming tribulation. Refer to books by Jack Van Impe (*Revelation Revealed*, 1982), Hal Lindsey (*The New World Coming*, 1984), and Tim LaHaye and Thomas Ice (*Charting the End Times*, 2001) for a thorough explanation.

Hatred, persecution, and death because of me (Jesus Christ)—During World War II, the Jews faced genocide at the hands of **Nazi Germany** or the **Third Reich**. In what has come to be called the **Holocaust**, 6 million European Jews (including 1.5 million children) were systematically exterminated in what the Nazis called the "final solution of the Jewish question." Hitler and his demonic followers literally killed two thirds of the Jewish people.

Such demonic, horrific behavior by human beings is a **supernatural evil** that permeates the world—an evil that "steals, kills, and destroys" with the final goal of eliminating the Jewish people, the church, and seizing control of God's authority or sovereignty. (See chapter 5, Nazi Germany and the Holocaust.) Evil is pervasive throughout history and this modern-day, historical event (the Holocaust) **leaves no doubt that a terrible supernatural evil is inescapable in this world if not for the saving grace of Jesus Christ—a holy, merciful God (love and goodness).** (See Prologue, Good and Evil.) Supporters of PC appeasement philosophy should take note that it took World War II to stop this demonic madness and keep end time prophecy on course to fulfillment.

> **Don't make the most terrible mistake of your life by turning away from the Creator God (Father, Son, and Holy Spirit). God is holy, righteous, and merciful,** and through our Lord Jesus Christ offers the gift of eternal salvation (John 3:16, 5:24, 14:6; Romans 10:9, 13; and Ephesians 2:8-9) to those who do not turn away.
>
> People lest not forget the Lord is **omnipresent, omnipotent, and omniscient** (Romans 8:29; Ephesians 1:4-5; 1 Corinthians 2:7) and *"the Lord is a warrior"* (Exodus 15:3)—*"He does whatever pleases Him"* (Psalms 115:3, 135:6; Job 23:13; Daniel 4:35, NIV), and *"He is to be feared"* (1 Chronicles 16:25; Psalm 96:4; Isaiah 8:13, NIV). [Bold added] See Preface, Who is God?

And in most recent times, both Christians and Jews have been persecuted worldwide, especially in the Middle East by Islamic extremists. Tens of thousands of Christians and Jews (entire families—mothers, fathers, and children of all ages) have been slaughtered without mercy. **Has humanity completely lost sight of what is good and true? The persecution of Jews and Christians is clearly the picture of monstrous and depraved mankind at its absolute worst.** (See Matthew 5:11, Matthew 24:9, and 1 Peter 4: 13-16.)

During the first half of the tribulation, the antichrist will persecute and put to death anyone who refuses to follow him (Matthew 24:9; Revelation 13:1-18), but *"he who stands firm to the end will be saved"* (Matthew 24:13, NIV). The last days are described as *"terrible times"* because of the increasingly evil character of people who continue to actively *"resist the truth"* (2 Timothy 3:1-9; 2 Thessalonians 2:3).

Christians are under increasing attack throughout the world today. Although in the United States Christians still enjoy freedom to worship God without physical suffering and persecution (cruelty of all types), there is **increasing ridicule, mocking, and**

discrimination, often at work and school. In many other countries such as China, Sudan, Africa, Saudi Arabia, North Korea, Russia, and many Muslim nations, Christians suffer much greater physical and emotional persecution (cruelty of all types) and often face death for their faith. During the tribulation, persecution and martyrdom will occur worldwide.

Many will turn away from the faith and betray each other—People often ask the question, why would a loving God create a world full of pain and suffering—**and then these same people use this rationale as an excuse to turn away from God. But the real question is,** "why would a loving God come into the world He created to suffer and die [suffer a terrible, agonizing death by crucifixion] to pay for my sin?"[17] Remember that it was man who chose to walk out of God's will.

Churches today are becoming more and more ecumenical (promoting unity among world religions), embracing the New Age merger of all faiths, and denying Christ as the only way to salvation. (This false idea is seen

Focus on material wealth as the standard for success. *Sketch by Anton Zakharov*

The **spiritual forces of evil in this world cause people to turn away**—to willfully forget without reason! (See 2 Peter 3:5-6, ASV.)

In Luke 8:10-12, NIV, Jesus described such people as *"though seeing, they may not see; though hearing, they may not understand."* The nature of mankind throughout history is to *'harden their hearts'* (Ephesians 4:18; Mark 8:17-18). It is sad that people who turn away without reason do not realize this verse applies to them.

There is no love without freedom. This world is a testing ground to either accept or reject the free gift of pardon through Jesus Christ. The **only unpardonable sin** is to reject the free gift of pardon offered by Jesus Christ, the promised Messiah...who stepped out of Eternity and became a guilt offering. He took the penalty for our sins upon Himself—but we have to believe it and accept it.

Man is given time here on earth to experience life, repent of sins, and make a "free will" choice for or against God by either accepting or rejecting the gift of pardon offered by the Son of God.

"Free will" will have been fulfilled during our life on earth (1 Corinthians 13:12; Revelation 21:1-5; Ephesians 1:4:2; 2 Timothy 1:9-10), and then in heaven a person will no longer be able to sin. Time here on earth is the "free will" testing ground for humans. **There is no love without freedom.**

For more information about this subject, see book by Roger Gallop, *Defeating Evil - God's Plan Before the Beginning of TIme.*

on many auto bumper stickers today espousing the same God for all religions—COEXIST.) Giving in to **PC doctrine**, people in the church have embraced homosexuality and transgender as an acceptable alternate lifestyle and preach tolerance and compromise in place of God's truth. This is today's **Laodicea church** (Revelation 3:14-22) **where the focus is on material wealth as the standard for success as well as scientific and philosophical rationalism (i.e., evolution and humanism).** This church calls itself Christian but "Christ sits in the back row." See chapter 10, Compromised Teaching of the Bible.

> **Political correctness (PC)** is a term primarily used to describe language, actions, or policies intended not to offend any particular group of people in society (except Christians and Jews); that is, to tolerate and fully embrace all ideologies so as not to offend. (See p. 152.) **Tolerance** used to mean "agree to disagree" but in today's politically correct world it means "acceptance" of all ideologies, life-styles, and behavior. See chapter 10, Political Correctness.
>
> The far left New Age church movement has lured parishioners into teaching tolerance of Islam—that is, embracing Islam with the idea that all people are under one faith and one God. It embraces the worshiping of 'mother earth' and believing in the atheistic, false doctrine of evolution (see the book, *evolution – The Greatest Deception in Modern History*) while demonizing a conservative belief in the Bible.

False prophets and deceiving spirits— Paul warned that in the last days there would be an obvious increase in **false teaching**, pagan religions, heresy (sacrilege or deviation from the Bible), deception, and occultism. *"The Spirit clearly says that in later times some will abandon the faith and follow **deceiving spirits and things taught by demons**"* (1 Timothy 4:1, NIV). [Bold added]

> *"For the time will come when people will not put up with sound doctrine. Instead, to suit their own desires, **they will gather around them a great number of teachers to say what their itching ears want to hear. They will turn their ears away from the truth and turn aside to myths**"* (2 Timothy 4:3-4, NIV). [Bold added]

We see this in the teaching of evolution— declared "as fact" in public schools and many secular colleges and universities throughout the U.S. and world. Although there is overwhelming scientific evidence supporting Creation (see chapter 1, Scientific Evidence for Divine Creation and the book by Roger Gallop, *evolution – The Greatest Deception in Modern History*), evolution is assumed and taught as truth because it is the only way secular teachers and scientists can "naturalistically" explain man's origin without a Divine Creator. Scientific evidence against evolution is simply ignored, rejected, or explained away by these secular, atheistic people.

In the last days there will be an increase in false messiahs and their deceptive teachings—it describes anyone who is a spiritual leader who claims to be God or a direct representative.

> *"Jesus answered: 'Watch out that no one deceives you. For **many will come in my name, claiming, 'I am the Messiah,' and will deceive many**. You will hear of **wars and rumors of wars**, but see to it that you are not alarmed. Such things must happen, but the end is still to come. **Nation will rise against nation, and kingdom against kingdom**. There will be **famines and earthquakes** in various places. All these are the **beginning of birth pains**'"* (Matthew 24:4-8, NIV). [Bold added]

> A list of Jewish, Christian, and Muslim messiah claimants is found on http://en.wikipedia.org/wiki/List_of_messiah_claimants. There are at least five false messiahs in the world today.[18] Also, "Islamic figures wreaking havoc in the world today" include Iran's Ayatollah Ali Khamenei; Abu Bakr al-Baghdadi, the leader of ISIS (reportedly killed in a U.S. airstrike); and Abubakar Shekau, the leader of Boko Haram.[19]

Increase of wickedness, and the love of most will grow cold—The last days (just before and during the tribulation period) are described as "**terrible times**" because of the increasingly evil nature of man and those who "oppose the truth." **The following Scripture seems to fit our modern age perfectly and it will only get worse.**

*"But mark this: There will be **terrible times** in the last days. People will be **lovers of themselves, lovers of money, boastful, proud, abusive, disobedient to their parents, ungrateful, unholy, without love, unforgiving, slanderous, without self-control, brutal, not lovers of the good, treacherous, rash, conceited, lovers of pleasure rather than lovers of God**—having a form of godliness but denying its power. Have nothing to do with such people"* (2 Timothy 3:1-5, NIV). [Bold added]

The Gospel and salvation message of Jesus Christ will be proclaimed throughout the whole world as a testimony to all nations, and then the end shall come—Although some countries do not allow proselytizing (not even in normal conversation with friends), today the gospel is preached not only by missionaries who travel to remote areas of the world (at the risk of persecution or death) but also on television (Hal Lindsey, Jack van Impe, and many others) to worldwide audiences, radio, and the internet (where there are many Christian websites proclaiming the "last days"). China and North Korea and countries in Eastern Europe and Russia and countries throughout Africa are hearing the gospel message through the advances of satellite communications.

The Bible has been translated into many languages and dialects and has been disseminated throughout the world and is available in many languages on the internet. Any Scripture (book, chapter, and verse) can be searched online in a just few seconds (https://www.biblegateway.com). Today, there are many web sites in many languages that proclaim salvation through Jesus Christ, signs of the end times, and His imminent return.

There are many Christian internet sites and television programs such as www.hopetv.org; 3angelstube.com; www.amazingfacts.tv; Billy Graham (http://billygraham.org/); Hal Lindsey (http://www.hallindsey.com/); and Jack Van Impe (http://www.jvim.com/). Via these internet sites, Biblical truths are being transmitted 24 hours a day in many languages throughout the world. They also publish books and Biblical literature and DVDs.

As is written in the Bible, *"And this gospel of the kingdom will be preached in the whole world as a testimony to all nations, and **then the end will come**"* (Matthew 24:14, NIV). [Bold added] This prophecy has already been fulfilled through television, radio, missionaries, the translation of the Bible into many languages, and the internet. *"And then the end will come"*—so the question is, are you ready? And *"The Lord is not slow in keeping his promise, as some understand slowness. Instead he is patient with you, not wanting anyone to perish, but **everyone to come to repentance**"* (2 Peter 3:9, NIV). [Bold added]

notes: Chapter 11

1. http://www.christianpost.com/news/5-false-messiahs-and-why-their-claims-to-be-christ-contradict-the-bible-97059/. Also see http://www.therefinersfire.org/challenging_false_messiahs.htm.

2. Hal Lindsey (September 18, 2015). The Hal Lindsey Report, News from Hal Lindsey Media Ministries. (www.hallindsey.org)

3. Ethnic conflict. Retrieved February 2016, from https://en.wikipedia.org/wiki/Ethnic_conflict and Ethnic Conflict. Retrieved February 2016, from http://regentsprep.org/Regents/global/themes/conflict/ethnic.cfm.

4. Earthquakes - What Are the Long Term Trends? (2011). Retrieved May 2016, from http://www.earth.webecs.co.uk/.

5. Carroll, L. (October 25, 2014). Worldwide Surge in 'Great' Earthquakes Seen in Past 10 Years. NBC News; as cited in Science News. Retrieved October 2014, from http://www.nbcnews.com/science/science-news/worldwide-surge-great-earthquakes-seen-past-10-years-n2336615.

6. Oskin, B. (June 2014). Earthquake frequency increasing: Rate of strong quakes doubles in 2014. Retrieved May 2016, from https://www.sott.net/article/281068-Earthquake-frequency-increasing-Rate-of-strong-quakes-doubles-in-2014 and Oskin, B. (Live Science, June 2014) Big Earthquakes Double in 2014.... Retrieved May 2016, from http://www.livescience.com/46576-more-earthquakes-still-random-process.html; and Don't Panic! Preliminary data suggest earthquakes are indeed increasing worldwide (posted Dec 2012). Retrieved May 2016, from https://theextinctionprotocol.wordpress.com/2012/12/31/dont-panic-preliminary-data-suggests-earthquakes-are-indeed-increasing-worldwide/.

7. USGS: Risk of earthquakes in 2016 increases, especially in Oklahoma (March 2016). Retrieved from http://www.foxnews.com/science/2016/03/28/usgs-risk-earthquakes-in-2016-increases-especially-in-okla https://theawakezone.wordpress.com/2016/04/17/earthquake-activity-has-increased/homa.html; and Earthquake activity has increased (April 2016). Retrieved May 2016, from https://theawakezone.wordpress.com/2016/04/17/earthquake-activity-has-increased/. Also see Gallop, R. (2016). *evolution - The Greatest Deception in Modern History*.

8. Guy-Allen, C. (March 10, 2014). The world's ten hungriest countries. Retrieved February 2016, from https://www.globalcitizen.org/en/content/the-worlds-10-hungriest-countries/Famine. Retrieved February 2016, from https://en.wikipedia.org/wiki/Famine; and Buerkle, T. (2006). 40 countries face food shortages worldwide. Retrieved February 2016, from http://www.fao.org/Newsroom/en/news/2006/1000416/index.html.

9. Sun, L.H. and Dennis, B. (May 27, 2016). Superbug dreaded by doctors found to have invaded the U.S., The Florida Times-Union, Jacksonville, Florida, A-10.

10. Reiter, R.R., et al. (1996). Three Views on the Rapture; Retrieved from http://www.christianbook.com/three-views-on-the-rapture/richard-reiter/9780310212980/pd/2129X?event=AFF&p=1011693&.

11. Hal Lindsey (November 6, 2015), op. cit.

12. European debt crisis. Retrieved February 2016, from https://en.wikipedia.org/wiki/European_debt_crisis.

13. International Monetary Fund; as cited in "About the IMF". IMF. Retrieved October 14, 2012, and February 2016, from https://en.wikipedia.org/wiki/International_Monetary_Fund.

14. Hal Lindsey (August 21, 2015), op. cit.

15. Hal Lindsey (June 5, 2015), op. cit.

16. From Nisan 445 BC Where Does the 483 Years End? Retrieved February 2016, from http://www.defendproclaimthefaith.org/Where_Does_483_Years_End.htm; and Daniel's Seventy Weeks prophecy: A detailed look at Daniel 9:24-27. Retrieved February 2016, from http://aboutbibleprophecy.com/weeks.htm; and Tribulation vs. Great Tribulation (June 2010). Gracethrufaith. Retrieved from http://gracethrufaith.com/ask-a-bible-teacher/tribulation-vs-great-tribulation/. Also see http://endtimepilgrim.org/70wks3.htm.

17. See Prologue of book, *evolution – The Greatest Deception in Modern History* by Roger G. Gallop, end note 2 (3rd paragraph).

18. http://www.christianpost.com/news/5-false-messiahs-and-why-their-claims-to-be-christ-contradict-the-bible-97059/. Also see http://www.therefinersfire.org/challenging_false_messiahs.htm.

19. Hal Lindsey (September 18, 2015), op. cit.

Chapter 12

The Seven Year Tribulation Period

> *"He will confirm a covenant with many for one 'seven'* [at the beginning of the tribulation period]. *In the middle of the 'seven'* [midway through the tribulation period] *he will put an end to sacrifice and offering. And at the temple he will set up an abomination that causes desolation, until the end that is decreed is poured out on him."* —Daniel 9:27, NIV

From this time forward, the next great events in store for planet earth are continued increase in the intensity of signs of the end times (currently happening) and removal of the church (a Divine act of deliverance) which could happen at any time. (See chapter 11, Rise of the Antichrist, for more information.) Following these events is the seven year tribulation which begins with a peace covenant between the antichrist and Israel. Midway through the tribulation, there is an event call the "abomination of desolation," and at the end of the seven year tribulation, the battle of Armageddon and the Second Coming of Christ with His Saints. Following the Second Coming is the Millennial Period, the Last Judgment, and the New Heaven and New Earth. These events are briefly described in this chapter.

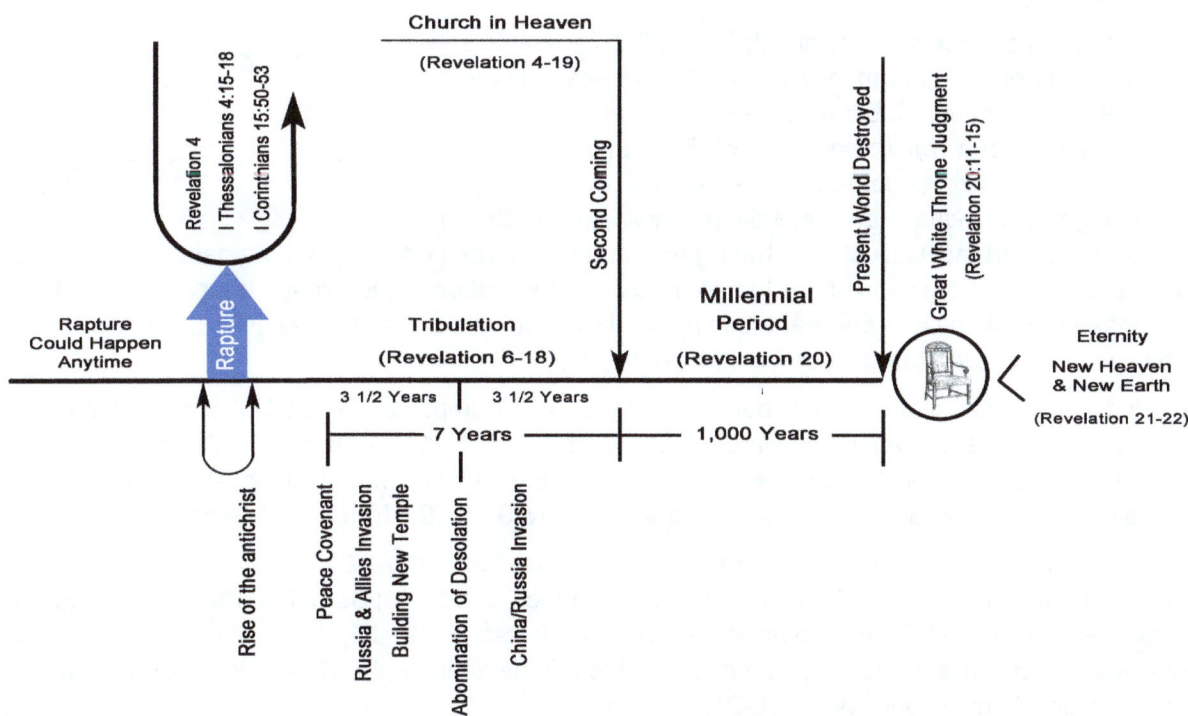

Rapture of the Church, the Seven Year Tribulation Period, and the Millennial Period.
See full timeline at the start of previous chapter. Sequence of events, not to scale

Seals, Trumpets, and Bowls

The Book of Revelation, chapters 4–22, describes the tribulation period with great symbolism of intensifying Divine judgments: **seals** (6:1 – 8:5), **trumpets** (8:7 – 11:19), and **bowls** (15:1 – 16:21). These judgments culminate with the final world battle, Armageddon—which ends with the Second Coming of Jesus Christ.

The first 3 ½ years begin when the antichrist (likely a European political leader) **guarantees Israel peace and protection.** In effect, Israel and the world will be at rest trusting in the EU military and political alliance. Israel will be lulled into an illusion of peace.

The second 3 ½ years begin when the antichrist stands in the newly constructed Jewish Temple in Jerusalem and demands to be worshiped "as God." In Scripture this is known as the "abomination of desolation." This last 3 ½ years comprise unspeakable global terror and nuclear catastrophe.

For a more detailed description of these events, refer to books by Jack Van Impe (Revelation Revealed, 1982) and Hal Lindsey (The New World Coming, 1984).

> **Tribulation** is a future seven year period when God decrees Divine judgment (seals, trumpets, and bowls) against all those who have rejected the free gift of pardon of Jesus Christ, and He will also complete His plan of salvation for Israel. It is a time of suffering, persecution, and global nuclear war immediately prior to the Second Coming of Jesus Christ. The first 3 ½ years begin with a seven year peace covenant between the antichrist and Israel (Dan. 9:26-27), and the second 3 ½ years is called the great tribulation.

Seals, trumpets, and bowls are judgments of intensifying pain and suffering during the seven year tribulation period. These judgments do not occur in a simple linear format but rather, they are consecutively layered or overlapping.

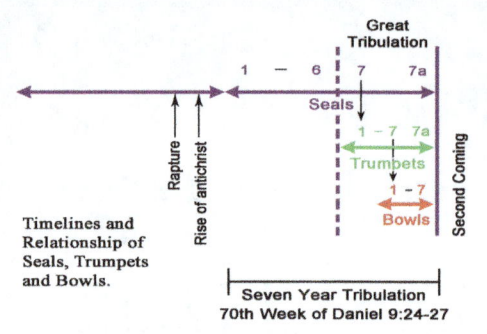

Timelines and Relationship of Seals, Trumpets and Bowls.

Seal 1 is the white horseman: the antichrist (vv. 6:1-2); Seal 2 is the red horseman: the Russian invasion (vv. 6:3-4); Seal 3 is the black horseman: famine (vv. 6:5-6); Seal 4 is the pale horseman: death, epidemics, and civil violence (vv. 6:7-8); Seal 5 is mass murder of believers (martyrdom); great persecution (vv. 6:9-11); Seal 6 is a great earthquake and celestial upheavals (vv. 6:12-17); Seal 7 opens the Trumpets. Just after the rapture and before the beginning of judgments, 144,000 Jewish evangelists (12,000 from each of the Jewish tribes; see Revelation 7:4-8) preach the gospel of Jesus Christ to the pagan world.[1] The new covenant (see Appendix B) with Israel will be established, and the Jews will again be God's representatives to spread the gospel.

Trumpet 1 is when 1/2 of the earth is burned up (vv. 8:1-2); Trumpet 2 is when 1/2 of sea creatures die (vv. 8:8-9); Trumpet 3 is when 1/2 of waters are polluted (vv. 8:10-11); Trumpet 4 is when 1/3 of celestial bodies are darkened (vs. 8:12); Trumpet 5 is the release of locusts/demons (vv. 9:1-11); Trumpet 6 is when 4 bound demons are released to kill 1/3 of humankind (vv. 9:13-19); Trumpet 7 opens up the Bowls.

Bowl 1 is horrible sores on those with mark of the beast (vs: 16:2); Bowl 2 is when every creature in the sea dies (vs. 16:13); Bowl 3 is when all waters are polluted (vv. 16:4-7); Bowl 4 is when the sun burns and scorches people (vv. 16:8-9); Bowl 5 brings complete darkness (vv. 16:10-11); Bowl 6 is when the Euphrates River dries up and kings of the east march toward the Middle East (vv. 16:12-15); Bowl 7 is a great earthquake and Armageddon (vv. 16:16-21).

Progression from seals to trumpets to bowls with **increasing intensity** of judgments upon the pagan world will culminate with the Battle of Armageddon (Revelation 16:12). Bowls will happen toward the end of the great tribulation (Revelation 16) and will end with the Second Coming of Jesus Christ.

First 3 ½ Years of the Tribulation Period

Sometime after the rapture, but before the beginning of the tribulation period, the antichrist manages to solve the economic debt problems besieging the European Union (EU) and the world, befriends Israel, and resolves the problems between Israel and Arabs. These resolutions propel the antichrist to the position of world dictator.

We are reminded that the Bible describes the antichrist's rise to power in largely economic terms. Following the rapture of the church (see chapter 11), **massive worldwide economic and social troubles will be the catalyst for the antichrist's meteoric rise** (similar to the time Germany willingly gave Adolf Hitler free reign prior to WW II). Because of the grim global economic and social turmoil, people will turn to anyone who they think has the answer or solution. Like Hitler, the antichrist will be charismatic and will convince everyone that he has the solution to the worldwide turmoil, and the nations of the world will blindly "throw the door open to him."[2] The only good news is that people who have accepted the free gift of salvation through Jesus Christ (prior to the rapture) will not suffer through the despair and misery of this tribulation period.

A peace covenant marks the beginning of the last week or 7 year tribulation period. The antichrist makes a strong and convincing covenant with Israel guaranteeing full military support, safety and security—a peace covenant that has alluded modern world leaders including every American president since Ronald Reagan. Israel is at rest because of the strong covenant (alliance) with the antichrist (European Union).

> "He will **confirm a covenant** with many for one 'seven' [**at the beginning of the tribulation period**]. In the middle of the 'seven' [**midway through the tribulation period**] he will put an end to sacrifice and offering. And at the temple he will set up an **abomination that causes desolation,** until the end that is decreed is poured out on him" (Daniel 9:27, NIV). [Bold added]

The **covenant** is a non-aggression pact between the antichrist and Israel; a military alliance that will enable the antichrist to gain power over the EU during the first 3 ½ years of the 70th week (Daniel 7:23-24, 8:23-25; Revelation 17:8-17), and it will assure Israel's protection and peace (Daniel 8:25, 9:27, 11:36-45).

The antichrist is a political and religious individual out of the EU (likely Rome) who is opposed to God the Father, Son, and Holy Spirit, and God's church. Although the only places in Scripture the name antichrist is used are 1 John 2:18, 22, 4:3; 2 John 7, the Bible is replete with the reality of the antichrist. The key passages are Daniel 7, 8, 11; Matthew 24; 2 Thessalonians 2; and Revelation 13, 17, and 18—"where the antichrist is referred to as the **beast, a little horn, a false Christ, that wicked one, and the man of sin.**"[3]

Invasion by Russia and Its Allies

Bible prophecy divides world military powers into four regions just before the end of the age. These four great world military powers are called **king of the North** (today's Russia including Kazakhstan), **king of the South** (today's Arab countries including Sudan, Libya, Egypt), **king of the East** (China and surrounding Asian countries), and **king of the west** (today's European Union and the U.S.). All directions in the Bible are described based on the geographic relationship to Israel—north, south, east, and west.

About 2,650 years ago the prophet Ezekiel said that one day Magog (modern Russia including Kazakhstan) and Persia (modern Iran) will form an alliance with several countries [namely, Cush (Sudan), Put (Libya), Gomer and Beth Togarmiah (Turkey), Meshech (Turkmenistan and Uzbekistan located east of the Caspian Sea), and Tubal (southern region of Russia)] and attack Israel shortly after the start of the first 3 ½ years. (See Ezekiel 38:1-8.) These nations are in position today.[4] See map of Russian Invasion on next page.

> "The word of the LORD came to me: 'Son of man, set your face against **Gog**, of the land of **Magog**, the chief prince of **Meshek** and **Tubal**; prophesy against him and say: This is what the Sovereign LORD says: I am against you, Gog, chief prince of **Meshek** and **Tubal**. I will turn you around, put hooks in your jaws and bring you out with your whole army—your horses, your horsemen fully armed, and a great horde with large and small shields, all of them brandishing their swords. **Persia, Cush** and **Put** will be with them, all with shields and helmets, also **Gomer** with all its troops, and **Beth Togarmiah** from the far north with all its troops—the many nations with you.'
>
> 'Get ready; be prepared, you and all the hordes gathered about you, and take command of them. After many days you will be called to arms. In future years you will invade a land that has recovered from war, whose people were gathered from many nations to the mountains of Israel, which had long been desolate. They had been brought out from the nations, and now all of them live in safety'" (Ezekiel 38:1-8, NIV). [Bold added]

Do Russian armies still utilize the horse calvary? Yes. Mechanized infantry can never equal the mobility of the horse in cross-country, difficult and diverse terrain such as Asia minor (southwestern part of Asia; Turkey), Armenia (south Caucasus region of Eurasia), Azerbaijan, Georgia, Iraq, and Syria. Motorized infantry can never swim rivers, climb mountains, cross rocky mountainous terrain, and traverse swampy areas with the efficiency and mobility of the horse. Russian cavalry forces have been involved in every war in which Russian troops have fought.

The Ezekiel passages appear to predict the use of small, tactical nuclear weapons alluded to in Ezekiel 38:20-22 and Revelation 6:3-4.

> "The fish in the sea, the birds in the sky, the beasts of the field, every creature that moves along the ground, and all the people on the face of the earth will tremble at my presence. **The mountains**

This first 3 ½ year period will not be a time of peace but rather, a time of war and great bloodshed. But **the invasion by Russia and its allies is not the battle of Armageddon** as described in the Book of Revelation (Revelation 16:16; see section Armageddon – The Great Tribulation). This Russian invasion (with its allies) takes place shortly after the start of the first 3 ½ years. See timeline at the start of this chapter.

will be overturned, the cliffs will crumble and every wall will fall to the ground. I will summon a sword against Gog on all my mountains, declares the Sovereign LORD. Every man's sword will be against his brother. I will execute judgment on him with plague and bloodshed; I will pour down torrents of rain, hailstones and **burning sulfur** *on him and on his troops and on the many nations with him"* (Ezekiel 38:20-22, NIV).

In Revelation, *"When the Lamb opened the* **second seal** *[see start of chapter], I heard the second living creature say, "Come!" Then another horse came out, a fiery red one [***Russia** *including Kazakhstan]. Its rider was given power to take peace from the earth and to make people kill each other. To him was given a large sword"* (Revelation 6:3-4, NIV). [Bold added]

Gog is a word for "ruler" or dictator which literally means "the man on top." Gog is the "chief prince" of the land of Magog which is today's Russia.⁵ Today's leader of Russia is Vladimir Putin. During the last several decades, Russia has maintained a very close relationship with Iran and has been directing and controlling Iran's nuclear weapons program. Also, Russia annexed Crimea from Ukraine in 2014 and

RUSSIAN INVASION
Gog and Magog War
Ezekiel 38 and 39

Note: Israel in Red

Russia severed diplomatic relations with Israel following the 1967 Six Day War and then aligned itself with Arab regimes, primarily Syria, and gave support to Palestinian militants (Hamas in the Gaza and Hezbollah, a paramilitary Iranian militia in Lebanon). Alliances of the **end times are being formed today!**

Russia is allied with Israel's enemies and strengthening an axis of power with Turkey, Iran, and Syria. Russia is now Turkey's second largest trading partner, and it has increased military and diplomatic cooperation with Syria. What is Russia's motivation? It is warm water ports, Arabian oil, and **mineral deposits in the Dead Sea**.⁶ See photo of the Dead Sea at the end of chapter.

then invaded Ukraine (February, 2022) with humiliating consequences for Russia. This botched invasion of Ukraine will ultimately lead to further Russian escalation in the Middle East in alliance with other nations such as Iran (not reckless aggression into NATO counties to the west and north). And finally, Put is today's Libya and Cush is today's Sudan.

Because of the power vacuum left by a retreating U.S. in Iraq and the Middle East, Russia is currently sending troops and armament into Syria: artillery and military transport vehicles, fighter jets, anti-aircraft batteries, missiles, and Navy ships. Russia has essentially established a base of operations in the Middle East—and Syria is immediately northeast of Israel! (And the Golan Heights is only 30 miles from Damascus.) Also, Russia continues to solidify its ties with Iran by supplying nuclear-related technology and supervision. This is not the fulfillment of Ezekiel 38 **but it strongly forecasts the coming invasion of Israel by Russia and its allies.**⁷

Will Turkey join with Russia and its allies? Turkey is not European, either geographically or culturally; and it is one of the largest nations and primarily Muslim. Fear of Islamic influence by EU nations will keep Turkey out of the EU. The coup attempt (July 2016) caused Turkey to align itself with Russia.

World in Denial - Defiant Nature of Mankind

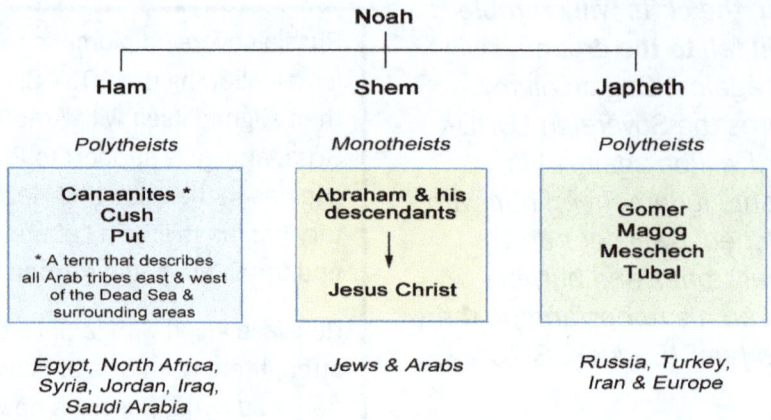

> The sons of Noah are Shem, Ham, and Japheth (Genesis 10:1) as shown above.
>
> All the names referred to in Ezekiel 38 are the sons of Japheth. After Noah's flood the sons of Japheth settled in the area of Rosh, what we know today as Russia.

Ezekiel puts utmost emphasis that Israel's great enemy would come from the "uttermost north" or "far north" (Ezekiel 38:6, 15-16, and in 39:2).

> "...will come from your place in the far north, you and many nations with you, all of them riding on horses, a great horde, a mighty army. You will advance against my people Israel like a cloud that covers the land. In days to come, Gog, I will bring you against my land, so that the nations may know me when I am proved holy through you before their eyes" (Ezekiel 38:15-16, NIV).

> "I will turn you around and drag you along. I will bring you from the far north and send you against the mountains of Israel" (Ezekiel 39:2, NIV).

Ezekiel is prophesying thousands of years in advance about a nation that has not come into existence. In order for these end time events to occur Russia would have to be a strong and fearsome nation with a formidable military. God is against Russia because it is an atheistic nation—and it is an enemy of Israel and an ally to Israel's enemies.[8] Russia is certainly aware of this prophecy but it doesn't care. Why? King David summarizes the problem with an atheistic mindset in one verse: *"The fool has said in his heart, 'There is no God'"* (Psalm 14:1, NIV). And there is nothing they can do about it anyway—God is in control.

The Russians with their Islamic allies invade the Holy Land with the intention of annihilating Israel—wiping Israel off the face of the map. God makes it clear that He is "dragging Russia and its allies" into Israel for a harsh reality check: *"I will bring you against My land."* The ensuing defeat of the Russian army and its Islamic allies is going to be an extreme "object lesson" (proof of God) for Russia and the world.[9] What is the lesson? A compelling demonstration to the world that God is sovereign, the Jews are God's chosen people, and that His covenant with Abraham, Isaac, and Jacob is 'forever' and 'everlasting.'

The European Union will make a weak, pathetic attempt to help defend Israel while the U.S. simply watches—similar to what the U.S. is currently doing in this region of the world. But God will miraculously deliver Israel out of the hands of this overwhelming military force. He will use a great earthquake (38:19); confusion and infighting amongst the troops of the invading nations (38:21); disease (38:22); and torrential rain, hailstones, fire, and burning sulfur (38:22) to repel the attack. This is something that God does, not the Israeli Defense Force.

"I will make known my holy name among my people Israel. I will no longer let my holy name be profaned, and the nations will know that I the LORD am the Holy One in Israel" (Ezekiel 39:7, NIV).

"This is the word of the Lord concerning Israel. The Lord, who stretches out the heavens, who lays the foundation of the earth, and who forms the spirit of man within him declares: **I am going to make Jerusalem a cup that sends all the surrounding peoples reeling.** *Judah will be besieged as well as Jerusalem. On that day, when all the nations of the earth are gathered against her,* **I will make Jerusalem an immovable rock for all the nations.** *All who try to move it will injure themselves"* (Zechariah 12:1-3, NIV). [Bold added]

At the end of Ezekiel 39, in verse 29, God "... will pour out my [His] *Spirit on the house of Israel..."* and show the world that God of Israel is sovereign and holy.

Demise of Damascus - During or before this time, Damascus will become a *"fallen ruin...the land will be a desolation"* as described in Isaiah 17—it will be laid waste and never inhabited again. *"See, Damascus will no longer be a city but will become a heap of ruins."* Destruction will happen suddenly in the darkness of one night— *"At evening time, behold, there is terror! Before morning, they are no more."* In Isaiah's day the sword, spear, and bow were their most advanced weapons, and weaponry capable of annihilating a massive city in just one night was non-existent (unheard of).

Laying waste and being *"removed from being"* (v. 1); *"heap or ruins"* (v. 1); *"will no longer be"* (v. 1); *"will disappear"* (v. 3); and *"all will be desolation"* (v. 9) is all due to a nuclear event and radioactive contamination preventing future use of the area. "Damascus is the oldest continuously inhabited city in the world that has never been totally destroyed." Obviously, this prophecy has not yet been fulfilled. Syria is absent from this Russian invasion, **a hint or warning that Isaiah 17 will have already occurred.** The destruction of Damascus could happen anytime.[10]

Rebuilding the Third Temple
(Future Temple)

After almost 2,000 years in exile, the Jewish people were able to return to their homeland, Israel, on May 14, 1948, and then acquired the ancient City of Jerusalem during The Six Day War (June 5-10, 1967). The Temple Mount is the ground where the Israelis want to rebuild their Third Holy Temple—but currently a Muslim shrine, known as the Dome of the Rock, lies on or near the site of the Temple. Although the Israelis captured the City, the Muslims were allowed to police (or maintain control) of the mosque and surrounding area (including al Aqsa mosque and Dome of the Chain; see sketch next page), and they certainly have no intention of allowing the Jews to rebuild their Temple.

The Temple has to be **rebuilt prior to the last 3 ½ years of the tribulation period** because of an event involving the antichrist called the **"abomination of desolation."** When this event happens (described in the next section), there is a literal countdown of 42 months before the return of Jesus—the Second Coming. After the Temple is rebuilt, the antichrist will seat himself in the Temple of God proclaiming himself to be God and taking credit for the economic recovery and consolidation of nations and the supernatural defeat of Russia and its allies. From that time on, the **"great tribulation"** begins with mass persecution of Jews and Christians throughout the world.

World in Denial - Defiant Nature of Mankind

The Jewish Temple has to be rebuilt in order for all remaining end time prophecies of the Bible to be fulfilled. This rebuilding effort will likely take place during the first 3 ½ year period immediately following the humiliating defeat of Russia and Iran and the demise of Damascus. The Russians and Islamic nations will be reeling from the loss. Although it is certainly possible that an earthquake (Ezekiel 28:19) will topple the mosque, the mosque will be no more. **The Jewish people already have detailed plans** to rebuild the Temple given the most opportune time. Apparently the rebuilding effort will take less than 1 ½ years once the way is supernaturally cleared.

> **Why, considering the vast numbers of acres of land in Islamic countries, did the Arabs select the Temple site of God's chosen people as one of their holy places?**
>
> This is a carry-over of the ancient family feud between Ishmael and Isaac. In Genesis 22:1-19, Abraham offered his son Isaac in total faith in the word of God on Mount Moriah—the site of the Temple Mount, Solomon's Temple (c. 957 BC), and the Second Temple (c. 516 BC).[11]
>
> The Muslims claim it was Ishmael, not Isaac, who their father Abraham offered as a sacrifice. So in commemoration, Abd al-Malik authorized the costly construction of the mosque.[12] The Dome of the Rock was built c. AD 685 to 691 as a shrine for Muslim pilgrims but interestingly, Mohammed never traveled to Jerusalem nor have any Muslims claimed Jerusalem as its capital.
>
> See photo and drawings, p. 104, chapter 7, The City of Jerusalem: The Temple Mount and the Western Wall.

Temple Mount (Mt. Moriah)

Sketches by Roger Gallop

Temple Mount is trapezoidal in shape, about 976 ft x 1571 ft, or about 35.2 acres.

City of Jerusalem - Present Day

World In Denial - Defiant Nature of Mankind

> The First Temple was built c. 957 BC by King Solomon but it was destroyed in 586 BC by the Babylonians. The Temple was then rebuilt a second time c. 516 BC and then destroyed by the Romans in AD 70 when the Jews were dispersed to the four corners of the earth.
>
> The **Dome of the Rock** is a shrine located on the Temple Mount in the Old City of Jerusalem. It was initially completed in AD 691, and it is now one of the oldest works of Islamic architecture and "Jerusalem's most recognizable landmark."
>
> Some archeologists believe that the Temple site is just north of the Muslim shrine directly in line with the Eastern Gate (see sketch on previous page).[13]

Dome of the Rock, Jerusalem
Photo by Roger Gallop, March 14, 2016

There are many groups already working on architectural and structural plans for rebuilding the new Temple. They already know the location of the site of the Second Temple. The blueprints are completed, the Temple garments have been made, and most of the clothing, instruments, and other artifacts required for Temple worship have been prepared.

Scenarios for the rebuilding of the Temple are as follows:

1. Following the defeat of Russia and its Islamic allies, there will be a window of opportunity for the Jews to rebuild the Temple. It is possible that the mosque will be destroyed during the Russian invasion. After Russia and Iran's defeat and the devastation of Damascus (in fulfillment of Isaiah 17), Islamic forces will be afraid to make any aggressive military movements toward Israel and the Temple Mount.

The supernatural destruction of the Russian army and its allies will cause an outpouring of worship and great enthusiasm amongst the Jewish people who will take the opportunity to quickly reconstruct the Temple (even with unwalled villages).

2. If the site of the first two Jewish Temples is north or south of the Dome of the Rock, some say the third Temple could be rebuilt without disturbing the Dome of the Rock, but it is highly unlikely that God will allow the Muslim shrine to remain. The Dome of the Rock will likely be destroyed supernaturally or during the Russian invasion.

Second 3 ½ Years of the Tribulation Period

Jesus refers to an "**abomination of desolation**" of a future Temple in Matthew 24:15-22, and this is more clearly spoken of in Luke 21:20-24. The beast (the antichrist) will take authority and set up an image of himself in the newly constructed Temple (Daniel 9:27; 2 Thessalonians 2:1-4; Revelation 13:1-18). When this happens, as Jesus said, *"then let those who are in Judea flee to the mountains..."* Those in Jerusalem are advised to flee for their lives when they see the beast take a seat of authority in the Temple (Matthew 24:15-22). See Scripture next section. The antichrist will rule from Jerusalem for 42 months (3 ½ years), the latter half of the tribulation, called the "**great tribulation.**"

This temple event will be televised throughout the world due to the pride, arrogance, and lust for power of the antichrist. The antichrist, who will be Satan incarnate, will now seat himself in God's Holy Temple for the next 3 ½ years and at this time he will begin **mass persecution and slaughter of Jews and Christians.** See Appendix C, Satan's Attempts to Seize Total Control. During this time, **he will literally kill two thirds of the Jewish people—**and this period will be worse than the Nazi Holocaust where 6 million Jews were killed.

> The man of lawlessness will *"exalt himself...so that he sets himself up in God's temple, proclaiming himself to be God"* (2 Thessalonians 2:1-4, NIV). [Bold added] With Russia no longer an obstacle to the antichrist's ambitions for ruling the world, he will drop the charade and will begin persecution and slaughter of Jews and Christians.

Persecution and Desolation

Matthew 24:15-22 describes the second 3 ½ year period as a time of terrible persecution of the Jewish people. Given our understanding of the Holocaust, it's difficult to fathom such a time of even greater horror. This second 3 ½ year period is when humanity's decadence and moral depravity will have reached its fullness (like the Canaanites when Joshua and the Jewish people crossed the Jordan River into the Promised Land in 1406 BC) with God judging accordingly.

> "Therefore when you see the **ABOMINATION OF DESOLATION** which was spoken of through Daniel the prophet, standing in the holy place (let the reader understand), **then those who are in Judea must flee to the mountains.** *Whoever is on the housetop must not go down to get the things out that are in his house. Whoever is in the field* **must not turn back** *to get his cloak. But woe to those who are pregnant and to those who are nursing babies in those days! But pray that your flight will not be in the winter, or on a Sabbath. For then there will be a* **great tribulation** **[second 3 ½ years],** *such as has not occurred since the beginning of the world until now, nor ever will. Unless those days had been cut short, no life would have been saved; but for the sake of the elect those days will be cut short"* (Matthew 24:15-22, NASB). [Bold added]

*"When you see Jerusalem being surrounded by armies, you will know that its **desolation is near**. Then let those who are in Judea flee to the mountains, let those in the city get out, and let those in the country not enter the city. For this is the time of punishment in fulfillment of all that has been written. How dreadful it will be in those days for pregnant women and nursing mothers! There will be great distress in the land and wrath against this people. They will fall by the sword and will be taken as prisoners to all the nations. **Jerusalem will be trampled on by the Gentiles until the times of the Gentiles are fulfilled"** (Luke 21:20-24, NIV). [Bold added]*

*"... In the middle of the 'seven' [seven year tribulation period] he will put an end to sacrifice and offering. And on a wing of the temple he will set up **an abomination that causes desolation,** until the end that is decreed is poured out on him"* (Daniel 9:27, NIV). [Bold added]

For additional Scripture, see Daniel 11:31 and 12:11.

According to Revelation 13, the antichrist will control the economy and commerce by forcing people to take the **"mark of the beast"**—and with today's fast-paced microchip technology, miniature microchips that can easily be placed under the skin are available now. Through the use of highly sophisticated supercomputers, the antichrist will have detailed information on everyone on the planet just like in the television series, Person of Interest, or in the recent motion picture, Snowden, this technology is already here in today's world.

In Luke 21:24 (ESV) [Bold added], Jesus speaks of future events, including the destruction of Jerusalem and His return. He says that *"Jerusalem will be trampled underfoot by the Gentiles, until the **times of the Gentiles are fulfilled.**"* A similar phrase is found in Romans 11:25 (ESV), which says *"a partial hardening has come upon Israel, until the **fullness of the Gentiles** has come in."*

"Times of the Gentiles" are all the years between the Babylonian Empire of Nebuchadnezzar (586 BC) and the glorious return of Christ to establish His kingdom. **This is the era of Gentile domination.** In Revelation 11:2, John indicates that Jerusalem will be under Gentile rule, even though the temple has been restored during the first 3 ½ years of the tribulation. In fact, Jerusalem will be under Gentile control until the Second Coming.

The **Mark of the Beast** is a term in the Book of Revelation, chapter 13. The number of the Beast is 666.

There is no mention of America in the Bible as an essential country in the last days—but many Bible prophecy scholars believe that America fits the profile of political Babylon aligned with the political Antichrist of the EU in the last 3 ½ years of the 7-year tribulation period (as described in Revelation 18, Isaiah 18:1-2, Jeremiah 50-51). For example, Isaiah depicts a latter day nation:
 1) that has an insignia of wings,
 2) a land beyond the sea from Israel,
 3) a land widely spread out, and
 4) whose rivers are spoiled.

Armageddon
The Great Tribulation

This is a time of great tribulation as described in Matthew 24:15-26, Luke 21:20-24, and Revelation, chapters 6-22. Throughout Scripture the great tribulation is referred to by other names such as the **Day of the Lord** (Isaiah 2:12, 13:6-9; Joel 1:15, 2:1-31, 3:14; 1 Thessalonians 5:2); **trouble or tribulation** (Deuteronomy 4:30; Zephaniah 1:1); the **great tribulation**, which refers to the more intense second half of the seven year period (Matthew 24:21); **time or day of trouble** (Daniel 12:1; Zephaniah 1:15); **time of Jacob's trouble** (Jeremiah 30:7).

> In Christian eschatology, the **great tribulation** is the second 3 ½ years of the future **seven year tribulation period**—a time when God will finish His discipline of Israel and finalize His judgment of the unbelieving world.
>
> The great tribulation will be the worst time ever seen on earth (Matthew 24:21). In fact, if those days were not cut short by the return of Christ, no one would survive the bowl judgments in Revelation 16 and nuclear holocaust.

In Revelation 7:14 (beginning of the Trumpet judgment), *"the great tribulation"* is used to indicate the period spoken of by Jesus. The context in which tribulation is used in Matthew 24:21, 29 denotes the terrible suffering and nuclear war.

> *"For then there will be great distress, unequaled from the beginning of the world until now—and never to be equaled again"* (Matthew 24:21, NIV).

> *"Immediately after the distress of those days, 'the sun will be darkened, and the moon will not give its light; the stars will fall from the sky, and the heavenly bodies will be shaken'"* (Matthew 24:29, NIV).

During the past two decades, China has been expanding its economic and military dominance while America has become irrelevant with anemic economic and do-nothing foreign policy. (See chap 9, Economic Decline, item #8.)

The U.S. military has recently been demoralized after 20 years in Afghanistan with an incompetent chaotic withdrawal on August 31, 2021, (described by many as an absolute debacle). This inept retreat left thousands of civilians (over 100 Americans and over 100,000 Afgan-American allied interpreters in hiding), and left approximately 85 billion dollars of advanced military hardware behind.[14] This withdrawal debacle has literally opened the door to China which is now perfectly situated geographically, politically, and militarily to fulfill its prophetic role in the end times.

In recent times China has become the largest military in the world asserting a **200 million-man infantry.** This vast army (allied with surrounding countries) is forecast to invade the Middle East in the second 3 ½ year period during the **great tribulation.** In Revelation 9:13-16 (continuation of the Trumpets), it states:

> *"And the sixth angel sounded, and I heard a voice from the four horns of the golden altar which is before God, Saying to the sixth angel which had the trumpet, Loose the **four angels which are bound in the great river Euphrates.** And the four angels were loosed, which were prepared for an hour, and a day, and a month, and a year, for to slay the third part of men. And the number of the army of the horsemen was **two hundred thousand thousand:** and I heard the number of them"* (Revelation 9:13-16, NIV). [Bold added] The last verse is the 6th trumpet of judgments.

The word **"Armageddon"** appears **only once in the entire Bible** and is found in Revelation 16:16 (Bowl judgments). According to the Book of Revelation, this will be the place where armies gather during the final battle of the second 3½ years. This site is located at the Mount of Megiddo across the Jezreel Valley about 20 miles southwest of the Sea of Galilee. In the Old Testament, this is called "the Valley of Jehoshaphat."[15]

In Revelation 16:12-21, it states:

*"And the sixth angel poured out his vial upon the great river Euphrates; and the **water thereof was dried up, that the way of the kings of the east might be prepared.** [13]And I saw three unclean spirits like frogs come out of the mouth of the dragon, and out of the mouth of the beast, and out of the mouth of the false prophet. [14]For they are the spirits of devils, working miracles, which go forth unto the kings of the earth and of the whole world, to gather them to the battle of that great day of God Almighty. [15]Behold, I come as a thief. Blessed is he that watcheth, and keepeth his garments, lest he walk naked, and they see his shame. [16]And he gathered them together into a place called in the Hebrew tongue **Armageddon**. [17]And the seventh angel poured out his vial into the air; and there came a great voice out of the temple of heaven, from the throne, saying, It is done. [18]And there were voices, and thunders, and lightnings; and there was a great earthquake, such as was not since*

Jezreel (YIZRE'EL) Valley; looking North from Mount of Megiddo.
Photos by Roger Gallop, March 9, 2016

men were upon the earth, so mighty an earthquake, and so great. ¹⁹And the great city was divided into three parts, and the cities of the nations fell: and great Babylon came in remembrance before God, to give unto her the cup of the wine of the fierceness of his wrath. ²⁰And every island fled away, and the mountains were not found. ²¹And there fell upon men a great hail out of heaven, every stone about the weight of a talent: and men blasphemed God because of the plague of the hail; for the plague thereof was exceeding great" (Revelation 16:12-21, KJV). [Bold added] Verse 12 is the 6th bowl of judgments.

The **Satanic trinity** consisting of **Satan**, his son the **antichrist**, and the demonized spiritual leader called the **false prophet** will mobilize the nations of the world to war in response to the invasion by China and its allies. (See glossary for description of these entities.) *"But news from the east [China] and the north [Russia] shall trouble him; therefore he shall go out with great fury to destroy and annihilate many"* (Daniel 11:44, NIV).

Although Russia will be badly crippled by the first invasion at the beginning of the first 3 ½ years, Russia will join China in this final nuclear onslaught, Armageddon. Nations of the European Union, the U.S., Canada, Australia, and other countries may send armies to help Israel repel the military offensive by China, Russia, and allied countries. These armies will clash for the final battle of Armageddon at the Valley of Jezreel, or Plain of Megiddo. See photos on previous page.

The River Euphrates in Iraq will be dried up so the army of the King of the East (China) can easily cross as it moves west. It is interesting that a severe drought has been drying up the Euphrates since 1999—the worst drought in Iraq this past century. An arid region in the Tigris-Euphrates Basin continues to grow drier due to consumption of water for drinking and agricultural activities. Also, Turkey is building dams upstream—all signs of the tribulation period and Armageddon.¹⁶

Also, the Dead Sea continues to grow drier for the same reasons—drought, consumption of water for drinking and agriculture. Remember Russia's motivation to invade the Middle East is **warm water ports, Arabian oil, and mineral deposits in the Dead Sea.**¹⁷ See adjacent photo.

Dead Sea; looking north from western shoreline.
Photo by Roger Gallop, March 12, 2016

Despite lack of Bible literacy or any knowledge of Bible prophecy, fascination with Armageddon continues to grow—apocalyptic movies (secular) of WW III. People seem to have **a deep knowing that something is wrong with the world**—that something will soon happen, but few people have any Biblical understanding. The Bible, on the other hand, gives specific events and signs leading up to the seven year tribulation and the last 3 ½ years, the great tribulation or Armageddon, and how people can escape these last seven years.

The Second Coming of Jesus Christ and the Millennial Period

At the end of the seven year tribulation, the antichrist with an alliance of nations will launch an offensive to repel the invasion by China and her allies. Near the end of this great military battle of nations (Armageddon), there will be astronomical upheaval (Matthew 24:29), and the nations of the world will see Christ *"coming on the clouds of the sky, with power and great glory"* (Matthew 24:29-30, NIV). **Those who become saved during the tribulation period will be gathered out of the world by the angels** (Matthew 24:31).

The Second Coming is when Jesus returns at the end of the great tribulation period (together with believers who died in the past and those raptured just before the seven year tribulation period) to defeat the antichrist and all nations that are aligned against the Lord (including China and Russia and their allies)—and ultimately destroying evil and establishing His millennial kingdom. This invasion from Heaven is described in Revelation 19:11-16, NIV.

"I saw heaven standing open and there before me was a white horse, whose rider is called Faithful and True. With justice he judges and wages war. His eyes are like blazing fire, and on his head are many crowns. He has a name written on him that no one knows but he himself. He is dressed in a robe dipped in blood, and his name is the Word of God. The armies of heaven were following him, riding on white horses and dressed in fine linen, white and clean. Coming out of his mouth is a sharp sword with which to strike down the nations. 'He will rule them with an iron scepter.' He treads the winepress of the fury of the wrath of God Almighty. On his robe and on his thigh he has this name written: **KING OF KINGS AND LORD OF LORDS**" (Revelation 19:11-16, NIV). [Bold added]

Ironically, the nations that align with the antichrist and the kings of the East and its allies will unite and turn their aggression away from each other toward the invading multitude from Heaven. In verse 19, the antichrist and his armies *"gathered together to wage war against the rider on the horse and his army."* Jesus Christ and His legion of angels will destroy the antichrist and his armies including the kings of the East and Russia, and the beast and the false prophet will be thrown into the lake of fire (Revelation 19:11-21), and all Israel will be saved (Romans 11:26).

"And I saw an angel standing in the sun, who cried in a loud voice to all the birds flying in midair, 'Come, gather together for the great supper of God, so that you may eat the flesh of kings, generals, and the mighty, of horses and their riders, and the flesh of all people, free and slave, great and small.' Then I saw the beast and the kings of the earth and their armies **gathered together to wage war against the rider on the horse and his army.**

But the beast was captured, and with it the false prophet who had performed the signs on its behalf. With these signs he had deluded those who had received the mark of the beast and worshiped its image. The two of them were thrown alive into the fiery lake of burning sulfur. The rest were killed with the sword coming out of the mouth of the rider on the horse, and all the birds gorged themselves on their flesh" (Revelation 19:17-21, NIV). [Bold added]

Christ will then bind Satan in the Abyss for 1,000 years and He will rule His earthly kingdom for a thousand-year period—the Millennial Period (Revelation 20:1-6).

"And I saw an angel coming down out of heaven, having the key to the Abyss and holding in his hand a great chain. He seized the dragon, that ancient serpent, who is the devil, or Satan, and bound him for a thousand years. He threw him into the Abyss, and locked and sealed it over him, to keep him from deceiving the nations anymore until the thousand years were ended. After that, he must be set free for a short time. I saw thrones on which were seated those who had been given authority to judge. And I saw the souls of those who had been beheaded because of their testimony about Jesus and because of the word of God. They had not worshiped the beast or its image and had not received its mark on their foreheads or their hands. They came to life and reigned with Christ a thousand years" (Revelation 20:1-4, NIV).

There will be two groups of people in the Millennium—those that return with Christ to reign and rule during the Millennium in their immortal bodies and those who survived the Tribulation and trusted Jesus Christ. This latter group of people and those born throughout the 1,000 years will be mortal and will live to the extent of years likened to Adam (Isaiah 65:22), many hundreds of years or more. Isaiah paints an incredibly peaceful picture of a Golden Age of Christianity; however, those born in this Millennial period must receive Christ as Savior just as people in prior dispensations (see p. xii).

At the end of the thousand years, Satan will be released for a short while, and he will need to be defeated once again and then cast into the lake of fire (Revelation 20:7-10) for eternity. **Why is Satan released for a short while?** The answer is found in the Prologue, Freedom of Choice (p. xvii) of this book and in the book by Roger Gallop, *Defeating Evil, God's Plan Before the Beginning of Time*, section titled Planet Earth - God's Testing Ground (p. 63).

Those living during the millennium will have retained the old Adamic sin nature which has been a part of man since the fall of Adam and Eve. These people must make a "free will" choice for or against God by accepting or rejecting the free gift of pardon offered by the Son of God. But, unbelieveably, even after ten centuries of tranquility, millions of people will follow Satan as he deceives nations worldwide.

Christ then judges all unbelievers (Revelation 20:10-15) at the Great White Throne Judgment (see the timeline at the start of chapters 11 and 12)—and those who have not accepted the free gift of pardon will be cast into Hell—outer darkness; separation from God. Jesus Christ will then usher in a new Heaven and new earth and the New Jerusalem—**and everything will be renewed—the eternal dwelling place of believers. There will be no more sin, sorrow, or death** (Revelation chapters 21–22).

"And God will wipe every tear from their eyes; and there will be no more death, neither sorrow, nor crying, neither shall there be any more pain: for the former things are passed away" (Revelation 21:4, NIV).

The Second Coming of Jesus Christ will not occur until certain end times events have taken place: most imminent is the rapture of the church; then the emergence of the antichrist in the European Union; a peace covenant with Israel; invasion of the Middle East by Russia and its Islamic allies; rebuilding of the third temple; and then the "abomination of desolation" at the beginning of the second 3 ½ years followed by the great tribulation period (Matthew 24:15-30; Revelation chapters 6–18). Although the tribulation period is not imminent, **the rapture of the church is imminent and may occur at any time.** For information regarding the difference between the rapture and the Second Coming, see Appendix D, The Rapture and the Second Coming.

> *"God blesses the one who reads the words of this prophecy to the church, and he blesses all who listen to its message and obey what it says, for the time is near"* (Revelation 1:3, NIV).

notes: Chapter 12

1. Lindsey, H. (1973, 1984). *There's A New World Coming.* Eugene, OR: Harvest House Publishers, 114. Other resources include books by other distinguished theologians (e.g., Jack Van Impe, Tim LaHaye and Thomas Ice, John Hagee, and many others).

2. Hal Lindsey (June 5, 2015). The Hal Lindsey Report, News from Hal Lindsey Media Ministries. (www.hallindsey.org)

3. Gritters, B. (last modified, June 2001). The Antichrist. Retrieved February 2016, from http://www.prca.org/pamphlets/pamphlet_3.html.

4. Missler, C. (August, 2006). Magog Revisited. Retrieved February 2016, from http://www.khouse.org/articles/2006/663/; and Hal Lindsey (April 24, 2015), op. cit.

5. Ibid.

6. Hagee, J. (2006). *Jerusalem Countdown: A Warning to the World.* Lake Mary, FL: FrontLine, 104-105.

7. Hal Lindsey (September 18, 2015), op. cit.

8. Hagee, op. cit., 102-103.

9. Hagee, op. cit., 107.

10. Hal Lindsey (May 31, 2013), op. cit.

11. The sacrifice of Isaac put Abraham through an excruciating trial of faith, but Abraham had complete devotion and trust in God. Abraham told his servants "we" will return to you—both he and Isaac. Abraham believed God would either provide another sacrifice or would raise Isaac from the dead. This foretells of God's sacrifice of His only Son, Jesus Christ, on the cross at Calvary for the sins of the world.

Because of God's agape love for humanity, He required of Himself what He did not require of Abraham. This site is where King Solomon later built the first Temple, but today the Muslim shrine (The Dome of the Rock) is located at or near the site where Muslims claim it was Ishmael, not Isaac, who was offered as a sacrifice. See Sacrifice of Isaac – Bible Story Summary. Retrieved February 2016, from http://christianity.about.com/od/Old-Testament/a/JZ-Sacrifice-Of-Isaac.htm.

12. Abd al-Malik, in full abd Al-malik Ibn Marwān, born AD 646 in Medina, Arabia—died AD 705, Damascus, fifth caliph of the Umayyad Arab dynasty in Damascus.

13. Lindsey, H. (1983). *A Prophetical Walk Through the Holy Land*. Eugene, OR: Harvest House Publishers, 64-75.

14. Hal Lindsey (September 19, 2021), op. cit.

15. Hagee, op. cit., 119.

16. Chillymanjaro (March 13, 2013). The Watchers; as cited in http://thewatchers.adorraeli.com/2013/03/13/tigris-and-euphrates-rivers-is-losing-water-reserves-at-a-rapid-pace/. (Creative Commons Attribution-Share Alike)

17. Hagee, op, cit., 104-105.

epilogue

questions and answers

1. Is there an intellectual basis for faith in Jesus Christ, the Son of God?

This question was asked by Josh McDowell in his book, *Evidence That Demands a Verdict*.[1] Theological scholars, students, and adults over the span of history and esteemed scientists in all fields of science answer this question with a resounding, Yes!

My personal faith in the God of the Holy Bible is based on a number of reasons: 1) overwhelming scientific evidence for Divine Creation as presented in the book, *evolution – The Greatest Deception in Modern History*; 2) unity, historical accuracy, preservation, and uniqueness of the Bible; 3) testimony of Old Testament prophets who foresaw historical events thousands of years into the future; and then 4) the fulfillment of prophetic events in Old and New Testament times; 5) physical signs in today's world that directly pertain to fulfillment of end time Bible prophecy; 6) the Moral Law (see preface; and chapter 3, section Human Nature and the Moral Law in the book, *evolution - The Greatest Deception in Modern History*) and the undeniable presence of good and evil, 7) corruption and moral depravity of mankind with its ensuing pain and suffering throughout history and especilay in today's world; and 8) the fundamental need for redemption.

Another scriptural reason is found in Romans 1:18-21 (NIV), *"The wrath of God is being revealed from heaven against all the godlessness and wickedness of men who suppress the truth by their wickedness, since what may be known about God is plain to them, because God has made it plain to them. For since the creation of the world God's invisible qualities—His eternal power and divine nature—have been clearly seen, being understood from what has been made, **so that men are without excuse**. For although they knew God, they neither glorified Him as God nor gave thanks to Him, but their thinking became futile and their foolish hearts were darkened"* (Romans 1:18-21, NIV). [Bold added]

If one sets aside evolutionary bias or pre-conceived notions about the origin of man, the earth, and the universe, overwhelming scientific evidences for creation are enough to convince most people that evolution is a false doctrine. Also, if one takes the time to read the Bible (multiple times if possible), it becomes obvious that man **could never have written the Bible without Divine help**—man would never admit or exclaim to the world his continual corruption and moral depravity throughout history.

Further, fulfillment of Old Testament prophecy is enough to convince most people that God is sovereign and at work in the lives of individual human beings and nations alike. And then the presence of good and evil (an unquantifiable but undeniable presence in our world) speaks to the supernatural conflict between God and Satan—between good and evil.

> "Human beings can absorb many pressures in life, but lack of hope is not one of them. The world in which we live has no hope. Looking back, we see an unending history of war, hatred, and cruelty, all of which reveals the inhumanness of mankind. The very study of history is a study of war and man's inhumanity to his fellow man. The whole world yearns for peace, but knows no peace. Mankind's problems continually worsen, leaving people without hope."[2]

Not only does the Bible provide that hope, but it tells us about the end times in which we now live through Bible prophecy and what we must do to be saved—which gives us hope and confidence in the future.

Evidence supporting Divine creation (scientific, prophetic and historical accuracy, unity, and preservation) and the Deity of Jesus Christ is incontrovertible. If someone just takes the time, McDowell says that he has "never heard a single individual—who honestly considered the evidence—deny that Jesus Christ is the Son of God and the Savior of men."[3] While a large segment of the world remains indifferent, many are ferocious in their anti-Biblical and anti-Christian sentiment.

Do you ever wonder why people have such an anti-God and anti-Biblical inclination? What drives them to think and behave this way? The fact is there is an **undeniable tendency by all human beings to sin and rebel (committing acts of evil to varying degrees) without reason**—thus, the book *World in Denial - Defiant Nature of Mankind*—a tendency or drive that would lead most rational people to believe there is a force in the world the exact opposite of a holy, righteous, and merciful God.

> **Agape love** is a self-sacrificing love found only in humans and God. It is described in John 3:16 (NIV), *"For God so loved the world that he gave his one and only Son, that whoever believes in him shall not perish but have eternal life."* The word "love" translated in this verse is agape. When 1 John 4:8 says *"God is love,"* the Greek New Testament uses the word agape to describe God's love.

Some people ask, "why would a loving God create a world full of pain and suffering," and then use this reasoning as an excuse not to believe—but the real question is, "why would a loving God come into the world He created to suffer and die to pay for my sin?" Wickedness and depravity with its pain and suffering are "man's fault, not God's."[4] From the beginning, God planned that his Son [Jesus Christ] should deal the death blow to Satan, evil, and suffering to reverse the Curse (see chapters 2 and 3 of the book, *evolution - The Greatest Deception in Modern History*), redeem a fallen humanity, and repair a broken world. Allowing

> **Sin** is breaking the moral law (see chapter 3, Human Nature and the Moral Law in the book, *evolution – The Greatest Deception in Modern History*) or any one of the Ten Commandments, or a departure from goodness. **Evil** is sin, iniquity, wickedness, immorality, or corruption. "Evil, in its essence, refuses to accept God as God and puts someone or something else [idolatry] in His place... For this reason, the Bible treats idolatry as the ultimate sin, since it worships as God what is not God."[5]

> **Terrorism** is the face of evil today—the horrific beheadings, crucifixion, torture, and persecution of Christians, Jews, and apostate Muslims (including women, children, and their families) by Islamic extremists in the Middle East and throughout the world. Also, **Immorality** and deviant behavior are being tolerated and accepted as the 'new normal' by much of our youth in America and worldwide.

evil, hence pain and suffering, "was a necessary price to achieve a far greater eternal result."[6] (See the book by Roger Gallop, *Defeating Evil - God's Plan Before the Beginning of Time*.)

Rebellious and idolatrous history of humanity, brutality, and the natural tendency for moral decay, is graphically portrayed in the Bible (Old and New Testaments): the paganistic cultures of the antediluvian period (c. 4004 BC to 2385 BC); in the time of Mesopotamia (c. 2200 BC); and in ancient Egypt and Assyria (c. 2000 BC); with the Canaanite people of the Middle East (c. 1600 BC to 1400 BC); and empires of Babylonia (c. 612 BC to 539 BC), Medo-Persia (c. 538 BC to 334 BC), Greece (c. 334 BC to 146 BC), and Rome (c. 146 BC to AD 476). Also, rebellion, idolatry, moral decay, brutality, and persecution are found in historical accounts of the Dark Ages (c. 6th to 14th century), World War I and World War II, and by today's continual worldwide ethnic conflicts.

Consider the U.S. and world today, with its political corruption, lying, deceit, slander, public displays of moral depravity, bizarre behavior, violent crimes against humanity, abortion, theft, adultery, drug-taking, drunkenness, gambling, greed of all kinds, prostitution, sexual perversions, trafficking of children and teenagers for sex, wars and rumors of wars, and terrorism. It has been the nature of mankind throughout history to 'harden their hearts' (Ephesians 4:18; Mark 8:17-18). This hardening of the heart is a supernatural phenomenon, an unseen battle between good and evil we witness in the news and in our everyday lives. The evil nature of mankind is also portrayed by the exceedingly repugnant behavior of some clergymen over the ages—physical cruelty, collusion with political dictators, and abhorrent sexual abuses—detestable behavior that has alienated many from the Christian faith.

The problem has never been with the God of the Holy Bible but with the corruption and moral depravity of humankind. Take a moment to read Romans 1, verses 18–32—<u>it reads like a commentary of today's world</u>.

2. What are the Abrahamic and Mosaic Covenants and New Covenant, and who are God's "chosen people"?

The Abrahamic Covenant is the first covenant between God and Abraham. (Genesis 12:1-5, 7, 13:14-15) This is an **unconditional covenant**—that is, there are no conditions that have to be filled by human beings.

> **Unconditional Covenant:** The Lord came to Abram with the **first covenant** (Genesis 12:1-3; 13:14-15) commonly known as the **Abrahamic Covenant.** (See chapter 2, section Abraham and His Sons Isaac and Ishmael.) God promised him, *"To your offspring* [descendants] *I will give this land"* (Genesis 12:7, NIV).
>
> This is also an **'everlasting covenant'** as promised in Genesis 13:14–15, 17:19-20; Deuteronomy 28:46, 29:29; and Psalm 105:8-10. The covenant cannot end; it remains in effect **forever**, and that "makes it fundamental to Bible prophecy."[7]

The Mosaic Covenant is conditional between the Jewish people and God: *"Now if you obey me fully and **keep my covenant**, then out of all nations you will be my **treasured possession**. Although the whole earth is mine, you will be for me **a kingdom of priests and a holy nation**. These are the words you are to speak to the Israelites"* (Exodus 19:5-6, NIV). [Bold added]

Under the Mosaic Covenant, the responsibility of the Israelites is to obey all of the statutes, ordinances, and decrees established by God—obedience added to faith. The **responsibility of God** is to bless Israel when they obey those laws and commandments, and to curse Israel when they do not.

The Jews are God's chosen people (Exodus 19:5-6) with the primary mission of spreading the word of God to the rest of the world. The reason for their exile, in 586 BC by the Babylonians for 70 years and then in AD 70 by the Romans for 1,878 years, was 1) because of their stubborn persistence in breaking the Mosaic covenant with God (Deuteronomy 5:1-5; Exodus 31:18); 2) their continual disobedience and adoption of pagan religious practices of surrounding Gentile nations (including idolatry, moral depravity, child sacrifice in fire, and worship of demonic gods); and then 3) their rejection of the Messiah, Jesus Christ in AD 32.

After much patience, God imposed the **curses of the covenant** (exile and humiliation), which were a warning to them from the beginning (see Leviticus 26:14-39 and Deuteronomy 28:15-68 in chapter 3, Blessings for Obedience and Punishment for Disobedience). Then what followed were the Dark Ages, World War I, World War II and the horrific atrocities by Nazi Germany during the Holocaust, and then today's continual worldwide ethnic conflicts and atrocities by ISIS and other terrorist factions such as al-Qaeda and Hamas.

The Mosaic Covenant is **a temporary covenant** because man is incapable of keeping the Mosaic law (commandments and decrees).

In Jeremiah 31:31, *"Behold, the days are coming, declares the Lord, when I will make **a new covenant** with the house of Israel and the house of Judah"* (Jeremiah 31:31, NIV). [Bold added] The New Covenant, in contrast to the Old, is 'spiritually' based, and it promises eternal life full of love and glory **for those who accept the gift of pardon through Jesus Christ.** See New Covenant in glossary and Appendix B.

Unlike the Mosaic Covenant, the Abrahamic covenant is **binding forever** despite the disobedience and failings of the Jewish people of the Old and New Testament and modern Israelis. **The restoration of Israel on May 14, 1948, validates that the Lord will keep His covenant with the Jews forever, and we are in the last days as forecast in the Bible.**

3. What is the difference between punishment and persecution?

Punishment (discipline) is the authoritative imposition of an unpleasant outcome upon an individual or group in response to unacceptable behavior. **Persecution** is the systematic mistreatment (without cause) of an individual or group (by another individual or group) driven by intense hatred or hostility. The most common forms are religious persecution, ethnic persecution, and political persecution, though there is some overlap among these terms.

Persecution is not from God—it comes from evil (sin, iniquity, wickedness, immorality, lawlessness, and corruption) within the hearts of mankind. And why does God tolerate evil and persecution, and why did He allow evil empires to execute punishment on the Jewish people? This is addressed in question #17.

4. Why does God punish human beings for their disobedience?

Throughout history, humanity has turned their back on the Lord while worshiping false idols and doing evil continually. This **downward tendency (sin drift)** began at the time of Adam and Eve and continued unabated during the antediluvian (pre-Flood) days. (See chapter 2, The Ethical Question of War; chapter 3, Punishment for Disobedience; and chapter 5, Why This Fierce Punishment for Disobedience?)

In Genesis 6:5 (NIV), *"The Lord saw how great man's wickedness on the earth had become, and that every inclination of the thoughts of his heart was only evil all the time. The Lord was grieved that He had made man on the earth, and His heart was filled with pain. So the Lord said, I will wipe mankind, whom I have created, from the face of the earth—men and animals, and creatures that move along the ground, and birds of the air—for I am grieved that I have made them."*

This pre-flood period reached a point of continuous utter depravity. The degradation and wickedness of the antediluvians have been affirmed by an astonishing collection of Scriptural testimony. (See Genesis 6:1-6, 11-13; Luke 17:26-27; 1 Peter 3:20; 2 Peter 2:5; and Jude 14-15.)

This same **downhill tendency of humanity (sin drift)** continued with post flood humanity of Mesopotamia (Tower of Babel) and then the paganistic, idolatrous culture of the Canaanites and surrounding countries. The conquest of the Canaanites by the Israelites was because the sins of these paganistic powers were overflowing—*"whose measure of sin was now full"* (Genesis 15:16, NIV).

The religious practices of these paganistic people included **child sacrifice in fire, idol worship, religious prostitution, orgies, and divination embedded in the worship of demonic gods.** God was long-suffering and tolerant in his judgment, even with the exceedingly wicked Canaanites.

> God is holy, righteous, and merciful, and through **our Lord Jesus Christ offers the gift of eternal salvation** (John 3:16, 5:24, 14:6; Romans 10:9, 13; and Ephesians 2:8-9) to those who do not turn away and are willing to accept the free gift of pardon through faith—so by grace [mercy] you are saved through faith (Ephesians 2:8-9).
>
> People lest not forget the Lord is **omnipresent, omnipotent, and omniscient** (Romans 8:29; Ephesians 1:4-5; 1 Corinthians 2:7), and **"the Lord is a warrior"** (Exodus 15:3)—**"He does whatever pleases Him"** (Psalms 115:3, 135:6; Job 23:13; Daniel 4:35, NIV), and *"He is to be feared"* (1 Chronicles 16:25; Psalm 96:4; Isaiah 8:13, NIV). [Bold added] See Preface, Who is God?

5. What are the beginning signs of the end times?

Matthew 24:4-8 (see Luke 21) refers to signs (birth pangs) **during a period before** the seven year tribulation period. These signs are the *"beginnings of sorrows"* (KJV) or **"the beginning of birth pangs"** (NIV). They include deceivers, wars and rumors of wars, and famines, earthquakes, and pestilences. These verses set the stage for the coming tribulation.

> "Jesus answered: 'Watch out that no one deceives you. *For many will come in my name, claiming, 'I am the Messiah,' and will deceive many.* You will hear of **wars and rumors of wars,** but see to it that you are not alarmed. Such things must happen, but the end is still to come. *Nation will rise against nation, and kingdom against kingdom.* There will be **famines and earthquakes** in various places. All these are the **beginning of birth pains**'" (Matthew 24:4-8, NIV). [Bold added]
>
> "There will be **great earthquakes, famines and pestilences** in various places, and fearful events and great signs from heaven" (Luke 21:11, NIV). [Bold added]

Earthquakes, volcanoes, and extreme historic weather events (flooding, tornadoes, fires, drought, mudslides, etc.) are occurring with greater frequency worldwide. Extreme weather events across the U.S. (and the world) are reported nightly on national news outlets. Also, pestilences and plagues throughout many parts of the world and U.S., or diseases thought to be eradicated, are making a dramatic return amongst the rise of new ones[8] (e.g., antibiotic resistant superbugs, zika virus, ebola, whopping cough, measles, cholera, tuberculosis, malaria, legionnaires disease, lyme disease, toxic shock syndrome, chronic fatigue syndrome, lassa fever, bubonic plague, and the COVID-19 pandemic, etc.) And famine is always present somewhere on a local or regional scale and the list goes on.

Obvious signs (see next question) are the restoration of the State of Israel on May 14, 1948, and their repossession of the ancient City of Jerusalem during the Six Day War on June 5–10, 1967; increase in worldwide terrorism, violence, and lawlessness; and disappearance of the moral code in society, government, and public schools.

6. What are the "super signs" of the end times (leading to the tribulation period)? (See chapter 8, Prophetic Super Signs Before the Seven Year Tribulation.)

The pre-tribulation Super Signs include:

1) the miraculous rebirth of Israel on May 14, 1948; and the possession of the City of Jerusalem on June 5–10, 1967;

2) tiny Israel surrounded by hostile Arab (Islamic) nations;

3) increase in arrogance, immorality, violence, and terrorism - worldwide;

4) rise of Russia and her alliance with Iran, Turkey, Syria, and other Islamic states; and

5) advent of modern transportation and supercomputers.

1) Miraculous rebirth of State of Israel and possession of City of Jerusalem

With the seemingly impossible restoration of the State of Israel on May 14, 1948, after almost 2,000 years of worldwide exile (banishment or dispersement) and the repossession of the City of Jerusalem during the Six Day War (June 5–10, 1967) in fulfillment of Bible prophecy, the odds of such an occurence is **Zero** without Divine intervention. (See questions 7 and 8 in epilogue concerning probability.)

Moses (1526 to 1406 BC) predicts the dispersement and restoration of the Jewish people (validation of the Abrahamic covenant) in Deuteronomy 30:1-5 (NIV). Also, the restoration was in direct **fulfillment of Old Testament Scripture** (see chapter 6; Ezekiel 28:25-26, 34:13, 36:22-24, 33-36, 37:1-6, 11-14, 21-22, 39:27-29; Amos 9:14-15; and Isaiah 11:11-12, 43:5-7). New and Old Testament Scripture pertaining to the rebirth of Israel is found in chapter 6.

The return of more than a million Jews to the Promised Land is one of the most extraordinary miracles of all time.[9] **To any open minded person, this is prophetic proof of Divine intervention and God of the Holy Bible.**

2) Tiny Israel is surrounded by at least 20 Arab (Islamic) countries

Arab nations initiated nine unprovoked attacks against Israel: 1948 - 1949 War of Independence (3), 1967 Six Day War (1), 1973 Yom Kippur War (1), 2006 Lebanon War (1), and the Gaza Wars of 2008, 2012, 2014 (3). (The 1956 Sinai and Suez Crisis and 1982 Lebanon War are not included; see chapter 7.) Israel defended itself each time and won (except 2006 Lebanon War which ended in a stalemate). After each war the Israeli army withdrew from most of the areas it captured. Returning captured lands in "defensive wars" is unprecedented in world history and demonstrates Israel's motivation to reach peace even at the risk of fighting for its very existence. (See chapter 8, Israel Surrounded by Hostile Arab Nations.)

Israel is only 2.5 times the size of Rhode Island, 1/19th the size of California, and only slightly larger than the Canary Islands. **The combined territories of Arab countries are 640 times greater in size than Israel** (see map in chapter 8 comparing size with Arab and Muslim countries), **Arab countries have huge oil reserves**, and **Arab population is 60 times greater than Israel's.**[10] (About 6 million Jews vs. more than 400 million Arabs in surrounding lands.) Yet Israel is the most disputed piece of land on the planet—and why? Because it is the Promised Land of the Holy Bible—it is a supernatural phenomenon.

What makes such a tiny country so great? How did they return as a nation after almost 2,000 years? It is **because the hand of God is on Israel.** This one fact alone seems to elude the mind-set of leaders of Arab nations as well as leaders in the European Union and U.S. and other nations of the world.

Why this fervent, everlasting hatred of the Arabs toward the Jews? It is about the lost birth right of Ishmael to his half-brother Isaac about 4,100 years ago—a feud that initiated this everlasting hatred of the Arabs (Muslim people) toward the Jews and a continual effort by the Arabs to take the land of Israel by force. Such unrestrained, unbridled motivation over thousands of years is a 'supernatural phenomenon.' Throughout history and certainly in today's world, the Islamic faith has been used to keep the Arab's ancient hatred of the Jews at a continually high fervor. (See chapter 2, The Seed of Everlasting Hatred.)

Since 1948 Israel had full support from the U.S. but this changed under the 2009-2016 administration. The U.S. Secretary of State (second term) made unilateral concessions with Iran and other nations having a direct effect on Israel but without Israel's involvement or blessing. This cool and disdainful U.S. policy toward Israel will

> Anonymous quote: "If the Arabs (Muslims) put down their weapons today, there would be no more violence. If the Israelis put down their weapons today, there would be no more Israel."[11]

ultimately have dire consequences for the U.S. and the world. (See chapter 8, God Blesses Israel with a Warning to Others Nations; and chapters 9 and 10, Decline of the United States.)

The proposed UN resolution (December 2014) to establish a Palestinian state by requiring the Israelis to withdraw to June 1967 borders utterly ignores Israel's security. **Who would rationally conceive of such a proposal?** And during a summit in France (June 2016), "the United States joined other nations [Israel was not invited] in calling Israel an 'occupying force' ...[and recommending that Israel] retreat to 1967 lines. Those lines are indefensible. **The U.S. administration [2009 -- 2016] and most of the nations of the world cling to a delusion.**"[12] [Bold added] (See chapter 8, Stated Goals of Arab Nations.)

Israel has only sought peaceful coexistence with its neighbors who are ferociously dedicated to its destruction. **The conflict between Israel and surrounding Arab countries is not about land or oil but it is all about the everlasting (supernatural) quarrel between the peoples of Ishmael and the peoples of Isaac!** This stark reality seems to be misunderstood by the United States, the European Union, and other nations of the world including the Arabs.

And what are the facts that support the legitimacy of the State of Israel? See chapter 8, The Fallacy of an Arab Palestinian State.

3) Increase in arrogance, immorality, violence, and terrorism - worldwide

The last days are described as "terrible times" because of the increase in arrogance, immorality, violence, and terrorism, and the increasingly evil nature of man because of those who actively and ferociously *"oppose the truth"* (2 Timothy 3:1-5; also see 2 Thessalonians 2:3). There will be an increase of wickedness, and the love of most will grow cold.

> *"But mark this: There will be **terrible times** in the last days. **People will be lovers of themselves, lovers of money, boastful, proud, abusive, disobedient to their parents, ungrateful, unholy, without love, unforgiving, slanderous, without self-control, brutal, not lovers of the good, treacherous, rash, conceited, lovers of pleasure rather than lovers of God**—having a form of godliness but denying its power. Have nothing to do with such people"* (2 Timothy 3:1-5, NIV). [Bold added]

And then in verse 7, Paul describes the secular, liberal university elite: *"...always learning but never able to come to a knowledge of the truth."*

We see this with many people today who teach the false doctrine of evolution (see the book by Roger Gallop, *evolution – The Greatest Deception in Modern History*) and hold fast to atheistic beliefs. All those who teach the false doctrine of evolution have entrenched themselves in an atheistic, demonic mindset—and there is no escape for them. All this fits our modern age exactly.

> And then just a few verses later in verse 13, Paul warned, *"...evil men and impostors will go from bad to worse, deceiving and being deceived"* (2 Timothy 13, NIV). [Bold added] Those days are here, and it will only grow worse. Isaiah 5:20 says, *"Woe to those who call evil good, and good evil."* (Also see 2 Thessalonians 2:3.)

In the last days there will be **scoffers** and **a moral breakdown** described in 2 Peter 3. This type of ridicule (scoffing and mocking) of the Sovereign God and Divine Creator is prevalent worldwide—most especially in the media, on television, and in movies when they continually **"take the Lord's name in vain."**

Cursing the Lord is a grievous sin (Matthew 12:32). There is apathy in this secular world with no true sense of belief or understanding.

> *"Above all, you must understand that in the last days* **scoffers will come, scoffing and following their own evil desires.** *They will say, 'Where is this 'coming' he promised? Ever since our ancestors died, everything goes on as it has since the beginning of creation.' But* **they deliberately forget** *that long ago by God's word the heavens came into being and the earth was formed out of water and by water. By these waters also the world of that time was deluged and destroyed. By the same word the present heavens and earth are reserved for fire [nuclear war], being kept for the day of judgment and destruction of the ungodly"* (2 Peter 3:3-7, NIV). [Bold added]

Violence is raging across our globe, most notably, the indiscriminate shootings in the U.S., in every state and city, and in every country throughout the world. Horrific acts of terrorism are continually committed by ISIS and al-Qaeda terrorists across the globe and throughout the Middle East. See chapter 8.

> Russia is allied with Israel's enemies and has increased military and diplomatic cooperation with Syria and Iran. **What is Russia's motivation? It is warm water ports, Arabian oil, and mineral deposits in the Dead Sea.**[13]

Is this significant? Yes, and right under the nose of world leaders who do not seem to have a clue what's going on, either Biblically or strategically. If you recall, about 2,600 years ago the prophet Ezekiel (Ezekiel 38 and 39) said that one day Magog and Persia—modern day Russia and Iran, as well as other surrounding countries—would form an alliance that would eventually attack Israel in the first battle of the seven year tribulation.[14]

We are very close to the 'tipping point' of the seven year tribulation, but much of the world seems oblivious and unconcerned about such events (*"though seeing, they may not see; though hearing, they may not understand,"* Luke 8:10-12). Russia is building a new axis of power with Iran, Syria, and Turkey—Israel's enemies—and actively asserting itself into the Middle East via these countries, and the U.S. is looking away.

4) Rise of Russia and her alliance with Muslim states

The rise of Russia as a superpower after WW II (1950 to 2015) is fulfillment of Bible prophecy, most notably in Ezekiel 38 and 39. Russia has invested heavily in military hardware and close Muslim alliances, most particularly Arab Muslim nations hostile to Israel. Not only has Russia (Gog and Magog) established strategic bases of operations in these countries, but it is actively and publically (in the news) establishing itself as the partner and protector of Iran and Syria.

5) Advent of modern transportation and supercomputers

Daniel 12:4 foretold of **continuous travel from one place to another and an unprecedented increase in knowledge which could only apply to today's modern 'computer age' world.** The fulfillment of end times prophecies seemed impossible until the advent of automobiles, airplanes, and supercomputers which in turn promoted space travel and DNA research including medical diagnostics and pharmaceuticals—all examples of the rapid increase in knowledge in our generation.

*"But you, Daniel, **shut up the words and seal the book**, until the time of the end. **Many shall run to and fro, and knowledge shall increase**"* (Daniel 12:4, NIV). [Bold added]

Daniel was told that his visions were prophetic, and **fulfillment would not be understood by him or anyone of his day until the end of the age. Today, this prophecy is obvious to those reading this Scripture.** The angel also informed Daniel that as the end of this era approached, knowledge about prophecy would greatly increase because so much would be seen (via television, the internet, books, newspapers, magazines, etc.). **Then the angel informed Daniel that the outcome would be sealed until the time of the end—that is the days in which we are currently living.**

*"I heard, but I did not understand. So I asked, 'My lord, what will the outcome of all this be?' He replied, 'Go your way, Daniel, because the **words are rolled up and sealed until the time of the end**. Many will be purified, made spotless and refined, but the wicked will continue to be wicked. **None of the wicked will understand, but those who are wise will understand**'"* (Daniel 12:8-10, NIV). [Bold added]

Daniel observed that **at the end of the age the wise would understand. In Biblical terminology the 'wise' are people who study what God has to say and become open-minded to its meaning through the Holy Spirit. Are we living in the end times? Yes, absolutely.** The next great event, the removal ('snatching-up'; rapture) of the church from the earth (described in chapter 11) could occur at any moment.

There are many great books available today that discuss in detail end time Bible prophecy and the rapture—books by Hal Lindsey, Jack Van Impe, Tim LaHaye and Thomas Ice, and many other theology scholars.

7. And what is the probability of fulfillment of prophecy concerning Jesus Christ?

There could possibly be a few prophecies fulfilled in other men but not in all 61 major prophecies (as listed in chapter 4, The Life and Ministry of Jesus Christ). The probability of only eight prophecies being fulfilled (place of birth; time of birth; manner of birth; betrayal; manner of death; peoples' reaction such as mocking, spitting, staring, etc.; piercing; and manner of burial) in any one man is 1 in 10^{17} and the chance of 48 prophecies is 1 in 10^{157}—**or chance is Zero without Divine intervention.**[15]

8. What is the probability of a Jewish state being restored after 1,878 years of worldwide banishment?

Only a Divine miracle could bring about the restoration of Israel—and that miracle was promised in Bible prophecy (Deuteronomy 30:1-5; Isaiah 43:5-7, 66:7-8; Ezekiel 34:13, 36:22-24, 37:1-6, 11-14, 21-23, 39:27-29; Hosea 3:4-5; Jeremiah 31:10, 31:35-36; and Amos 9:14-15). (See chapter 8, Rebirth of the State of Israel.) Although it took two world wars, the miracle occurred after 1,878 years as the hand of God directed world events with the restoration of Israel on May 14, 1948—and within the lifetime of many people living today.

The hand of God is on the Jewish people and the State of Israel. The covenant between God and Israel is **forever** and **everlasting**. (See question #2 in this section and chapter 6, The Fallacy of Replacement Theology, for Scripture.) **The restoration of Israel further validates that the Lord will keep His covenant with the Jews forever, and <u>we are in the last days</u>**.

God exiled the Jewish people worldwide for their continual disobedience, idolatry, and moral depravity during Old Testament times and then finally for rejecting the Messiah and Savior, Jesus Christ—but the Lord God, Creator of the heavens and the earth, has miraculously restored the State of Israel as foretold in Bible prophecy (see chapter 6, Miraculous Rebirth of the State of Israel). What are the odds of a Jewish state and repossession of the City of Jerusalem after worldwide exile—the answer is **Zero without Divine intervention.** The world and its world leaders, especially those in the United States, **do not seem to understand or comprehend this reality.**

9. How could Old Testament Bible prophets forecast events thousands of years into the future?

We know for sure that no one in recent history could do such a thing—there are no prophets in today's world. **How could these Old Testament prophets know thousands of years in advance the Jewish nation would be destroyed and its people scattered worldwide for almost 2,000 years only to be restored in just one day?** In fact, **they did not "know" the future—as prophets, they simply wrote down what they were told by God.** Scripture is God-breathed: 2 Timothy 3:16; 2 Peter 1:21; Genesis 2:7; Exodus 24:3, 4, 7; Jeremiah 36:1-4; 1 Corinthians 14:37; Revelation 1:1, 2, 10, 11, 19; and Ephesians 3:3-5.

But God knew the future because God is omnipotent, omnipresent, and omniscient—He knew you (that is, all human beings) in ancient times (Romans 8:29; Ephesians 1:4-5; 1 Corinthians 2:7) and foreknew the choice you will make in your lifetime (to believe Jesus Christ as your Lord and Savior and to choose good or evil—that is, choose to live a righteous life or a sinful life), although you still have freedom of choice today. **These prophecies, fulfilled thousands of years later, offer indisputable evidence of the truthfulness, inspiration, and reliability of the Bible.**

10. Do these signs of the end times pertain to the U.S.?

There is no mention of America as an essential country in the last days. The U.S. has been losing its role as the leader of the free world over the last several decades—it is no longer the same vibrant, morally upright country as it was following WW II (late 1940s and 1950s). The 2017-2020 administration wanted to "make America great again" but it was too late—too much water had flowed over the dam.

Exactly how the U.S. is finally removed from its political position as world leader is speculation: nuclear attack by terrorists, cyber attacks, economic collapse, or Divine judgment for its role in dividing or compromising Israel and Jerusalem (see Camp David Accords... and The Oslo Accords in chapter 7); or the nuclear and monetary giveaway with Iran (see chapter 10, referencing the Joint Comprehensive Plan of Action adopted October 18, 2015); or the painfully incompetent withdrawal from Afghanistan by August 31, 2021, after a 20 year unsuccessful occupation—or rapture of the church (see chapter 11).

11. What are the signs of the decline of the U.S.? (See chapters 9 and 10.)

1) increase in violence and immorality;

2) economic decline;

3) political correctness;

4) moral decline of public schools and universities;

5) compromised teaching of the Bible.

1) Increase in violence and immorality

The trend of the U.S. since the 1960s and 70s has been an increase in violence, lawlessness, and immorality in every city and state. Just read the newspapers or listen to national news or go to the movies or watch television or travel to any of our cities in the

U.S. and listen to the local news. All states and cities throughout America (including many of our neighborhoods) are filled with crimes of all types, people living on the streets, shootings and murder, and rampant illegal drug use, pornography, and XXX businesses which proclaim our godless, paganistic, and immoral society. And once the door is cracked open, moral decay will only get worse—the slippery slope downhill. This sign of violence and immorality will continue to rapidly increase in intensity just before and during the tribulation period.

For anyone who has watched television with the array of 'adults only' programs and even the sexual oriented advertisements on television (certainly not shown 30 years ago), or gone to the movie theatre, or seen the array of pornographic magazines in bookstores—we know that the U.S. is in dire trouble, but few in leadership positions seem concerned or even care. We are on the **'slippery slope' toward increased depravity**. The same troubles are found worldwide on every continent and more so in Europe.

We see evil all around us, in every country, state, city, and neighborhood, but most notably the **indiscriminate shootings and other forms of senseless violence in every American city**. *"Because of the increase in wickedness, the love of most will grow cold, but he who stands firm to the end will be saved"* (Matthew 24:12, NIV).

Many argue that one of the great signs of America's decline is the disintegration of the core foundation of any society—**marriage and the family**. The racial conflicts we have witnessed in Ferguson, Missouri, and Baltimore, Maryland, and elsewhere throughout the U.S. have **more to do with the breakdown of the American family and the absence of a Christian father and 'love and caring' in the family, teaching sons and daughters Christian moral values and the absolute truth and importance of understanding the saving grace of our Lord Jesus Christ.**

The immorality rampant in society today is a symptom of mankind's rebellion against God—whether we want to admit this or not. In every city, town and neighborhood in the U.S. and world, abortion, homosexuality, drug abuse, trafficking of child prostitutes, and child molestation are proof that *"**evildoers and impostors will go from bad to worse**"* (2 Timothy 3:13). [Bold added]

There will be an increased intensity of this sign during the end times and during the future tribulation as it was in the days of Noah. Since 2000 there has been an **abrupt shift in 'what is considered normal'** toward a shocking and terrifying evil in the world. Our society today is **redefining morality of what is right and what is wrong**, and year by year, morality has grown significantly worse.

2) Economic decline

With a national debt of 28.8 trillion dollars and total debt of 86 trillion as of September 2021 (19.97 trillion dollars and total debt of 66.88 trillion dollars as of February 2017) and with a free entitlement mindset (welfare, disability, **bloated pensions for the top managers and executives** in almost every city and county), the United States is clearly in an advanced state of decline and is heading down the same path as Greece and other socialist countries. The American economy is being eroded from within by liberal-minded, greedy, inept politicians and bureaucrats, and an ever-increasing massive entitlement state.

Our economic foundation is rotting, and our nation is collapsing under the weight of bloated entitlement debt. And let's make it clear—entitlement programs such as social security and Medicare **require employees to pay monies in advance from their paycheck (matched by their employers) into these programs for future compensation. (The employer must also pay a payroll tax for unemployment insurance which provides income for workers whose jobs have been terminated through no fault of their own.) These are entitlement programs because they have been paid in advance in accordance with state and federal regulations, and *workers are entitled to future compensation*.**

Unfortunately, these monies are being siphoned into free handout government programs such as welfare, food stamps, Medicaid, social services, etc. Please do not misunderstand: there are individuals with medical issues and families with children that **absolutely need government help to survive and get a new start in life**, but unfortunately, there are those who can work and choose not to work, preferring to defraud the system (which hurts all of us, especially those in real financial need).

Social security liability of 21.4 trillion dollars as of September 2021 (15.31 trillion as of September 2016) is climbing because of the ineptitude of government. In this progressive society, non-working healthy adults and illegal aliens often receive better government treatment and seem to have more advantages than the average working American.

We are not the same country that we were prior to 1980. Today, Americans are "proud, selfish, greedy, arrogant, ungrateful, treacherous [deceitful], and completely addicted to entertainment and pleasure... [and] Our country is literally falling apart around us...."[16]—economically, politically, morally, socially, and structurally (referring to our infrastructure such as deteriorating roads, bridges, sewer lines, and public buildings). Most Americans are so plugged into their smart phones and music that they are completely unaware of what is really happening to our economy and the world.

Most of the new money that the Federal Reserve has printed (out of thin air—called "quantitative easing") has gone directly into the stock market, further enriching corporate managers and executives on Wall Street, all sitting on an economic and inflated stock market bubble ready to collapse. This is what happened at the start of the Great Depression of 1929—and when a stock market crash finally happens, it will be catastrophic to our economy and the world. It is said that the top 25 U.S. banks have over 200 trillion dollars of exposure (total amount of unsecured loans; debt exceeds revenue), and when the "house of cards comes crashing down there is no way that anyone will be able to prop it back up."[17]

The United States is in the middle of a long-term economic decline due to mounting debt (due to foreign trade deficits, bloated pensions, and giveaways)—and until the American people truly understand how bad our economic situation is, we will never accept the austere solutions needed to correct the problems.

So what are our government leaders doing to solve these economic failures? The 2017-2020 administration wanted to "make Americal great again" but it is too late. And previous administrations told us over and over that a "recovery" has already begun and everything is fine—but the reality is, the U.S. economy is in a much worse situation than most Americans realize (despite "bubble" inflated stock market surges). Although there will be economic "ups and downs" as we move along, people generally realize we are in the middle of a long-term economic decline.[18]

The U.S. economy is declining a little each day although financial stock market types continue to be over-optimistic (because they are the ones who are reaping the vast monetary benefits of "quantitative easing"—again, paper money with no security or anything to back it up), and most Americans don't seem to understand the enormous debt problem and the entitlement and welfare (non-entitlement) dilemma. "While professing to care for the interests of the average person, **the underlying motivation** for the vast majority of the governing class or establishment is first and foremost **self-aggrandizement and the acquisition of wealth**. While a few may be motivated by ideology, the preponderance are not."[19]

3) Political correctness

Political correctness is a term primarily used to describe **language, actions, or policies intended not to offend any particular group of people in society (except Christians and Jews)**—that is, **to appease, tolerate, and fully embrace so as not to offend**. The problem is, some language, actions, or policies advocated by the government and certain organized groups are morally corrupt, and embracing such ideas is normalizing paganistic behavior.

> God of the Bible is sovereign and "governs all nations, bringing them into being (Amos 9:7, NIV) and **calling them into account** (Amos 1:3-2:3). He is the Great King who rules the whole universe (Amos 4:13, 5:8, 9:5-6). Because He is all-sovereign, the God of Israel holds the history and destiny of all peoples and the world in His hands. ...He is Lord over all."[20] [Bold added]

The policy of appeasement leads to a shift in moral values, including rejection of God of the Holy Bible, and ultimately leads to a paganistic and excessive society. Empires throughout history (e.g., Canaanites, Egyptians, Assyrians, Babylonians, Medes-Persians, and Romans; see chapters 2 - 5) became extremely paganistic and immoral and collapsed under the weight of moral depravity.

Political correctness is a tool used to appease or promote all religions "together." Today, this misconceived idea is fully displayed on automobile bumper stickers with symbols of many religions—the idea that there is one God for all religions (e.g., COEXIST), in turn promoting a one world religion and that there are many ways to heaven. Contrary to this sacrilegious ideology, the Bible teaches that there is only one way to salvation through Jesus Christ who says in John 14:6 (NIV), *"I am the way, the truth, and the life. No one comes to the Father except through me."* The Bible warns: there is only one way to heaven.

> God will deal with sin either by grace or by wrath. John 3:36 (NIV) says, *"Whoever believes in the Son has eternal life, but whoever rejects the Son will not see life, for God's wrath remains on him."* Those who do not accept Jesus Christ as their Savior will remain under the Lord's wrath.

The far left New Age movement has lured people into believing that tolerance of all religions including Islam is a good thing—all the while the Muslim faith is the most "intolerant" of all major religions. Tolerance used to mean "agree to disagree" but in today's politically correct world it means "endorsement" or "acceptance" of all religions, ideologies, life-styles, and behavior except, of course, Christianity and Judaism.

For more information about social decay in America, see the website: The Last Days of America? 25 Signs of Extreme Social Decay.

4) Moral decline of public schools and universities

Government leaders, school administrators, and the community continue to wonder and speculate why the public school system (specifically, middle schools and often high schools) has failed to educate its students. They come up with a variety of reasons:

1) **unqualified teachers (False assumption);** 2) **no accountability for underachieving schools (both True and False)**; 3) **wasted funds by the school system (True)**; 4) **non-effective, exotic education plans devised by state judiciaries, legislatures, and bureaucracies (True)**; 5) **one class level for all students holds the best and brightest back (False)**; and 6) **too much emphasis on test scores (True)**.

The problems overlooked by the school system are the following: 1) overworked and overwhelmed teachers; 2) chronic disruptive student behavior which destroys the classroom learning environment, and 3) **lack of moral and behavioral standards**. Solutions to these problems are provided in chapter 10, Public Middle Schools and High Schools.

In today's public schools there is no protocol for enacting swift, harsh punishment for chronic misbehavior and no strict moral and behavioral standards (i.e., the Ten Commandments) which were taken out of the classroom years ago—

yet school administrators and government leaders continue to "scratch their heads" and ponder the cause and solutions for failing schools and then come up with exotic, useless solutions that have nothing to do with solving the problem of chronic misbehavior.

So what is going on in public universities? Prior to the 1950s (post WW II), America was a nation where sexual morality was based on the norms of the church, and in the 1960s and 70s the idea of coed dorms in universities was unthinkable. More than 20 universities and colleges across America now allow undergraduates of the opposite sex to share on-campus dorms and dorm rooms. **This is the decades-long drift away from gender separation in college dorms, hallways, and even bathrooms.**[21]

Again, it must be restated that when foundations are challenged, **when the doors are cracked open, the tendency is for evil to creep in (e.g., transgenderism, LGBT), and this ultimately has an impact on our sense of normality—our ability to distinguish between good and evil.** If the foundations of the church were challenged all at once in a major way, people would reject the message, but **when the challenge comes little by little people eventually accept it as normal.** This sense of normality has eroded our educational system on all levels.

The enormous volume of sexual assault on U.S. college campuses is a reflection of campus culture awash in sexual immorality and the wickedness in an assailant's heart.[22] This illustrates the truth of Jeremiah 17:9 (NIV) that *"the heart is more deceitful than anything else, and incurable -- who can understand it?"*

Will man change his heart? **No. The downhill slide of immorality began more than several decades ago, and only God's wrath and punishment (like in the days of the Old Testament when people turned from God to paganistic cultures) will change men's hearts and set a new course.** See question 16 as a sequel to this dilemma.

5) Compromised teaching of the Bible

The Philadelphia church (Revelation 3:7-13) has endured patiently (3:10) and is still present in the world today—holding fast to the truth of Jesus Christ, and it will be here until the end, but it is not the dominant church. We certainly see these churches today. See chapter 10.

The predominant church today is the Laodicea (Revelation 3:14-22) with lukewarm faith (3:16) with its **focus on material wealth as the standard for success. This church has been caught up in scientific and philosophical rationalism (i.e., evolution and humanism)** and although it still calls itself Christian, "Christ sits in the back row."

Christian churches in America have lost many of their members over the last several decades, and this trend is especially striking among young Americans. According to a recent survey by America's Research Group, of the 95% of 20 to 29 year olds of the protestant faith who attended church regularly with their families during their years in elementary and middle school, only 55% attended church regularly during high school, and only 11% attended church regularly when in college.[23]

12. Is it a strategic mistake for countries such as the U.S. to turn their backs on the State of Israel?

Yes. In Genesis 12:2-3 (NIV), God makes certain promises to the Jewish people (see Scripture in previous section). In verse 3, the Lord states *"...I will bless those who bless you, and whoever curses you I will curse...."* God knew that the Jews would be subject to attack, **so He forewarns peoples and nations who do not support Israel, especially anti-Semitic nations and organizations (e.g., Iran, surrounding Arab countries, Russia, and many others).**

A previous U.S. administration (2009-2016) turned its back on Israel through anti-Semitic attitudes and policies which was a

very grave strategic mistake. Many people in the U.S. do not understand or grasp the consequences pertaining to Biblical Scripture.

Since 1948 Israel had full support from the U.S. but during the 2009-2016 administration the U.S. made unilateral concessions with Iran and other nations concerning the very survival of Israel, but without Israel's involvement (see start of chapter 10, Decline of the United States, and section, Appeasement of Evil Political Ideologies). This cool, disdainful, and arrogant policy toward Israel will ultimately have dire consequences for the U.S. and the world. The 2017-2020 administration made great strides in mending the relationship between the two countries.

> The United States has supported Israel since 1948 and has been blessed—but U.S. politicians and citizens should take note that **turning their back on Israel will bring great economic calamity to this nation.**

You would hope that people within the U.S. administration (referring more so to the previous administration) would have some practical understanding of Bible prophecy. But unfortunately, many people turn away and *willfully forget* without reason. In Luke 8:10-12 (NIV), such people *"though seeing, they may not see; though hearing, they may not understand."* And in Matthew 13:14, NIV, *"You will be ever hearing but never understanding; you will be ever seeing but never perceiving."* This describes a great part of humanity today.

Many within the U.S (including its leadership) do not seem to understand the truth and reality of Bible history and Bible prophecy—that God made **an irrevocable, unconditional covenant** with the Jews to return them to the land of Israel in the years just prior to the return of Jesus Christ for His church (rapture; see chapter 11) and the seven year tribulation. Additionally, **God promised to bless all those who bless and protect His chosen people (the Jews)—the descendants of Abraham, Isaac, and Jacob. Conversely, God promised to curse, harm, or abandon all those who do not** (Genesis 12:3). The nations that support the descendants of Abraham will be blessed, and the nations that curse the sons of Abraham have been or will be cursed.[24]

13. Why are so many people apathetic (indifferent, uninterested, unconcerned, and even bored) about the reality of a Sovereign God and their destination after death?

Given the miraculous return of the State of Israel on May 14, 1948; repossession of the ancient City of Jerusalem as its capital during the Six Day War on June 5-10, 1967; the ever-increasing economic debt of the U.S. (28.8 trillion dollars national debt and 84.8 trillion dollars total debt, September 2021), the European Union, and the rest of the world; the prophetic alliance of Russia and Iran; and the world's focus on that region of the world, **you would think people would take notice and open their Bibles, and read and study and discern the truth.**

> If a person's mind is closed to Scripture, no amount of evidence (scientific and theological) will change his/her mind. This *"hardening of their hearts"* (Ephesians 4:18) against God is an unseen battle between good and evil— a phenomena we actually witness in the news and in our lives every day.

The spiritual forces of evil prevalent in this world cause people to turn away—to *"willfully forget"* without reason! (See 2 Peter 3:5-6, ASV.) In Luke 8:10-12 (NIV) [and this bears repeating again], Jesus described such people as *"though seeing, they may not see; though hearing, they may not understand."* [Bold added] (Also see Matthew 13:14.) If a person's mind is closed to Scripture, no amount of evidence will change his mind.

Many people dismiss such claims because they have **"an enormous predisposition against the supernatural."**[25]

One would logically assume that maintaining an open mind and seeking the truth about the Divinity of our Lord Jesus Christ and Creation as described in the Book of Genesis would be of <u>utmost importance</u> to every person living today, **especially when Heaven or Hell is on the line.** After all, in the scheme of things, **life here on earth is a very short time (a vapor in the wind) when compared to eternity,** *"...a mist that appears for a little while and then vanishes"* (James 4:14, NIV). [Bold added]

Seeking answers to questions concerning life after death should be at the top of everyone's list of life's questions—but sadly, it is not. Most people avoid reading the Bible or attending church because this corrupt, immoral, and secular world is telling us there is no hope. But scientific evidence, in fact, supports creation as stated in Genesis, and the Bible is telling us through fulfilled Old and New Testament prophecy there is certainty of life after death. The question is, where is your destination?

Take time to read the Bible (devote a few minutes a day) and read those books listed at the bottom of the copyright page of this book.

14. Is there an unpardonable sin?

Yes, there is. And for those who turn their back to the Lord, this question becomes of utmost importance.

The only unpardonable sin is to reject God's love and free gift of pardon by rejecting the Lord Jesus Christ, the promised Messiah, who willingly died for our sins...who stepped out of Eternity (*"from old, from everlasting"*... see Micah 5:2) and became a Man. He suffered a terrible death on the Cross to save us (humanity) from our sins and the wrath of God—from the eternal loneliness, darkness, and torment of Hell—but only if we accept the gift of pardon through faith and repentance of sins. The Bible tells us that Heaven is available to everyone.

John 3:16 (KJV), *"For God so loved the world, that he gave his only begotten Son, that whosoever believeth in him should not perish, but have everlasting life."* And John 3:18 (NIV) states, *"Whoever believes in him is not condemned, but whoever does not believe stands condemned already because they have not believed in the name of God's one and only Son."* In this verse God gives every human being the right to believe or not believe that Jesus Christ is the Son of God and to choose good or evil (that is, choose to live a righteous life or sinful life). "Believes" implies choice. **Unbelief (choosing against God and rejecting the gift of pardon) is the only unpardonable sin.**

God is long suffering: *"The Lord is not slow in keeping his promise, as some understand slowness. He is patient with you, not wanting anyone to perish, but everyone to come to repentance"* (2 Peter 3:9, NIV). Jesus said, **"But unless you repent, you too will all perish"** (Luke 13:3, NIV). [Bold added]

<u>**Can anyone be so arrogant, biased, and indifferent that they are unwilling to read the Bible and come to a personal understanding of the truth, and then unwilling to accept this free gift of pardon and eternal salvation? But this is exactly the case for many in the world today**</u>.

God will deal with sin either by grace or by wrath. John 3:36 (NIV) says, *"Whoever believes in the Son has eternal life, but whoever rejects the Son will not see life, for God's wrath remains on him."* Those who do not accept Jesus Christ as their Savior will remain under the Lord's wrath.

God hates idolatry, injustice, and rebellion but **delights in pardoning the penitent.** (See 2 Chronicles 30:18; Isaiah 55:7; Joel 2:12-17, and Micah 7:18.) In 1 John 1:9, KJV, *"If we confess our sins, he is faithful and just to forgive us our sins, and to cleanse us from all unrighteousness."* Also see John 3:16; 1 John 1:9; Romans 10:13.

15. What can we expect next on the prophetic timeline?

We have seen the prophetic restoration of the State of Israel on May 14, 1948, and their repossession of Jerusalem on June 5–10, 1967; and since 1985, the full integration of supercomputers and modern transportation (automobiles and supersonic airplanes) into our global society; rise of Russia and Iran as an alliance; a more aggressive China with enormous wealth and nuclear capability; withdrawal of the U.S. from the world scene; Israel attacked 9 times by hostile Arab nations; an increase in immorality, violence, arrogance, and lawlessness in the U.S. and worldwide; and normalization of deviant behavior through political correctness.

In the foreseeable future we can expect an increase in economic and political uncertainty and terrorism worldwide; unprecedented surges and declines in the stock market; an increase in the persecution of Christians and Jews (in the United States, Middle East, Europe, and much of the world); an even greater increase in violence, lawlessness, immorality; the continued moral decline in public schools and universities; the continued normalization of deviant behavior (e.g., transgenderism, LGBT); economic decline; and extreme weather patterns. Continued economic decline in the U.S. will be partially the result of the ever-increasing national debt (September 2021, 28.8 trillion dollars and total debt of 86 trillion; February 2017, 19.97 trillion dollars and total debt of 66.88 trillion dollars) and a socialistic entitlement mindset.

We also see a trend toward a world economic and religious system; Russia and Iran will continue to solidify their technological and military alliance (Ezekiel 38 and 39); and Russia will maintain an even greater presence in the Middle East with the goal of "exerting its control over the region";[26] and China will continue to gain worldwide prominence with a vast 200 million-man army (Revelation 9:16; Revelation 16:12). America is not mentioned in Bible prophecy, and what we are seeing today is America collapsing into irrelevancy (economically and militarily).

This is partially the result of America naively turning its back on Israel during 2009–2016 and then approving a disastrous nuclear Iran (via the Joint Comprehensive Plan of Action) that allows lifting of financial sanctions and very liberal compliance verification, all while leaving Israel completely out of the negotiations. (See start of chapter 10, Decline of the United States and section, Appeasement of Evil Political Ideologies.)

The next big prophetic event that will certainly get everyone's attention is when the church (true believers) is removed from the earth—snatched away in an event known as the rapture. (See 1 Thess. 4:13-18; 1 Cor. 15:50-54; Rev. 4:1-11.) Christian adults and young people and children will literally disappear, perhaps as many as 40 to 50% of the U.S. population (and a lesser percentage elsewhere in the world). Alien abduction will be blamed, and the world will move closer to a one-world government and religion. Most people remaining will have no clue what actually happened. See chapter 11.

Following the rapture, the Holy Spirit will no longer restrain the "lawless one" (antichrist) and the growth of evil (2 Thessalonians 2:6-7), although the Holy Spirit will continue to indwell and minister to those being saved during the seven year tribulation period. The church is saved from the wrath to come (1 Thessalonians 5:9)—like in the days of Noah (see question 16). Most theology scholars believe the rapture will occur immediately before the tribulation period.

In these last days economic conditions will become so grim that **people will literally turn to anyone who is charismatic and who they think has the answer or the solution. This is what happened to Germany just prior to WW II**. The economic situation became so grim that the people propelled Adolph Hitler into a totalitarian dictatorship. And like Hitler, the antichrist will charismatically (and supernaturally) convince practically everyone he has the answer and can solve their economic woes. True believers (the church) will not be here to suffer through the agony and chaos the **"man of lawlessness"** will bring upon this world.[27]

16. What are the parallels between the days of Noah and the Rapture?

Like it was in the days of Noah, today's world is filled with political corruption, lying, deceit, slander, public displays of depravity, violent crimes, abortion, theft, adultery, drug-taking, drunkenness, gambling, and greed of all kinds, not to mention wars, rumors of wars, and terrorism. **Does this sound familiar?** (Refer to Romans 1:18-22.) Just like in the days of Noah (pre-flood or antediluvian period—Age of Conscience), *"The Lord saw how great man's wickedness on the earth had become, and that every inclination of the thoughts of his heart was only evil all the time"* (Genesis 6:5, NIV).

The teaching echoed by Christ (Matthew 24:37-39; Luke 17:26-27) and the apostle Peter (2 Peter 3:6-7) in the **New Testament speaks of the destruction of mankind by flood and then by fire (nuclear war) at the time of Christ's return.**

> *"As it was in the days of Noah, so it will be at the coming of the Son of Man. For in the days before the flood, people were eating and drinking, marrying and giving in marriage, up to the day Noah entered the ark; and they knew nothing about what would happen until the flood came and took them all away. That is how it will be at the coming of the Son of Man"* (Matthew 24:37-39, NIV).

> *"Just as it was in the days of Noah, so also will it be in the days of the Son of Man. People were eating, drinking, marrying and being given in marriage up to the day Noah entered the ark. Then the flood came and destroyed them all"* (Luke 17:26-27, NIV).

The parallels between the days of Noah and the Second Coming are described by the apostle Peter as well:

> *"Know this first of all, that in the last days* **mockers will come with their mocking** *[we see this today], following after their own lusts, and saying, 'Where is the promise of His coming? For ever since the fathers fell asleep, all continues just as it was from the beginning of creation.' For when they maintain this, it escapes their notice* ["deliberately forget," NIV] *that by the word of God the heavens existed long ago and the earth was formed out of water and by water, through which* **the world at that time was destroyed, being flooded with water. But the present heavens and earth by His word are being reserved for fire [nuclear war], kept for the day of judgment and destruction of ungodly men"* (2 Peter 3:3-7, NAS). [Bold added and underlined]

The modern day Noah's Ark prior to the seven year tribulation is the rapture of the church (the next prophetic event on the horizon; see chapter 11) and the Second Coming of Christ (as described in chapter 12).

In the above Scripture, the apostle Peter spoke of a day in the future when men would *scoff* at the possibility of Christ's Second Coming as a cataclysmic, global intercession by God into world affairs. And the reason for this skeptical attitude is because of pagan rebellion and unbelief in God, and blind obedience to evolutionary doctrine. Essentially, it is the belief that God has never judged the world through a worldwide flood. Because we are told by atheistic academia and evolutionists that this is so, most people show little or no concern for God's future judgment as foretold in the Bible. See the book by Roger Gallop, *evolution - The Greatest Deception in Modern History (Scientific Evidence for Divine Creation)*.

> Many Bible scholars believe that we are at that prophetic time in world history with the miraculous rebirth of the nation of Israel on May 14, 1948, and with Jerusalem in the hands of the Jewish people following the Six Day War (June 5-10, 1967). The State of Israel and Jerusalem under Israeli control are necessary prerequisites for the fulfillment of end time prophecy.

17. Why does God allow evil empires such as the Assyrian (721 BC), Babylonian (586 BC), and Roman (AD 70) to execute punishment (Habakkuk 1:12) on a people (the Jews) more righteous than themselves? See chapter 5.

Let's first define evil, persecution, and punishment.

Evil—is sin, iniquity, wickedness, immorality, lawlessness, corruption, and persecution. It is breaking the moral law (see chapter 3, section Human Nature and the Moral Law in the book, *evolution – The Greatest Deception in Modern History*), or any one of the Ten Commandments, or a departure from goodness. When we think of evil we think of tyrants and dictators, and mass murderers, and people twisted into psychotic monsters who commit crimes against the innocent.

Evil includes the cruel persecution of the Jewish people by the Assyrians (721 BC), Babylonians (586 BC), the Greek ruler Antiochus Epiphanes (c. 175 BC), the Romans (AD 70), and then the horrific persecution and slaughter of the Jews by Nazi Germany during the Holocaust; ISIS cruelty and barbarism in the Middle East, Europe, and worldwide; and continued treachery, violence, and injustice during the dark ages and in recent times.

Persecution—is systematic mistreatment driven by intense hatred or hostility such as harassment, oppression (abusiveness), beating (striking), scourging, flogging, and any type of torture including crucifixion. An example is the Nazi Holocaust of World War II which is the face of evil, and ISIS barbarism in the Middle East.

Persecution is Not from God—*it comes from the evil within the hearts of mankind.*

Punishment (discipline)—is the authoritative imposition of an unpleasant outcome upon an individual or group in response to unacceptable behavior—and it obviously includes some measure of suffering and oftentimes death. **God inflicts punishment but He does not inflict persecution. And it bears repeating, persecution comes from the evil within the hearts of mankind.**

We must understand that God of the Bible is sovereign and "governs all nations, bringing them into being (Amos 9:7, NIV) and calling them into account (Amos 1:3-2:3). He also uses one against another to carry out his purposes (Amos 6:14). He is the Great King who rules the whole universe (Amos 4:13, 5:8, 9:5-6). Because He is all-sovereign, the God of Israel holds the history and destiny of all peoples and the world in His hands. ...He is Lord over all."[28]

Although the Jewish people are God's *"treasured possession"* (Deuteronomy 7:6-9, NIV) and will be *"a kingdom of priests and a holy nation"* (Exodus 19:4-6, NIV), they willfully and continually turned their backs on the Lord (from the time of Moses, c. 1526 - 1406 BC, through the time of Jesus) and rejected the Messiah, Jesus Christ (AD 32)—the author of life. Their disobedience and rejection of Jesus resulted in their worldwide exile (Diaspora) to the four corners of the world in AD 70.

Throughout the Old Testament the Jewish people were continually and willfully disobedient, idolatrous, and arrogant, and adopted pagan immoral cultures of surrounding nations including orgies, worshiping demonic gods, and child sacrifice. God's punishment (Deuteronomy 28:15-63) was in the form of harsh and prolonged disasters and eventual exile. "God makes it clear...that eventually the corrupt destroyer [the punisher, i.e., Assyria and Babylon] will itself be destroyed."[29] And it was so; the corrupt destroyers were themselves completely destroyed.

And then the question is asked, why did God allow persecution (mistreatment, oppression, and terrible cruelty) of the Jewish people by the evil punishers (Assyria and Babylon, and Nazi Germany)? And why does He allow this kind of evil to exist in this world?

God tells us about the entrance of evil into the universe. (See Ezekiel 28:11, 14-15; Revelation 12:3-9, 9:1; and Luke 8:30.) Rebellion by angelic beings led to the temptation and fall of mankind. Allowing evil, hence pain and suffering, "was a necessary price to achieve a far greater eternal result." [30] (p. 41-42, Alcorn)

People often ask (and use this question not to believe), why would a loving God create a world full of evil with its ensuing pain and suffering—but the real question is, "why would a loving God come into the world He created to suffer and die [Jesus suffered the wrath of God the Father] to pay for my sin?"

> For additional information, see the book by Roger Gallop, *Defeating Evil - God's Plan Before the Beginning of TIme (No Love Without Freedom...but Freedom Makes Evil Possible).*

As Alcorn explains, "From the beginning, God planned that his Son [Jesus Christ] should deal the death blow to Satan, evil, and suffering, to reverse the Curse [see chapters 2 and 3 of book, *evolution - The Greatest Deception in Modern History*], redeem a fallen humanity, and repair a broken world." (p. 51, Alcorn) *"The reason the Son of God appeared was to destroy the devil's work [to eliminate the evil in the world]"* (1 John 3:8, NIV).

In the Olivet Discourse, Jesus warned His followers (Christians and Jews) that they will suffer **tribulation and persecution** before the ultimate triumph of the Kingdom of God. This discourse is recorded in Matthew 24:1 – 25:46. Parallel passages are found in Mark 13:1-37 and Luke 21:5-36. (See chapter 6, New Testament Scripture Pertaining to the Rebirth of Israel.)

And in Luke 21:12 (NIV) Jesus warned, *"But before all this, they will seize you and **persecute you**. They will hand you over to synagogues and put you in prison, and you will be brought before kings and governors, and all on account of my name."* The apostle Paul warned that *"everyone who wants to live a godly life in Christ Jesus will be **persecuted**"* (2 Timothy 3:12, NIV).

Persecution by the Assyrians, Babylonians, and Romans was from the evil in the world and in the hearts of all human kind. Jesus said. **"If they persecuted me, they will persecute you also"** (John 15:20, NIV). All humans are subject to persecution, especially Christians and Jews.

Persecution of Jews and Christians throughout history and in today's world is clearly humanity **at its very worst**. "Evil's ultimate origin remains a mystery...[and] God has chosen to remain silent on this question." (p. 50, Alcorn) *"The secret things belong to the Lord our God"* (Deuteronomy 29:29, NIV). The question of evil and suffering will "ultimately make good sense, in the fullness of time." Through all the world's hate and injustice, there is a God who knows love and justice and, ultimately, He will wipe out the hate, persecution, and injustice; in short, there **is a righteous and holy God who will make things right. And that God is the God of the Holy Bible.**

> *"...our present sufferings are not worth comparing with the glory that will be revealed in us"* (Romans 8:18, NIV), and *"For our light and momentary troubles are achieving for us an eternal glory that far outweighs them all"* (2 Corinthians 4:17, NIV).

Scripture pertaining to persecution is found in chapter 5, Persecution is Not from God.

18. Why did Jesus have to be the sacrificial Lamb of God?

Because of sin (rebellion) by the first man, Adam, against his Creator (Genesis 3:6; Romans 5:12), creation was cursed by God (Genesis 3:14-19)—in effect leading to a contaminated and corrupt world. (See Appendix C.) All men are guilty of sin (Romans 3:23; 1 John 1:8,10), and sin always carries a death sentence, *"For the wages of sin is death, but the gift of God is eternal life through Jesus Christ our Lord"* (Romans 6:23; NIV). In Genesis 2:17, despite the serpent's denial (Genesis 3:4; you will not surely die), disobeying God ultimately results in death.

"God devised a way for [through] His love (agape love, a sacrificial love) to deliver sinners from His wrath [death] while not compromising His righteousness and justice. Jesus Christ took upon Himself a human nature (God incarnate), lived as a true man, and never once sinned. **He therefore qualified to voluntarily take upon Himself the penalty and punishment for our sins. He died in our place and secured a true forgiveness for each one who will receive it as a gift.** Salvation cannot be given if any human merit is attached to it. Salvation is an **absolute gift.**"[31]

God will deal with sin either by grace (mercy) or by wrath. John 3:36 (NIV) says, *"Whoever believes in the Son has eternal life, but whoever rejects the Son will not see life, for God's wrath remains on him."* Those who do not accept Jesus Christ as their Savior will remain under the Lord's wrath.

Only Jesus, the Son of God, could be the Mediator between God the Father and desperately sinful mankind, and without Jesus, there would be no reconciliation and no redemption [salvation; restoration] for humanity. The complexity of the concept of the God-Man in Jesus Christ is especially difficult to comprehend, but **it was necessary to redeem creation lost to sin.** God loved us so much that He provided a "second Adam" in His Son Jesus to take our place and become our "redeemer."[32]

Meaning of Genesis 3:15 (NIV)
Ref. Verse by Verse Commentary[33]

"And I will put enmity"—This verse concerns the fall of Adam and Eve. God is speaking to the serpent who is an embodiment of Satan. God desires no alliance with Satan and the two are mutually exclusive.

"between you and the woman, and between your seed **[Satan's seed]** *and her Seed* **[Jesus]**"—God draws a distinction between "your seed" (Satan's seed; spiritual descendants such as demons or fallen angels) and "her Seed" (Jesus). "Her Seed" refers to the humanity or the incarnation of Christ in human form through the virgin birth. The New Testament calls Jesus the "Seed" (Galatians 3:16).

"He shall crush your head, and you shall strike His heel."—God forecasts the defeat of Satan by the incarnation (God in human form) of Christ, the Messiah. The battle lines were drawn between God and Satan. *"He shall crush your head"* is a mortal wound. The power of Satan is crushed by the Cross of Christ. *"And you shall strike* [bruise] *His heel"* refers to the sacrifice of Jesus at the Cross (Isaiah 53:10).

At the fall of man (when man turned away from God in the Garden of Eden), God promised a solution to their sin. Sin was the reason for Christ going to the Cross, and at the Cross Christ crushed Satan's head. Christ not only fully paid for the sins of the world on the Cross but He defeated Satan as well (Colossians 2:14-15).

19. Why did wholesale attempts fail to eradicate the Jews as a people?

Satan's attempts to rule the earth and first and second heavens began at the Garden of Eden and later, upon realizing God's plan for redemption, he tried to kill the infant Jesus; attempted to deter the Messiah in the wilderness (Matthew 4:1-11; Mark 1:12-13; Luke 4:1-13); attempted to destroy the Hebrew race (persecution of Jews following their dispersion in AD 70 and persecution and slaughter of 6 million Jews in the Nazi Holocaust during WW II); and attempted to destroy the church (martyrdom of Christians). This question is described in detail in Appendix C, Satan's Attempts to Seize Total Control, and in the book by Roger G. Gallop, *Defeating Evil*, (Planet Earth - God's Testing Ground), chapter 4, Origin of Evil.

Satan knew that if these attempts or threats to eradicate the Jews ever succeeded, or if the Jewish people were never given the opportunity to form a new State of Israel on the world stage, prophecy and the word of God (Hosea 3:4-5; Jeremiah 31:10, 35-36) **would have become worthless—fulfillment of Bible prophecy requires the Jews' survival as a nation in Judea, in the land of Canaan.**

20. Why, considering the vast numbers of acres of Arab land did the Arabs select the Temple site of God's chosen people as one of their most holy places?

The Arabs' assertion of their right to the site is a carry-over from the ancient family feud. In Genesis 22:1-19, Abraham offered his son Isaac in total faith in the word of God at the Temple Site.[34] Muslims hold to this very same tradition but they claim it was Ishmael, not Isaac, who their father Abraham offered as a sacrifice. The Arabs also revere this site because they believe it was here that Mohammed (c. AD 570 to 632) ascended into heaven on his horse Buraq (Islamic mythology)—so in commemoration, Abd al-Malik, authorized the costly construction of the mosque.[35] The Dome of the Rock (mosque) was built c. AD 685 to 691 as a shrine for Muslim pilgrims, but interestingly, Mohammed never traveled to Jerusalem nor has any Muslim nation ever claimed Jerusalem as its capital.

Further, Muslims have placed a cemetery in front of the Eastern Gate (Golden Gate) and constructed the al-Asqa mosque across the Huldah Gates and the Southern Steps where Jesus often entered the Temple Mount. Why do such a thing? It is perhaps both an insult to the Jewish people and in hopes of preventing Jesus, the Messiah, from returning to Jerusalem through these very gates.

21. Is a Palestinian State legitimate?

The reader is referred to chapter 8, The Fallacy of an Arab Palestinian State, for a detailed answer.

22. Why would Satan embark on such rebellion against a Sovereign God if he knew his plan would be futile?

Although Satan could not foresee the future (he is not omnipotent, omnipresent, or omniscient as in the case of God the Father, the Son, and the Holy Spirit), he (Satan) was convinced he could win the battles and the war, and ultimately, be like God. For more information, see book by Roger Gallop, *Defeating Evil*, chapter 4, Origin of Evil.

Why doesn't Satan give up now and negotiate a "deal" of surrender or peace with God? Because of his extreme egotism and pride, and because there has been too much terrible damage over too long a period of time—there is no going back. But in fact, God desires no truce with Satan; and the two (God and Satan) are mutually exclusive (see Genesis 3:15 on previous page and in the prologue, Pain and Suffering and its Origin).

the Bible warns: there is only one way to heaven

Our eternal destiny is either Heaven or Hell—eternal and everlasting. For those who have turned their back on God—stop and seriously reconsider the consequences of your decision and motivation. Eternal life in the Kingdom of Heaven is freely offered during your time here on earth through our Lord Jesus Christ, the Messiah, who is *"King of Kings and Lord of Lords"* (Revelation 19:16, NIV). And according to Romans 9:5, Jesus is God in the fullest sense.

> In Revelation 1:8, NIV, *"'I am the Alpha and the Omega' says the Lord God, 'who is, and who was, and who is to come, the Almighty.'"* There is no better way to describe the continuous existence of being. And in John 1:1 (NIV), it states that *"In the beginning was the Word, and the Word was with God, and the Word was God. He was with God in the beginning."* God continuously existed before the beginning of all things.

Jesus shed His blood, suffered, and died on the Cross to save us from our sins and the wrath of God—from the eternal loneliness, darkness, and torment of Hell—but only if we accept the gift of pardon through faith and repentance of sins. The Bible tells us that Heaven is available to everyone—it doesn't matter who you are, how old you are, where you live, or what sins you may have committed. That is why Jesus is called Savior. He graciously offers life in Heaven (Paradise)—but there is **only one way** and it is through Jesus Christ—**not multiple ways** as some suggest who believe in the same God for all religions. We have to **sincerely repent of our sins and accept the gift of pardon by faith.**

In our present state, man is sinful and separated from God; **Jesus Christ is God's only provision for man's sin**; we must individually receive Jesus Christ as Savior and Lord; and we cannot 'earn' our way into Heaven by our 'good deeds.'

> *"For it is by grace you have been saved, through faith—and this not from yourselves, it is the gift of God—not by works, so that no one can boast"* (Ephesians 2:8-9, NIV).

> *"He who believes in Him is not judged; he who does not believe is judged already, because he has not believed in the name of the only begotten Son of God"* (John 3:18, NIV).

> *"For God so loved the world that he gave his only begotten Son, that whosoever believeth in Him should not perish but have everlasting life"* (John 3:16, KJV).

> *"I am the good shepherd. The good shepherd lays down his life for the sheep"* (John 10:11, NIV).

> *"Do not let your hearts be troubled. You believe in God; believe also in me. My Father's house has many rooms [mansions; abiding places]; if that were not so, would I have told you that I am going there to prepare a place for you? And if I go and prepare a place for you, I will come back and take you to be with me that you also may be where I am [in Heaven]. You know the way to the place where I am going"* (John 14:1-4, NIV).

The only unpardonable sin is to reject the free gift of pardon offered by Jesus Christ, the promised Messiah...who stepped out of Eternity (*"His goings forth are from long ago, From the days of eternity,"* Micah 5:2, NAS) and became a guilt offering. He became a sacrificial 'Lamb of God' on the Cross—the ultimate and final sin offering for Israel and the whole world... and bore our iniquities so we can be cleansed of all our sins. He took the penalty for our sins upon Himself—**but we have to believe it, accept it, and receive it in our hearts by faith.**

Invite Him into your life as Lord and Savior, believe He died on the Cross for all your sins, and rose from the grave. There will be no peace in our heart until we make peace with God through His Son, Jesus Christ, the promised Messiah, who died for us so we might have life after death in Heaven. Consider the following principles:[36]

> All men are guilty of sin and need forgiveness - Romans 3:23, 6:23; 1 John 1:8, 10.
>
> God desires to have all men turn from sin and be saved - 1 Timothy 2:4; 2 Peter 3:9; Titus 2:11, 12.
>
> Jesus died to make salvation available to all men - 1 Timothy 2:6; Hebrews 2:9; John 3:16; Matthew 11:28-30.
>
> To be saved, men must hear, believe, and obey the gospel - John 6:44, 45, 8:24, 32; Hebrews 5:9; 2 Thessalonians 1:8, 9; 1 Peter 1:22; Romans 1:16, 6:17-18, 10:14, 17.
>
> God desires for all men to learn the gospel so they have the opportunity to believe and obey - 1 Timothy 2:4; Matthew 28:18-20; Mark 16:15, 16; Luke 24:47; Acts 2:38-39, 17:30-31; Colossians 1:28.
>
> The gospel, revealed in the first century to the apostles, provides all that is good and all that we need to please God - John 14:26; 16:13; 2 Peter 1:3; 2 Timothy 3:16, 17; Acts 20:20, 27; Matthew 28:18-20; James 1:25.

All people need the gospel, God wants all people to have the gospel, and so the gospel was completely and accurately revealed in the first century. The Gospel of Jesus Christ has remained available throughout history, and it is available to all people today through missionary outreach and advanced communications in television, radio, and the internet.

God is long suffering: *"The Lord is not slow in keeping his promise, as some understand slowness. Instead he is patient with you, not wanting anyone to perish, but everyone to come to repentance"* (2 Peter 3:9, NIV). We thank God that He loves us enough to provide a way for us to escape the judgment for our sins. By accepting Jesus Christ as our Lord and Savior, and by the grace of God, we are granted forgiveness of sins, mercy, and salvation with the promise of everlasting life. (See John 3:16; Ephesians 2:8-9.)

In their remarkable book, *Charting the End Times,* Drs. Tim LaHaye and Thomas Ice describe The Way to Paradise:[37]

> "... those who go to Paradise and those who end up in Hades are sinners. The latter die in their sins, while those who reside in Paradise were forgiven of their sins sometime during their life. Jesus Himself gave us clear directions on how to obtain admittance to this glorious place when He said, *'I am the way, and the truth, and the life; no one comes to the Father but through Me'* (John 14:6, NIV). Only through Jesus Christ can we gain access to the Father, who is in heaven (where Paradise is now located). The Bible says that all men deserve to go to hell (Romans 3:23; 6:23), and only through faith in the Lord Jesus Christ and His finished work on the cross can we escape Hades and hell. John 1:12 says, *'As many as received Him, to them He gave the right to become children of God, even to those who believe in His name.'*
>
> To activate the eternal effects of God's forgiveness of sins through the death of His Son, a person must call on the name of the Lord and be saved (Romans 10:13). There is no other way—and no second chance."

final message

This final passage is borrowed from the Introduction to the Book of Psalms, The NIV Study Bible:[38]

"Under God creation is a cosmos—an orderly and systematic whole. What we distinguish as 'nature' and history had for them one Lord, under whose rule all things worked together. Through the creation the Great King's majestic glory is displayed. He is good (wise, righteous, faithful, amazingly benevolent and merciful—evoking trust), and he is great (his knowledge, thoughts and works are beyond human comprehension—evoking reverent awe). By his good and lordly rule he is shown to be the Holy One."

"As The Great King by right of creation and enduring absolute sovereignty, he ultimately will not tolerate any worldly power that opposes or denies or ignores him. He will come to rule the nations so that all will be compelled to acknowledge him. This expectation is no doubt the root and broadest scope of the psalmists' long view of the future. Because the Lord is the Great King beyond all challenge, his righteous and peaceable kingdom will come, overwhelming all opposition and purging the creation of all rebellion against his rule—such will be the ultimate outcome of history."

"As the Great King over all the earth, the Lord has chosen Israel to be his servant people, his 'inheritance' among the nations. He has delivered them by mighty acts out of the hands of the world powers, he has given them a land of their own (territory that he took from other nations to be his own 'inheritance' in the earth), and he has united them with himself in covenant as the initial embodiment of his redeemed kingdom. Thus both their destiny and his honor came to be bound up with this relationship. To them he also gave his word of revelation, which testified of him, made specific his promises and proclaimed his will."

God will deal with sin either by grace or by wrath. John 3:36 (NIV) says, *"Whoever believes in the Son has eternal life, but whoever rejects the Son will not see life, for God's wrath remains on him."* Those who do not accept Jesus Christ as their Savior will remain under the Lord's wrath.

It's not too late to choose eternal life. All that is required is acceptance of God's free gift of pardon through faith and repentance of sin. There is nothing you can do to earn grace [mercy]; Jesus has paid the price for you (Romans 3:24).

If what you see happening in the world makes you fearful or anxious, don't be. If you accept this free gift of pardon, you will inherit eternal life and won't be here during the seven year tribulation.

God is holy, righteous, and merciful and through our Lord Jesus Christ offers the gift of eternal salvation (John 3:16, 5:24, 14:6; Romans 10:9, 13). *"For it is by grace you have been saved through faith…"* (Ephesians 2:8-9, NIV).

People lest not forget the Lord is **omnipresent, omnipotent, and omniscient** (Romans 8:29; Ephesians 1:4-5; 1 Corinthians 2:7); **He is inside and outside the universe;** and *"**the Lord is a warrior**"* (Exodus 15:3)—*"**He does whatever pleases Him**"* (Psalms 115:3, 135:6, NIV; Job 23:13; Daniel 4:35), and *"**He is to be feared**"* (1 Chronicles 16:25, NIV; Psalm 96:4, NIV; Isaiah 8:13; Job 25:15-16). [Bold added] See Preface, Who is God?

notes: epilogue

1. Stoner, P.W. (1963). *Science Speaks*. Chicago: Moody Press; as cited in McDowell, i.

2. LaHaye, T. and Ice, T. (2001). *Charting the End Times*. Eugene, OR: Harvest House Publishers, 14.

3. McDowell, J. (1972). *Evidence that Demands a Verdict*. San Bernardino, CA: Campus Crusade for Christ, i.

4. Mitchell, T. (December 2011). Death and Steve Jobs. *Answers Update*, 18 (12), Hebron, KY: Answers in Genesis, 2 (answersingenesis.org).

5. Alcorn, R. (2009). *If God Is Good – Faith in the Midst of Suffering and Evil*. Colorado Springs, CO: Multnomah Books, 24-25.

6. Alcorn, R. (2009), op. cit., 41-42.

7. Hal Lindsey (February 13, 2015). Hal Lindsey Report, News from Hal Lindsey Media Ministries. (www.hallindsey.org).

8. Hal Lindsey (August 1, 2014), op. cit.

9. McDowell, J. (1972), op. cit., 328.

10. The World Bank. Retrieved from http://data.worldbank.org/country; Geography, Maps Don't Lie. Retrieved from http://www.mefacts.com/cached.asp?x_id=10190; Economy of the Middle East, https://en.wikipedia.org/wiki/Economy_of_the_Middle_East; and Israel, https://en.wikipedia.org/wiki/Israel.

11. The PBI, 1425 Lachman Lane, Pacific Palisades, CA 90272; as cited in http://www.heraldmag.org/2006/06nd_13.htm.

12. Hal Lindsey (June 17, 2016), op. cit.

13. Hagee, J. (2006). *Jerusalem Countdown: A Warning to the World*. Lake Mary, FL: FrontLine, 104.

14. Hal Lindsey (April 24, 2015), op. cit.

15. Stoner, P.W. (1963), op. cit.; as cited in McDowell, 175.

16. Snyder, M. (2012). 34 Signs That America is in Decline. Retrieved January 2016, from http://theeconomiccollapseblog.com/archives/34-signs-that-america-is-in-decline; and http://endoftheamericandream.com/archives/tag/economic-decline.

17. Snyder, M. (May 21, 2013). America's Bubble Economy Is Going To Become An Economic Black Hole. Retrieved January 2016, from http://theeconomiccollapseblog.com/archives/americas-bubble-economy-is-going-to-become-an-economic-black-hole; and Snyder, M. (March 20, 2013). Why Is The World Economy Doomed? The Global Financial Pyramid Scheme by the Numbers. Retrieved January 2016, from http://theeconomiccollapseblog.com/archives/why-is-the-world-economy-doomed-the-global-financial-pyramid-scheme-by-the-numbers.

18. Snyder, M. (November 9, 2011). 35 Statistics That Show The Average American Family Has Been Broke Down, Tore Down, Beat Down, Busted And Disgusted By This Economy. Retrieved January 2016, from http://endoftheamericandream.com/archives/tag/economic-decline.

19. McCann, S. (November 29, 2012). The Governing Class and Decline of America. American Thinker. Retrieved February 2016, from http://www.americanthinker.com/articles/2012/11/the_governing_class_and_the_decline_of_america.html#ixzz2DdCUjIsK.

20. Passage taken from the introduction to the Book of Amos, The NIV Study Bible (1985), New International Version, Zondervan Publishing House, Grand Rapids, MI 49506.

21. Arnoldy, B. (December 28, 2006). In dorms, men and women now room together. The Science Christian Monitor. Retrieved January 2016, from http://www.csmonitor.com/2006/1228/p02s01-legn.html.

22. Roach, D. (February 2, 2015). Analysis: Rape on college campuses. *Baptist Press*. Retrieved January 2016, from http://bpnews.net/44146/analysis-rape-on-college-campuses.

23. The Decline of Christianity in America (June 2009). The Last Days. Retrieved January 2016, from http://signsofthelastdays.com/archives/the-decline-of-christianity-in-america. Also see Lillian Kwon, Christian Post Reporter (June 29, 2009). Survey: Churches Losing Youths Long Before College. Retrieved January 2016, from http://www.christianpost.com/news/survey-churches-losing-youths-long-before-college-39433/.

24. Hal Lindsey (November 7, 2014), op. cit.

25. Burrows, M. (1956). *What Mean These Stones?* NY: Meridian Books, 291, 1; as cited in McDowell, J., 69.

26. Hal Lindsey (April 22, 2016), op. cit.

27. Hal Lindsey (June 5, 2015), op. cit.

28. Passage taken from the introduction to the Book of Amos, The NIV Study Bible (1985), New International Version, Zondervan Publishing House, Grand Rapids, MI 49506.

29. Passage taken from the introduction to the Book of Habakkuk, The NIV Study Bible (1985), New International Version, Zondervan Publishing House, Grand Rapids, MI 49506.

30. Alcorn (2009), op. cit., 41-42, 51; Mitchell, T. (December 2011). Death and Steve Jobs. *Answers Update*, 18 (12), Hebron, KY: Answers in Genesis, 1-2; Johnson, J. (November 2011). Human suffering: Why this isn't the "best of all possible worlds." *Acts & Facts*, 40 (11), Dallas, TX: Institute for Creation Research, 8-10 (ICR.org).

31. Hal Lindsey (December 30, 2016), op. cit.

32. Hal Lindsey (March 20, 2015; March 27, 2015; September 4, 2015), op. cit.

33. Richison, G.C. (December 23, 2001). Genesis 3:15; as cited in http://versebyversecommentary.com/christmas/genesis-315/

34. The sacrifice of Isaac put Abraham through an excruciating trial of faith, but Abraham had complete devotion and trust in God. Abraham told his servants "we" will return to you—both he and Isaac. Abraham believed God would either provide another sacrifice or would raise Isaac from the dead. This foretells of God's sacrifice of His only Son, Jesus Christ, on the cross at Calvary for the sins of the world. Because of God's agape love for humanity, He required of Himself what He did not require of Abraham. This site is where King Solomon later built the first Temple but today the Muslim shrine (The Dome of the Rock) is located at or near the site where Muslims claim it was Ishmael, not Isaac, who was offered as a sacrifice. See Sacrifice of Isaac – Bible Story Summary. Retrieved February 2016, from http://christianity.about.com/od/Old-Testament/a/JZ-Sacrifice-Of-Isaac.htm.

35. Abd al-Malik, in full abd Al-malik Ibn Marwān, born AD 646 in Medina, Arabia—died AD 705, Damascus, fifth caliph of the Umayyad Arab dynasty in Damascus.

36. Pratte, D.E. (1998, 2000). God Desires All Men to Know, Believe, & Obey His Will; as cited in http://www.gospelway.com/bible/bible_preservation.php.

37. LaHaye, T. and Ice, T. (2001), op. cit., 133-134.

38. Passage taken from the Introduction to the Book of Psalms (1985), The NIV Study Bible, New International Version, Zondervan Publishing House, Grand Rapids, MI 49506.

Appendix A
Glossary[1]

Abomination of desolation— midway through the seven year tribulation, the antichrist defiles the newly built Jewish temple and demands to be worshipped "as God." When this event happens there is a literal countdown of 42 months before the return of Jesus Christ (the Second Coming).

Abraham (according to a footnote in the NIV English translation of the Bible)— "Father of many nations." Abram is defined as "exalted father."

Abrahamic Covenant— the first covenant between God and Abraham. In the first covenant (Genesis 12:1-5, 7, 13:14-15) God promised Abraham, *"To your offspring* [descendants] *I will give this land"* (Genesis 12:7, NIV). This is an **unconditional covenant**—that is, there are no conditions that have to be fulfilled by human beings. See Mosaic Covenant.

> **Unconditional Covenant**— the Lord came to Abram with the **first covenant** (Genesis 12:1-3, 13:14-15) commonly known as the **Abrahamic Covenant.** (See chapter 2, section Abraham and His Sons Isaac and Ishmael.) God promised Abraham, *"To your offspring* [descendants] *I will give this land"* (Genesis 12:7, NIV). In an unconditional covenant there are no conditions that must be fulfilled by human beings. The covenant cannot end; it remains in effect **forever,** and that "makes it fundamental to Bible prophecy."[2]

AD (anno Domini)— "in the year of our Lord." The Anno Domini system was developed by a monk named Dionysius Exiguus (born in Scythia Minor) in Rome in AD 525.

Agape love— a self-sacrificing love found only in humans and God. It is described in John 3:16 (NIV), *"For God so loved the world that he gave his one and only Son, that whoever believes in him shall not perish but have eternal life."* The word translated "love" in this verse is agape. When 1 John 4:8 says *"God is love,"* the Greek New Testament uses the word agape to describe God's love.

Antediluvian (syn. Prediluvian; Latin for "before the deluge"; pre-Flood)— a term describing a period of time that preceded the Great Flood during the time of Noah as described in the Book of Genesis in the Bible. Postdiluvian period is after the flood. For more information, see the book by Roger Gallop, *evolution – The Greatest Deception in Modern History (Scientific Evidence for Divine Creation).*

Antichrist— see Satan and false prophet.

Apostasy— the abandonment or renunciation of a religious belief; **blasphemy** is the act of speaking sacrilegiously about God; and **heresy** is any provocative belief or theory that is strongly at variance with established beliefs.

Apostle (in Greek)— a 'messenger' while **Disciple** (in Greek) means 'student or follower.' Disciples were followers or students of Christ. Jesus chose the original twelve to travel and learn from Him; eventually, eleven plus one added later (Matthias; Acts 1:26) were sent to foreign lands to act as messengers (apostles) of the gospel.

Aram— a region mentioned in the Bible located in central Syria, including the city of Aleppo (aka Halab). Aram stretched from the Lebanon mountains eastward across the Euphrates, including the Khabur River valley in northwestern Mesopotamia on the border of Assyria.

Aramaic— the language of Semitic peoples throughout the ancient Near East. It was the language of the Assyrians, Chaldeans, Hebrews, and Syrians. Aram and Israel had a common ancestry, and the Hebrew patriarchs who were of Aramaic origin maintained ties of marriage with the tribes of Aram. The Hebrew patriarchs preserved their Aramaic names and spoke in Aramaic. The term Aramaic is derived from Aram, the fifth son of Shem, the firstborn of Noah. See Genesis 10:22. See chapter 2, Abrahamic Covenant (sketch).

Archaeology— the study of human activity in the past, primarily through the recovery and analysis of relics, monuments, tombs, and artifacts of ancient civilizations.

Armageddon— according to the Book of Revelation, the site of the final battle during the second 3 ½ years of the seven year tribulation period. It is the invasion by China and surrounding countries (possibly including Russia) while the U.S. (likely political Babylon) is most likely aligned with the European Union and the antichrist.

Assyria— a distinct ethnic group whose origins lie in northern Mesopotamia. They speak, read, and write distinct dialects of Eastern Aramaic exclusive to northern Mesopotamia and its immediate surroundings.

Babylon— in the 7th and 6th centuries B.C.E., the city of Babylon was the largest and wealthiest in the ancient world under the ruthless and ambitious King Nebuchadnezzar II. In the last days the U.S. will likely be 'political Babylon' aligned with the antichrist out of the E.U. (ref. Revelation 17) and 'religious Babylon' will be situated in Rome on seven hills (ref. Revelation 18).

Balfour Declaration (dated November 2, 1917)— a letter from the United Kingdom's Foreign Secretary Arthur James Balfour to Walter Rothschild, 2nd Baron Rothschild, a leader of the British Jewish community, for transmission to the Zionist Federation of Great Britain and Ireland.

> His Majesty's government viewed with favor the establishment in Palestine of a national home for the Jewish people and used their best efforts to facilitate the achievement of this objective—it being clearly understood that nothing shall be done which may prejudice the civil and religious rights of existing non-Jewish communities in Palestine, or the rights and political status enjoyed by Jews in any other country.

BC— before Christ.

Beth Togarmiah— today's Turkey. See Meshech and Tubal for more information.

Bond (Government Bond)— see National Debt.

Byzantine Empire— sometimes known as the **Eastern Roman Empire**, was the predominantly Greek-speaking continuation of the eastern Roman Empire during Late Antiquity and the Middle Ages. Its capital city was Constantinople (modern-day Istanbul), originally founded as Byzantium.

Caliphate— is a form of Islamic government led by a person (**caliph**) considered to be a political and religious successor to Muhammad, the original leader of the entire Muslim community. By using the language of Caliph and Caliphate, ISIS (Islamic State in Iraq and Syria) wants to establish itself as the leader of a worldwide Muslim movement without national boundaries.

Canaan— corresponds to the Levant, a large area in the eastern Mediterranean. Canaanites, the most frequently used ethnic term in the Old Testament, are commonly described as a paganistic people. See chapter 2, The Ethical Question of War.

Canonization— comes from the Greek word *kanon*, which means a *straight edge or ruler*. It is a rigorous review process using precise rules and standards.[3] The books of the Bible have been canonized and have been determined to be *Holy Scripture,* or the divinely inspired *Word of God.* Determining the standards was a process conducted first by Jewish rabbis and scholars and then later by early Christians. Ultimately, it was God who decided which books belonged in the Bible. For more information, see chapter 1, The Bible's Preservation.

Chaldeans— were people who lived in southern Babylonia which would be the southern part of Iraq today.

Cold War (1947 – 1991)— was a state of political and military tension after World War II between powers in the Western Bloc (the United States, its NATO allies, and others) and powers in the Eastern Bloc (the Soviet Union and its allies in the Warsaw Pact). It was termed as "cold" because there was no large-scale fighting between the two sides.

Constantinople— was located on the Bosporus Strait, the waterway that connects the Black Sea to the Mediterranean. Therefore, it was strategically placed, being both defended by water on three sides, and also well positioned to demand taxes from ships traveling the trade routes.

Coptic— is the language which represents the final stage of ancient Egypt. It now survives only as the liturgical (ceremonial) language of the Coptic Church. Coptic Christianity began in Egypt in the first century, making it one of the oldest Christian churches.

Covenant— is a binding agreement between two or more parties; in legal terms, it is a formal sealed agreement or contract. A **conditional covenant** mentioned in the Bible is the Mosaic Covenant whereby the blessings of the Lord are contingent upon Israel's adherence to the Law. The Mosaic Covenant was temporary. See chapter 2, The Mosaic Covenant, and appendix B, Establishment of a New Covenant. **Unconditional covenants** mentioned in the Bible are the Abrahamic and Davidic Covenants whereby God promises to fulfill blessings completely and absolutely regardless of other factors.

Crusades— were military campaigns sanctioned by the Latin Roman Catholic Church during the Middle Ages. In 1095 Pope Urban II proclaimed the First Crusade with the goal of restoring Christian access to holy places in and around Jerusalem. The crusades were not about restoring the Jewish homeland—land given to the Jews through the Abrahamic covenant—but rather, **the crusades were military campaigns to reclaim "Christian lands" captured by the Muslims.**

Cush— is Sudan. See Meshech and Tubal for more information.

Cyber attack— is an attempt by hackers to damage or destroy a computer network or system. Such attacks have become more sophisticated using sleeper programs easily embedded in computer programs or systems.

Disciple— see apostle for complete definition.

Dispensation in the Bible— a period of time in which God dealt/deals with mankind. The Scripture divides time (from the creation of Adam in Genesis to the *"new heaven and a new earth"* of Revelation 21:1) into seven unequal periods, usually called dispensations (Ephesians 3:2), although these periods are also called ages (Ephesians 2:7). These periods are 1) **Innocence** which extends from the creation of Adam in Genesis 2:7 to the expulsion from Eden, 2) **Conscience** which extends from expulsion from Eden to the flood, 3) **Government** which extends from the flood to Abram, 4) **Promise** which extends from Abraham to Moses, 5) **Law**, which extends from Moses and the Ten Commandments to the time of Jesus Christ, 6) **Grace** which extends from the crucifixion of Christ to the Second Coming, and 7) **Millennium** which extends from the Second Coming for another 1,000 years.

> These periods are designated in Scripture by a change in God's method of dealing with mankind with respect to sin and man's responsibility. Each of the dispensations may be regarded as a new test, and each ends in judgment, marking mankind's complete failure in every dispensation. Five of these dispensations, or periods of time, have been fulfilled—we are living at the close of the sixth, and facing the seventh and last dispensation, the Millennium.

Diaspora— describes the exile of the Jewish people from their homeland, first was for 70 years in 586 BC by the Babylonians, and second was worldwide exile for 1,878 years in AD 70 by the Romans.

Divine— intervention is a deity's (God the Father, the Son, or the Holy Spirit) active involvement in the affairs of humankind—nations, government, and people.

Dome of the Rock (AD 685 – AD 691)— is a Muslim shrine located on the Temple Mount in the Old City of Jerusalem; Dome of the Chain (AD 691) is a free-standing dome located immediately east of the Dome of the Rock; and al-Aqsa Mosque (AD 705 and rebuilt AD 754, 780) is located just south of the Dome of the Rock.

Electromagnetic pulse (EMP)— is a short burst of electromagnetic energy. It can be man-made or natural and occurs as a radiated, electric or magnetic field. Weapons are divided into nuclear and non-nuclear. The rapidly changing electric and magnetic fields may couple with existing electric and electronic systems to produce damaging current and voltage surges.

End times (also called end of time, end of days, last days, final days)— is a time period described in eschatology (see definition below) just prior to and including the seven year tribulation period prior to the Second Coming of Christ. In Judaism, the term "end of days" refers to the Messianic Age that includes an in-gathering of the exiled Diaspora and the coming of the Messiah.

Eschatology— is the study of the end of the age and the destiny of man as it is revealed in the Bible.

Evil— is sin, iniquity, wickedness, immorality, lawlessness, corruption, and persecution. It is breaking the moral law (see section Human Nature and the Moral Law in the book *evolution – The Greatest Deception in Modern History (Scientific Evidence for Divine Creation)*, or any one of the Ten Commandments, or a departure from goodness. When we think of evil we think of tyrants and dictators, and mass murderers, and people twisted into psychotic monsters who commit crimes against the innocent.

False prophet— is one who falsely claims the gift of prophecy or divine inspiration and uses that gift for evil ends. The false prophet of the end times is described in Revelation 13:11-15. He is also referred to as the "second beast" (Revelation 16:13, 19:20, 20:10) who promotes antichrist propaganda. Together with the antichrist and Satan, the false prophet is the third party in the 'unholy trinity.' Both the antichrist and false prophet are directly influenced by Satan. See Satan in the glossary.

Fatah— is the political and military organization of the PLO founded in the late 1950s by Yasser Arafat and Khalīl al-Wazīr with the mission of displacing the State of Israel using guerrilla warfare and forming a Palestine Arab state. Fatah is a more moderate party (as compared with Hamas) and currently controls parts of the West Bank. See Hamas in glossary.

Fedayeen (Arabic: "those who sacrifice themselves")— are Palestinian Arab guerrillas who operate mainly against Israel. Fedayeen are not normally connected to an organized government or military and often operate in areas with little or no government control.

Fig tree—represents the State of Israel politically reestablished in the Holy Land on May 14, 1948. See Matthew 24:32-35.

> Israel did not exist as a self-governing country for 2,534 years (586 BC + AD 1948) following the destruction of Jerusalem and the first Temple by the Babylonians in 586 BC and exile of the Jewish people to Babylon for 70 years—and then they did not exist as a distinct people in the Holy Land for 1,878 years (AD 70 - 1948) following worldwide exile (Diaspora) and the destruction of Jerusalem and the second Temple by the Romans in AD 70.

Gaza Strip— is a region on the eastern coast of the Mediterranean Sea that borders Egypt on the southwest for 11 kilometers (6.8 mi) and Israel on the east and north along a 51 km (32 mi) border. Gaza is part of the current Palestinian territory. (Palestinian territory also includes parts of the West Bank.)

Generation— is the average age of a man when his first son is born or one cycle in the succession of parents and children. A generation may vary depending on the time along Old and New Testament chronology. Today's generation is about 30 - 40 years.

Gentile— is an ethnonym (name applied to an ethnic group) that commonly means **non-Jew**.

Gog— is a word for "ruler," which literally means "the man on top" or dictator. Gog was the "chief prince" of the land of Magog which is today's Russia (today's Russia including Kazakhstan).[4] Gog is the name of an individual—and today's leader of Russia is Vladimir Putin.

Gomer— is located within modern Turkey. See Meshech (Meshek) and Tubal for more information.

Goodness (morality or virtue)— refers to qualities of character or conduct usually based on a code of conduct such as the Ten Commandments. (See Exodus 24:38; Deuteronomy 4:13; and prologue.)

Hamas— is a Palestinian Islamic political organization and militant group that has waged war on Israel since 1987, through suicide bombings and rocket attacks. Hamas seeks the destruction of Israel and the replacement of Israel with a Palestinian state. Hamas governs Gaza (independent of the Fatah controlled Palestinian Authority, PA; see Palestinian Liberation Organization, PLO, for more information)—and Hamas is the primary catalyst for aggression against Israel.[5] See Fatah in glossary.

> Hamas used suicide bombings against Israel in the 1990s and 2000s, although in recent years it has shifted to rockets and mortars. Unity talks between Hamas and the PA have broken down repeatedly—consequently, there is no unified PA which, in turn, complicates peace talks.

> In 2006, Hamas won a majority in the PA legislative elections and then refused to accept previous agreements the PA made with Israel, leading Hamas to withdraw from the PA and to govern Gaza independent of the PA. Since January 2013, Fatah controlled the PA which was renamed the State of Palestine after the UN voted to recognize Palestine as a non-member UN observer state.[6]

Hate— is an intense animosity or hostility that can be directed against individuals, groups of people, or beliefs or ideas. Hatred can manifest itself with the persecution of Christians, Jews, and the State of Israel as we see today. Love and hate are polar opposites and they have no quantifiable mass or energy.

Hebrew— was the language of the Jewish people in Biblical times, and most of the Old Testament was written in Hebrew. Prior to the restoration of Israel in 1948, Hebrew was a dead language. Although the language largely died out over time, it was revived in the 1900s, and in 1982 Hebrew became the official language of Israel. Today, Hebrew and Arabic languages are spoken throughout Israel. *"For then I will return to the people a pure language, that they may all call upon the name of the Lord, to serve him with one consent"* (Zephaniah 3:9, NIV).

Hebrews— are mostly taken as synonymous with the Semitic Israelites, especially during the pre-monarch period (Period of Judges; see chapter 3), when they were still nomadic.

Hellenistic period— is the period between the death of Alexander the Great in 323 BC and the emergence of the Roman Empire (c. 146 BC). It is often considered a period of transition—sometimes considered a period of degeneration and self-indulgence when compared to the virtuosity of the Greek classical era. The entire classic Greek culture was absorbed by the Romans who imitated the Greeks culturally, artistically, religiously, and politically including democratic ideas.

Heresy— is any provocative belief or theory that is strongly at variance with established beliefs or customs. A heretic is a proponent of variant claims or beliefs.

Herods of the Bible— were part of a ruling dynasty of Israel during the time of the Roman Empire. Unlike previous kings of Israel, the Herods were appointed by Roman emperors and the senate.

> **Herod the Great** (c. 37 BC to 1 BC) had begun an ambitious rebuilding program which included palaces, citadels, a theatre and an amphitheatre, bridges and public monuments, all done in order to promote his importance in the eyes of Rome. He sought to kill Jesus (Matthew 2) and tried to recruit the wise men to disclose the location of Jesus. See chapter 4, Life and Ministry of Jesus Christ (text box), for more information about the time period of Herod the Great.

> **Herod Antipas** (or Antipater) (c. 4 BC to 39 BC)— the son of Herod the Great, was tetrarch of Galilee (he governed one fourth of the kingdom of Judea and Samaria; other sons, Herod Archeiaus and Herod Philip, governed other portions of the kingdom). Pontius Pilate, the Roman governor of Judea, sent Jesus to

Antipas while Antipas was visiting Jerusalem at that time. Antipas presided over the trial and crucifixion of Jesus (Luke 23), and he also had John the Baptist beheaded (Matthew 14).

Herod Agrippa I the grandson of Herod the Great (Acts 12) persecuted the church and had the apostle James, the brother of John, put to death by the sword. James was the first apostle to be martyred.

Herod Agrippa II (the son of Agrippa I) was influential in saving Paul from being tried and imprisoned in Jerusalem.

How many Herods are in the Bible? See http://www.thegoodbookblog.com/2014/mar/03/how-many-herods-are-there-in-the-bible/.

Hezbollah— is a Shia Islamist militant group and political party based in Lebanon. Hezbollah was conceived by Muslim clerics and funded by Iran following the Israeli invasion of Lebanon in 1982 and was primarily formed to offer resistance to the Israeli occupation.

Its leaders were followers of Ayatollah Khomeini, and its forces were trained and organized by a contingent of 1,500 Iranian Revolutionary Guards that arrived from Iran with permission of the Syrian government. After the 1982 invasion, Israel occupied a strip of south Lebanon which was controlled by a militia supported by Israel, the South Lebanon Army. Hezbollah waged a guerilla campaign against them; with the collapse of the SLA, Israel withdrew on May 24, 2000. See chapter 7, 1982 Lebanon War.

Holocaust— is a term that describes the systematic extermination of 6 million European Jews (including 1.5 million children) by Nazi Germany or the Third Reich in what they called their "final solution of the Jewish question." Jewish fathers, mothers, children were identified, stripped of their possessions, separated from family members, shipped to concentration camps where they were starved, shot, hung, buried alive, put to death in gas chambers and ovens, injected with drugs and chemicals, and subjected to horrific, unspeakable medical experiments. This horror was part of a supernatural evil that permeates the world—an evil that "steals, kills, and destroys" with the ultimate goal of eliminating the church and seizing control of God's authority.

Hornet— used in these passages (Deuteronomy 7:20-21 and Exodus 23: 27-29) describes some agent that caused great panic amongst the Canaanites before the advancing Israelites. Some believe that the word hornet was used in a metaphorical sense as 'sheer panic' which would seize the people as a "terror of God" (Genesis 35:5). The Septuagint (Greek translation of the OT) renders the word a 'wasp'—but whatever it was, it caused great panic and confused the peoples of Canaan.

Humanism— is a belief that human beings are able to determine right and wrong through universal qualities such as reason—that is, prime importance is placed on human ability and self-reliance rather than the divine or supernatural. The basic philosophy of humanism is that man created himself, has control over his own destiny, and can rely on his own superior "intellect"—essentially, that man is God.

Idolatry— is the inclination of man to worship idols in place of God. Idols can take the form of religious statues: golden calf idols, bull idols, Greek idols, African idols, Hindu idols, Buddha idols, Mayan idols, Krishna idols, just to name a few. It can also mean worshiping the sun, moon, and stars ('the starry host'); material possessions (money, automobiles, boats, homes, etc.); sports, movie, and music celebrities; kings and queens; or even dictators. Some argue that even big businesses have turned their back on God and worship at the altar of the dollar. All of this is a form of idolatry.

Infidel— is a person who does not accept a particular faith, especially Islam.

Inquisition— is a period of intense questioning or investigation that is harsh or unfair. A court established by the Roman Catholic Church in the thirteenth century tried cases of heresy (belief strongly at variance with established beliefs) and other offenses against the church.

International Monetary Fund (IMF)— is an international organization headquartered in Washington, DC, comprising "188 countries working to foster global monetary cooperation, secure financial stability, facilitate international trade, promote high employment and sustainable economic growth, and reduce poverty around the world."[7]

ISIS— Iraq Syria Islamic State, an Islamic Sunni terrorist group known for its barbarism and brutality.

Islam— is a religion founded in the 7th Century AD by Muhammad (AD 580 – AD 632), an Arabian merchant from the city of Mecca. In the centuries leading up to the birth of Muhammad, Christianity had become the dominant faith of the Mediterranean, and its message was spreading to other regions of the world via major trade routes of that time. **Islam** denotes the religion or community of believers as a whole whereas **Muslim** distinguishes the person. See Muslim.

Israel— today is located on the site of the ancient kingdoms of Israel and Judah including Jerusalem except that these kingdoms also included areas east of the Jordan River. The Promised Land (Holy Land or Land of Israel) as defined in the Abrahamic Covenant (Genesis 15:18-21; see chapter 2) stretches from the Sinai Desert north and east to the Euphrates River which would include present-day Israel, Lebanon, and Jordan plus substantial portions of Syria, Iraq, and Saudi Arabia. Israel is the birthplace of the Hebrew language and the Abrahamic religions (Judaism and Christianity).

Jewish-Roman War (66–70 AD; sometimes called The Great Revolt)— was when the Roman Empire crushed Judah and destroyed the City of Jerusalem and the Second Temple in AD 70—and then the Romans crushed a second Jewish rebellion for independence in a three-year war ending in AD 135. In AD 70 the Jewish people were dispersed to the far corners of the earth because of their disobedience to God and rejection of the Messiah, the Lord Jesus Christ.

Jihad— is war or struggle against unbelievers; that is, non-Muslims.

Jihadist— is one engaged in jihad, especially one engaged in armed opposition to Christians or Jews—and such opposition is perceived as fanatical or employing means that are unlawful. Jihadist is one who considers using unlawful means in pursuit of an ideology; a fanatic or terrorist.

Judaism— encompasses the religion, culture and way of life of the Jewish people. It is an ancient monotheistic religion with the Torah as its foundational text. Judaism is considered an expression of the 'covenant relationship' that God established with the people of Israel through Abraham, Isaac, Jacob, and Moses.

Judea— the biblical, Roman, and modern name of the mountainous southern part of the Holy Land of Israel. It corresponds to the ancient Kingdom of Judah, also known as the Southern Kingdom with it capital Jerusalem. The Northern Kingdom retained the name Israel with its capital **Samaria**. See chapter 4, Divided Kingdom.

Knesset— is the unicameral (one parliamentary chamber or house) legislature of Israel located in Jerusalem. As the legislative branch of the Israeli government, the Knesset passes all laws, elects the President and Prime Minister, approves the cabinet, and supervises the work of the government.

Last days (also called end times, end of time, end of days, final days)— is a time period (described in eschatology; study of Bible prophecy) just prior to and including the seven year tribulation period preceding the Second Coming of Christ. In Judaism, the term "end of days" refers to the Messianic Age that includes an in-gathering of the exiled Diaspora and the coming of the Messiah.

Levant (eastern Mediterranean)— a term occasionally employed to refer to events, peoples, states or parts of states in the same region, namely Cyprus, Egypt, Iraq, Israel, Jordan, Lebanon, Palestine, Syria, and Turkey.

Love— is an intense feeling of affection. There are four forms of love: friendship (platonic), romantic, natural affection (familial), and agape. The first three can be understood in terms of shared mutual benefit that is found in all animals. Agape is a self-sacrificing love found only in humans and God. It is described in John 3:16 (NIV), *"For God so loved the world that he gave his one and only Son, that whoever believes in him shall not perish but have eternal life."* The word translated "love" in this verse is agape. When 1 John 4:8 says *"God is love,"* the Greek New Testament uses the word agape to describe God's love.

Melchizedek (translated as "my king is righteous")— was a king and priest who blessed Abram in chapter 14 of Genesis. In Christianity, according to Hebrews 2, Christ is identified as a priest forever in the order of Melchizedek, and so Jesus assumes the role of High Priest forever.

Magog – see Gog.

Maronites— are an ethno-religious group situated in the Levant (eastern Mediterranean), mainly in the area of modern Lebanon. They derive their name from the Syriac Christian Saint Maron whose followers migrated to the area of Mount Lebanon from their previous location of residence around the area of Antioch, establishing the nucleus of the Maronite Church. Maronites were able to keep their Christian religion and even their distinctive Aramaic language.

Masoretic Text— is the authoritative Hebrew text.

Medes (538 BC)— were an ancient Iranian people who lived in northwestern Iran (known as Media) and who spoke the Median language. See chapter 4, Medo-Persians.

Meshech (Meshek)— is Turkmenistan and Uzbekistan east of the Caspian Sea. **Tubal** is the southern tip of Russia east of Ukraine, **Gomer** and **Beth Togarmiah** are in Turkey, and **Persia** is Iran. During the last several decades, Russia has maintained a very close relationship with Iran and has been supervising and directing Iran's nuclear weapons program. And finally, **Put** is today's Libya, and **Cush** is today's Sudan. **Magog and Gog** refer to Russia (including Kazakhstan) and a Russian leader, respectively. See map, chapter 12, Invasion by Russia and Its Allies.

Millennial Period— is a dispensation period extending from the Second Coming of Jesus Christ for 1000 years (p. xii).

Mongol Empire (AD 1215 – AD 1453)— emerged from the unification of nomadic tribes in the Mongolia homeland under the leadership of Genghis Khan (c. AD 1206 - AD 1227), who was ruler of the Mongols. The empire grew rapidly under his rule and his descendants invaded in every direction and became one of the largest empires in human history.

Moral Law— a universal law of decent behavior or morality—a law of "right and wrong" behavior.

Mosaic Covenant— is a **conditional covenant** whereby the responsibility of the Israelites was to obey all the statutes, ordinances, and decrees established by God, and the responsibility of God was to bless Israel when they obey those statutes and to punish Israel when they do not. Moses was the intermediary between God and the Jewish people. The covenant was temporary and was replaced with the New Covenant with Jesus Christ. (See New Covenant in glossary and appendix B.)

> **Conditional Covenant:** *"'Now if you obey me fully and keep my covenant, then out of all nations you will be my treasured possession. Although the whole earth is mine, you will be for me a kingdom of priests and a holy nation.' These are the words you are to speak to the Israelites"* (Exodus 19:5-6, NIV).

Mount Moriah— is the specific site on which Abraham offered his son Isaac in Genesis 22. Traditionally, Moriah is interpreted as the site of the Temple Mount whereas others believe it also includes the elongated ridge to the south (the Eastern Hill). See chapter 12, Rebuilding the Third Temple.

Muhammad (AD 580 – AD 632)— an Arabian merchant from the city of Mecca, founded the Islamic religion and was therefore the original leader of the Muslim community. In the centuries leading up to the birth of Muhammad, Christianity had become the dominant faith of the Mediterranean, and its message was spreading to other regions of the world via the major trade routes of that time.

Muslim— is a person who follows the religion of Islam, a monotheistic and Abrahamic religion based on the Quran (Koran)—it is a religion of submission, acceptance, or surrender. Muslims consider the Quran to be the word of God as revealed to the Islamic prophet Muhammad. **Islam** denotes the religion or community of believers as a whole whereas **Muslim** distinguishes the person.

National debt— is the amount owed by the U.S. federal government. The measure of the public debt is the value of the outstanding Treasury securities (government debt instruments such as Treasury bills, notes, bonds, etc. issued by the U.S. Dept of the Treasury to finance the national debt). Currently, the national debt is a staggering 28.8 trillion dollars (September 2021) and the total debt is 86 trillion dollars (September 2021) which includes household, business, state and local governments, banks, and the Federal government. **Government bond** is a security or IOU to the investor (debt obligation) issued by the U.S. government with a promise to pay periodic interest payments and to repay the face value on the maturity date. See U.S.DebtClock.org.

Nazi Germany or the Third Reich— are common English names for the period of history in Germany from 1933 to 1945 when it was a dictatorship under the control of Adolf Hitler and the Nazi Party (NSDAP).

New Covenant— is a promise that "God would forgive sin and have a close, unbroken relationship with His people [Jeremiah 31:31-34]. The promise was first made to Israel and then extended to everyone [Jews and Gentiles] who comes to Jesus Christ in faith [Matthew 26:28; Hebrews 9:15]."[8] See Appendix B, Establishment of a New Covenant.

> Under the New Covenant, which Jesus sealed with His own blood, **everyone is offered salvation by grace through faith**. *"And it shall come to pass, that whosoever shall call on the name of the Lord shall be saved"* (Acts 2:21, KJV) and *"For whosoever shall call upon the name of the Lord shall be saved"* (Romans 10:13, KJV).

Olivet Discourse— is the teaching of the end times by Jesus Christ on the Mount of Olives and warning to His followers (Christians and Jews) that they will suffer tribulation and persecution before the ultimate triumph of the Kingdom of God. This discourse is recorded in Matthew 24:1 – 25:46. Parallel passages are found in Mark 13:1-37 and Luke 21:5-36. See chapter 6, New Testament Scripture Pertaining to the Rebirth of Israel.

Original Covenant – see Abrahamic Covenant.

Oslo Accords— are a set of agreements between the government of Israel and the Palestine Liberation Organization (PLO): the Oslo I Accord, signed in Washington, D.C., on September 13, 1993, and the Oslo II Accord, signed in Taba (small Egyptian town near the northern tip of the Gulf of Aqaba) in 1995. The Oslo Accords marked the start of a peace process aimed at achieving a peace-treaty based on United Nations Security Council Resolutions 242 and 338. The Oslo Accords resulted in the recognition by the PLO of the State of Israel, and the recognition by the State of Israel of the PLO as a representative of the Palestinian people.

Palestine— is identified today as a geographic region in Western Asia between the Mediterranean Sea and the Jordan River. But interestingly, the name "Palestine" is not found in the Bible. The name was identified with the "Philistines," a war-like tribe to the SW along the coast but an older name for Palestine is synonymous with "Canaan," a term most frequently used in the Old Testament. See start of chapter 5 for more information.

Palestinian Authority (PA) was formed in 1994 pursuant to the 1993 Oslo Accords between the Palestine Liberation Organization (PLO) and Israel. The PA was an interim body comprising the **Fatah** and **Hamas** parties, and it was established to govern certain areas of the Gaza Strip and the West Bank. It is headquartered in Ramallah, West Bank, located 10 km (6 miles) north of Jerusalem.

> **Fatah**— is the political and military organization of the PLO founded in the late 1950s by Yasser Arafat and Khalīl al-Wazīr with the mission of displacing the state of Israel using guerrilla warfare and forming a Palestine Arab state. Fatah is a more moderate party (as compared with Hamas) and currently controls parts of the West Bank.

> **Hamas**— is a Palestinian Islamist political organization and militant group that has waged war on Israel since 1987 through suicide bombings and rocket attacks. Hamas seeks the destruction of Israel and to

replace Israel with a Palestinian state. Hamas governs Gaza (independent of the Fatah controlled PA), and it is the primary catalyst for aggression against Israel.[9]

Hamas used suicide bombings against Israel in the 1990s and 2000s, although in recent years it has shifted to rockets and mortars. Unity talks between Hamas and the PA have broken down repeatedly—consequently, there is no unified PA, complicating peace talks significantly.

Palestine Liberation Organization (PLO)— is an organization founded in 1964 for the purpose of the "liberation of Palestine" through armed struggle. It is headquartered in Ramallah, West Bank, and recognized as the "sole legitimate representative of the Palestinian people" by over 100 states with which it holds diplomatic relations, and has enjoyed observer status at the United Nations since 1974. The PLO was considered by the United States and Israel to be a terrorist organization until the Madrid Conference in 1991. In 1993, the PLO recognized Israel's right to exist in peace, accepted UN Security Council Resolutions 242 and 338, and rejected "violence and terrorism"—in response, Israel officially recognized the PLO as the representative of the Palestinian people.

Difference between PLO and PA? The PLO is recognized internationally as the sole legitimate representative of the Palestinian people. The Palestinian Authority (PA) is an interim administrative body established as a result of the Gaza–Jericho Agreement (follow-up treaty to the Oslo I Accord) in which details of Palestinian autonomy were concluded. The PA was only supposed to have lasted for 5 years, and its leaders were mostly Fatah members, the largest faction of the PLO. For the difference between Hamas and Fatah, see chapter 7, The Gaza Wars, and Palestinian Authority.

Passover— is an important Jewish festival. The Jewish people celebrate Passover as a commemoration of their liberation by God from slavery in Egypt and their freedom as a nation under the leadership of Moses. It commemorates the story in the Book the Exodus.

In Exodus, the Bible tells that God helped the Children of Israel escape from their slavery in Egypt by inflicting ten plagues (Exodus 7-12) upon the ancient Egyptians before the Pharaoh would release his Israelite slaves; the tenth and worst of the plagues was the death of the Egyptian first-born.

The Israelites were instructed to mark the doorposts of their homes with the blood of a slaughtered spring lamb and, upon seeing this, the spirit of the Lord knew to pass over the first-born in these homes, hence the English name of the holiday.

When the Israelites were freed, they left in such a hurry they could not wait for bread dough to rise (leaven). Thus, in commemoration of Passover, no leavened bread is eaten during Passover, which is called the feast of unleavened bread in the Torah or Old Testament. Thus Matzo (flat unleavened bread; not prepared with rising agents such as yeast) is eaten during Passover and it is a tradition of the holiday.[10]

Persecution— is the systematic mistreatment (without cause) of an individual or group (by another individual or group) driven by intense hatred or hostility. **Persecution comes from the evil within the hearts of mankind.** The most common forms are religious persecution, ethnic persecution, and political persecution with some overlap between these terms. Harassment, oppression (abusiveness), beating (striking), scourging, flogging, and any type of torture including crucifixion are factors that establish persecution. An example is the Nazi Holocaust of World War II which is the face of evil.

Persia— is Iran. See Meshech and Tubal for more information.

Pharisees— were primarily teachers of the law, elders, and middle-class businessmen, and **Sadducees** were primarily aristocrats holding important and powerful positions such as chief or high priests. These Jewish sects flourished from 1st century BC to 1st century AD.

Pharisees— believed that God controlled all things, although individuals had freedom of choice; they believed in the resurrection of the dead; they believed in an afterlife with appropriate reward and punishment on an individual basis; and they believed in a spiritual world. (As a comparison to current times, many businessmen and their employees and blue collar workers tend to fall into this category.)

Sadducees— were self-sufficient, prideful and arrogant, and denied God's involvement in everyday life; they denied any resurrection of the dead; they denied the afterlife; and they denied the existence of a spiritual world. (As a comparison to current times, many of our political leaders and wealthy individuals including those in the private sector who are CEOs of large wealthy corporations tend to fall into this category.)

Pogrom— is a Russian word meaning "to wreak havoc, to demolish violently." Historically, the term refers to violent attacks by local non-Jewish populations on Jews.

Political correctness (PC)— is a term primarily used to describe language, actions, or policies intended not to offend any particular group of people in society (except Christians and Jews); that is, to appease, tolerate, and "fully embrace all groups" so as not to offend. The problem with PC is that some groups are intrinsically evil. See chapter 10, Political Correctness.

It is a tool that has been used to appease or promote all religions (except Christians and Jews), alternative sexual lifestyles (e.g., transgenderism, LGBT), political ideologies, or speech. Today, **this idea** is fully displayed on automobile bumper stickers with symbols of all religions promoting a one world religion with many ways to heaven (e.g., COEXIST). Contrary to this sacrilegious belief, the Bible teaches that the only way to salvation is through Jesus Christ (John 14:6, NIV).

Prophecy— involves Divine inspiration, interpretation, or revelation of future events that is 100% accurate. Old Testament prophecy describes events hundreds or many thousands of years in advance.

Prophet of the Old Testament— is an individual who actually spoke with God and received Divine knowledge and, in turn, served as an as an intermediary with humanity, delivering knowledge from the Lord God.

Punishment (discipline)— is the authoritative imposition of an unpleasant outcome upon an individual or group in response to unacceptable behavior—and it obviously includes some measure of suffering and sometimes death. God inflicts punishment but does not inflict persecution. Disobedience - see chapter 5, Why This Fierce Punishment for Disobedience.

Put— is today's Libya. See Meshech and Tubal for more information.

Ramadan— is the ninth month of the Islamic calendar; Muslims worldwide observe this as a month of fasting.

Rapture— refers to the belief that believers will be raised from the earth to meet the Lord Jesus in the air just prior to the seven year tribulation period. The concept has its basis in various interpretations of 1 Thessalonians 4:13-18; 1 Corinthians 15:51-53; Revelation 4:1-11. The church, made up of all who have trusted in the Lord Jesus Christ, will not be present during the tribulation. See chapter 11, Rapture of the Church, and Appendix D, The Rapture and the Second Coming.

Pretribulation rapture (PTR)— is the belief that the rapture will occur before the seven year tribulation; **midtribulation rapture** is the belief that the rapture will occur at the midpoint of the seven year tribulation; and **posttribulation rapture** is the belief that the rapture will occur at the end of the tribulation.

At the PTR, the church will meet Christ in the air, and soon thereafter the antichrist is revealed and the tribulation begins. In other words, the Rapture and Christ's Second Coming (to set up His kingdom) are separated by at least seven years. According to this view, the church does not experience any of the tribulation.

PTR is supported in Scripture in that the church is not appointed to wrath (1 Thessalonians 1:9-10, 5:9), and believers will not be overtaken by the Day of the Lord (1 Thessalonians 5:1-9). The Church of Philadelphia was promised to be kept from *"the hour of trial that is going to come upon the whole world"* (Revelation 3:10). Note that the promise is not 'preservation' through the tribulation but rather, 'deliverance' from "the hour of trial" or the tribulation.

PTR also finds support in what is not found in Scripture. The word "church" appears nineteen times in the first three chapters of Revelation but, significantly, the word is not used again until chapter 22. In other words, in the entire description of the tribulation in Revelation, the word "church" is **noticeably absent**. In fact, the Bible **never uses** the word "church" in a passage relating to the tribulation.

PTR is the only interpretation which clearly maintains the distinction between Israel and the church and God's separate plans for each. The seventy "sevens" of Daniel 9:24 are decreed upon Daniel's people (the Jews) and Daniel's holy city (Jerusalem). See chapter 11, Daniel's 70th Week. This prophecy makes it plain that the seventieth week (the tribulation) is a time of purging and restoration for Israel and Jerusalem, not for the church.

PTR view seems to be the most in keeping with God's character and His desire to deliver the righteous from the judgment of the world. Biblical examples of God's salvation include Noah (see chapter 10 in the book, *evolution - The Greatest Deception in Modern History*), who was delivered from the worldwide flood; Lot, who was delivered from Sodom; and Rahab, who was delivered from Jericho (2 Peter 2:6-9).

Replacement Theology— is a fallacious belief that states the Old Covenants made with the descendants of Abraham, Isaac, and Jacob were forfeited when the Jews rejected Jesus as the Messiah and forced His execution. They believe that the church has replaced the Israelites as God's representatives on earth and inherited a New Covenant. (See chapter 6, The Fallacy of Replacement Theology, and Appendix B, Establishment of a New Covenant.)

Those holding to replacement theology believe that Old Testament prophecies have already been fulfilled and conclude that the present State of Israel is destined to destruction which, in turn, fosters anti-Semitic attitudes and persecution of the Jews which we see today. Unbelievably, such people in the Christian community are actually sacrilegiously rooting for the destruction of Israel.

Most mainstream theologians such as Hal Lindsey and Jack Van Impe denounce replacement theology because God made certain "unconditional promises" to the descendants of Abraham, Isaac, and Jacob (see chapter 2, The Abrahamic Covenant and The Mosaic Covenant) which were reaffirmed to Moses and other prophets. The Abrahamic Covenant is binding forever despite the disobedience and failings of Jews of the Old and New Testaments and modern Israelis. **The restoration of Israel on May 14, 1948, further validates that the Lord will keep His covenant with the Jews forever, and we are in the last days.**

Sadducees – see Pharisees.

Samaria— see Judea.

Samaritan Pentateuch— is the first five books of Moses (the Pentateuch) traditionally written in the Samaritan alphabet. There is no reason why copies of the Torah might not have been available in northern Israel when the Assyrians led a great many of its people into exile in 721 BC. See chapter 4, Assyrian Empire Conquers the Northern Kingdom (Israel).

Satan (meaning "adversary" or sometimes "devil")— a figure who brings evil and temptation and is known as the "deceiver" who leads humanity in the wrong direction—away from the true God of the Holy Bible. The Bible tells us about the entry of evil into the universe—how Lucifer and 1/3 of the angels chose to rebel against God the Creator by attempting to usurp God's power or authority (Ezekiel 28:11, 14-15; Revelation 12:3-9, 9:1; and Luke 8:30). Rebellion by these angelic beings led ultimately to the temptation and fall of mankind. In the Hebrew Bible and the New Testament, Satan is primarily an accuser and adversary of God and humanity—he possesses demonic powers but he is not omnipresent, omnipotent, or omniscient. See Appendix C, Satan's Attempts to Seize Total Control.

Satanic trinity (unholy trinity)— consisting of Satan, his 'son' the antichrist, and his demonized spiritual leader called the false prophet.

Antichrist— found only in 1 John 2:18, 2:22, 4:3, and 2 John 7. Many antichrists (false teachers) will appear as the Messiah between the time of Christ's first appearing and the seven year tribulation period—

but there will be 'one great antichrist' who will rise to power during the end times, or "last hour," as stated in 1 John. He will deny that Jesus Christ is the Messiah; he will deny God the Father and God the Son; and he will be a liar and a deceiver. At the end of the seven year tribulation period, Jesus will appear in His Second Coming to imprison the antichrist, who will be the greatest false messiah in Christianity. Just as Christ is the Savior of humanity, his adversary in the end time will be an entity of "concentrated evil."

False prophet— one who falsely claims the gift of prophecy or divine inspiration and uses that gift for evil ends. The false prophet of the end times is described in Revelation 13:11-15. He is also referred to as the "second beast" (Revelation 16:13, 19:20, 20:10) who promotes antichrist propaganda. Together with the antichrist and Satan, the false prophet is the third party in the '**unholy trinity.**' Both the antichrist and false prophet are directly influenced by Satan.

Scientific method— common steps that scientists use to gather information to solve problems. These common steps include observation, prediction (hypothesis), data collection, experimentation (to test the hypothesis under controlled conditions), and conclusions. **Empirical analysis** is verification through repeated testing.

Seleucid Empire (c. 312 BC to 63 BC)— was a Hellenistic state (in the Syrian region) ruled by the Seleucid dynasty following the division of the Macedonian dynasty created by Alexander the Great.

Semitic— was a language of West Asian origin. It referred to peoples of ancient Southwestern Asian descent including the Akkadian Empire (2334 BC — 2154 BC) in ancient Mesopotamia, the Phoenicians, Hebrews (Jews), Arabs, and their descendants.

The language of the Jewish people shifted from Hebrew to Aramaic sometime between 721 BC - 500 BC. Therefore, we know that Jesus, his disciples, and contemporaries spoke and wrote in Aramaic. The message of Christianity spread throughout Israel, Syria, and Mesopotamia in this Semitic tongue. See Aramaic in glossary.

Septuagint— is the primary third century BC Greek translation of the Old Testament. It is the oldest Greek version of the Old Testament, translated by Jewish scholars during the reign of Ptolemy II Philadelphus (king of Ptolemaic Egypt from 285 to 246 BC).

Sharia— is the religious system (law) governing the members of the Islamic faith. It is derived from religious precepts of Islam, particularly the Quran and Hadith.

Shepherd— is symbolic of Jesus and all the patriarchs, but it is also a practice for dealing with the difficulty and challenges of unifying and leading a very large group of people.

Shia and Sunni— see Sunni and Shia-Islam.

Sin— is breaking the moral law (see chapter 3, Human Nature and the Moral Law in the book, *evolution – The Greatest Deception in Modern History*), or any one of the Ten Commandments, or a departure from goodness.

Sin is evil, iniquity, wickedness, immorality, or corruption. "Evil, in its essence, refuses to accept God as God and puts someone or something else [idolatry] in His place...For this reason, the Bible treats idolatry as the ultimate sin, since it worships as God what is not God." (p. 24-25, Alcorn)

Rebellious and idolatrous history of humanity and the natural tendency for moral decay are graphically portrayed throughout the Bible (Old and New Testaments). Examples include paganistic cultures of the antediluvian period (c. 4004 BC to 2385 BC); in the time of Mesopotamia (c. 2200 BC); in ancient Egypt and Assyria (c. 2000 BC); Canaanite people of the Middle East (c. 1600 BC to 1400 BC); and the empires of Babylonia (c. 612 BC to 539 BC), Medo-Persia (c. 538 BC to 334 BC), Greece (c. 334 BC to 146 BC), and Rome (c. 146 BC to AD 476); and in historical accounts of the Dark Ages (c. 6th to 14th century), World War I and World War II (including the Holocaust), and by today's continual worldwide ethnic conflicts.

Consider the world today, with its political corruption, lying, slander, public displays of moral depravity, bizarre behavior, violent crimes against humanity, abortion, theft, adultery, drug-taking, drunkenness, gambling, greed of all kinds, prostitution, sexual perversions, trafficking of children and teenagers for sex, wars and rumors of wars, and terrorism. Beheadings and massacre of children and their families in the Middle East and worldwide is the face of evil today.

The nature of mankind throughout history is to 'harden their hearts.' (See Ephesians 4:18, Mark 8:17-18.) This *"hardening of their hearts"* (Ephesians 4:18) is a supernatural phenomenon, an unseen battle between good and evil we witness in the news and in our everyday lives. The evil nature of mankind is also portrayed by the exceedingly repugnant behavior of some clergymen over the ages—physical cruelty, collusion with political dictators, and abhorrent sexual abuses—detestable behavior that has alienated many from the Christian faith.

Immorality is tolerated and accepted as the norm by our youth. The problem has never been with the God of the Holy Bible but with the corruption and moral depravity of humankind. Take a moment to read Romans 1, verses 18–32—it reads like a commentary of today's world.

The problem of evil and suffering has been addressed by theologians and authors throughout the centuries; more prominently by C. S. Lewis, in *The Problem of Pain*; by best-selling author Randy Alcorn in his book, *If God Is Good – Faith in the Midst of Suffering and Evil* (2009, Colorado Springs, CO: Multnomah Books); by Dr. Carl Wieland in his book, *Beyond the Shadows - Making Sense of Personal Tragedy* (2011, Atlanta, GA: Creation Book Publishers); and by Dr. N. L. Geisler in his book, *If God, Why Evil?* (2011, Bloomington, MN: Bethany House Publishers).

South Lebanon Army or South Lebanese Army (SLA)— was a Lebanese militia during the Lebanese Civil War which split from the Army of Free Lebanon. After 1979, the militia operated in southern Lebanon under the authority of Saad Haddad's Government of Free Lebanon. It was supported by Israel during the 1982–2000 South Lebanon conflict to fight against the Palestine Liberation Organization (PLO) and Hezbollah.

Sunni and Shia-Islam— Sunni and Shia Islam are the two major denominations of Islam. An approximation is that 85–90% of the world's Muslims are Sunni and 10–15% are Shia with most Shias belonging to the Twelver tradition and the rest divided among many other groups. Sunnis are a majority in most Muslim communities: in Southeast Asia, China, South Asia, Africa, and most of the Arab world. Shia make up the majority of the citizen population in Iraq, Iran, Azerbaijan, and Bahrain, as well as a politically significant minority in Lebanon.

Supernatural— is that which is not subject to the laws of physics or that which is said to exist outside or beyond our natural world. (An eternal universe; eternity implies something supernatural.)

The spiritual forces of evil cause people to turn away—to willfully forget without reason! (See 2 Peter 3:5-6, ASV.) In Luke 8:10-12 (NIV), Jesus described such people as **"though seeing, they may not see; though hearing, they may not understand."** [Bold added] Also see Matthew 13:14. For whatever reason, **if a person's mind is closed to Scripture, no amount of evidence will change his mind.** This **"hardening of their hearts"** (Ephesians 4:18, NIV) against God is a supernatural phenomenon, an unseen battle between good and evil we witness in the news and in our everyday lives. Many people dismiss such claims because they have "an enormous predisposition against the supernatural."[11]

Syriac (Syriac Aramaic)— is a dialect of Middle Aramaic that was once spoken across much of the Fertile Crescent (region in the Middle East which curves from the Persian Gulf, through modern-day southern Iraq, Syria, Lebanon, Jordan, Israel, and northern Egypt) and Eastern Arabia. Aramaic is a family of languages or dialects belonging to the Semitic family. More specifically, it is part of the Northwest Semitic subfamily which also includes Canaanite languages such as Hebrew and Phoenician.

Taliban— is an Islamic Sunni fundamentalist militant group in Afghanistan and Pakistan.

Temple Mount— is one of the most important religious sites in the City of Jerusalem. This site has been used for thousands of years by the three primary religions: Judaism (since 1400 BC), Christianity (since AD 32), and Islam (since 7th century AD). The present site is dominated by three monumental structures from the early Umayyad period (AD 661 – 750): the al-Aqsa Mosque, the Dome of the Rock, and the Dome of the Chain.

Thermodynamics— is the study of heat power—heat is "energy in transit." It is the branch of physics that examines kinetic energy, or the efficiency of energy transfer, or energy transformation; for example, hot to cold; high pressure to low pressure; solar energy to fossil fuel to mechanical energy to electrical energy to light energy. When we eat, our bodies transform energy stored in food (potential energy) into energy to do work (kinetic energy). When we run or walk, think, read or write, we "burn" food energy in our bodies. Cars, planes, boats, light bulbs, and machinery also transform energy into work. Work is moving, lifting, warming, or lighting something. See chapter 2 in the book by Roger Gallop, *evolution - The Greatest Deception in Modern History (Scientific Evidence for Divine Creation)*.

> **The First Law of Thermodynamics** (Law of Conservation of Matter) states that matter/energy cannot be created or destroyed. Although the amount of matter/energy remains the same, energy can be transferred from one form to another. For example, it can change from solar energy to fossil fuel to mechanical energy to electrical energy to light energy; or from hot to cold; high pressure to low pressure, etc. This law confirms that creation is no longer occurring which, in turn, implies that creation existed at sometime in the past. In today's world, there is no creation of new matter/energy rising to higher levels of organized complexity!

> **The Second Law of Thermodynamics** states that matter/energy in the universe available for work is decaying or running down. While the *quantity* remains unchanged, the *quality* of matter/energy has the tendency to decline or deteriorate over time. This is commonly known as **The Law of Increasing Entropy.** While usable energy is used for growth and repair, it is "irretrievably lost in the form of unusable energy." Aging and death are implicit in the 2nd Law (see p. 19 of above reference book). This law is a fundamental contradiction to the doctrine of evolution. **Many scientists believe the 2nd Law is enough to disprove evolutionary theory** and <u>is one of the important reasons why many esteemed scientists have abandoned evolutionary doctrine in favor of creationism</u>.

Times of the Gentiles— are all the years between the Babylonian Empire of Nebuchadnezzar (586 BC) and the glorious return of Christ to establish His kingdom. In Revelation 11:2, John indicates that Jerusalem will be under Gentile rule, even though the temple has been restored during the first 3 ½ years of the tribulation. In fact, Jerusalem will be under Gentile control until the Second Coming. In Luke 21:24, Jesus speaks of future events, including the destruction of Jerusalem and His return. He says that *"Jerusalem will be trampled underfoot by the Gentiles, until the times of the Gentiles are fulfilled"* (ESV). See chapter 12, sections Second 3 ½ years of the Tribulation Period and Persecution and Desolation (text box), and Appendix B, Establishment of a New Covenant, for more information.

Transgenderism— a person feeling that they are not the same gender (= sex) as the one they had or were said to have at birth.

Tribulation— is a future seven year period in which God will decree Divine judgment on a pagan world—on all those who have rejected Him and [He] will complete His plan of salvation for Israel. It is a time of great trouble and suffering in the last days immediately prior to the Second Coming of Jesus Christ. It is a time of unprecedented war and nuclear catastrophe—the first 3 ½ years begins with a 7-year peace covenant between the antichrist and Israel, and the second 3 ½ years is called the great tribulation. See chapters 11 and 12.

Tubal— is the southern tip of Russia east of Ukraine; **Meshech (Meshek)** is Turkmenistan and Uzbekistan east of the Caspian Sea; **Gomer** and **Beth Togarmiah** are in Turkey; and **Persia** is Iran. During the last several decades Russia has maintained a very close relationship with Iran and has been supervising and directing Iran's nuclear weapons program. And finally, **Put** is today's Libya and **Cush** is Sudan. **Magog and Gog** refer to Russia (including Kazakhstan) and a Russian leader, respectively. See map, chapter 12, Invasion by Russia and Its Allies.

Umayyad— was the second of the four major Islamic caliphates established after the death of Muhammad. This caliphate was centered on the Umayyad dynasty (AD 661 – AD 750) from Mecca, a city along the Red Sea in Saudi Arabia.

United Nations Partition Plan for Palestine— was a proposal developed by the United Nations which recommended a partition to follow the termination of the British Mandate. On November 29, 1947, the U.N. General Assembly adopted a resolution recommending the adoption and implementation of the Plan as Resolution 181(II).[12]

Western Wall or Wailing Wall— is located in the Old City of Jerusalem at the foot of the western side of the area known as the Temple Mount (as known to the Jews). The Temple Mount is the holiest site in Judaism and is the place to which Jews turn during prayer. Parts of the wall are remnants of the ancient wall that surrounded the Temple's courtyard during the time of Jesus prior to AD 70. The Western Wall is arguably the most sacred site recognized by the Jewish faith other than the Temple Mount itself.

Yahweh ("the Lord")— is a form of the Hebrew name of God used in the Bible. The name came to be regarded by Jews (c. 300 BC) as too sacred to be spoken, and the vowel sounds are uncertain. In the Old Testament, Yahweh occurs 6,519 times. This name is used more than any other name of God.

Yom Kippur, also known as Day of Atonement— is probably the most important day of the year for the Jewish people. Many Jews who might otherwise not attend customary services will stop work, fast, and attend services. Central themes are centered on atonement and repentance—because, according to custom, it is during this time that God decides the fate of each person, so Jews ask for forgiveness for sins and are encouraged to make reparations.

Zion— symbolizes the Jewish people; or a hill in Jerusalem on which the Temple was built (Mount Moriah; the Temple Mount).

---

notes: Appendix A - Glossary

1. Glossary definitions were obtained from Wikipedia, the free encyclopedia, under the Creative Commons Attribution Share-Alike License and GNU Free Documentation License. Other sources include other websites, theology books, and personal sources.

2. Hal Lindsey (February 13, 2015). Hal Lindsey Report, News from Hal Lindsey Media Ministries. (www.hallindsey.org).

3. All About Truth. Retrieved 2014, from http://www.allabouttruth.org/bible-manuscripts-faq.htm) and http://www.gotquestions.org/canon-Bible.html.

4. Magog Revisited by Chuck Missler. Retrieved February 2016, from http://www.khouse.org/articles/2006/663/.

5. Palestinian National Authority, from Wikipedia. Retrieved February 2016, from http://en.wikipedia.org/wiki/Palestinian_National_Authority and http://www.vox.com/cards/israel-palestine/hamas.

6. Ibid.

7. International Monetary Fund, from Wikipedia. Retrieved February 2016, from https://en.wikipedia.org/wiki/International_Monetary_Fund.

8. 5What are the different covenants in the Bible? Retrieved February 2016, from http://www.compellingtruth.org/covenants-in-the-Bible.html.

9. See end note 5.

10. Passover from Wikipedia. Retrieved February 2016, from https://en.wikipedia.org/wiki/Passover.

11. Burrows, M. (1956). *What Mean These Stones?* New York: Meridian Books; as cited in McDowell, J., 69.

12. United Nations Partition Plan for Palestine. Retrieved February 2016, from https://en.wikipedia.org/wiki/United_Nations_Partition_Plan_for_Palestine.

Appendix B
Establishment of a New Covenant

What is the New Covenant?[1]

A quotation from Jeremiah 31:31-34 contains a prophetic announcement and definition of the new covenant which is different from the Mosaic covenant. (See chapter 2, The Mosaic Covenant.)

*"'The days are coming,' declares the LORD, 'when I will make a **new covenant with the people of Israel and with the people of Judah.** It will not be like the covenant I made with their ancestors when I took them by the hand to lead them out of Egypt, because they broke my covenant, though I was a husband to them,' declares the LORD. 'This is the covenant I will make with the people of Israel after that time,' declares the LORD. 'I will **put my law in their minds and write it on their hearts.** I will be their God, and they will be my people. No longer will they teach their neighbor, or say to one another, 'Know the LORD,' because they will all know me, from the least of them to the greatest,' declares the LORD. 'For **I will forgive their wickedness and will remember their sins no more'"** (Jeremiah 31:31-34, NIV). [Bold added]*

New Covenant is a promise that "God would forgive sin and have a close, unbroken relationship with His people [Jeremiah 31:31-34]. The promise was first made to Israel and then extended to everyone [Jews and Gentiles] who comes to Jesus Christ in faith [Matthew 26:28; Hebrews 9:15]."[2] .

The new covenant is distinguished from the older covenant: God will write the law in the minds and on the hearts of those in the new covenant, and God will forgive their iniquities. The new covenant has **an internal spiritual transformation** resulting in a new relationship with God.

Old Covenant (Mosaic) versus New Covenant[3]

The Old Covenant (Mosaic Covenant; a conditional covenant) was an agreement that was initially made at Mount Sinai with the Jewish people. **It required strict obedience of God's law.** It promised that the people would be physically blessed (health, wealth, freedom, success, etc.) or cursed (e.g., plagues, poverty, captivity, misfortune, etc.) **depending on their devotion to all of God's written commandments and statutes.**

The New Covenant, in contrast to the Old, is 'spiritually' based, and it promises eternal life full of love and glory **for those who accept the gift of pardon through Jesus Christ.** See epilogue, The Bible Warns: There is ONLY ONE WAY TO HEAVEN. The book of Hebrews tells us WHY this new covenant offered through Jesus Christ is better than the old Mosaic Covenant of the Old Testament.

"For if there had been nothing wrong with that first covenant [Mosaic covenant], no place would have been sought for another. But God found fault with the people and said: 'The days are coming, declares the Lord, when I will make a new covenant with the people of Israel and with the people of Judah'" (Hebrews 8:7-8, NIV).

"By calling this covenant 'new,' he has made the first one obsolete [Mosaic covenant]; and what is obsolete and outdated will soon disappear" (Hebrews 8:13, NIV).

"For this reason Christ is the mediator of a new covenant, that those who are called may receive the promised eternal inheritance—now that He has died as a ransom to set them free from the sins committed under the first covenant [Mosaic covenant]" (Hebrews 9:15, NIV).

The **new covenant** makes **three promises:**

1. Jesus Christ offers the promise that ALL sins will be forgiven. There is forgiveness of sins only through the new covenant (Jeremiah 31:31-34; Zechariah 13:1).

> *"In the same way, after the supper He took the cup, saying, 'This cup is the new covenant in My blood, which is poured out for you'"* (Jeremiah 31:31-34, NIV). *"This is My blood of the covenant, which is poured out for many for the forgiveness of sins"* (Matthew 26:28, NIV). It is only through the death of Jesus Christ the Savior on the Cross that such an incredible gift of forgiveness can be offered to man.

God is holy, righteous, and merciful, and through our Lord Jesus Christ offers the gift of eternal salvation (John 3:16, 5:24, 14:6; Romans 10:9, 13; and Ephesians 2:8-9)—so by grace [mercy] you are saved through faith (Ephesians 2:8-9).

In fact, God makes the promise that once our sins are forgiven, they will NEVER be recalled or remembered. *"For I will forgive their wickedness and will remember their sins no more"* (Hebrews 8:12, NIV).

2. God will spiritually instill within man the need and desire to obey Him. Ancient Israel was not given the ability to obey their Creator both in the letter and spirit of the law (Jeremiah 31:31-34). God promises that through the power of His Holy Spirit, **He will personally write His laws and ways on the minds of all mankind.**

> *"I will put My laws into their minds, and write them on their hearts. I will be their God, and they will be My people"* (Hebrews 8:10, NIV). (Also see Ezekiel 36:26-27.)

3. God's children will receive an eternal inheritance upon accepting this gift of pardon.

> *"And for this reason Christ is the Mediator of the New Covenant, for those who are called may receive the promised eternal inheritance..."* (Hebrews 9:15, NIV).

For more information about the purpose of mankind, best possible solution, God's testing ground and making the right choice, see book by Roger Gallop, *Defeating Evil - God's Plan Before the Beginning of Time* (chapter 8 and epilogue.)

In Luke 21:24 (ESV), Jesus speaks of future events, including the destruction of Jerusalem and His return. He says that *"Jerusalem will be trampled underfoot by the Gentiles, until the **times of the Gentiles are fulfilled.**"* [Bold added] A similar phrase is found in Romans 11:25 (ESV). **"Times of the Gentiles"** are all the years between the Babylonian Empire of Nebuchadnezzar (586 BC) and the glorious return of Christ (the Second Coming) to establish His kingdom.

The Christian church has already received the new covenant but the **new covenant** will soon be offered to ALL Israel. When and how will this be done?

God's Purpose for Israel

When the Jews were exiled for their continual disobedience and rejecting the Messiah Jesus Christ, the focus of spreading God's word shifted to the church (Gentiles). But with the removal of the church at the rapture, the focus of spreading the gospel will shift back to the Jewish people, God's "chosen people" (Deuteronomy 7:6-9). At this point in time (following the rapture), the Jewish people will begin to fully acknowledge the truth of the new covenant—the gospel of Jesus Christ. "The Jews will once again be responsible, as God's representatives, to take His message to the world. But this time these 144,000 Jews [see chapter 12, Seals, Trumpets, and Bowls; Revelation 7:4-8] will do in only seven years what their nation has failed to do in all its history—evangelize the whole world!"[4]

"God made humans for a particular reason and purpose. Out of His perfect (agape) love, He wants to share ALL He has, forever, with as many [human] beings as possible."[5]

God's purpose for Israel:[6]

1) receive and record God's revelation to man,
2) protect and preserve the accuracy of the Scriptures,
3) serve as the human family for the Messiah, Jesus Christ,
4) witness to the world there is only one true God, the God of the Holy Bible, and
5) spread the gospel of Jesus Christ, the Messiah, throughout the pagan world (with 144,000 Jewish evangelists).

Because the Jewish people remained disobedient and rejected Jesus in AD 32, the Jewish people were exiled worldwide and the focus of spreading the word shifted to the church. This focus will soon shift back to the Jewish people.

See chapter 6, The Fallacy of Replacement Theology, for additional information.

---

notes: Appendix B

1. What is the New Covenant? Retrieved February 2016, from http://www.biblestudy.org/basicart/what-is-the-new-covenant.html and New Covenant. Retrieved February 2016, from http://www.biblestudytools.com/dictionary/new-covenant/.

2. What are the different covenants in the Bible? Retrieved February 2016, from http://www.compellingtruth.org/covenants-in-the-Bible.html.

3. Old Covenant versus New Covenant. Retrieved February 2016, from http://www.biblestudy.org/beginner/old-covenant-versus-new-covenant.html.

4. Got Questions.org. What are the times of the Gentiles? Retrieved September 2016, from http://gotquestions.org/times-of-the-Gentiles.html.

5. What is the New Covenant? op. cit.

6. Lindsey, H. (1973, 1984). *There's A New World Coming,* Eugene, OR: Harvest House Publishers, 101-103.

Appendix C
Satan's Attempts to Seize Total Control

This takes us to the topic of Satan and the first rebellion against the one true God of the Holy Bible. Just as he led 1/3 of the angels to rebel in Heaven (see end notes, p. xvi of book, *evolution -- The Greatest Deception in Modern History*), Satan has attempted to lead all mankind to become willfully disobedient and destroy the Hebrew race and the church. This is well described by Tim LaHaye and T. Ice in their book, *Charting the End Times*.[1] Also see epilogue, question #18, Why did Jesus have to be the Sacrificial Lamb of God? and #19, Why did wholesale attempts fail to eradicate the Jews as a people?

1. In the Garden of Eden

In the beginning at the Garden of Eden, God created man in God's image (Genesis 1:27), and He created a world without death and suffering (Genesis 1:31). God also **allowed man to be a free moral being**—that is, He gave man the ability **"to choose what is true, what is right, what is good."**[2] The first man, Adam, decided to walk out of God's will (Genesis 3)—a moral decision that brought death and corruption to a perfect creation (Genesis 3:14-19; Romans 5:12, 6:23) and ultimately to all of humanity. Wickedness and depravity with its pain and suffering are "man's fault, not God's." People ask why would a loving God create a world full of pain and suffering—but the real question is, "why would a loving God come into the world He created to suffer and die to pay for my sin?"[3]

The Bible tells us about the entry of evil into the universe—how Lucifer and 1/3 of the angels chose to rebel against God the creator by attempting to usurp God's power or authority.[4] (See Ezekiel 28:14-15; Revelation 12:3-9, 9:1; and Luke 8:30.) These fallen angels sinned by desiring more authority and power than what was appointed to them by God. Rebellion by these angelic beings led ultimately to the temptation and fall of mankind. Allowing evil, hence pain and suffering, "was a necessary price to achieve a far greater eternal result."[5]

> "...our present sufferings are not worth comparing with the glory that will be revealed in us" (Romans 8:18, NIV) and "For our light and momentary troubles are achieving for us an eternal glory that far outweighs them all" (2 Corinthians 4:17, NIV).

At this point in time (c. 4004 BC; Garden of Eden), Satan was not aware of God's plan of redemption for mankind. Satan believed that once evil (sin) was loosed upon the world, mankind would be forever immersed in sin with no viable solution for God—there was no plan that included the defeat of evil without the destruction of freedom, love, and mankind who was now separated from God. Satan believed he would rule the earth, mankind, and the first and second heavens. For more information, see the book by Roger Gallop, *Defeating Evil - God's Plan Before the Beginning of Time*, chapter 4, Origin of Evil, section Rebellion - Methodical and Calculated.

This was Satan's first successful attempt to seize God's authority by deceiving Adam and Eve. But Satan was not aware of God's plan of redemption until much later, *on or before* the time of Moses when Moses wrote the Pentateuch (c. 1446 BC to c. 1406 BC)—the first five books of the Bible including Genesis 3:15.

"In Genesis 3:15 we find the first prediction relative to the Savior of the world, called '*the seed of the woman.*' In the original oracle **God foretold the age-long conflict which would be waged between the 'seed of the woman' [Jesus Christ, Lord and Savior] and 'the seed of the serpent' [Satan]** and which will eventually be won by the 'seed of the woman.' This primitive promise indicates a struggle between the Messiah of Israel, the Savior of the world, on the one hand, and Satan, the adversary of the human soul, on the other. It foretells complete victory eventually for the Messiah."[8] [Bold added] (See epilogue, questions 18 and 19, for more on Genesis 3:15.)

As Alcorn explains, "From the beginning, God planned that His Son [Jesus Christ] should deal the death blow to Satan, evil, and suffering, to reverse the Curse, redeem a fallen humanity, and repair a broken world."[7] *"The reason the Son of God appeared was to destroy the devil's work"* (1 John 3:8, NIV).

2. Polluting the Bloodline of Adam

During the Days of Noah (the Antediluvian period before the Great Flood; c. 4004 BC to 2385 BC, or 1,619 years), Satan attempted to pollute the pure bloodline of Adam, the first man (4004 BC to 3074 BC, or 930 years). He allowed fallen angels (demons in human form) and human women whom they found tempting to live together and have relations, thus producing "Nephilim," or fallen ones, in an attempt to spoil the "seed of the woman" [Jesus Christ]—thus, thwarting God's plan of redemption. This can be found in Genesis 6:1-4 and Jude 7, and "this is likely the [primary] reason why God resorted to the extreme measure of sending a flood to destroy the whole human race, with the exception of Noah's family. Through Noah's family God preserved the purity of the original bloodline of humans...[and this] cannot happen again because God imprisoned those [particular] fallen angels in Tartarus (2 Peter 2:4-10)."[8]

3. The Tower of Babel

The Tower of Babel (Genesis 11:1-9) was an attempt by Satan to establish a worldwide, idolatrous (pagan) religion in Babel, the largest city and the center of the world's population at that time—with the goal of preventing mankind from worshiping the one true God. God blocked this attempt by Satan by confusing the people's language, causing them to separate into small groups and scatter worldwide. The confusion of language and scattering of the people ended Satan's attempt at a one-world, pagan religion. For more information, see the book, *evolution – The Greatest Deception in Modern History*, chapter 10, The Postdiluvian Period.

4. Temptation of Job

As we see in the Book of Job we can take refuge in the fact "that Satan cannot take a believer's life unless God permits [it]"[9]— but Satan can make our lives miserable and tempt us for a short time, but God, through the Holy Spirit, will give us **strength and perseverance** during such times.

5. Attempting to Eradicate the Hebrew Race

When Moses was born (1526 BC) Pharaoh ordered the killing of all male Hebrew babies (see chapter 2, Moses and Aaron)—yet God saved Moses and preserved the Hebrew race and the bloodline of the Messiah. Also, Satan attempted to destroy all the Jews during their exodus from Egypt while they were in one place (see chapter 2). And Satan also attempted to destroy the Hebrew race through the slaughter of over 6 million Jews (including 1.5 million children) during what is known as the Holocaust during WW II. (See chapter 5, Nazi Germany and the Holocaust.)

6. Attempting to Kill the Messiah

Satan attempted to kill the infant Jesus by having Herod Antipas (4 BC - AD 39; son of Herod the Great) slaughter all the babies in Bethlehem—but Joseph and Mary were provided a means to escape to Egypt, and they eventually returned when the threat had passed (Matthew 2:16-18).

7. Attempting to Deter the Messiah

Further Satan tempted Christ before the crucifixion (see Matthew 4 and Luke 4); Satan continued his spiritual attacks throughout the ministry of Jesus, culminating in the supreme trial (temptation) at the Garden of Gethsemane (Luke 4:13, NIV; refer to end note in NIV Bible and Matthew 26:36-46); and attempts on Jesus' life that failed (stoning, John 8:58-59; plotting to kill Jesus, Matthew 12:14; Mark 3:6, 6:4, 14:1; Luke 4:28; John 5:18, 7:1, 11:53, 12:10). Ultimately, Jesus defeated Satan through His crucifixion and resurrection.

In the Garden of Gethsemane (John 12:27; Matthew 4:11; Mark 1:13; Luke 22:41-44), Jesus faced the terrible prospect of becoming sin (a sacrificial lamb, or sin offering that turns away wrath that God feels toward sin; see note below) as redemption for all mankind (2 Corinthians 5:21). He considered praying to God the Father to save Him from this horrible, most excruciating death, but He refused to pray for mercy. This was the reason He had come to earth in the form of man—to die for the sins of fallen humanity.

> Note: "His [God's] justice is satisfied because the perfectly righteous man, Jesus Christ, took the **wrath** of God's offended righteousness and justice in the place of all men."[10] [Bold added] (See epilogue, question #18 and John 3:36.)

8. Attempting to Destroy the Church

Through persecution and false teaching, "500 million believers have been martyred during the past 2,000 years, yet the church is still the largest religious body in the world." False doctrines (2 Timothy 4:3-4) include the belief in 'evolution' described in the book, *evolution – The Greatest Deception in Modern History*. During the coming tribulation period, Satan will use both persecution (Revelation 6:9-11) and false teachers (Matthew 24:23-26) in his endeavor to deceive people about the reality of God and Jesus Christ.

---

notes: Appendix C

1. LaHaye, T. and Ice, T. (2001). *Charting the End Times*. Eugene, OR: Harvest House Publishers, 32-34.

2. Johnson, J. (November 2011). Human suffering: Why this isn't the "best of all possible worlds." *Acts & Facts*, 40 (11), Dallas, TX: Institute for Creation Research, 8-10. (ICR.org)

3. Mitchell, T. (December 2011). Death and Steve Jobs. *Answers Update*, 18 (12), Hebron, KY: Answers in Genesis, 1-2. (answersingenesis.org)

4. Alcorn, Randy (2009). *If God Is Good – Faith in the Midst of Suffering and Evil*. Colorado Springs, CO: Multnomah Books, 48-49.

5. Alcorn, R., op. cit., 41–42.

6. Alcorn, R., op. cit., 51.

7. McDowell, J. (1972). *Evidence that Demands a Verdict*. San Bernardino, CA: Campus Crusade for Christ, 151.

8. LaHaye, T, op. cit., 32.

9. Ibid.

10. Hal Lindsey (August 12, 2016). The Hal Lindsey Report, News from Hal Lindsey Media Ministries. (www.hallindsey.org)

Appendix D
The Rapture and the Second Coming

What are the important differences between the rapture and Second Coming?[1] (Refer to timelines sketch.)

1. **The rapture is when Jesus Christ returns to remove the church (snatch away all believers in Christ) from the earth** as described in 1 Thessalonians 4:13-18 and 1 Corinthians 15:50-54. Believers who have already died (their soul and spirit are in Heaven; 2 Corinthians 5:8) will have their physical bodies resurrected at the rapture and, together with raptured believers who are still living, will meet the Lord in the air. This will all occur in a just moment of time.

This event occurs before the tribulation period. How do we know? Before the tribulation (Revelation, chapters 1-3) the church is mentioned 7 times, but during the tribulation (Revelation, chapters 6-19) **the church is not mentioned**.

Also, chapters 2 and 3 of Revelation speak of the churches, *"He who has an ear, let him hear what the Spirit says to the churches"* (Revelation 2:7, 11, 17, 29, 3:6, 13, 22) while in chapter 13:9, it states, *"If anyone has an ear, let him hear."* This is the same warning **except the church is noticeably absent**. God would not have omitted the church if it was still on the earth. During the tribulation—also called "the time of trouble for Jacob" (Jeremiah 30:7)—God will again turn His primary attention to Israel (Romans 11:17-31).

2. **The Second Coming occurs after the seven year tribulation** (Revelation chapters 6-19) with the physical presence of Jesus. Again, the rapture occurs before the tribulation (1 Thessalonians 5:9; Revelation 3:10) in the clouds (atmosphere). At the Second Coming (following the seven year tribulation), all believers (those that previously died and raptured believers) together with angelic armies will return with the Lord to the earth (Revelation 19:14). The Second Coming will be visible to all (Revelation 1:7; Matthew 24:29-30).

3. **The rapture is the removal of believers from the earth as an "act of deliverance"** (1 Thessalonians 4:13-17, 5:9) similar to the deliverance of Noah and his family during the Great Flood (see chapter 10, The Great Flood c. 2385 BC, in the book, *evolution – The Greatest Deception in Modern History*) as described in Matthew 24:37-39, NIV.

> *"As it was in the days of Noah, so it will be at the coming of the Son of Man. For in the days before the flood, people were eating and drinking, marrying and giving in marriage, up to the day Noah entered the ark; and they knew nothing about what would happen until the flood came and took them all away. That is how it will be at the coming of the Son of Man"* (Matthew 24:37-39, NIV).

The rapture (1 Corinthians 15:50-54) will occur in a moment in time—and people left behind will surely panic as they notice that people (loved ones including young children) are missing, and they will undoubtedly blame this on an alien abduction (an on-going theme of many movies and television programs today). **There will be a worldwide economic collapse which will initiate the rise of the antichrist.**

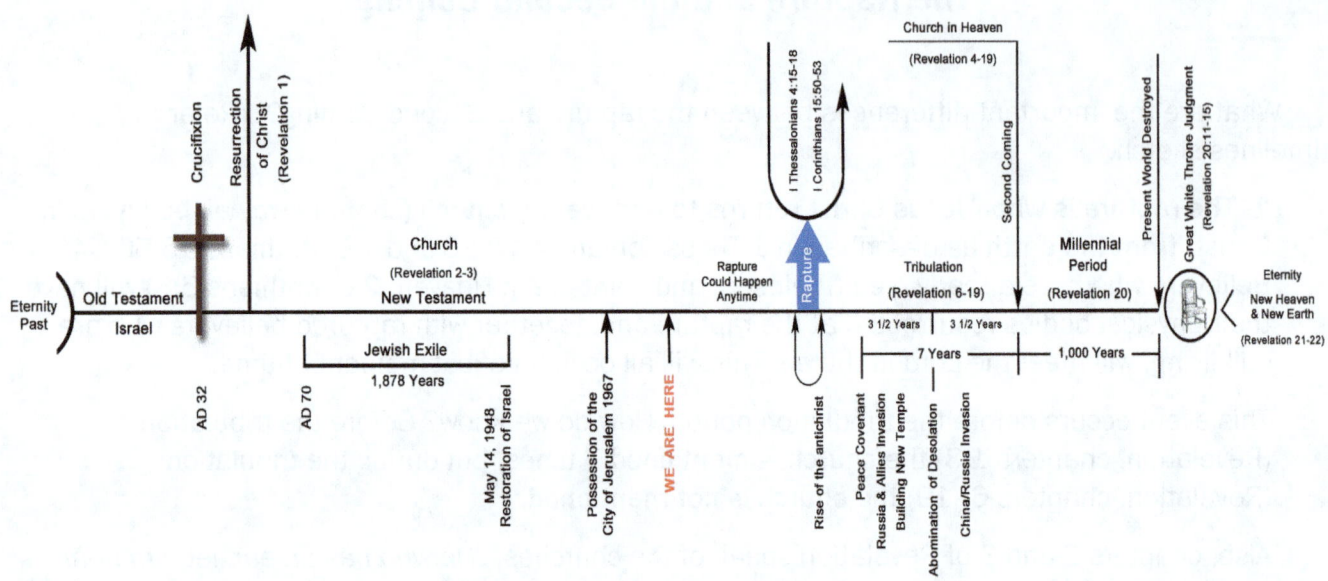

4. **The rapture is imminent**—it could take place at any time. **It is the next great prophetic event.** (Titus 2:13; 1 Thessalonians 4:13-18; 1 Corinthians 15:50-54)

In summary, the rapture is the return of Christ in the clouds to remove all believers from the earth before the seven year tribulation period—the time of God's wrath. The Second Coming is the return of Christ to the earth to bring an end to the seven year tribulation and to defeat Satan, the antichrist, and the false prophet, and their evil world empire.

In His first coming, Jesus arrived in humble circumstances as the "**suffering Servant.**" In His second coming, Jesus will arrive with the armies of heaven as the "**conquering King.**" (See Isaiah 53; also Isaiah 7:14, 9:6-7; and Zechariah 14:4.) In His first coming, Jesus Christ came to earth as a baby in a manger in Bethlehem, just as prophesied in the Old Testament (see chapter 4, Prophecies Pertaining to Jesus Christ). Jesus fulfilled many of the prophecies during His birth, life, ministry, death, and resurrection, but there are some prophecies that remain unfulfilled. **The Second Coming of Christ will fulfill these remaining prophecies.**

During the time of Jesus (1 BC - AD 32), the Pharisees did not understand the need for a suffering Messiah—they only looked toward a "warrior King" who would deliver them from Rome's oppression. Although the message of a suffering Messiah and crucifixion was prophesied in the Old Testament, **the Pharisees did not recognize Him and did not accept Him.** They were sadly mistaken when they believed that approval by God **was based on observance of Judaic laws**—and therefore, **they believed there was no need for repentance.** When Jesus began preaching about **sin and repentance** (see chapter 4, Jesus Christ Teaches About Sin and Repentance), they rejected the message and ultimately had Him crucified.[2]

After Jesus ascended into Heaven, the angels declared to the apostles, "'Men of Galilee,' they said, 'why do you stand here looking into the sky? This same Jesus, who has been taken from you *into heaven, will come back in the same way you have seen him go into heaven'"* (Acts 1:11, NIV). Zechariah 14:4 identifies the location of the Second Coming as the Mount of Olives. Matthew 24:30 (NIV) declares, *"At that time the sign of the Son of Man will appear in the sky, and all the nations of the earth will mourn. They will see the Son of Man coming on the clouds of the sky, with power and great glory."* Titus 2:13 describes the Second Coming as a *"glorious appearing."* Israel and the whole world **will mourn** for not having accepted the Messiah, Jesus Christ.

For additional information about the Millennial Period (1000 year period following the Rapture), see chapter 12, section The Second Coming of Jesus Christ and The Millennial Period (p. 199).

> Zechariah 12:10 and Revelation 1:7 describe the Second Coming as one who has been pierced, and the Jewish people will one day grieve bitterly realizing their terrible mistake.

Mount of Olives; looking east from the Temple Mount. Orthodox Church of Maria Magdalene in left foreground (golden spire) and Church of Dominus Flevit in upper right (small, gray spire).
Photo by Roger Gallop, March 14, 2016

---

notes: Appendix D

1. What is the difference between the Rapture and the Second Coming? http://www.gotquestions.org/difference-Rapture-Second-Coming.html.

2. Morrisson, J.L. (2002). A Perspective About the End Times. Scripture Insights. Retrieved from http://www.scriptureinsights.com/EndTimes.html.

Index

Abomination of desolation, 185-186, 191, 194, 200

Abrahamic Covenant, 17, 18, 31, 35, 84, 91, 122, 204, 207

Agape love, x, 201, 203, 247

Alexander the Great, 58-59

Antichrist, 58, 81, 146, 167, 171, 175-177, 179, 185–187, 191, 194-195, 198-200, 218, 251-252

Anti-Semitism, 74-75, 81, 93-94

Apostle, 5, 7, 12-13, 61, 70, 225, 253

Arab occupation, 78

Arab Palestinian State (Fallacy of), 121, 125

Armageddon, 33, 81, 167, 185-186, 188, 196-198

Asaph, 53-54, 101, 119, 126

Assyrian Empire, 7-8, 40, 52, 74, 125, 153, 214, 220-221

Babylonian, 7, 40-41, 52-55, 57, 71, 74, 105, 119, 125, 131, 153, 193, 195, 204, 214, 220-221, 247

Balfour Declaration, 80, 83, 123-124

Bible's historical accuracy, xiv, 5, 202

Bible's preservation, xiv, 6-7, 11, 202

Bible's prophetic accuracy, 12

Bible's uniqueness, xiv, 12, 202

Bible's unity, xiv, 4, 57, 202

Blessings, warnings, disobedience, chapter 3

British/French control, 79-80

Caliphate, 78, 130, 141-142, 155

Canaan, xv, 17-18, 20, 22, 25-26, 28-33, 36-37, 41-42, 44-46, 67, 71, 73, 90, 93, 103, 118, 120, 122, 137, 153, 194, 203, 205-206, 213, 223

Camp David Accords, 108

China, xxi, 14, 125, 145-147, 149, 175, 180, 182, 186, 188, 196, 198-199, 218

Compromised teaching, 162, 211, 215

Crusades, 4, 78

Daniel's 70th week, 60, 177-178

David, 4, 47-49, 51, 92, 101, 103-105, 119, 122, 125, 190

Dead Sea Scrolls, 6-8

Decrees and warnings, chapter 3

Diaspora, ix, 14, 40-41, 69, 74, 117, 127, 131, 167

Disciple, 5, 12, 61, 66, 168-169

Disobedience, 27-29, chapters 3-4, 72, 204-205

Dispensations, xii, xiii

Divided kingdom, 51, 57

Divine Creation, xiv, 1, 14, 202-203

Dome of the Rock, 48, 57, 78, 80, 99, 103-104, 122, 191-193, 223, 228

Eastern Gate, 48, 80, 104, 193, 223

Economic decline, 143, 145, 147, 149, 211-213, 218

End times, ix, xiv, 13-14, 36, 84, 87, 92, 94, 115, 117-118, 127, 131-133, 167, 169-170, 172, 176, 182, 185, 189, 200, 203, 206, 209-212, 221, 252

Ethics of war, 31

Ezra, 53, 55-56

Fatah, 110, 113-114, 126, 137, 142, 170

Federal Reserve, 144, 146-147, 213

Fig tree, budding of the, 87

First Temple, 48, 101, 105, 119, 193

Freedom of choice, xvi, 59, 211

Gaza Strip, 98-100, 108, 110-114, 119

Gaza Wars, 110, 113, 115, 124, 169, 207, 237

God's chosen people, ix, xiii, 14, 20, 24, 45, 67, 81, 90-91, 102, 118-119, 135, 190, 192, 195, 204, 216, 223, 247

> Glossary pages are not listed in the index.

Golan Heights, 99-100, 107-108, 111-112, 115, 119, 124, 189
Great tribulation, 33, 176, 178, 186, 188, 191-194, 196, 198, 200
Grecian Empire, 58-59
Hamas, 110, 113-115, 126, 131, 136-137, 142, 170, 189
Hellenistic Period, 58-59
Herod Antipas, 249
Herod the Great, 60, 103, 105, 249
Hezbollah, 109, 112-13, 115, 126, 131, 136-137, 142, 170, 189
Holocaust, 75, 81, 91, 93, 118, 130, 154, 179, 186, 194, 196, 205, 220, 222, 249
Immorality, xv, xx, 4, 52, 74, 117, 127-128, 138, 140, 153, 162, 203, 206, 208, 211-212, 215, 218, 220
Indifferent, 216
Inquisition, 74-75
Islamophobia, 155
Jacob's trouble (time of), 171, 176, 196
Jerusalem (First Century BC), 63
Jerusalem (present day), 192
Jerusalem, 47-49, 103-106
Jesus Christ, ix, xii, xiv, xviii-xix, 11, 24, 30, 32, 36, 60-69, 72, 76, 87, 91, 118, 122, 162, 167, 171-172, 174, 179, 182, 186, 199-200, 202, 206, 210-212, 214, 217, 222, 224-226, 245-247, 251-253
Jezreel Valley, 196
Joint Comprehensive Plan of Action, 136, 142, 211, 218
Jihadist, 122, 136-137, 142
Josephus, Titus Flavius, 60, 71
Judea, 41, 51, 59, 60, 71, 74, 77, 84, 121-122, 194-195, 223
Last days, see end times
Lebanon War (1982), 108
Lebanon War (2006), 112
Levant, 77, 79, 109, 121, 170
Maccabean revolt, 58

Mark of the beast, 195
Maronites, 109
Medo-Persians, 55, 125
Megiddo, 33, 196-198
Melchizedek, 103
Millennial Period, 199
Mongol Empire, 79
Moral code (Law), x-xi, xxi, 36, 73-74, 152, 203, 220
Moses and Aaron, 23
Mount of Olives, 87-88, 167-168, 221, 251
National debt, iii, 135, 143-144, 147, 149, 175, 212-213, 216, 218
Nature of mankind, xiv-xv, 204
Nazi Germany, 75, 81, 113, 121, 137, 142, 154, 169, 179, 205, 220
Nebuchadnezzar, 41, 53, 105, 131, 195, 247
Nehemiah, 56
Netanyahu, 151-152
New Covenant, 36, 91, 118, 186, 245-247
Noah, x, xiii, xvi, 5, 12, 18, 31-32, 67, 139-140, 171-173, 190, 212, 218-219, 251
Old Covenant vs. New Covenant, 245-247
Olivet Discourse, 87, 167, 172, 221
Oslo Accords (1993, 1995), 108, 110, 114, 135, 211
Ottoman Empire, 79-80, 103, 122
Pain and suffering, ix, xiv, xvi-xviii, 180, 186, 202-203, 221, 248
Palestine Liberation Organization (PLO), 108-110, 114
Palestine, 71-72, 77-80, 83-84, 94, 97, 110-111, 113, 121-124
Palestinian Authority (PA), 99-110, 113-114, 119
Parthians, 77
Period of Judges, 46, 83, 123
Persecution, xv, xxi, 74-76, 81, 93-94, 121, 162, 167, 179-180, 182, 186, 191, 194-195, 203, 205, 218, 220-222, 250
Pharisees, 59, 61, 68-69, 252

> Glossary pages are not listed in the index.

Pogrom, 74-75

Political correctness, 130, 136-137, 142, 153-158, 160, 172, 180, 211, 213-214, 218

Possession of Jerusalem by Israel (June 5-10, 1967), 99-100, 111, 119, 167, 206-207, 216, 218

Pre-tribulation signs, chapters 8, 9, 10; 206-210

Probability of fulfillment, 66, 207, 210

Prophecies fulfilled; rebirth of Israel, 12-14, chapter 6, 97, 117-118, 123, 167, 206-207, 219

Prophecies pertaining to Jesus Christ, 60-69

Prophet, xiv, xxii, 4-5, 7, 12-14, 29, 46-47, 52-55, 57, 60-61, 67-68, 84, 90-92, 94, 101, 119, 131-132, 178, 181, 188, 198-199, 202, 209, 211, 252

Psalm 83, 54, 101, 119, 126

Public high schools and universities, 158-162, 214-215, 218

Punishment, ix, xiii, xvii, 37-38, 40-41, 45, 55, 59, 72-74, 76, 128, 159, 161, 204, 214, 219

Qumran Mountains, 8-9

Ramadan, 107

Rapture of the church, ix, 13, 87-88, 133, 167, 171-174, 176, 185-187, 195, 199-200, 210, 218-219, 247, 251-253

Rebirth of Israel, 12-14, chapter 6, 97, 117-118, 123, 167, 206-207, 219

Rebuilding the Temple (second), 55-56

Rebuilding the Temple (future), 191-193

Rejection of Jesus Christ, ix, 60, 68-69, 72, 91, 105, 122, 153, 177, 205, 213

Replacement theology (fallacy of), 91-93, 118, 123, 163, 201, 210

Roman Empire (Roman Republic), 41, 58-59, 77, 79, 105, 176

Russia, xxi, 12, 14, 18, 71, 74-75, 79, 117, 125-126, 129, 131-132, 141, 169-170, 175, 180, 182, 186-194, 198-200, 206, 209, 215-216, 218

Sacrificial Lamb, xviii, 61, 222, 224, 250

Sadducees, 59

Samaria, 51, 61, 121

Samaritan pentateuch, 8

Satan (attempts at control), 129-130, 222-223, 248-250

Saul, 47-48, 51, 119, 122, 125

Schools, public, 158-162, 214-215, 218

Scientific evidence for creation, 1-3

Scientific method, 1

Seals, trumpets, and bowls, 186

Second Coming, xii, 13, 69, 80, 88, 117, 127, 131, 167, 173-174, 176, 185-186, 199-200, 219, 251-253

Seleucid Empire, 11, 58

Septuagint, 8, 44, 66

Seven churches, 162-163

Repentance, xxii, 66-68, 94, 107, 182, 217, 225, 252

Sinai War (1956), 98-99, 124, 169, 207

Six Day War (June 5-10, 1967), 99-100, 111, 119, 167, 206-207, 216, 218

Solomon, 4-5, 47-49, 51, 84-85, 101, 105, 119, 122, 125, 193, 201, 228

South Lebanese Army, 109

Southern Steps (Huldah Gates), 48, 104-105, 223

Super signs, chapters 8, 9, 10; 206-210

Surrendering land for peace (1982, 2005), 112

Temple Mount, 48-49, 57, 78, 88, 99, 103-105, 119, 167, 191-193, 223, 253

Temple rebuilding (timeline), 168-169, 185, 191-193, 252

Ten Commandments, xii-xiii, xv, xvii, xix-xx, 25-26, 28, 35-37, 53, 57, 73-74, 153, 161, 203, 220, 245

Terrorism, xv, xx, 110, 129-130, 137, 141, 155, 170, 173, 203-204, 208, 218-219

Third (future) Temple, 191-193

Timeline (prophetic), 168-169, 185, 252

Times of the Gentiles, 195, 247

Transgenderism, 129, 135-136, 155, 160, 162, 215, 218, 239

> Glossary pages are not listed in the index.

Transjordan, 83-84, 97, 123-124

Tribulation (first 3 1/2 years), 187-193

Tribulation (second 3 1/2 years), 194-200

Tribulation period, 176-182, chapter 12

Turko-Persian Empire, 78

Turning away, 30, 51-52, 54, 90, 94, 115, 128, 138, 140, 179, 248

Twelve sons of Jacob, 21, 23

Twelve tribes of Jacob, 21-22

Ukraine, 75, 126, 132, 169, 189

United Kingdom, 47-49, 83, 101, 108, 119, 122-123

United States, xvii, xxi, 40, 93, 108, 110, 115, 120-121, 124-125, 130, 132, chapters 9 and 10, 179, 208, 210, 212-213, 215-216, 218

Universities (colleges), 161-162

Unpardonable sin, 217, 224

Violence, iii, xii, xvi, xx, 74-75, 110, 124, 138, 140-141, 147-149, 155, 162-163, 172, 186, 208, 211-212, 218, 220

War of Independence (1948-1949), 97-98, 101, 124, 169, 207

West Bank, 98-100, 108, 111-115, 119, 124

Western Wall, 99, 103-104, 192

Yom Kippur War (1973), 107, 124, 169, 207